Wilhelm Scherer, Friedrich Max Müller

A History of German Literature

Volume 1

Wilhelm Scherer, Friedrich Max Müller

A History of German Literature
Volume 1

ISBN/EAN: 9783337205386

Printed in Europe, USA, Canada, Australia, Japan

Cover: Foto ©Thomas Meinert / pixelio.de

More available books at **www.hansebooks.com**

A HISTORY

OF

GERMAN LITERATURE

BY

W. SCHERER

TRANSLATED FROM THE THIRD GERMAN EDITION

BY

MRS. F. C. CONYBEARE

EDITED BY

F. MAX MÜLLER

VOLUME I.

Oxford

AT THE CLARENDON PRESS

1886

INTRODUCTION.

THIS work is a history of German literature from the earliest times to the death of Goethe.

The first chapter traces the roots of German nationality back to the period preceding the Aryan separation, and presents a picture of the intellectual condition of our forefathers at the time when they became known to the Romans.

The second chapter treats of the rise and development of the German hero-legends in the epoch of the migrations, and during the Merovingian period.

The third chapter is devoted to the Mediæval Renaissance, under the rule of the Carlovingians and the Ottos, the so-called Old High-German period, the chief literary achievements of which consisted in prose and verse translations from the Bible, in short political songs and poetic tales, and in the Latin dramas of the nun Rosvitha.

The fourth to the seventh chapters embrace the classical period of Middle High-German lyric and epic poetry, extending from about the eleventh to the middle of the fourteenth century.

The eighth and ninth chapters include the next three hundred years, the period of transition from Middle High-German to New High-German. To this epoch belongs Luther's translation of the Bible; the poetry of the period inclined to the drama, but no great literary masterpiece was produced.

The tenth to the thirteenth chapters are devoted to the unfinished epoch in which we live, the New High-German period which began with the close of the Thirty Years' War. Its strength lies in lyric and epic poetry; and, in tracing its development from Paul Gerhardt to Goethe, I have given more space to it than to the earlier centuries.

CONTENTS.

VOLUME I.

CHAPTER I.

CHAPTER III.

CHAPTER IV.

CHAPTER V.

CHAPTER VII.

CHAPTER VIII.

VOLUME II.

CHAPTER XI.

CHAPTER I.

THE ANCIENT GERMANS.

ABOUT the time when Alexander the Great was opening new fields to Greek science by his invasion of India, a learned Greek, Pytheas of Massilia, started from his native town, sailed through the straits of Gibraltar, along the western coast of Spain and France, and, passing Great Britain, discovered at the mouth of the Rhine a new people—the Teutons.

Pytheas of Massilia discovers the Teutons at the mouth of the Rhine 4th century B.C.

Towards the end of the second century B.C., these same Teutons made themselves formidable to the Romans. A little later we find the great race to which they belonged designated by a Gallic name—*Germans*, which is supposed to mean ' the neighbours.'

Julius Cæsar defeated them, and yet gained no real footing in their country, which lay on the right bank of the Rhine. He gives a sketch of his barbaric enemies in his history of the Gallic War, but could furnish only an imperfect account of their intellectual condition. Their religion seemed to him pure nature-worship. He notices—as characteristic features of this nation of hunters and warriors—the freedom of their life, their want of all sense of duty and of propriety, their incapability of self-control, the pleasure they took in hardening themselves against physical suffering, their delight in marauding expeditions, and their ambition to lay waste all lands bordering on their own. In all this he expresses neither admiration nor contempt, but simply records his observations.

Julius Cæsar.

Further intercourse, in peace and war, soon made the Germans better known to the Romans. In the first century of our era, in the first glorious years of the Roman Empire, our forefathers

B

excited at Rome an interest, springing partly from fear, partly from admiration. The Stoic saw in the unbroken power of these children of nature the realisation of his ideal of morality; the aristocratic champion of liberty welcomed in the Germans the fulfilment of his hopes, while the far-seeing patriot recognised in them a menace to his country. In the winter of 98–99 the historian Tacitus collected all that was known about them in his celebrated *Germania*. In that work he directed the attention of the Romans to this remarkable nation, whose affairs kept the newly-elected emperor Trajan absent from the capital, where his presence was ardently desired. He drew at the same time, by way of contrast, a picture of the moral consequences of that excessive luxury which surrounded himself and those whom he addressed. There is in his account something of the tone of the pastoral poem, by which effete civilisation strives to satisfy, through the imagination, its longings after primitive innocence.

The Germans of Tacitus know no riches other than their herds; the possession of silver and gold and the practice of usury have no attractions for them. Their dress is simple, their military equipment imperfect. They value warlike adornments as little as splendid funeral rites. Their food consists of fruits, game, and milk. They are exceedingly hospitable, and live not in towns, but each one by himself, wherever wood or field or spring attracts him. They are strangers to sensational shows and to artificial allurements of the senses. They reverence their women, lead pure lives, and hold the marriage tie sacred.

Although the noble Roman's description contains many idyllic elements, yet it is not fair to call the whole of it a mere idyll. Tacitus appears to have had abundant material before him, drawn from immediate observation, and but slightly coloured by his own opinions. The life of the Germans is thoroughly known to him; he sketches the outlines of their constitution, their military customs, their religion and manners. He does not suppress their faults: their indolence in time of peace, their dislike of hard work, their immoderate love of drink, gambling, and fighting. He gives a summary of the numerous tribes and clans into which the nation was politically divided, and produces the impression of an inexhaustible and steadily increasing power, upon which a few isolated Roman victories could have no lasting effect. In short, it is evident that his picture is on the whole a faithful one, in which pleasing and repugnant features are mingled; and he leaves to posterity a valuable record—valuable for general history, as giving an idea of the character of that people, which was hereafter to destroy the Roman empire, but especially valuable to us who are descended from them.

THE ARYAS.

Tacitus raises the question whether the Germans were immigrants, or had sprung up on their own soil. He decides in favour of the latter hypothesis, because it seemed to him impossible that the barren land which they inhabited could ever have attracted immigrants from another country.

Modern science gives a different answer. It infers from the relationship of languages the relationship of nations, and the existence of a primitive race which spread and ramified by migration. It infers from cognate words the existence among those primordial tribes of the things which those words designate, and thus shows us the degree of civilisation reached by them before they branched off into different nations. It infers from kindred mythologies and from similarity of poetical themes the existence of a primordial mythology and poetry, and endeavours to distinguish in this dark but rich background the beginnings of the separate nations, known to us in later and historical times. We are thus able to trace the antecedents of our forefathers. The conquerors of Rome fought without knowing it against a people who had once spoken the same language as themselves, and had migrated with them from Asia to Europe.

The Germans were formerly a small tribe of a great race, sometimes called the Indo-Germanic race, but which we may designate by the name, probably used by themselves, of Aryan. The Germans Most of the European peoples, Celts, Romans, Greeks, belong to the Germans, and Slavs, and in Asia the Persians and Aryan Indians, sprang from this common source, and re- family. present the whole united body of the Aryan race, in contradistinction to the similar ethnographical groups of the Semitic and Turanian races.

Before their dispersion the primitive Aryas had already passed out of the lowest stage of civilisation. They were shepherds, and The ancient acquainted with the first elements of a rude agri-
Aryas. culture. Their poetry was truthful, graphic, and full of imagery, and contained the germs of a connected view of things. Their language endowed even lifeless objects with sex. Most of them looked upon the sky and the sun as male, on the moon and the earth as female, and thus the foundation was laid for a human conception of the whole of nature. Personifications and allegories Primitive arose quite naturally, and explanations of remarkable Aryan my- phenomena or events in nature were drawn from thology. the analogy of human experience. Peculiarities in animals were accounted for by fables, and remarkable occurrences in nature, both regular and irregular, such as the alternation of day and night, the change of the seasons, or tempests, were explained in the same manner. These men saw a reflection of their own simple life in all that surrounded them, and in this naive way tried to account for whatever they could not understand. They created a rich mythology, reflecting the main incidents of a pastoral life, such as feuds caused by the capture of cattle or women, or raids upon rich owners. The sound of the thunder is the battle-cry in the strife between the gods and giants. The former are favour- able to man and take his part, the latter, embracing all the adverse powers of nature, threaten his happiness.

All poetry is worthless which does not represent the visible life that surrounds us. The Aryas began by giving poetical expres- sion to the conditions under which they lived, by finding words to describe the uncommon as well as the common, and by arranging together events which displayed the same characteristic features, till at last they were able to give them a typical and permanent form of expression.

These were the first modes of their poetical activity, the basis of all further poetical invention. When an independent existence has once been imparted to images of surrounding life, we get anecdotes, fables, and stories ; and out of this lowest stratum of Aryan thought and imagination spring the human elements of the myth, and perhaps also certain tragic elements of the later epic poetry. Such is, for instance, the noble invincible hero, invulnerable except in one spot, where he is wounded at last by treachery, like Achilles and Siegfried; or father and son fighting together, unknown or only half known to each other, and yet forced to fight like Laios and Œdipus, Rostem and Sohrab, Hildebrand and Hadubrand. Primitive forms of Aryan poetry.

We find, moreover, that worldly wisdom and experience embodied itself at a very early stage in the most various forms. The same experience may on the one hand originate a story, and on the other hand give rise to some reflection, which is handed down as a proverb. Observations of natural objects might take the form of riddles. Lastly, the selfishness of man invented all sorts of formulas to secure the fulfilment of his wishes from the gods and from his fellow men. The old Aryas had medicinal charms for ruling the powers of nature, and making them subservient to the wants of man. They had love songs, dwelling on the harmony or on the sharp contrasts between the joys and sorrows of the human heart and the varying phases of nature. They had hymns which were sung in chorus; songs in praise of celebrated men; songs glorifying the deeds of their gods, and imploring their aid. Such songs glorifying the gods were sung at sacrifices, and, along with invocations and prayers, formed the noblest class of ancient poetry. They were the solemn accompaniment of those public religious ceremonies on which depended the weal or woe of a nation, a tribe, or a family. Music and dancing were combined with this poetry. The crowds of worshippers danced as they sang their sacred songs, and rhythm and metre are, in fact, a remnant of the dance which once formed an integral portion of poetry and music. The half line with its four beats, peculiar to the oldest German poems, along with the form of stanza in which it appears, is found in the old hymns of the Rig-Veda, and conjures up before the trained fancy of the scholar a picture of old Aryan times. We see a circle of men gathered round the place of sacrifice; they move four steps forward and four backward, or four to the right Origin of rhythm and metre.

and four to the left. Measured song accompanies their movements.
And every such movement, from the point of departure till the
return to that point, corresponds to a line of eight beats or feet, or
to double as many syllables in the song which accompanied it.

GERMANIC RELIGION.

In prehistoric times some tribes of the Aryan race migrated into
Europe. These tribes developed gradually into nations no longer
able to understand each other's speech. The several
nations again split up into tribes, and their language
was divided into dialects containing the germs of other
new languages. The Germans were one of these
nations. They established themselves at first in North Germany,
spreading as far as Scandinavia, and in later times tried to advance
to the Rhine and South Germany. Everywhere they drove back the
Celts, and at last found themselves face to face with the Romans.

Migration and dispersion of the Aryas.

From this time onward we are tolerably well informed as to the
degree of civilisation which our forefathers had attained; indeed
we are able to form a conjecture as to their intellectual development before the time when they become historically known to us. At
least we can discover a few main facts in the history of their religion.

We can distinguish an early epoch, during which they worshipped the Heaven, the Aryan Dyaus, the Greek
Zeus, as the highest deity. We can distinguish a
second epoch, in which the worship of the heaven-god
was confined more and more to the tribe of the
Suebi, the later Suabians, whose oldest settlements
on the middle Elbe may be looked upon as the first
home of the Germans in Europe. The new tribes which started
thence chose their own favourite gods, whose sanctuary was the
central meeting-place of the tribe. The eastern nations, the
Vandals and Goths, worshipped a divine pair of brothers, resembling Castor and Pollux. The tribes on the North Sea, the
forefathers of the future conquerors of England, worshipped a goddess Nerthus, who in modern times has been wrongly called Hertha
and relegated to the Baltic coasts. The tribes on the Rhine, the

Three epochs in the religious development of the early Germans.

later Franks, worshipped the storm-god Wodan as their leader
and protector. Finally, we can distinguish a third epoch in which
this Wodan has been set above all the other gods. The Germanic
tribes on the Rhine attained a higher degree of culture through
intercourse with their Celtic neighbours, and Wodan, the god of
their tribes, impersonates their highest culture. The storm-god,
who hurries through the air with the departed spirits, now becomes
a god of knowledge, of poetry, the giver of understanding, of
victory, and of all good. The worshippers of Wodan probably
acquired a more refined art of war and better weapons from the
Celts. Wodan himself carries a spear, and gives to those whom
he loves precious swords, to be taken away again at his pleasure.
When he is represented as the author of victory, this implies that
victory ultimately rests with intelligence.

The higher civilisation of the Rhenish tribes, and with it the
worship of Wodan, spread to all the Germans. A common
mythology sprang up, which later on enabled the Formation of
Romans to identify certain German deities with some a common
of their own gods. Wodan, the most honoured, German
and, at the same time, the swift traveller, was iden- mythology.
tified with Mercury. Friya, the German Venus, was his wife.
The old heaven-god Tius had retired to the position of god of
war, and might therefore be compared with Mars. His former
task of conquering the giants in the tempest is transferred to an
entirely new god, *Donar*, in Old English Thunor, the personification
of thunder, who was invested with certain grotesque and rude
characteristics. Armed with the hammer, he reminded the Romans,
by his constant struggle with monsters and robbers, of the ad-
venturous club-bearer Hercules, or, according to a Its warlike
higher conception of him, of the thunderer Jove him- character.
self. Almost all the Germanic gods and goddesses have a warlike aspect. They carry on a perpetual strife with giants and
dragons, and at the end of all things they are themselves destroyed
by the world-consuming fire, *Muspilli*.

The reader must bear in mind that the accuracy of some of these
statements is disputed. It is not certain that the German Olympus
bore such a warlike character in all epochs. Side by side with

the fiercer traits are found gentler ones, which probably point to a time when milder sentiments prevailed.

The later northern mythology assigns the goddess of peace to the rude Thunderer as his wife; and, after the last dread struggle **Peaceful** between gods and giants, after the general con- **elements in** flagration, in which the sun is blackened and the **the later** earth disappears, a hope is held out to the souls of **Icelandic** **mythology.** the faithful of an eternal realm of peace. Then the earth, green and beautiful, will rise again from the sea, and corn will spring up unsown; all evil will disappear, and sinless gods will reign for ever.

We possess many proper names used by the various German tribes, and comparison shows us that they are of the highest **Proper** antiquity. The names given to boys and girls may **names.** be compared to those of patron saints given in later times in the Catholic Church; they pointed to examples of virtue, as ideals after which they were to strive. Thus these old German proper names show us what our forefathers held to be most truly good and beautiful. The names of men express those qualities which secure success in life, wisdom, strength, fortitude, the virtues of the warrior and the ruler, but above all the resolute will which pursues its object with fervour **Two classes** and determination. The names of women, on the **of names of** other hand, fall into two distinct groups. In the **women.** names of the one group nature and beauty are combined; they tell of love, gentle grace, purity, and constancy. The other group shows us women rejoicing in battle, bearing arms, and waving their torches as they rush on to victory. Such warlike women, the Walkyries, are also found in German mythology. Tacitus attests the respect paid by the Germans to women, and their belief in woman's sanctity and prophetic power. He represents the women as counselling, inspiriting, and tending the men; but later historians tell of some women who took part, fully armed, in battle. The same age and soil can hardly have originated such divergent ideals of womanhood. These names, fraught with such opposite moral significance, probably point to two different epochs in the spiritual growth of the nation.

The one appointed to women their special sphere, and bowed in reverence before the weaker sex; the other prized in women successful emulation only of masculine qualities.

A similar change in moral views seems to be reflected in the name and myth of the sun. There must have been a time when love of beauty and reverence for women predominated, and then it was that the Aryan sun-god was changed into a goddess. Later on the same goddess received the name of Sindgund, that is, 'she who must fight her way.' She then adopts the hero's dress, and under this aspect is also called Brunhild, i.e. 'the fighter in armour.' The myth further tells us how the sun goes of an evening to her home in the west, and how the heaven-god of a morning wakes the sleeping goddess, who appears on the summit of the hills in glowing flame—in rosy dawn. The hero, who later on took the place of the heaven-god in the legend of Brunhild, was called Siegfried.

Sun myths.

Siegfried.

His name implies that he fights for victory, in order to secure peace, and he too is, therefore, one of the symbols of that milder view of life which we must distinguish in the history of our forefathers. He is the ideal of a hero and of a perfect man; the gods and the good spirits are favourable to him. The clever dwarfs educate him; he learns the trade of a smith, and a godlike woman initiates him in sacred wisdom. He is early surrounded by the glory of wonderful deeds; riches and power are his portion; love beautifies his life; but he falls by the treachery of a powerful enemy, and his early death raises him to still higher glory. The character of Siegfried lived on for centuries in the imagination of the poets. His praises were first sounded, it appears, by those same Franks who spread the worship of Wodan. And in the age of the migration of the German tribes and of the introduction of Christianity among them, the story of Siegfried was bequeathed by the expiring mythology to the folk-lore, which has preserved it to the present day.

Oldest Remains of Poetry.

'This I heard as the greatest marvel among men, that once there
was no earth, nor heaven above, the bright stars gave no light,
the sun shone not, nor the moon, nor the glorious sea.' With
some such words as these begins a literary relic of the eighth
The Wesso- or ninth century, ending in a prayer, the so-called
brunner 'Wessobrunner Gebet.' It is the beginning of a
Gebet. Saxon poem, written down in Bavaria. The same
primitive chaos is still more clearly depicted in a Norwegian poem
Völuspá. Völuspá :—There was neither sand nor sea nor cool
wave; there was no earth nor heaven above; there
was a yawning gulf, and no firm land anywhere. Such a coincidence of ideas in poems coming from different and distant localities, leads us to infer a common origin of the highest antiquity.
We seem to hear in them an echo of primitive Germanic times,
when our forefathers were heathens. Such echoes are rare, and
are therefore worthy of careful attention.

The first line of the Bavarian Manuscript runs thus:—

'Dat gafrégin íh mit firahím firiwízzo méistá.'

If these words are read aloud, the three f's at once strike
the ear. The three similar initial letters serve to ornament
Alliteration. and bind together the eight feet of the line. This
alliteration may be regarded as an indispensable
element of versification in all old German poetry. It gives to
the verse not melody, but a characteristic sound; it does not
beautify it, but makes it compact and strong. Such alliteration
results from a tendency early found in the Germanic nature, which
renders all art difficult to us—a tendency, namely, to prize originality
more than beauty, substance more than form. This feature has
even stamped itself on our language. Already in very early times
the accent was laid on the root-syllable, and all inflections tended to
disappear. The word *mensch* (man) was once *mannisko*; now the
three syllables are reduced to one, at the expense of all euphony.
Only the first sound of the root-syllable is considered in alliteration,
no notice being taken of the vowels, so that the chief place is held
by the consonants. The consonants have been well called the

bones of speech, while the vowels fulfil the office of the flesh, imparting colour and beauty. The old German ear, however, had little feeling for beauty and colour.

Apart from its alliteration and the changes which language has undergone, German poetry remains at this epoch essentially Aryan. It has the same technical means at its disposal, and is moulded in the same forms. The chorus in which the multitude takes part is still the leading type. Individuals are subordinate to the whole body of singers, though in the course of time they separate from them, as chief singers, dancers, or actors. The choral song comprised lyric, epic, and dramatic elements, and was accompanied by march and dance, sometimes even by pantomime.

Essentially Aryan character of the earliest German poetry.

Choral songs played an important part on all the great occasions of private and public life. Choral song received the wedded bride, and conducted her to her husband. The praises of the dead were celebrated in a solemn funeral chorus. The march into battle and the sacrificial procession were attended with choral song. The departure for battle was itself a kind of sacred procession, when all who took part in it sang the praises of a saving god, *Donar* (Thunor), the slayer of monsters. Their loud battle-cry, which they called *barditus*, was supposed to be an imitation of thunder, the 'beard speech' of the god. They also sang the deeds of their ancestors, and drew courage from the example of their forefathers. Little is told us about the sacrifice itself, but remnants of heathen worship lingered on for a long time, and with them some poor fragments of songs. Thus for example, in Mecklenburg, the reapers still leave a few ears of corn uncut; these they tie together, besprinkle them, form a circle round them, and taking off their hats, call on Wodan, 'Wode, Wode, now fetch thy horse food, now thistle and thorn, in a year's time corn.'

Choral songs.

Tacitus tells us of a solemn procession of the goddess Nerthus. She was thought to be present in a covered car drawn by cows and accompanied by a priest. She was received everywhere with reverence, and on her advent weapons were laid aside amid general peace and rejoicing. The Roman historian, however, makes no mention of songs. The Langobardi again, to the great wrath of Pope Gregory the Great, offered the head of a goat, with songs and dances, to some heathen deity, or, as he says, to the devil. Lastly, in comparatively modern times, it was the custom in many places for a hammer, a fox, or a crow to be carried about with singing. All these are relics of the old heathen symbolism, and of primitive religious processions.

Again a myth might be represented dramatically, as the struggle between summer and winter is sometimes represented even in our day. Summer appears dressed in ivy or periwinkle, Winter in straw or moss. They fight until Summer is victorious. Then vanquished Winter is stripped of his covering, which is scattered to the winds, and a wreath or branch of summer flowers is carried round in procession. The chorus sings songs, to encourage and praise the conqueror, and uses words of which the meaning is now half lost, ' Stab aus, stab aus, blas dem Winter die Augen aus.'

The same dramatic setting might be given to Thunor's conflict with the giants; or again, Wodan's marriage with Friya and the awakening of the sun-maiden might be made to furnish material for small pantomimic scenes, in which chosen actors represented what was expressed in the words of the songs. When the actors sang, and established themselves along with, but independently of the chorus, dialogue and with it the beginning of the drama were created.

Such songs and representations were not restricted to solemn occasions, but could also be used in social gatherings and at festivals. Amongst children's games there are still many with dramatic action, founded on some fairy tale or fable of animal life. In the same way myths were probably dramatised in primitive times.

But choral poetry is not the only kind of poetry at this period. The other Aryan forms of poetry also continue to exist. **Lyrics and** The maiden greets her lover thus: ' I wish thee as **riddles.** much joy as there is foliage in spring; I wish thee as much love, as the birds find delight and food; I wish thee as much honour as the earth bears grass and flowers.' At social

gatherings riddles were set, founded on simple observation of
nature, like the following:—

> 'There came a bird featherless,
> Sat on a tree leafless;
> There came a maiden speechless,
> And eat the bird featherless
> From off the tree leafless.'

This signifies the sun eating up the snow. In a simpler form the
same riddle occurs in Vedic times. 'What is the best medicine
for snow?' The answer is, 'the Sun.'

In time of need, the help of heaven is invoked by a charm
which consists in relating a mythical incident analogous to the earthly one. The repetition of the
saving words which proved effectual in the myth is supposed to
secure an equally favourable result in the actual earthly difficulty.
This is illustrated in the two charms found at Merseburg.

The first refers to the horse of the god Phol or Balder, and
introduces us to a whole company of gods. It runs
thus: 'Phol and Wodan rode into the forest; suddenly
Balder's horse sprained its foot. Sindgund and her
sister Sunna uttered a charm over him. Volla and her sister
Friya did the same; but all in vain. Then Wodan, who understood
such things well, uttered his charm. He charmed away the sprain
in the bone, the blood, and the joint. He uttered the potent
formula, "Bone to bone, blood to blood, joint to joint, as if they
were glued."'

Of course the meaning is that the desired effect immediately
followed, and that the formula would produce the same result in
all similar cases. This formula is of common Aryan origin. An
old Indian charm begins 'Let marrow join to marrow, and also
limb to limb; may what thou hast lost in flesh and bone, grow
again; marrow be joined to marrow, skin to skin; let blood come
to the bones, and flesh to the flesh, let hair join hair, and skin
skin.'

Wodan, the god of wisdom, is also, as we see, the chief physician.
Even the art of the four heavenly women, who understand wounds
as the German wives did, is far inferior to his.

Marginal notes: Charms. — The two Merseburg charms.

The second Merseburg charm is said to have power to loose a prisoner's bonds. It describes the activity of the heavenly women, the Walkyries, in the battle. They are divided into three detachments; the first bind the prisoners in the rear of the army which they favour, others engage the foe, the third group appear in the rear of the enemy, where the prisoners are secured, and touching their fetters, utter the formula of deliverance : 'Escape from your bonds, flee from the enemy.'

There were charms also for protection and blessing, commending men to the protecting hand of the gods when starting on a journey, or cattle when sent to pasture.

But above all, it was the principles which regulated life, and underlay morality and law, that were embodied in poetic form.

Poetical elements in primitive law. There were no written laws, but the priest proclaimed the fixed laws as approved by the people. He was the 'mouth-piece' and guardian of the laws. These promulgations of the law often described in detail the circumstances of actual life, which the law covered, and this gave rise to real poetry, whose charm lingers even in the later written code. For instance, certain Frisian law-documents enumerate the 'three needs' or conditions under which the inheritance of a fatherless child may be alienated, and in doing this bring before us a touching picture of misery. 'The first "need" is, when the child is taken prisoner and carried away bound, northwards over the sea, or southwards beyond the mountains; the mother may then part with her child's inheritance, and thus set her child free and save his life. The second "need" is when years of dearth come, and famine reigns in the land, and the child is dying of hunger; then the mother may alienate his inheritance and buy him therewith corn and cattle, that his life may be spared, for hunger is the sharpest of swords. The third "need" is, if the child is naked and houseless, and the cloudy night and ice-cold winter peep through the hedges, and all men hurry to their hearths and homes, and the wild beasts take refuge in the hollow trees and rocky caves; the innocent child cries and laments its nakedness and wails because it has no shelter, and because its father who would protect it against cold winter and gnawing hunger is lying in the dark depths of the earth, in his oak coffin fastened down with four nails, and hidden away; then the mother may alienate and sell her child's inheritance.'

All solemn legal proceedings were accompanied by poetry. Oaths were sworn in alliterative verse. The sentence of banishment was uttered in alliterative language. The culprit is to be a fugitive and an outcast, everywhere and always: wheresoever fire burns, and grass is green, child cries for its mother or mother bears a child, as far as ship sails, shield glitters, sun melts snow, feather flies, fir-tree flourishes, hawk flies through the long spring day, while the wind lifts its wings, wheresoever the welkin spreads, or the world stands fast, winds roar and waters flow into the sea.

Indeed, all legal formulas were full of alliteration. And some expressions uniting two terms each having the same initial letter, remain even in our time, such as house and home, spick and span, weal and woe, hand and heart, stock and stone, kith and kin, bed and board, wind and weather.

CHAPTER II.

GOTHS AND FRANKS.

Two classical periods are usually recognised in the history of German literature; but it is probable that there were in reality three. It is true that nothing but fragments of a single song

Three classical periods of German Literature. remains to us from the first period, but to the historian lost poems are often as important as those still extant, if their former existence can be proved and their influence on after ages established. That first period was richer indeed in inventive genius than any that followed it; the characters which it created are full of moral grandeur, and are well known to us through the later Epics, though the songs which first told of them can never be recovered. Such was the creative force of language that these earliest poetic types lived on through long ages, nay, even when they seemed to have died out, revived again with fresh and undiminished vigour. The poetical stories of that first classical period were revived in the epic poems of the twelfth and thirteenth century, in the Nibelungenlied, Gudrun, Hugdietrich and Wolfdietrich and others. These stories are usually designated as the German hero-legends.

The whole scheme of our history of literature becomes perfectly clear, if we bear in mind that it has attained those culminating points, separated each from the other by about 600 years.

About the year 600 A.D.—if I may be allowed to fix a date, which should only be taken approximately—after the total change effected in Europe by the destruction of the Empire of the West, at a time when the Germans had not forgotten their own

First classical period, circa A.D. 600. migration, though they had begun to feel the strong intellectual influence of conquered Rome,—the Germanic national Epic attained its highest development. More fortunate in this respect than the Germans, the English possess in Beowulf a fine and well-preserved specimen of

what Germanic poetry could accomplish at that period. About the
year 1200, as we have already said, the half-forgotten
stories of the hero-legends appear again, and are
embodied in the well-known poems, the Nibelungenlied and Gudrun. The same period produced lyric
and epic poets of the first order, whose artistic training was at least
in part based on French models. Such are Wolfram von Eschenbach, Gottfried von Strassburg, and Walther von der Vogelweide.

*Second clas-
sical period,
circa
A.D. 1200.*

About the year 1800 Germany had its Goethe, its Schiller, and
other poets and scholars, who absorbed in themselves
the rays of French, English, classical and their own
old national culture, and added them in a purified
form to the intellectual life of the nation. The old
heroic songs revived again, the Nibelungen legend acquired new
fame, new poets made use of the old materials, and the brothers
Grimm became the leaders of a new science, which sought to
recover for the present the vanished creations of the past.

*Third clas-
sical period,
circa
A.D. 1800.*

These three culminating points of development imply a struggle
to reach these points, an ascent followed by a descent. As
far as we can judge, the tenth and sixteenth centuries were the times of deepest depression in
German literature. Literary culture was then at its
lowest ebb; poetry excited no general interest, but
became a medium of party strife, or a mere mechanical
exercise, or a source of coarse amusement. The
poetry of these periods was not entirely wanting in creative genius;
it had vast materials at its disposal, and even created certain moral
types of great grandeur, though they were mostly the offspring of
hatred or rude jest. But the charm of form is totally absent from
it; it is too superficial, too indifferent to outward beauty; it did
not care to go deep enough to attain perfection and refinement;
it left, in fact, the best it had, as formless material to be put into
shape by a happier generation.

*Two periods
of depression
in German
literature,
10th and 16th
centuries.*

The times of deepest depression are likewise separated from
each other by 600 years. The course of our history of literature
may therefore be reduced to the simplest scheme: three great
waves, trough and crest in regular succession.

Alas! only too regular. Treasures were scarcely won when they were lost again, and the nation had to begin once more from the beginning. The religious epic flourished in the ninth century, but was completely forgotten by the twelfth. The perfection of form found in the thirteenth century had entirely disappeared in the fifteenth. Poets of little talent had a hard struggle to purge their verse of the grosser elements of the sixteenth century and recover purity of form and refinement of language. We ourselves feel at the present day that there is a risk of the German nation degenerating from the ideals which, in Goethe's time, constituted its greatness and its pride. Other nations are more fortunate in this respect, and know better how to preserve their literary traditions.

Both the second and the third of the classical periods are marked by a spirit of free criticism which triumphs over all prejudices. Respect for foreign nations increases, regardless of political differences. Men are liberal enough to feel that appreciation of foreign merits is no sin against national pride. Thus it was that the more developed sense of form, characteristic of the Romanic nations, exercised a beneficial influence on the Germans, purified their taste, incited them to imitation, yet withal developed their originality. Hand in hand with this tolerance of foreign nationalities, went religious toleration and abandonment of rigid conventionalities in life and literature. Moral judgment became more liberal, and at the same time a higher sense of honour sprang up, and led to a nobler type of humanity. The individual soul became inspired with a noble self-consciousness, springing from the consciousness of pure intentions. In good society the lower passions are silenced. Women are worshipped with a pure enthusiasm. 'Honour the women' is Schiller's precept, and Walther von der Vogelweide sang :—

Characteristics of the second and third classical periods.

'Pure women are sweet as honeyed flowers. What shall compare unto the sight of them? Verily they are fairer than aught in air, or earth, or in green fields.'

Women themselves are at pains to develop their nature within the limits of their sex. They do not try to disguise their weakness

as strength, or openly to compete with men, but are content
with the indirect influence which nature gives them.   They
do not enter into public life, but they exert their influence on
men, and through them on the world.   Their smile rewards
the hero, the orator, the poet.   They are the guardians of good
manners, they demand self-restraint and culture.   In their service
poetry is spiritualised, and produces its best in epic, romance, and
lyric song.

THE HEROIC SONGS.

Young nations, like children, have no memory; they live in the
present, in pleasure and pain, in hopes and wishes.   But great
suffering and great dangers make a deeper impression on them;
whoever appears as a deliverer in time of need is praised, and, if
a tragic fate should overtake him, he lives on for a time in song.
This was the case with the Cheruscan Arminius, the liberator of
Germany, at least so Tacitus reports, and he also remarks that
with the Germans songs took the place of sober annals.   But
the songs in praise of Arminius soon died away, and no lasting
tradition gathered round his memory.

The historical consciousness of the Germans dates from their
great migration, which also gave life and substance to their
heroic poetry.   The rich legends which form the material of great
national epics always owe their origin to gigantic national con-
vulsions.   It was so with the Greeks and Indians; it was so with
the Teutonic race.

We can distinguish two elements, a mythological and an historical, in the Germanic hero-world.   On the one hand there are
gods who take the form of men, without descending altogether
to the level of common humanity; on the other hand there
are historical heroes, whose greatness seemed more
than human, half divine, to the popular imagination
fired by the fame of their exploits.   To the first
class belong Siegfried and the fabulous genealogies,
through which the German princely families traced
their descent from Wodan or other gods.   To the
second class belong those names of heroic legend which are

Mythological and histori-cal element in the old German hero-legends.

attested by history, the historical leaders of the national movement against Rome. The German migration is like a deluge, which gradually encroached on the frontiers of the Roman empire and eventually submerged it entirely. Internal weakness, depopulation, dearth of talent, led the Romans to surrender one position after another to the Germans, who gradually came to occupy all the **The German** most responsible posts in the state, from that of the **Migration.** mercenary on the frontier to the imperial throne itself. It was a strange experience for these barbarians, and one which must have enormously increased their national pride, and stamped itself deeply on their memory. Their horizon was enlarged; the individual acquired more importance; remarkable men arose; and foreign civilisation, mingling in countless ways with native barbarism, called forth the strongest contrasts. With the growth of their own self-consciousness their early heroic ideals too became more and more individualised. They lost their vagueness, and, in acquiring variety and a character of their own, became genuine personal types with distinct individual characteristics.

But this is the mere dawn of historical consciousness. We are still far from exact history or even from that degree of faithfulness which we find in the most meagre chronicles. It is partly the knowledge that is wanting, partly the power of exact observation. It is true the Germans possessed runic writing; they attributed mysterious virtue to the letters, and used them for casting lots, for spells, and for short inscriptions, but never for historical annals **Orally trans-** or other consecutive records. The only organ of **mitted songs.** tradition was unwritten poetry, handed down by memory. But in their poetry they follow an idealising method, and make it general and mythological. The characters and incidents receive a typical form, often far removed from reality. The poets wandered from place to place, taking the songs with them, and the story became more vague the further it was transplanted from home. Exaggeration could hardly be avoided. The characters were mixed up and the dates confused. The older characters were absorbed in those of the immediate past, whose figures thus assumed larger proportions, and became the centre of various legends. Thus a cycle of stories gathered round a single name. The frequent coincidence of names rendered this confusion easier; and when their great men had been raised to equal dignity with the old heroes, mythical and historical persons were blended together, and the cycle of legends became larger than ever.

The traditions of German heroic poetry extend over more than 300 years, and are drawn from various German tribes. Historical King Ostrogotha reigned over the Goths about the elements in year 250, and was the contemporary of the emperors the heroic Philip and Decius. Ermanaric governed the Ostrogoths about 100 years later, and was a very warlike king, ruling over a large extent of territory. The invasion of the Huns drove him to despair, and he fell by his own hand before the year 374. Soon after the year 400 the Burgundians founded a mighty empire in the most fertile part of the Upper Rhine, where Cæsar had already fought with the Germans, near Spiers, Worms, and Mayence. The Roman Aëtius, who ruled Gaul with the aid of his Hun allies, defeated the Burgundians by means of these barbarians in a terrible battle about the year 437; 20,000 men fell, amongst them their king Gundicarius (Gunther). The Burgundians seemed to be annihilated, and soon after retreated to Savoy. About the same time Attila was king of the Huns and Ostrogoths, to the terror of the world. His name is Gothic, the arrangements of his court were Gothic, and he reckoned among his knights Theodomer, the king of the Ostrogoths. The West had just learnt all the terror of this 'Scourge of God,' when news came of his sudden death (453), and in the following year his followers succumbed to the attacks of the Germans (454). Twenty-two years later Odoacer deposed the last shadow of a Roman emperor; and again, twelve years later, Theodoric led the Ostrogoths into Italy and Odoacer fell by his hand. About the same period the Merovingian Clovis founded the kingdom of the Franks; about the year 530 his sons destroyed the Thuringian empire; and his grandson Theodebert extended his kingdom so far, that, starting from Hungary, he planned an attack on the Byzantine emperor. The Merovingians also offered a successful resistance to the Vikings, who were the terror of the North Sea, and who appeared

even at the mouths of the Rhine. From another quarter the
Longobards in little more than a century reached Italy, having
started from Lüneburg, in the neighbourhood of Brunswick, and
their King Alboin took possession of the crown of Italy in 568.

These wonderful transferences of power, and this rapid founding
Distortion
of history
by the poets. of new empires, furnished the historical background
of the German hero-legends. The fact that the move-
ment was originally against Rome was forgotten;
the migration was treated as a mere incident in the internal
history of the German nation. There is no trace of chronology.
An English bard of the eighth century, who transports himself
into the heroic period, says that he has been at Alboin's court,
that Gunther gave him an arm ring, and that he met Ostrogotha at
the court of Ermanaric. Legend adheres to the fact of the enmity
between Odoacer and Theodoric, but it really confuses Theodoric
with his father Theodomer, transplants him accordingly to Attila's
court, and supposes that he was an exile there in hiding from the
wrath of Odoacer. Attila becomes the representative of every
thing connected with the Huns. He is regarded as Ermanaric's
and Gunther's enemy, and as having destroyed the Burgundians.
These again are confused with a mythical race, the Nibelungen,
The Nibe-
lungen
legend. Siegfried's enemies, and thus arose the great and complicated scheme of the Nibelungen legend. While
in the Nibelungen legend historical and mythical
elements are mingled, the Theodoric legend, on the contrary, is
in its main features historical, and the legend of King Orendel
affords an example of pure myth. In the oldest version of the
Nibelungen legend—that, namely, which penetrated into the
North and was there preserved—Attila bears the blame of the
slaughter of the Burgundians. But as early as the seventh century certain German songs related the story in an essentially
different manner. In these songs not Attila, but his wife Kriemhild, Siegfried's widow, the sister of the Burgundian kings, plans
the murder. In the same version the attractive character of the
Markgrave Rüdiger is introduced for the first time into the
legend, and it is probable that this whole variation arose in
Austria, being connected with that general amplification of the

heroic song, which brought it to its highest level of perfection and inaugurated the first golden age of German poetry.

The oldest *mythical* legends, dating from a period before the migration, give us the typical hero Siegfried, frank and bold, cut off in the bloom of his youth by his wicked and perfidious enemy Hagen.

The oldest *historical* legends, down to about the middle of the fifth century, show us nothing but repulsive characters, drawn doubtless from the life of those rough times. Ermanaric and Attila represent the type of the covetous, cruel, ambitious sovereign. Such tyrants have generally at their side a faithless and intriguing counsellor, to whose influence the worst deeds of the sovereign are attributed. Sibicho, the counsellor of Ermanaric, became later on in German a·by-word for faithlessness. Beside him, we also find in Ermanaric's service Wittich and Heime, faithless warriors, of cold, gloomy nature, venal and cunning, shrinking from no expedient, however dishonourable.

A very different type of ruler meets us later on. Theodoric, who treacherously destroyed his opponent, but afterwards became a beneficent sovereign, is represented in the legend as a man of clear judgment, gentle, yet strong. He is a benign and just ruler, and his banishment from throne and kingdom and home **Milder character of the later legends.** excites our pity. The faithless Sibicho is contrasted with a careful monitor, the faithful Eckhart. Faithful servants, like old Hildebrand, play a great part in these later legends. Rüdiger is animated in battle by the noblest motives, and comes unsullied out of a tragic struggle of conflicting duties. Women, as in Gudrun, become the peace-makers between families at feud with one another. Or else it is a woman who stirs up the quarrel and knows how to make manly strength subservient to her own ends. Attila loses his selfish cruelty; and whatever horrors Kriemhild may be guilty of in the later legend, she is always actuated by loyalty to her husband, and only fulfils the duty of avenging the death of the noblest of heroes. Under all circumstances, we see in the position assigned to her a lofty recognition of woman's power. This idea also reflects the life of the time. The history of Merovingian France tells of a Brunhild and a Fredegonde, as the history of the Bourbons tells of a

Maintenon and a Pompadour. The wives of these Merovingian sovereigns met with express recognition at the hands of historians, as also did the influence they exercised on affairs. In countless deeds of horror a woman is said to be the cause; the narrators seem accustomed to the question 'Where is the woman?' But by the side of these demon-like forms, we find another type of woman, modest, chaste, and gentle, who, although perhaps of lowly birth, may be raised to the throne and there spread blessings all around her. It was a rule of common law that double as much wergeld (blood-money) should be paid for the murder of a woman as for that of a man; and the reason of this is often expressly stated—because she cannot defend herself with weapons. To tear the diadem from the head of a young girl, or even to loosen the plaits of her hair, was according to Bavarian law to be punished as heavily as an attempt to poison a freeman. In many other ways too feelings of humanity asserted themselves. A Gothic king of Spain is reported to have exclaimed after a victory, 'How miserable am I, that so much blood must flow in my time.' It was regarded as barbarous not to be willing to make compensation for any wrong done. We have instances of men who made it their work in life to buy and liberate slaves. One cannot say that it is the gentleness of Christianity that is here at work; the influence of Christianity worked in a very different way in other times. But here, as in other cases, humanity and respect for women go hand in hand. Only in this milder atmosphere could the heroic songs have developed their moral tendency, and the grandeur of the epic, the delight in polished manners and in eloquent speech, have grown up.

German heroic song begins with the Goths, and ends with the nations of the Frankish kingdom. The poets who first sang the epic songs to their harps belonged to the court. Wandering minstrels spread abroad the praise of princes, and were the teachers of the community. The Byzantine ambassador Priscus describes a feast of Attila at which he was present. After the dinner, when it grew dark, torches were lighted, and two men, who stood opposite to Attila, sang songs, in which they celebrated his victories and warlike

Poets at the court of Attila.

virtues. The guests gazed intently on the singers, some delighting in the poems, others excited by the thoughts of combat which
they inspired, while the aged, who could no longer share in the
deeds of daring which they loved, burst into tears. It is a picture
like that of Ulysses among the Phæacians, when Demodokos sings
the deeds of the heroes, and Ulysses hides his face and weeps. What
has become of those songs of Ermanaric, Attila, and Theodoric,
all those poems which once so strongly stirred German hearts?
Charlemagne caused them to be written down, as Collection
Pisistratus did the Homeric epics. But the next of hero-songs
generation had already forgotten them. In the ninth under Charle-
century we come again on traces of them, after which magne, but
they drop quite out of sight. We must give up the soon lost.
collection of Charlemagne as lost for ever: this most important
record of the German national epics is destroyed, and we are
reduced to guess-work. All we know is, that the epic singer
appeared before his audience like an orator, that he discarded the
traditional strophic form, and that his song flowed on without
break through the so-called Long-verses. He did not sing
rhythmically, but rather declaimed in recitative.

The old picturesque and vivid modes of expression, which primitive German poetry probably once possessed in common with the
Aryan, disappeared in the ballad-like poetry which followed upon,
and celebrated the stormy epoch of German migration; and later
on, when long narrative poems were revived, the old skill was not
recovered.

We possess in Germany itself but one poor literary fragment
from the whole of this first classic period of epic legend and poetry;
this fragment is the song of Hildebrand.

The aged Hildebrand has gone with Theodoric into exile among
the Huns. Years afterwards he returns to Italy at the head of an
army of Huns. His son Hadubrand advances to op- The song of
pose him. The poet begins abruptly: 'I have heard Hildebrand.
that Hildebrand and Hadubrand challenged each other to battle.' It
seems as though he were treating a theme which he might assume
to be generally known. Son and father arm themselves, and ride
to meet each other. Hildebrand asks who his opponent is, and

receives the answer, Hadubrand, son of Hildebrand. Then a second enquiry from Hildebrand and a clearer answer from Hadubrand make it plain to the old man that his opponent is his own son. He tries to avoid the combat, tells his name, and offers bracelets as presents. Hadubrand rejects them with disdain, and takes the old man for a crafty deceiver, who only wishes to entice him on within range of his spear. As for his father, he has heard that he was killed in battle. Hildebrand still tries to pacify him. He sees, indeed, that Hadubrand does not need his gifts, for he wears beautiful armour, and no doubt has a generous master; but he tries to induce him to seek out another opponent such as he can easily find in the army of the Huns, quite as distinguished as himself. Then Hadubrand taunts him with cowardice, and this he cannot bear; he sees he must fight, and laments in despair the cruelty of his fate which dooms him, after thirty years of wandering, and after a thousand escapes, either to be slain by his own son, or to become that son's murderer. Here the combat begins; they dash against each other with couched spears, which glance off from the shields; then they dismount, and with their swords hack each other's shields in pieces. The conclusion of the poem is lost. We may suppose that the old man conquered, and stood over the dead body of his son. He had destroyed his own race.

The poet knows how to place his subject before us in the most impressive manner. He takes little interest in the outward incidents. He just describes the arming of the two combatants, but in the fewest words possible. He goes straight to the point which seems to him the most important. What he delights in is the development of question and answer. He tells us specially that Hildebrand was the first to speak, because he was the worthiest and the oldest. He knows that it is an advantage in narrating long speeches that they should be interrupted or accompanied by action: he therefore introduces the episode of the bracelets, which Hildebrand takes from his own arms and offers to his opponent.

Apart from its mere technical excellence the dialogue is so skilfully handled, that we perceive at once the character, the coming destiny, and the tragic end of the human beings who take part in it. The poet has reproduced the naïve manners of a childlike age, in which men are allowed to praise themselves, in which possessions, presents, booty, are the objects of an undisguised selfish cupidity. Hildebrand parades his own extensive acquaintance with men. The prize of battle is the armour of the vanquished; ornaments are offered to soften the stubborn temper of the opponent. The poet not only knows how to introduce without effort a number of facts which lie outside the framework of the story, but he also understands the art of developing character, and of making speeches and actions its natural outcome. Hildebrand is the picture of old age as Hadubrand is of youth. The former is cautious, deliberate, prudent; the latter is hasty, eager for combat, suspicious, and obstinate. The answers which Hildebrand receives to his cautiously put questions have the effect of forcing on him still further caution. But in order that we may entertain no doubt of his valour, Hadubrand, who suspects the courage of his foe, is made to allege that his father was always too fond of fighting. Tragic irony could not go further than in this admirable contrast between father and son; between the father who knows his son, and the son who knows not his father; the father striving to reveal his kinship, the son repudiating it; the father filled with love for the son before him, the son full of affection and admiration for the father whom he believes to be dead; and the two engaged in mortal conflict with one another.

Hildebrand is decidedly the hero of the poem. His whole early history is touched upon. Our pity is excited for him, so long separated from his family, and now, at the risk of dishonour, forced to engage in mortal conflict with the man whom he knows to be his own son. Yet the poet utters no word of sympathy, he works on us only by a bare statement of the facts in the formal style which he has adopted. Hildebrand's cry of despair when the fight is inevitable, stands alone in the poem: in this cry the unspeakable anguish of the father's heart is concentrated. The fearful mental struggle, the fearful deed which must be done under the imperious demands of honour—these are the chief ideas which filled the imagination of the poet. He thus evidences the moral spirit of the old heroic songs. Small as is the fragment left to us, it is a noble fruit, and from it we may infer the grandeur of the tree which bore it.

ULFILAS.

At the very time when heroic song was taking a higher flight, Christianity began to exert its influence on the Germanic nations.

Influence of Christianity on German legend. The latest legends have nothing heathen about them, and when we find that in these legends women play an important part, we must remember that at this time pious women were already contributing as nuns to the sanctification of life. At the king's court the monk now stands side by side with the minstrel. The forms of the old gods fade before the image of the Crucified. The migration began with the

The Goths. Goths. Among them heroic song first sprang up, and they were also the first converts to Christianity. The Goths were the most advanced of the old German tribes. Their brief career foreshadowed the later and fuller development of the Franks. Nay, the problems which the Goths had to face were such as have occupied men's minds both in the middle ages and in modern times, and they recur again and again throughout German history. These problems are imperial power, the religious training of the people, toleration of nationalities and of creeds.

Heroic song began with the Ostrogoths; but it was the Visigoths who were first converted to Christianity. We can only guess at the causes which influenced the people to forsake their old gods.

Religious consequences of the migration. The most important was the migration itself, and the changed conditions which arose from the total change of locality. To leave their homes, to leave the sanctuary of their tribe, where they assembled for their religious festivals, and the sacred groves in which the gods dwelt,—this in itself was a great wrench. A time of great deeds, but also of great suffering ensued. The excitement of the struggle for existence might nerve and elevate the hearts of king and nobles, yet the mass of the people were without doubt exposed to extreme distress. They invoked the old gods, and finding no succour began to lose faith in them. Why should they not try the new gods, to whom the Greeks and Romans raised innumerable churches and altars, the gentle and merciful God, the God of the poor and needy, who had Himself suffered the greatest indignities? Even the Roman emperor bowed before this God; and He must surely be the most powerful Deity to whom the emperor himself could appeal for help. While these were probably the feelings of the people, their chiefs, on the other hand, had good political reasons for offering homage to the God of the Byzantine empire; they might thus acquire land and gain favour with the emperor. So the vigilant Christian missionaries found ready listeners in chiefs and people.

The Visigoths were the tribe most closely connected with the Empire of the East. In the great struggle between Arius and Athanasius, which agitated the Church in the fourth century, the imperial power inclined for a time to the side of Arianism. Constantius in particular, the son of Constantine the Great, favoured this more easily comprehensible form of church doctrine, and the Eastern bishops of that time were mostly Arian in their opinions.

The form of Christianity therefore which lay nearest to the Goths was Arianism. Thus it was that at the Synod   Ulfilas, of Antioch in the year 341, the Arian Wulfila or   circa 350. Ulfilas, as the Greeks call him, was consecrated bishop of the Goths, that is of the Visigoths to the north of the lower Danube. Ulfilas was about thirty years old. He was no ordinary theologian of the time: he had not been spoilt by the schools of the rhetors. We possess his later confession of   His faith, in which he attempts to modify the doctrine of   Arianism. the Trinity in the direction of a simple monotheism,—a striking proof of the freshness and vigour of his understanding. Seven years after his consecration misfortune befel the young community. The new religion roused the suspicion of the Gothic king, and a bloody persecution followed. The emperor Constantius allowed the survivors to emigrate to Mœsia, in the neighbourhood of Nicopolis, not far from the Hæmus mountains. These emigrants were called the Little Goths. Ulfilas laboured among them till his death. He died in 381 in Constantinople, whither he had gone to defend the doctrines of Arius. When he led the emigrants over the Danube in 348, he seemed to his contemporaries a second Moses at the head of his people. By his hand, as a biographer expresses it, God had wrought for the followers of His

only-begotten Son, to deliver them from the hand of the barbarians, just as formerly He saved His people, through Moses,
from the hand of the Egyptians, and led them through the Red
Sea. And in fact Ulfilas stands alone in the history of the conversion
of the Germanic tribes. He is in the sphere of religion what
Theodoric the Great is in the sphere of politics. At one moment
the Ostrogoths are a homeless people; a few years elapse and
they are reigning in Italy, their king becomes the successor of the
Roman emperors, and endeavours to enter upon the whole inheritance of Roman politics and Roman power. He and his
people appropriated at one stroke all that Rome had attained to
in political knowledge and statecraft. The highest ideal known
to declining Rome in the intellectual sphere was Christianity,
and the possession of the Bible has the same significance in the
intellectual and religious sphere that the possession of Italy and
Rome has in the political. The former, Ulfilas by one effort
secured to the Visigoths. He was master of three languages:
he preached in Greek, Latin, and Gothic; and he devoted this
His Transla- gift to the noblest purpose. He is reported to
tion of the have translated the whole Bible, only omitting the
Bible into Books of the Kings as likely to encourage the
Gothic. warlike propensities of his people. This translation he effected for those who were till then destitute of the first
beginnings of a written literature. Nay, till he taught them, the
Goths did not even know what reading meant, and Ulfilas had
to translate the word by 'singing.' He created a style of writing
which could be painted on parchment for a people who till then
had only scrawled single signs, or a few consecutive words on
wood or stone. He formed his alphabet by supplementing the
Runes from the Greek alphabet, or the Greek alphabet from the
Runes. The translation is a literal reproduction in Gothic of the
Greek text. He united the greatest reverence for the holy Book,
with a due regard for the laws of his native language. The
language itself here came to his aid; the Gothic syntax stood in
closer relationship to the Greek than modern or even old German
stands to the Gothic. Ulfilas had doubtless fellow-workers; the
few remaining fragments of the Old Testament show a different

hand from the Gospels, and these again from the remains of the
Pauline Epistles. But the idea, the example, the supervision, the
merit, are his.

Ulfilas did not write for the Little Goths alone. The entire conversion of the Visigoths was, notwithstanding the **Wide extent**
first persecution, only a question of time ; and the con- **of German**
version of the Visigoths was destined to react upon **Arianism.**
a large number of Germanic tribes. All the tribes of the Eastern
branch were gradually drawn under the influence of Arianism.
So it was with the Ostrogoths, with the Heruli, Skiri and Rugii
of Austria and Bavaria, and also with the Vandals in Spain.
Even the Burgundians, who had formerly been Roman Christians, inclined for a time towards Arianism, and the less closely
related Longobards seem, while they ruled on the Danube, to have
superficially adopted Arianism, after the example of their Austrian
neighbours.

We may assume that the Gothic Bible and the intellectual
power of Ulfilas reached as far as the limits of German Arianism.
No German of Catholic persuasion ever attempted anything like it.
Wycliffe in England, and Luther in Germany, are the first who can
be compared with him. The partial or complete translations
which arose before Wycliffe and Luther suffered from two causes :
firstly, from the exaggerated respect felt for Latin as the sacred
language ; secondly, from the papal decrees, which later on forbade
the use of the Bible.

What we possess in the Gothic language besides the Bible is
insignificant. It consists of an interpretation of St. **Other lite-**
John's Gospel founded on Greek commentaries, a **rary frag-**
fragment of a Gothic Calendar, a few documents, at- **ments in**
tested by Gothic priests in Gothic, a Gothic toast in **Gothic.**
a Latin epigram, and a few isolated words in Latin writings.
Probably the written literature was confined to the careful copy-
ing and faithful rendering of the Bible, or to the amending and
altering of the sacred text. These alterations consisted in changes
based on the authority of a Latin translation or in the addition of
synonyms and the choice of fresh expressions. But even when
writers advanced to commentaries, they still kept within the lines

which Ulfilas had laid down. The MSS. which have been preserved are probably of Italian origin: the most valuable of all, the famous 'Codex argenteus' at Upsala, in silver letters on purple parchment, may have been in the possession of the Ostrogothic kings themselves.

In the territory of the Skiri and Rugii, the progenitors of the Austro-Bavarian race, we find in the ninth century in a Salzburg MS. traces of a knowledge of the Gothic alphabet and Bible. And it is evident that isolated ecclesiastical words, such as Heide (heathen), Pfaffe (priest), Kirche (church), were first coined in Gothic, and thence passed into the German language, where they still survive. Thus the German language has received at least some small legacy from Gothic Arianism, although the Arian churches themselves have all perished.

The chief enemy which those tribes which had embraced Arianism had to contend against was the Roman Church. They succumbed before the opposition of this and other hostile elements. But the Bible of Ulfilas has acquired an entirely new importance. Franciscus Junius printed and published it in the seventeenth century, and áfter Jacob Grimm in the nineteenth had made it the basis of the comparative grammar of all the Teutonic languages, it became the true key to German antiquity. Ulfilas is our best guide to the secrets of German primitive times; he alone has survived his whole people. The Gothic songs which once formed the centre of our heroic legends, the songs of Ostrogotha, Ermanaric, Theodomer, and Theodoric, have long since died away; the Gothic Bible, in its noble fragments, lives on, a sacred relic, unchanged, and now imperishable.

The Merovingians.

The more roving and warlike of the German tribes showed Christianising of the German tribes. themselves the most ready to embrace Christianity; they had been uprooted, and their heathen traditions shaken. Rome, though conquered in the field, became intellectually the mistress of her conquerors. The rule of the emperors came to an end, that of the popes was gradually established. The Arian phase of German faith was followed by a Roman Catholic one, at least among the Franks, Alemanni, Anglo-Saxons, and Bavarians, who had all distinguished themselves in the famous German movement against Rome. The more stationary Hessians, Thuringians, and Frisians, held out for a long time; the Saxons were converted by force, after a weary struggle, towards the end of the eighth century, while with the Scandinavians the process of conversion began later, and was still more arduous.

In the beginning of the sixth century the songs concerning Siegfried and Attila spread as far as Scandinavia, but after that period the various German tribes became more and more separated from each other. The wide influence exercised by Theodoric did not descend to his successors. Under the Merovingian dynasty the Franks took up the task of consolidation, and com- **The Franks.** pelled the whole of middle and South Germany to acknowledge their supremacy. The ground was thus prepared for fresh conversions. The Christianity of the Franks, which was due to accidental causes, was not of a very strict character. The clergy were drawn into secular life. No vigorous opposition was offered to the remnants of heathenism, nor was literature employed in support of religion. The Merovingian period, which brought German popular heroic song to perfection, cannot point to a single literary document in the German language. No Ulfilas arose; no missionaries were sent out. The example of proselytism had to be first set from outside, by a small people, which now for the first and only time exerted its influence on the intellectual development of Europe, i.e. the Irish.

In the first half of the fifth century St. Patrick brought Christianity to the Irish from Scotland, and the Irish monasteries became a centre of civilisation and Christian missions, independent of Rome. and often directly opposed to her. They sent forth Columbanus, an apostle full of zeal, and yet of liberal views. He **Irish mis-** recommended the study of the ancient poets just as **sions in** much as that of the early fathers of the church, and **Germany.** quoted the authority of Juvenal, as lending support to the Gospel maxims. He himself wrote in old Greek metre. and was well versed in classical literature and mythology. The maxims of life which he gives to his monks are fit for a brotherhood of philosophers.

This Columbanus became in the seventh century the Apostle of the Alemanni. His disciple, Gallus, founded the monastery of St. Gall. They were followed by many others of their countrymen, whose zeal roused the emulation of the Frankish clergy, and prepared the way for the conversion of the Bavarians and Thuringians. The Merovingian empire thus became on the whole a Christian empire. But down to the eighth century, to the time of St. Boniface, all strict church discipline was wanting. Christianity was only one element of civilisation by the side of others, and did not yet claim the exclusive dominion over men's minds. German heroic song attained at this time its highest development.

In the matter of poetic form, Germany was indebted to the **Rhyme, a** *Romanic* nations; it was from them that German **product of** poetry received the ornament of rhyme. We find **the Romanic** the first traces of rhyme in Germany in the ninth cen- **nations.** tury; but then it is already used to adorn Christian hymns which were meant to supplant the popular songs. It is most probable that rhyme had been employed for some time in the popular songs, for the writers of these early Christian hymns would hardly have made the strange matter of their poetry yet more strange by clothing it in an unaccustomed form. As epic poetry with its stately alliterative verses gradually disappeared, rhyme came more and more into fashion. But it first found its way to Germany from outside.

Popular Latin poetry had long employed nothing but rhyme. The Christian hymns, intended to be sung by the masses, adopted the same form. It is also found in Irish poetry, and all the Romanic nations, the Northern and Southern French, the Spaniards, and Italians submit to its fetters. This melodious, sensuous adornment was evidently a product of that obscure epoch which laid the foundations of mediæval life. It came to Germany through the medium of music, and German poetry could not resist its influence. Attractive Italian or French melodies wandered to Germany, and German poets set German words to them, as the Minnesänger

and the poets of the Renaissance did in later periods. And with
these melodies, songs, and dances there also came rhyme. We find
it first of all on the Upper Rhine, from whence it spread over the
rest of Germany.   The fact that rhyme is found in German poetry
is as substantial a proof of the early influence of Romanic culture,
as the foreign words used in German to designate   Influence of
wine-culture and house-building, words which came   Romanic
into the German language at about the same period   civilisation
as the introduction of rhyme.   This points to a dis-   on Germany.
tinguishing feature of the first classical period of German literature,
and one which recurs again in the second and third classical periods,
—it was the Romanic nations who shaped the æsthetic sense of
the Germans.

Yet another event belonging to this epoch continues to exert its influence to the present day, and is one of the most important incidents
of German history ; I refer to the dialectal separation   Separation
between South and North German, which must have   of High- and
begun about the year 600.   Then arose the still exist-   Low-German
ing difference between High- and Low-German dialects,   dialects,
and there was no educated language, no literary speech   circa 600.
to bridge over the gulf.   Two German languages were formed,
and those who spoke them might easily have separated into two
nations.

Low-German *dat* and *wat*, by the side of High-German *das* and
was ; Low-German *ick* instead of *ich*, *open* instead of *offen*, the
modern Berlinese *duhn* instead of *thun ;* these and countless similar
consonantal differences place Low German on the same level as
Dutch, English, Danish, Swedish, and Norwegian.   And all these
languages have really kept to the original form of Germanic speech,
while High German has separated itself from this common foundation.   At first it was only a separate dialect, but afterwards, when
used as the literary language, it slowly gained a sure supremacy.
The movement seems to have originated in the mountainous districts.   The Alemanni, the Bavarians, and Longobards, were the first
to fall under its influence ; the Franks, Hessians, and Thuringians
were only gradually drawn into it.   Lower down the Rhine it was less
powerful, and the Netherlands remained entirely untouched.

Jacob Grimm has given the name of *Old High German* to the language which thus arose, and which continued to develop down to the eleventh century. And if we enquire what were the causes of this consonantal change, or 'Lautverschiebung' as Grimm calls it, we shall find an answer in the general character of the Old High-German dialect. Among all the Teutonic languages, whether of older or more modern times, none can compare for melody with this dialect, as seen in the rhyming poets of the ninth century. The cold, serious, sober ninth century is here using an instrument bequeathed to it by an older, gentler, and more æsthetic age. The language was rich in vowels, melodious and plastic as Italian, and therefore in its very nature suited to rhyme. But the delight in vowels led to the neglect of the consonants. The immoderate striving after euphony dissolved the firmer elements of words, and this was the real origin of the change of consonants in High German.

Old High German.

This separation of High German has exercised a momentous influence in German literature and German history. To it may be attributed in great measure the difficulty which the Germans have found in creating a united national literature and culture. For centuries all German poetry could only count upon a local and limited public; and even to the present day the people of the various provinces are more abruptly divided from each other than elsewhere, South Germans and North Germans in particular standing in many respects in sharp contrast.

It was the subjection of the Saxons by Charlemagne which hindered the High and Low Germans from becoming two nations. The cruel propagation of the Christian faith was in the end an advantage to the German nation. The giant will which kept together Italy, Gaul, and Germany, also united Saxons, Franks, Hessians, Thuringians, Alemanni, and Bavarians. At the same time the Germanic element in the empire was strengthened by the addition of the Saxons. More regard was now paid to the kinship of races, as may be seen from the division of the empire among the sons of Louis the Pious. At Strassburg, on February 14, 842, the Western Franks under Charles the Bald took their oath in French, while the Eastern Franks under Louis the German took theirs in

German. And the German Empire, strictly speaking, only began to exist after the Treaty of Verdun in 843.

The mother-tongue of Charlemagne was High German; he himself, his family, and his court, spoke mostly High German, and it is to this circumstance that the High-German dialect owes that supremacy which it has asserted since then almost without interruption. Under Charlemagne we first find the expression '*deutsch*,' i.e. popular (from *deot*, people), used to designate the popular language of German origin in distinction to Latin and the Romance languages.

The consciousness of German nationality first asserted itself at the time of the revival of the Empire of the West under Charlemagne.

CHAPTER III.

THE OLD HIGH-GERMAN PERIOD.

UNDER Charlemagne we come to the first connected records in the German language, and these seem to have been called forth by The Anglo- the needs of Christian teaching. Under his succes-
Saxons. sors complete Christian poems were produced. But in all this the Franks, Saxons, and other German tribes only followed in the steps of another Germanic people, who led the way both by their example and direct influence — the Anglo-Saxons. Before St. Columbanus crossed to the continent, the Roman Church had gained a strong footing in the same corner of Europe from which the Irish missions had started.

In the beginning of the seventh century Pope Gregory the Great succeeded in winning over the Anglo-Saxons to Christianity. Numerous learned and poetical works bear witness to the extraordinary
Beowulf. talent of this people. Their popular epic, the 'Beowulf,'
gives the story of a noble hero who came to succour foreigners in distress, fought victoriously with destructive water-demons, was crowned by his people, and finally succumbed in a fight with a dragon. Into this framework are woven varied pictures of life, marked by the true epic love for full details of manners, speech, and modes of warfare. The same creative power which is here displayed in the treatment of a national legend also exercised
Bede. itself on the new materials offered by Christianity. In
Bede the Anglo-Saxons possessed a scholar of the first order, who had mastered the whole science of his time, and embodied it in various school-books which soon became very popular.

In Aldhelm they had a Latin poet of much feeling and refinement. Cædmon is named as the oldest Anglo-Saxon Christian poet who wrote in the vulgar tongue; Cynewulf is known to us by various excellent works.   Grand paraphrases in Old English verse of parts of the Old and New Testaments are still extant, as well as wonderful legends, like Cynewulf's 'Andreas,' in which the union of Christianity with the spirit of the popular epic produces noble effects.   It was this circle of life and culture that sent out St. Boniface.   He was no Bede; he was a man of narrow spirit and small education, but certainly a hero, and *St. Boniface.* well fitted to realise the ideal of a Christian apostle and martyr. He was quite different from St. Columbanus, whose fellow-country-men he persecuted everywhere in Germany; he even accused them to the Pope, because they held such fearful heresies as belief in the roundness of the earth, and the existence of the antipodes.   He is the representative of a different nationality, a different church sys-tem, a different age.   He did not make many new converts among the Germans, but held the reins tight over those already converted. He was inexorable in rooting out all traces of heathen worship, and also set his face against all the more liberal elements of Chris-tianity.   He established a regular system of sacerdotal rule, and put all under the dominion of Rome.

Charlemagne, with his great love of power and care for his people, continued in his church policy the work which Boniface had begun, and in this the Anglo-Saxon Alcuin was his *Charlemagne* most trusty counsellor.   Charlemagne's decrees of *and the first* the year 789 were intended to insure outward unifor- *German* mity in matters of religion, and called forth the first *prose.* German prose writings, translations of the baptismal vow, of the Creeds, the Lord's Prayer, and Confessions.   These again gave rise to other literature, chiefly of a religious character, but merely borrowed from the Latin; many of these translations show a remarkable and quickly acquired facility, and they were a great aid in the composition of sermons which Charlemagne demanded from the clergy by decisive injunctions.   Little was done towards acquiring a complete German Bible.   People only cared to possess the life of Christ, for which one gospel was enough.   That according to St. Matthew, which was selected for the purpose, was reproduced in a translation at once beautiful and impressive.   At

the same time poetry was applied to religious subjects. Short
prayers in verse were produced, and the stories of the Creation and
Fall seem to have been favourite themes. The end of the world is
described in a poem of which the greater part has come down to us.
'Muspilli.' The author, who is a layman, adopts the prophetic
tone of the preacher. He sets before his readers as
effectively as possible church doctrines which he barely understands,
and renders them attractive to the warlike nobles whom he addresses.
The following is a short outline of the poem :—Two hosts, angels
and devils, fight for the departing soul ; Antichrist fights with Elias ;
the former is conquered, the latter wounded, and the drops of his
blood set on fire forest and mountain ; all water is dried up, heaven
melts in the glow, the moon falls, the world is consumed by fire—
'Muspilli,' as the poet calls it, using the old heathen term for the
final conflagration of the world. The poem draws a terrible picture of the pains of hell, and an equally attractive one of the joys of
heaven. It points with solemn warnings to the last judgment
when all crimes will come to light and be avenged. The penance
of fasting is recommended as a protection against final punishment. The sins which the poet specially has in view are murder,
bribery of judges, quarrels about boundaries—all of them aristocratic sins.

THE FIRST MESSIANIC POEMS.

In the ninth century Christian poetry took a higher flight, and
selected as its theme the life of the Saviour. It undertook to
render the gospel of love into German verse, and dared to pro-
claim to a warlike people, through the mouth of its God, ' Blessed
are the peacemakers.'

The ninth century produced two Messianic poems, which were
written during the reigns of the son and grandson of Charlemagne:
a Saxon one by an unknown poet, and a Frankish one by Otfried.
Both show us the highest theological culture of the time, as represented by the school of Fulda.

The monastery of Fulda was founded by St. Boniface, and we

know pretty accurately all the circumstances of its foundation.
His pupil Sturmi, who had lived for some time as a   The Mon-
hermit, was charged to select a site, and his bio-   astery of
grapher describes him riding alone on his ass through   Fulda.
forest and desert, scanning with sharp eyes mountain and valley,
and seeing nothing but huge trees and desert plains, wild animals,
and all kinds of birds. At night he makes an enclosure for his
ass, while he himself sleeps securely after making the sign of the
cross on his forehead. 'Thus,' we are told, 'the holy man set out to
fight against the devil, well provided with spiritual weapons, clothed
in the armour of righteousness, his breast protected by the shield
of faith, his head covered with the helmet of salvation, his waist
girt with the sword of the word of God.' This figure of the *Miles
Christianus*, the Christian knight and vassal of God, often meets us
again in later times, in Erasmus, in the drama of the sixteenth
century, and in Albert Dürer's pictures.

Sturmi was, like Boniface, a true soldier of God. He was the
first Abbot of Fulda. In the campaigns of Charlemagne he was
the first missionary to the Saxons. A MS. at Fulda preserves the
formula in which these heathen were forced to abjure 'Donar,
and Woden, and Saxnot, and all the other monsters who are their
companions.'

From 822 Rabanus Maurus presided over the monastery as fifth
Abbot. He was a narrow and intolerant man, who afterwards
attained to the highest ecclesiastical dignity in Germany, and
became Archbishop of Mainz (847 to 856). He made Fulda
the first and most esteemed school of Germany. In his time the
monastery filled the position of a leading university and was the
resort of all who were eager to learn. The works of Rabanus are,
from our point of view, scientifically worthless; he has hardly any
original thoughts, and only transmits those of others. But creative
minds were very rare in the ninth century, and even encyclopædic
learning is a merit. Rabanus directed the school of Fulda from
804, and as Abbot retained part of the teaching in his own hands,
particularly the expounding of the Scriptures. About 820 he wrote
a commentary on St. Matthew's Gospel, which was much used in
the two old Messianic poems I have mentioned. And it seems

that he himself had the idea of making his mother tongue the vehicle of religion. A Latin life of Christ, compiled from all four Gospels, but based mainly on St. Matthew, was translated into German in his time, and probably at his instigation; and Otfried von Weissenberg, the author of the Frankish Messianic poem, acknowledges himself as his pupil.

The older Saxon Messianic poem—usually called the ' Heljand ' (Heiland) ' Saviour,' was composed about the year 830, and, as an old record tells us, at the instigation of the emperor Louis the Pious. It contains about 6000 alliterative lines, and has been extravagantly praised; but an impartial critic will form a more sober estimate of its value. The poet stands on the same level as the Anglo-Saxon priests, who had already in the eighth century treated Bible-subjects poetically in their mother tongue. Intellectual intercourse still existed between the Saxons of England and those of North Germany. The German poet could learn much from the English, but he went even further than they did in transferring the spirit and costume of the secular epic to subjects which from their nature were but little fitted for such treatment. The secular epic, as it existed among the Anglo-Saxons, makes the sovereign and his circle the centre of interest. The relation between the king and his followers is a feudal one : he gives them lodging and food, equips them with arms, gives them presents out of his treasure; in return for this they are bound to be faithful to him even to death. This relation, known already to Tacitus, is transferred by the poet to Christ and his disciples, and he makes use of the same means of description and representation as would be employed in secular poetry. But between the moral ideas of Christianity and those of the Germanic hero world there was a wide gulf which no art could bridge. The warlike deeds commemorated in the secular epic have nothing in common with the peaceful and suffering life of the Saviour. It was impossible to reconcile the code of honour which suffered no insult to pass unavenged with the moral code which bade men present the other cheek to the smiter. The poet carefully omits this humiliating command; but he could not in the same way suppress the story of the flight of the disciples after the betrayal. They were guilty of

The Heljand, circa 830.

one of the blackest crimes known to the German moral code, and yet they were holy men for whom the poet wishes to inspire veneration. He therefore tries to justify their conduct in the strangest manner. He denies that it was cowardice which made them forsake the Son of God, and says they could not avoid doing so, because the prophets had long before foretold that this would happen. Strange fatalism this! A true German would have accused those prophets of lying. As a compensation the poet lays great stress on the passage where Peter cuts off the ear of the servant Malchus; this single warlike action supplied by the narrative is painted in fullest detail. In other ways, too, the poet pays great regard to the feelings of his audience. He places the Jews in the most unfavourable light, but is careful to say nothing against the heathen before his newly-converted countrymen; he omits any passages of the Bible likely to offend their sense of honour, and in one passage he actually distinguishes the adversaries and followers of Christ as Jews and heathens. He makes the most of incidents, such as banquets and storms, which lent themselves to the established methods of epic description. But we cannot say that he has a creative imagination. He neither invents new details to enlarge the story, nor does he elevate us by the spirit in which he treats it. The involuntary travesty by which he clothes biblical figures in the garb of his countrymen, like the painters of the fifteenth century, may be called naïve or original; at all events it forms for us the chief charm of the poem. We should, however, value it less if we possessed a plentiful supply of secular poetry of the same time and place; and we must bear in mind that this manner of treatment was a simple necessity with the poet, if he wished to secure any real influence for his poem. There still remains much which is contrary to the spirit of an epic, and which he could not, and indeed did not try to remove. Christ is always the chief speaker; his speeches are often long and unbroken, and instead of deeds we have maxims. Whether Christ is addressing his disciples, or the author his public, preaching still preponderates.

In short, this Heljand, which has been compared to Homer, and has been declared the most sublime work which Christian poetry has ever produced, nay the only real Christian epic—

this Heljand is really no epic at all, but just the didactic poem which its author meant it to be. It is a free translation of the Bible with a running commentary added, composed in the only style which was at the author's command, if he did not wish to make a literal prose translation. He is only a narrator because his didactic object required it. His work is meant to edify, and we must look upon him as a preacher and no more.

This applies still more to his successor, Otfried, whose 'Gospels' appeared about 870, and were dedicated to King Louis the German. They are arranged in five books, the idea being that they should purify and sanctify the five senses.

Otfried's Gospels, circa 870.

The books are divided into chapters headed by Latin inscriptions, and in a Latin introduction the author informs us of his aims and principles; in fact, the composition claims to be a learned work in all respects. Strangely enough, this monk of Weissenberg meant in writing it not only to furnish a book for reading, but also hymns for singing, and he hoped that these hymns would supplant the secular songs which he held in abhorrence. He has not that simple earnestness which distinguishes the author of the Heljand. The exaggerated method of biblical interpretation then in vogue, which could leave no fact to its own merits, but attributed to every event a special symbolical, moral meaning, either retrospective or prophetic, interrupts the narrative at every step in a most unpleasing manner. Besides this, Otfried introduces psychological reflections and even personal sentiments, and strives to attain a touching eloquence. We will mention a single example. When the three Wise Men after having seen the Holy Child, return to their home by another way, Rabanus Maurus, Otfried's teacher, remarks in his commentary 'Even so must we do; our home is Paradise, we have left it through self-will and disobedience, we must return by tears and obedience.' Otfried expands this thought after he has asserted in the strongest way that words fail him to describe Paradise; he proceeds with much rhetorical repetition to represent earthly life as a sad exile; he tells us how he has himself tasted the bitterness of exile. But such lyrical touches do not often occur. At the end of the work he represents once more, in all its details, the glory of heaven as opposed to the misery

of earth. Old age, which he laments, seems to weigh on himself; he suffers from failing strength, ennui and—cough. Then
he lays down his pen, or, as he himself expresses it, he ends his
voyage, guides his vessel back to the coast, lets down the sail, and
his oar is henceforth to rest on the shore.

Either in narrative or reflection Otfried seldom expresses himself
in telling or appropriate language. In this he is inferior to an
otherwise insignificant, short, ballad-like poem of this period, which
describes the meeting of Christ and the woman of Samaria at the
well. But his disagreeable diffuse style does not hinder us from
enjoying the music of his rhymed verses, though in this it must
be owned the merit lies more with the language than with the poet.
In the beginning of his work he is more fresh and concise.
His description of the Annunciation is very graphic. He also
draws a picture, charming for its fresh naturalness, of the Virgin
as a young mother. He lends greater reality to the massacre of
the Innocents by introducing many probable details, and never
fails to enlarge on women's lamentations.

But we do not find these pathetic and didactic elements balanced
by passages expressing natural pleasure in life. Yet Otfried is
proud of the glory of the Franks, he praises the country and
people, and we see that national pride guides his pen. He is not
so much a monk as to suppress his patriotic feelings. The chapter
entitled 'Why the author wrote this book in German,' is perhaps
the most interesting in the whole work.

Otfried establishes a peculiar literary canon according to which
piety is all-important for sacred songs, for then angels help the
poet. He praises the literary art of the Greeks and Romans, and
especially commends their poetry for its smoothness and polish.
They would have presented the sacred story in an equally beautiful
form ; why should not the Franks do the same? For they were
as brave and warlike as the Romans and Greeks; they were wise
and skilful, rich and industrious, and all nations—unless separated
from them by the sea—stood in awe of them. They came from
Macedonia and were related to Alexander, who subdued the world:
therefore even the Medes and Persians would come off badly, if
they fought with them.

These patriotic sentiments are not merely personal on the part of Otfried. He only expresses in a naïve poetic form thoughts which had long lived among his people, and had found utterance in an official document at the head of the chief collection of Frankish laws, the *Lex Salica*. 'The glorious nation of the Franks,' it is there said, 'was founded by God the Creator, brave in war, faithful in covenants, wise in counsel, of high stature, white skin, and great beauty, bold, quick, and keen.' And then Christ's protection and favour are invoked for empire, rulers, and army, on the following grounds :—' For this is the strong and brave people, who by hard fighting broke the heavy yoke of the Romans from off their neck, and who, after they had been baptized, adorned with gold and precious stones the bodies of those holy martyrs whom the Romans burnt in the fire, mutilated by the sword and flung to the wild beasts.'

Such utterances as these enable us to realise in some measure the thoughts which must have been present to Charlemagne when he seized the crown of the Cæsars. And an equally strong pride in their Saxon nationality must have inspired Otto the Great and his successors, when they followed the example of Charlemagne, and when the far-reaching dominion of the Franks seemed for a time to be renewed in the Saxons.

The Mediæval Renaissance.

In the year 1000, the youthful Emperor Otto the Third had the vault of Charlemagne in the Cathedral at Aix-la-Chapelle opened, and descended into it. He took the golden cross from the neck of the corpse, and some of the clothes, then had the remains reverently put back into the coffin, and retired.

The youth of twenty-one who, half-reverential, half-bold, thus ventured to disturb the repose of the great emperor, was animated by the same spirit as his mighty predecessor. The old glory of the Romans was present to both, and both were inspired by the thought that the universal empire of the Romans had passed to the Germans. The mediæval Renaissance has two culminating periods, the first under Charlemagne, the second under the Ottos.

The political aspect of this Renaissance is represented by the
revival of the Empire of the West; the artistic side is represented by palaces and churches formed on late Roman and Byzantine models, and in part actually constructed out of antique
materials. The literary aspect of the Renaissance is seen in
improved schools, in the revival of classical studies, in the writing
of Latin history and poetry, in which phrases borrowed from
Suetonius and Virgil were made to serve new purposes. Charlemagne was praised in the same terms as Cæsar Augustus, and
the founding of Aix was likened to the founding of Carthage in
the Æneid.

Aix is the classical home of the mediæval Renaissance, and,
according to Charlemagne's idea, was to be a second Rome, a
Christian Athens. The Italian campaigns had made Charlemagne
acquainted with the education received by the laity in the South,
and this had roused him to emulation. From the year 781 he
strove to make his court the centre of all the Latin cul-   Court of
ture of the time. There we find the Italians Paulinus Charlemagne.
and Petrus of Pisa ; the Lombard Paulus Diaconus, the historian of
his people ; the Anglo-Saxon Alcuin, the first theologian, philosopher, and teacher of his age ; the Spanish Goth Theodulf, the first
poet of his time ; the Irishman Clement ; the Franks Angelbert and
Eginhard. Charles and his most intimate scientific friends had
regular meetings after the manner of an academy. They exchanged
poetic epistles, set scientific problems, and propounded enigmas.
As in later academies, the members had special academic names ;
Charles himself was called David, Angelbert the new Homer, and
Alcuin the new Horace. Like later academies, they imagined
themselves in the pastoral world, and two of the courtiers were
called Menalcas and Thyrsis. No wonder that the antique idyll
was revived in this circle, and in connection with it there arose
the ‘ Streitgedicht,’ or poem in dialogue (called *conflictus* in Latin),
which was so much in vogue in the Middle Ages. The antagonism
of summer and winter was a favourite theme in such poetry.

The consciousness of living in the midst of a Renaissance of
vanished glories might well fire the hearts of men of that day.
Thus a young poet describes the great Emperor, as looking down

from the battlements of his palace at Aix, on the kingdoms subject to his sceptre, on the changed aspect of the world, and the revival of ancient civilisation. 'Already,' he exclaims, 'golden Rome is born again on the globe.'

No one has a better claim to be compared with Charlemagne than Alfred the Great of England. And they both have this in common, that they did not devote themselves exclusively to Latin literature, but valued the productions of their own country. Charlemagne surpassed all his court in many-sidedness and literary patriotism. He caused the German heroic songs to be written down, and began himself to compile a German grammar; but no lasting results followed these efforts. The culture of the laity, which he had so much at heart, seems not to have been quite lost in the next two centuries; the higher classes could at least introduce scraps of Latin into their conversation. But the heroic songs were forgotten, and the grammar was never finished. Henceforth the monasteries were the chief homes of culture. The **Monastery of St. Gall.** monastery of St. Gall is one of the best-known centres of civilisation in the middle ages[1]. The foundation of St. Gall dates from the seventh century; its most flourishing period lasted from the end of the ninth on through the tenth century. About 883 an old monk collected and wrote down a number of anecdotes about Charles the Great, which he derived from oral tradition. We see how the figure of the Emperor was gradually enveloped in the mist of legend, which however did not diminish, but rather increased, his regal grandeur. Among the younger contemporaries and cloister brothers of this unknown monk there were many able men, who far surpassed him in learning. They devoted themselves mostly to writing Latin hymns, they were good musicians, and their monastery was celebrated for its school of sacred song. They also began to translate the Psalms into German rhymed verse, but of this, unhappily, little is left to us.

So soon as the troubles which darkened the opening decades of the tenth century had passed away the spirit of Charlemagne's

---

[1] A good picture of this age is given in the modern novel 'Ekkehard,' by Victor Scheffel.

age revived. The literary fame of the monastery was connected with the names of the monks, Ekkehard the First, who died in 973. and Notker Teutonicus, who died in 1022. The former revived the Germanic hero-song, in Latin hexameters, it is true, after the example of Virgil; the latter continued the German prose of the Carlovingian epoch, and made the grammatical correctness and purity of the German language his chief concern. Ekkehard's 'Walter of the Strong Hand' (Waltharius manu fortis) **Ekkehard's** was not, as Scheffel pretends, composed in romantic **'Waltharius.'** solitude, but was produced on the school bench, about 930, as a theme set and corrected by the teacher. It is a remarkable poem, not so much on account of the classical form given it by the author, as by reason of the materials, the old song, or songs, which he made use of. There are passages in it which remind us of the Iliad. The poet does not merely speak, but narrates in a broad, graphic, and truly epic style. A number of single combats take place at the mouth of a cave in the Vosges mountains, and the peculiar features of each, as well as the different kinds of weapons, and the way in which they were used, are carefully described. Walther is defending his betrothed Hildegund, whom he has carried off with rich treasures from the Huns, against the twelve heroes of Worms led by King Gunther. A message from Gunther, demanding his submission, is rejected by Walther, though at the same time he offers one hundred golden bracelets, if Gunther will leave him in peace. Hagen, Gunther's vassal, but also Walther's old companion in arms, finds himself placed between conflicting duties. He advises that the bracelets should be accepted, for he has had a dream foreboding evil from this combat. But Gunther reproaches him with hereditary cowardice. Hagen thereupon holds aloof from the fight, like Achilles; he rides away to a hill, dismounts from his horse and looks on calmly, as one hero after another vainly rushes to the attack and meets his death. Hagen himself has to mourn the loss of his nephew whom he had warned in vain. Eleven warriors have fallen: then at length the king is able by prayers and entreaties to prevail with him, and the following day, when Walther leaves his cave, Hagen avenges his nephew's death; he and Gunther together fall on the hero, and after they have all been cruelly mutilated, peace is concluded. Gunther has lost a leg, Walther his right hand, Hagen his right eye. Hildegund approaches, binds up their wounds, and presents them with wine which she has herself tasted. Walther and Hagen exchange rough jests and renew their friendship.

A cold, stern spirit pervades the whole poem, but it shows remarkable artistic taste. The poet has produced a work of the first order, and it is a great pity that we can only enjoy it in a Latin form. There is a perfect connection and unity throughout the whole poem. Here too, as in the Song of Hildebrand, the interest turns on the fact that two heroes, bound together by close ties, cannot avoid fighting with each other; but this time the issue is not tragic. The quarrel does not proceed from unavoidable circumstances, but from the covetousness of King Gunther, who disturbs the friendship of the two invincible heroes; he represents the evil principle in the poem, and is therefore painted as black as possible by the poet. The chief characters furnish us with a moral lesson, and at the same time most of the secondary characters have a clear individuality of their own. Though friendship between men is the leading motive of the poem, yet love of women is not absent. There is a beautiful description of Walther sleeping with his head in Hildegund's lap, while she watches against the approach of danger. When she thinks the Huns are coming she sinks on her knees before Walther, begging him to kill her, so that she may not fall into the hands of any other man. There is also much beauty in the account of the night between the first and second day of fighting. Walther entrenches himself in a cave, lays each dead man's head beside the body, drives in the captured horses and ties them up with boughs. Then he again sleeps the first part of the night in Hildegund's lap, while she keeps herself awake by singing; the remainder of the night he lets the maiden sleep, while he watches. Jacob Grimm justly remarks that this scene is one of the most perfect in the whole of our early poetry.

The young Ekkehard has, it would seem, very faithfully reproduced his original. Monkish sentiments are not inseparably interwoven into the fabric of the poem, but occur incidentally; for instance, Walther, during the night, is made to pray for the souls of the slain; a long moral reflection on covetousness is put into the mouth of Hagen; and again Walther, after proud heroic words, is made to fall down at once on his knees, and with Christian humility to entreat pardon of God.

The second monk of St. Gall, who contributed to the development of German literature, Notker, surnamed the German, or the thick-lipped, is also no mere monkish author. He wrote much himself, and inspired those around him to write also. In his prose translation of the Psalms with explanatory notes, he followed that same taste for annotated paraphrases of Scripture, which in the ninth century had given the first impulse to German poetry. Besides late Roman philosophical works, the monks even ventured to approach Aristotle. But it is still more interesting to find among this monkish literature a text-book of rhetoric, giving examples taken from German popular songs, and a text-book of logic, illustrating various syllogisms by German proverbs. The most interesting and characteristic work of this Renaissance literature is unfortunately lost to us, namely, a German version of the ' Andria ' of Terence.

Works of Notker and other monks.

The comedies of Terence were favourite reading at this time, as is proved by the writings of the nun Roswitha, the first German poetess and the first dramatist since the Roman epoch. Her name transports us at one step to North Germany, and the circles connected with the Court of the Ottos.

Roswitha of Gandersheim.

The women of the mediæval Renaissance were the intellectual rivals of the men. The daughters of Charlemagne received a classical education; the Duchess Hadawig of Suabia, a strong-willed woman and unconventional in her habits, even went so far as to learn Greek. So we are not surprised to find a nun imitating Terence, and adding to his six comedies six new ones in Latin prose, in which themes of very doubtful propriety are often touched on. I shall say nothing about her life of 'Otto the Great,' or about her ' Sacred Legends,' though amongst them we find that of Theophilus, the mediæval Faust; for the fact that she gave a dramatic form to such legends is of far greater importance. Roswitha dramatised legends in the same manner as Shakespeare

dramatised tales. She always leaves virtue triumphant in the end,
Roswitha's plays. but she leads us fearlessly through the very depths
of wickedness. Roswitha is anything but prudish,
yet she never sinks to mere coarseness; the consciousness of
a good aim makes her regardless of conventional prejudices.
Her pieces are short sketches, with rapid action and constant
change of scene. She hardly attempts any development of character, but she knows how to depict emotions, to reproduce
conflicting feelings, and to make these the source of action in
the play. Her dialogue is lively, her speeches never too long,
and her piety never obtrudes itself upon us. She often contrives
her scenes very skilfully; she has an eye for what will produce
a good effect and appeal to the audience, and many varieties of
the later drama are foreshadowed in her works. 'Gallicanus,' for
instance, is an historical tragedy in two parts, in which the contrast between a Christian and a heathen emperor is shown in the
persons of Constantine and Julian the Apostate. The play entitled 'Dulcitius' borders upon farce. The Governor Dulcitius,
having to guard three holy virgins and future martyrs, falls in love
with them, and tries to embrace them; but God blinds him, so
that he embraces cooking-vessels instead, and appears black all
over; his guard fly from him, taking him for the devil himself;
he is thrown down the steps of the imperial palace, and at length
is roused by his wife from his delusion. The play of 'Abraham'
paves the way for the popular sentimental drama. A hermit of
this name, disguised as a knight, rescues his niece from the slough
of evil, into which she has sunk deep without being utterly lost.
'Callimachus,' finally, is an example of a love tragedy, with a curious
likeness in some parts to Shakespeare's 'Romeo and Juliet.'
Callimachus is in love with Drusiana, the wife of the prince Andronicus. His friends reprove his passion; they tell him that
Drusiana is baptized and is a pupil of the apostle John, and, in
spite of her marriage, under a vow of chastity, so that it would
not be possible to gain her affections. Nevertheless, he declares
his passion to her; she indignantly repels him, and in the agony
of her doubt whether to confess this declaration of love to her
husband or not,—for she fears mischief in either case,—she prays

to God for death, which is at once granted her.   The last scene, again reminding us of 'Romeo and Juliet,' leads us into Drusiana's grave.   There Callimachus also lies dead, slain by the wrath of God upon the threshold of crime.   But the miraculous interference of St. John restores both to life, and wins the once too passionate but now purified lover to Christianity.

The mediæval Renaissance was indissolubly connected with the empire.   With the decline of the Carlovingian empire learning also decayed.   But with the restoration of the empire under Otto the Great a fresh impulse was given to literary efforts.   Historians arose, and intellectual life revived in the monasteries and round the episcopal sees.   By his marriage Otto II was connected, through his wife Theophania, with Greek learning, and their son, Otto III, formed grand but fantastic projects of intellectual achievement, in which he was encouraged by the first scholar of the age, the Frenchman Gerbert, just as Charlemagne had been by the great Alcuin.   Otto III despised Saxon barbarism; his mind delighted to dwell far away from his own times, among the triumphs of the Cæsars.   Eternal Rome itself should be the seat of his government, the Code of Justinian should again rule the globe.   His palace stood on the Aventine, and he was surrounded by Byzantine ceremonial.   But his short life was spent in dreams, which he could not even make his people share.   According to his own wish he was buried in the cathedral at Aix, side by side with his great ancestor Charlemagne.

Connection of the Mediæval Renaissance with Imperialism.

THE WANDERING JOURNALISTS.

We have noticed the varied and fruitful literary activity of the monasteries.   But the professional German poet of the ninth and tenth centuries did not live in the monasteries; in fact he had no fixed home.   He was a roving minstrel, who wandered from place to place to gain his livelihood.   We cannot describe him more exactly than by calling him the journalist of the time.   The singers who, 1200 years back, wandered from one court to another, bringing with them the latest news, have as good a right to be designated journalists as the correspondents of a modern newspaper.

When the nobler poets of the age of the migration died out, they were replaced by the 'gleeman' (Spielmann), who resembled the Roman *mimus*. He represents a somewhat lower order of journalism ; his office may be compared with that of an illustrated comic paper, the illustrations being acted by himself. He was a clown, with something about him of the actor and conjuror. He accompanied the dance on his instrument, and sang at court and in the streets. But he always sang about the latest events. The grand heroic legend with its high ideals was losing favour with the general public ; it became more and more meagre, and finally took refuge in the peasant's hut. The present entirely engrossed men's attention as in the epoch of the migration. The poets became the organs of public opinion, and therefore also the organs of those who wished to govern public opinion. We know little of these minstrel poems of the ninth century, but we may suppose that they were not entirely devoid of serious and lofty thoughts. We can, however, gain an idea of what they were like from a poem by a priest commemorating the victory of the Carlovingian monarch, Louis III, over the Normans, on August 3, 881. The poem is called the 'Ludwigslied.'

The Gleemen.

The Ludwigslied, 9th century.

The author does not confine himself to this single event, but sketches in bold outlines the entire life of his hero. He chooses for this purpose a mythic form, taking as his model certain stories of the Old Testament, in which God is described as holding direct intercourse with men. Louis, he tells us, lost his father when a child, but God supplied the loss. He adopted him, became his teacher, and then gave him rule. Then, minded to put his youth to trial, He suffered the Normans to cross the sea, and punish the Franks for their sins. The king was far away, but God saw their distress, and bade him go thither. 'Louis, my king, help my people, who are sore oppressed by the Normans.' Then said Louis, 'Lord, if death does not hinder me, I will do all that thou commandest.' Forthwith he departs, rides against the Normans, and rests his authority, before his people, on the fact that God has sent him.

The story is energetically told, the language is terse and pregnant, and the interest never flags, nearly every half line introducing
a new incident.   The poet's religious bias is apparent throughout;
the evil that befalls the people is a Divine judgment, and is felt as
such; all sinners do penance.   Two dialogues precede the battle,
one between God and Louis, the other between Louis and his
followers.   The poet lingers over these, but not in so marked a
manner as the author of the 'Hildebrandslied.'   The whole poem
is conceived in the true biblical spirit, all the incidents being divinely
ordained.   The enemy is described merely as the instrument of
God, and Louis is His minister.   Only in the beginning of the
battle do we get a glimpse of the masses of the people; they join
in the war-song, the fray begins, the angry blood rises to their
cheeks, the Franks leap for joy.   But then our attention is immediately recalled to the king—'No one fought like Louis, brave
and bold, according to his wont.   He hewed down one, he ran
through another; he gave his enemies bitter wine to drink: woe
to them—their lives are at stake.   Praised be the power of God,
Louis was victorious.'   The poet has nothing more to relate; he
concludes by invoking blessings on the king.

This song was intended for edification, not for amusement
or instruction.   The minstrel poetry of the next, **Minstrel
Poetry
of the
10th century.** the tenth century, offers a complete contrast.   It
was frivolous and comic, gay and bold, whilst
maintaining the same energy of diction that we
noticed in the Ludwigslied.   Conciseness, point, and epigram
are its main objects, and a witty saying forms the favourite ending
for a narrative.   Short satiric poems were much in vogue; one of
these, on a broken-off betrothal, has been preserved.   Another
poem, descriptive of a chase, gives a very amusing picture of the
hunted boar.   He has feet as large as a cart-wheel, bristles as high
as trees, and tusks twelve ells long.

But these short fragments really tell us little about the minstrel poetry.   We can happily learn more from the **Historians
of the
10th century.** historians of the end of the tenth century, who profited
by the poetic activity of the minstrels.   They had often
no other sources of information but these poems, and expressly

mention the fact that remarkable events were handed down in song. The bloody feud of the Babenbergs and Conradins in the time of Louis the Child (899-911) was celebrated in song even as late as the twelfth century. There was a rich cycle of legends about Henry the Fowler (918-936). After a victory of his Saxons over King Conrad's (911-918) brother, the glee-men exclaim, 'Is hell large enough to hold all the slain?' Otto the Great (936-973) had a vassal Kuno, Count of Nieder-lahngau, who, on account of his smallness, was nicknamed 'Kurzibold.' He was the special favourite of these wandering minstrels; being a good subject for mirth and humour. He had by nature such an abhorrence of women and apples, that he would not lodge on his journeys in a place where he had met with either. Long afterwards, it was a popular saying for anyone who did not seem susceptible to love, 'He cannot eat apples.' Kuno had a bold heart in his little body; he is said to have vanquished, like a new David, only with a lance instead of a sling, a gigantic Slav, who had challenged him to fight. The minstrels also sang of incredible deeds of valour performed by him in the war against the two dukes, Giselbert of Lorraine and Eberhard of Franconia. Once, when the army of these dukes was crossing the Rhine at Breisach and they were meanwhile playing chess on the bank, Kurzibold attacked them with only twenty men. He sank the boat into which Duke Giselbert sprang, by boring a hole in it with his lance : Eberhard he slew on the bank, reproaching him for his faithlessness.

Otto the Great was always wont to swear by his beard. This gave rise to the story of a Suabian knight, who once dragged him to the ground by his beard, threatened his life, and thus obtained pardon for a murder which he had committed; he was, however, banished and not received back into favour till after he had saved the emperor's life in Italy, by springing from the bath in his tent and rescuing him from an ambush into which he had fallen. The minstrel-poetry is not over particular in its choice of materials, as may be seen from this tale of rude violence.

The revolt of Otto the Great's son, Ludolf, no doubt furnished another theme to the minstrels of the time. The songs they composed about it formed the basis of the later legend of Herzog Ernst, which attained such prominence in Middle High-German poetry.

Besides kings, princes, and nobles the gleemen also sang the praises of remarkable ecclesiastics such as Bishop Ulrich of Augsburg and Benno of Osnabrück. Some of these gleemen themselves sprang from the ranks of the clergy. Good-for-nothing clergy and those who were averse to the discipline of any special order joined the body of wandering singers. They then turned their knowledge of Latin to account; they wrote Latin poetry or mixed Latin with German, thereby recommending themselves to a more cultivated audience. They were particularly fond of praising music. One of them gives a somewhat biassed account of the reconciliation of Otto the Great with his brother Henry; another celebrates the wonderful escape of Otto II (973–983) after a lost battle. A third describes the victory over the Hungarians on the field of the Lech, and praises all three Ottos. A fourth neglects subjects of public interest for coarse tales of Swabian cunning. Even Oriental tales are included in his *répertoire,* as well as incidents which we find again in Boccaccio: but the bare narrative is all that these poets care about, and they take no pains to shape and elaborate it.

Clerical Gleemen.

Every humorous topic is welcome to the gleemen. They even seize on sacred legends, and divest them of their religious meaning. We have large fragments of a German Martyrdom of St. George, which to our ideas is a perfect comedy, and reads like a modern parody. St. George is struck down with a wonderfully sharp sword, but he jumps up immediately and begins preaching again. He is bound, put on the wheel, torn in ten pieces, but he jumps up again at once and resumes his preaching. He is ground to pieces, burnt to ashes, thrown into a well, over the mouth of which great stones are rolled, the heathen run round it, mocking him; but he jumps up once more and resumes his discourse. The outward form in which these extraordinary adventures are clothed is more polished than one might expect. The merry company of gleemen became more and more welcome in good society; this refined their taste, and helped to keep up among them a poetical tradition. It is true this intercourse did not raise them morally. The whole epoch is wanting

Song of the Martyrdom of St. George.

in moral refinement; all the characteristic anecdotes have something cold-blooded, coarse, and jocular about them. To outwit another was evidently the acme of intelligence, just as it was the highest of pleasures to laugh at the dupe.

Summing up the different modes of literary activity, by means **General literary character-istics of the 9th and 10th centuries.** of which these minstrels partly led, partly flattered the taste of their age, and taking no account of their dramatic attempts, of which we know nothing, we may say that these modes chiefly consisted of historical ballads, tales, legends, fairy stories, farces, fables of animal life, in a word of short narratives. Of works of greater calibre than these, the ninth and tenth centuries offer hardly any trace. For instance, no romances or epics were composed, nor any poems too long to have been improvised and having an intricate and well-worked-out plot. There is no new creation, but merely a handing on of old material. In the monastery of St. Gall, attempts were made to present German heroic songs in a classical form, and romances written during the last decadence of classical literature were still read, such as the historical romance of Alexander the Great, and the romance of Apollonius of Tyre. But it is not till the eleventh century that we meet with any really creative works of fancy. We are then on the threshold of a new epoch, and the new-born spirit of chivalry invests these works with a peculiar charm. Their tone is gentler and more elevated; the narrative is more elaborated and is rich in materials drawn from contemporary manners and events.

At the same period, the gleeman assumes a new character. **Influence of chivalry on letters begins in 11th century.** He is still the wandering journalist, but he now strives also to elevate, not only to amuse. Above the low jesters, who still found a grateful audience in less cultivated circles, there arose a class of more refined poets, who attached themselves to the knights, and wandering from court to court, from castle to castle, diffused and fostered more ideal sentiments; they revived the German heroic legends, and shed a new glory on the half-forgotten names of Siegfried, Kriemhild, and Theodoric. Thus the idealised heroes of the Merovingian poets gave the first impulse to the idealism

of chivalry. In the tenth century German poetry was entirely
popular, in the eleventh it again became aristocratic. In the
tenth century, the only mark of education was the knowledge
of Latin; in the eleventh century a national culture arose, and
even a German verse was capable of literary polish. In the tenth
century the Renaissance of classical antiquity was exclusively
predominant, in the eleventh came the revival of German heroic
song, and with it the golden age of Middle High-German poetry.

CHAPTER IV.

CHIVALRY AND THE CHURCH.

In the year 1043, the marriage of Henry III with Agnes of
French Poitiers was celebrated at Ingelheim. Henry dis-
marriage of missed the minstrels, who had collected in crowds, as
Henry III, was their wont on such occasions, in the hope of
1043. obtaining a rich reward. They withdrew sorrowfully,
but the king gained the approbation of the clergy, whose stern
monastic views he favoured and promoted. Yet even amongst
the clergy there were patriotic men who shook their heads at his
marriage. There was already a tendency among the upper classes
to imitate French dress and manners, and they feared that this
French marriage would strengthen that tendency and prejudice
the simplicity of old German manners.

Happily their fears were realised. From the eleventh century
onward through the twelfth we notice an increase of French
French influence. We need only examine the German
Influence. vocabulary to assure ourselves of this; foreign words
force themselves in everywhere. All refinements in weapons and
dress, in dwellings and cookery, in war and play, in the chase and
dance, have French names.

German chivalry developed itself in all respects after the French
model. In this development the Normans played an important
part, in so far as they became the connecting link between the
Romance and Teutonic nations. As the Germans of Germany
The proper had their migration, so, 600 years later,
Northmen. the Germans of Scandinavia had their Viking ex-
peditions. As the Goths and their companions had helped to
bring about the dissolution of the Roman Empire, so these
Northmen aided in the destruction of the empire of Charlemagne.
In the second half of the ninth century these northern seafarers

founded the Russian state; soon after, we find them plundering the coasts of the Black and Caspian Seas, and serving
in the body-guard of the Greek Emperor. Passing the Faroe
Islands and Iceland, they reached North America. In the beginning of the tenth century, they founded a new state in Normandy,
where they soon became thoroughly French, though, with Scan-
dinavian boldness, they still formed extensive plans of conquest.
Their character presented a marvellous union of love of change
with sturdy perseverance, of wild imagination with sober common
sense, and this union of contrary qualities was the source of their
extraordinary power.

Normandy in the eleventh century sent forth the conquerors of
Southern Italy, Sicily, and England. Side by side with the super-
human form of Gregory the Seventh stand the characteristic figures
of William the Conqueror and Robert Guiscard. Both of them were
his allies, both were designed by him to be his tools, but neither
proved to be sufficiently pliable. The Normans, who arrived on
French soil as heathens, became the champions of Christianity.
The French songs, celebrating Charlemagne's struggles with the
Saracens, became the Norman war-songs. It was among the
Normans that the spirit of Christian chivalry and of the Crusades
grew up. The Norman knight was the type of a perfect warrior;
and German poetry of the eleventh century derived its modern
ideal of a hero from the Normans.

Knighthood was an institution which bridged over the old gulf
between freedom and slavery; it broke the barriers of caste, and
received both soldiers and civilians within its ranks. *Chivalry.*
It is true that at first the word Ritter (knight) only
designated the rider, and more especially the man who did military
service on horseback; but the word soon came to imply the idea
of noble, refined life, and thus became a term for denoting the
ideal of manhood. Knightly society meant refined society; such
society not only gathered round the emperor and the king, but
also round the small reigning princes, so numerous throughout
Germany. Chivalrous life meant the life of the courts. The
German words 'hübsch' (pretty) from 'höfisch' (courtly), and
'höflich' (courteous), point back to a period when the courts of

the nobility were the only homes of culture and refinement. In these circles was developed that beautiful Middle High-German language, whose charm and melody still survive for us in the poetry of that time.

Already in the eleventh century knightly society was the public, whose tastes poets chiefly considered in their productions. The poetry of this date either pictures the manners of chivalry, or endeavours to exert an influence on the minds of the aristocracy. Thus far chivalry played but a passive part in the new development of poetry. In the eleventh century we know of no poet who was at the same time a knight, though knights would sometimes play the music for dancing. It is only in the second half of the twelfth century, after the glorious years of political prosperity under Frederick Barbarossa, that knights began to take an active part in literature. Music and poetry then became recognised elements in the culture of the aristocracy, and the representatives of the highest and most refined life were at the same time the poets of the period.

LATIN LITERATURE.

To the beginning of the new epoch belongs a Latin poem, written about 1050, of which unfortunately only fragments have been preserved to us. It seems to have originated in Bavaria, and furnishes an excellent clue to the changes wrought in society by chivalry.

This poem is called 'Rudlieb,' and is the oldest chivalrous Latin romance of 'Rudlieb,' circa 1050. Romance known, and at the same time the first European work of pure fiction. It begins that series of romances which was continued without interruption down to Don Quixote, and was revived again by Wieland.

Rudlieb is, however, at the same time connected with the old German hero-legends. The interest attaching to a banished hero is a relic of Merovingian times, when the love of home was almost sentimental. The exile was designated by the word 'Recke,' which afterwards acquired a more general meaning. The poem of 'Rudlieb' relates the history of such a 'Recke.' The general outline of the story, however, reminds one strongly of the prosperous career of many a Norman adventurer, whom domestic troubles drove to seek his fortune in foreign lands.

Rudlieb, early left fatherless, has not, like Hadubrand, a good master at home; promises are made to him and never performed, and he is left to cope with enemies single-handed. He therefore leaves his country and enters the service of the king of Africa. After staying there ten years, he is recalled by a letter from his mother. The king gives him sound parting advice, which stands him in good stead in the sequel of the story. After many adventures he reaches home. A young servant standing on the watch-tower joyfully announces the arrival of his master. The hero is now to marry, and his relations suggest a maiden who is secretly in love with a priest. Rudlieb knows this, and whilst pretending to woo her, contrives by means of presents, which clearly prove his knowledge of her secret, to make her angrily reject his suit. He is, however, destined to find the right bride. A dwarf whom he gets into his power shows him the treasure of two kings, Immung and his son Hartung. Rudlieb kills both, Herburg, Immung's daughter, the heiress of a mighty empire, becomes his wife, and the former exile thus wins a throne.

Thus far we can make out the course of the story, and its origin is also pretty clear. A number of incidents drawn from popular tales, as well as traits derived from the heroic legends, are grouped round Rudlieb. In order to expand the story, he is brought into contact as friend or servant with various persons, the incidents of whose lives offer material for further description. Notwithstanding this wealth of incident, artistic unity is not lost sight of. There is a good deal of method in the composition. At the commencement, as is natural, the hero's future is left quite dark. But as soon as he leaves the African court, the writer anticipates and sketches a plan which is gradually carried out. This anticipation is seen, for instance, in the king's counsels to Rudlieb, which are all to be fulfilled in the course of the story. Whenever the hero follows them, it is to his advantage. The king also gives him two loaves filled with gold, the smaller of which is only to be opened in the presence of Rudlieb's mother,

the larger in the presence of his bride.   This incident again opens
a vista of expectations to be fulfilled, and uncertainties to be
removed.   Finally, the crowning successes of the hero are solemnly
foreshadowed in his mother's dreams and the dwarf's prophecies.

In other respects the author's art is somewhat inferior.   His
characters lack individuality, and the narrative is not as objective
The author's as epic narrative should be, for the poet constantly
style.   obtrudes his personality upon us in his moralisings
and descriptions.   But epic breadth and richness of detail are
present in a degree which *German* poetry only attained at the
close of the twelfth century.   The meagre style of the tenth
century has suddenly given place to redundance.   A picture
is given us of a society which cultivates refined manners, a
society whose members, though conscious of belonging to a
community, retain the feeling of their separate individuality, and
assert it by what is called a proud bearing.   The poet also,
being a member of this society, feels tempted to describe both
individual characters and social forms.   We see the knights
engaged in various occupations, and are made thoroughly acquainted with their manner of life.   In describing a foreign
country the poet naïvely reproduces what he was acquainted with
at home.   Though he assigns to Africa its camels and crocodiles,
its apes and parrots, yet otherwise everything is just the same
there as in Germany; he does not make it an Oriental fairy-land
full of geographical and ethnographical marvels.

In the romance of 'Rudlieb' there are signs that the social
influence of women is beginning to assert itself, though their
standard of propriety is not as yet very high.   The conversation
and jests of both men and women are still rude and coarse, but
all licence is condemned, even loud laughter is reproved, and
society requires from women moderate mirth and gentle smiles.
Their good breeding must show itself even in their deportment.
Stateliness is felt to add a charm to women, and this feeling is
expressed by a simile often repeated in later German poetry; a
woman in the bloom of youth is compared to the moon, and
a maiden is said to draw near like the rising moon.   Humane
sentiment, too, which always springs from respect for women, is

perceptible throughout the whole poem. The judge is merciful to a repentant sinner, the conqueror to the defeated foe. There is no honour in avenging an injury; vengeance in the highest sense is the taming of one's own anger. Hospitality and benevolence are highly praised. Great compassion is felt for widows and orphans, and it is considered the duty of a knight to protect them. Family affection is highly prized and honoured. Christian sentiment, though never repressed, is yet never obtruded upon us. One passage alone betrays the monkish origin of the work: the victorious king of Africa refuses all presents for himself and his followers, but excepts the twelve abbots who accompany him, 'For they,' he says, 'will richly repay any gift with their prayers.'

This romance soon spread from the cloister to wider circles. Minstrels introduced it into German songs, and continued the story further. They gave to Rudlieb and Herburg a son, Herbort, and told how this Herbort carried off a Norman maiden, the beautiful Hildeburg, how he defeated the pursuers, and how she dressed his wounds. Herbort also kills the giant Hugebold with the sword Eckesachs, given to his father by the dwarf. Two other heroes, Goldwart and Seewart, likewise fall by his hand, and finally he defends his wife against Theodoric and his followers. Here we have clearly an imitation of the legend of Walther and Hildegund, only the king of the Goths has taken the place of the king of the Burgundians.

Such was the intrinsic freshness and popularity of this romance that it ultimately won the ear of the people in spite of the Latin dress in which it first appeared. Nor was it only the lighter forms of literature that profited by this poem. The same epic talent which its author displays characterises, as might be expected, the annals and chronicles written by some of his learned brother monks.

The historical writers of the eleventh and twelfth centuries show a great improvement in style. They have more power of characterisation, and do not paint everything in the same colours. Religious and political zeal imparted fresh life to the records of contemporary history, and also called forth artistic capabilities. Yet only a small number of historians arose, and of these none can be called

Historical writing in the 11th and 12th centuries.

really great, except perhaps Bishop Otto von Freising, of the Babenberg family, the author of a universal history, and the
biographer of Frederick Barbarossa. He was not, indeed, a Thucydides, or even a Livy, but he wrote universal history from St. Augustine's point of view, and was thus able to give
an impressive conclusion to his work. All temporal events are to
him but a prologue to eternity, and he therefore adds to his narrative of earthly destinies a description of the Last Judgment. His
soul is filled with a sublime sense of the mutability of all earthly
happiness; yet this does not hinder him from paying due attention
to transitory matters, and painting earthly things in glowing
colours. He is a true artist, and adopts to a certain extent
the forms and devices of ancient historical writing. Thus, he
employs the artifice of imaginary speeches, and graphically describes the situation of countries and towns, as well as the manners
and customs of their inhabitants. His powerful descriptions of
battles and sieges transport us into the very midst of the scenes
which he is describing. He permits himself to introduce a strong
personal element into his narrative, which lends it a peculiar charm.
Ecclesiastical transactions, theological disputes, which he considers
of importance, are often very irrelevantly brought in. The reflections
in which he indulges savour strongly of scholastic philosophy, but
always attest the genius of the writer. His narrative of the Second
Crusade, in which he himself took part, begins, like a lyric poem,
with a description of the beauties of Spring, the season at which
the Crusaders set out. He says he will not relate the sad issue of
this Crusade, as he does not intend to write a tragedy, but a merry
history. This merry history is the life of Barbarossa, while his earlier
Universal History is written in a somewhat tragic tone. It seems as
if the freshness and vigour which characterised Barbarossa's government had communicated itself to his biographer, so that Bishop Otto
appears more closely connected with the joyous secular spirit of
chivalry than any other of his clerical brethren of the same rank.

The chief strength of chivalrous poetry lay in romances and lyrics,
and the romance later on exercised an influence on the style of historical writing. But both in romances and lyrics clerical poets set
the example, and Latin works prepared the way for the classics of

[margin note: Otto von Freising.]

chivalry.   It is certain that 'Rudlieb' was written in Germany, but
hitherto it has proved impossible to assign any fixed locality to the
Latin lyrics of this period. Germany, France, Italy, and England all
produced them in the eleventh and twelfth centuries; Latin lyrics,
their Latin dress conceals all traces of their origin,   Goliardic
and the vagrant clerk or dissolute student, who lived   poetry.
by writing and reciting these poems, wandered with them from
country to country.   'Rudlieb' was clearly intended for a knightly
audience, but the same cannot be said of this vagrant lyric poetry.
Already in the eleventh century the old nobles complained that the
younger generation would no longer learn Latin. The ' Vagrant,'
the ' Golias,' or ' Goliard,' amused the Bishop and Abbot, not the
noble.   But these poets did not always confine themselves to
Latin; in Germany they also cultivated German poetry, and
initiated the knights in the art. The roving singer preserved the
tradition of true art, and nowhere showed himself more free, more
unrestrained, more genial, than in Latin verse. The Goliard had
a strong love of life and all its pleasures, was a great drinker and
gambler, and dangerous to the peace of maidens; he tried to
supplant the knights in the favour of ladies, as is already seen in
'Rudlieb.' He knew no self-respect, and was an incorrigible
sinner, but his irregular life furnished material for a poetry, remarkable for its wild fun, its power of graphic description, and its unfet-
tered beauty of form. Coarseness and tenderness, blasphemy and
piety, all moods are at the command of these singers. The bright
ornament of rhyme seems as suitable to their poems as to the ancient hymns of the Church. Their poetic ideas are in great part
drawn from the ancient treasure-house of Greek and Roman lyric
poetry, which was thus opened to the national literatures of
Western lands. In these Latin lyrics we already find the main
features of the mediæval songs ; the contrast or harmony between
external nature and the lover's feelings is described after the manner
of Horace, and the tradition was handed on from the Latin poetry
to the French minstrels and the German Minnesänger.

'The Goliards' also established a truer conception of gentility, the source of our modern ideal of what is morally
noble. Virtue, they said, was the only title to nobility; nobility

requires us to exercise self-restraint, to raise those who are fallen, not to break the natural law of right, to fear nothing but disgrace. 'The Goliards' not only indulged in general satire, but especially directed their gibes against the vices of the clerical orders. They picture Rome as the ocean with all its terrors, Scylla and Charybdis, the Sirens and Syrtes; the Cardinals are pirates, outwardly resembling St. Peter, but inwardly like Nero. They sell Christ's inheritance, thieves and their associates have seized on the pastoral office, the Church has become a den of vice, the God of vengeance must soon come and strike with His sword and drive the buyers and sellers out of His temple. The 'Goliards,' like the German gleemen, recorded contemporary events in their poetry ; they followed the battles and treaties of the Emperors, they took an active interest in Oriental affairs, and celebrated in song the fate of the Kingdom of Jerusalem.

All varieties of this 'Goliardic' poetry and its best efforts culmi-
'The Arch- nate in one poet, who has been called the *Arch-poet*,
poet.' and who introduces us, like Otto von Freising, to the circle of Frederick Barbarossa. Of knightly descent, this poet enjoyed the special favour of the Imperial Chancellor and Archbishop of Cologne, Reinald von Dassel, a highly cultivated and energetic statesman and warrior, who inspired the emperor with the idea of a universal monarchy, which should triumph over the Papacy.

In the full and varied life of the second half of the twelfth century, the ideas of the Mediæval Renaissance re-asserted their power by the side of the other tendencies of the age. We sometimes feel ourselves transported back into the world of Charlemagne. If the Arch-poet wishes to characterise classical times, he mentions Homer and Aristotle; if he desires to contrast Christianity with them, he instances St. Augustine. And it was the same in politics as in the intellectual sphere. Barbarossa wished to be the successor
Growth of of the Cæsars, not in name only, but in reality.
Imperialism. Roman Jurisprudence, flourishing at the University of Bologna, sought to derive absolute authority from the old laws of the Roman empire, and for this reason Barbarossa granted his special protection to the professors and students, and even to the wandering scholars of that University (1158). After the destruction

of Milan (1162) he adopted the full title of Charlemagne; he considered the kings of France, England, Spain, and Hungary as Regents of his provinces, and the Pope as a mere imperial official. By canonising Charlemagne, and causing his bones to be publicly exhibited at Aix before a great concourse of people (1165), he as it were declared him to be the patron saint of the Hohenstaufen policy.

Reinald, as chief minister, was always with the Emperor, and his *protégé*, the Arch-poet, has reproduced the stirring thoughts of those years, in noble verses relating the fall of Milan. He addresses the Emperor as Lord of the world, the king appointed by God above all other kings; he praises him as the protector alike of the high and the lowly, and as the guardian of security and order. The Emperor, he exclaims, has overthrown the rebels, like Charlemagne, with his avenging spear. The Emperor's fame spreads quickly; the Greek Emperor trembles before him, as the flock before the lion, Apulia voluntarily submits to him, Sicily longs for him and despises its own tyrant. Even in this poem the Arch-poet does not forget to extol his master, the mighty Chancellor, and in other poems he is extravagant in his praises, ascribing to him the wisdom of Nestor, the eloquence of Ulysses, and omnipotence in all affairs of state. But unfortunately we always find these words of praise accompanied by petitions for help, complaints of hunger, cold, illness, the dearness of wine and the shabbiness of his apparel. In one splendid poem, full of beauty and humour, he relates that he was caught up into heaven, and heard St. Martin, the type of liberality, reproaching the Chancellor, and threatening to accuse him to God, ' but my tears,' he continues, 'moved him, for I wept bitterly, as I often do, and begged him to spare thee, and since I wept so faithfully for thee, thou oughtest on this feast-day to give me a noble present.'

The Arch-poet's song on the Fall of Milan.

The ' Confessions ' of the Arch-poet have survived for centuries in the student songs, especially his verses describing the reveller who wishes to die in the tavern. ' Meum est propositum in taberna mori,' says the Arch-poet, or, as Bürger translated it, ' I am resolved some day, by yea and nay, to

Drinking songs.

die before the tap ; ' and in the song of Goethe's reveller,
(' Tischlied '), we still catch an echo from this old Latin poet.
But the Arch-poet has an ulterior purpose in his Confessions ;
he wishes to convince his benefactor that he is really going
to reform, and his honest self-accusation is to gain his pardon.
Women, dice, and wine are his sins ; he is like a leaf in the wind,
like a rudderless ship, like a bird fluttering in the air ; no chains or
locks can hold him ; he seeks his equals, and associates with the
wicked. Still there is a charm in his verses, and they will live as
long as merry Tavern life exists in Germany.

The serious thoughts on imperial grandeur and worldly power,
which appear in the Arch-poet's melodious Latin rhymes, also found
expression in a dramatic form, and were brought before the public
in a dramatic poem, full of lofty symbolism and happy fancy.

Old Latin　The Antichrist of the Revelation was a character
drama of　which had much attraction for the minds of mediæval
Antichrist.　scholars and poets. He was inseparably connected
with all descriptions of the end of the world, and we already find
him in Old High-German verse. As early as the tenth century
men believed that the Roman Emperor would one day lay down
his crown at Jerusalem, and that when his empire was at an end
Antichrist would appear. A gifted poet, of strong imperial views,
seized on this idea, in order to impress upon the world, in a drama,
that its salvation depended on the Emperor.

The piece is something between the oratorio and the opera. It
is sung throughout, the text and the melody being often repeated,
thus producing a great simplicity in design and execution. Dumb
action plays an important part. Battles, court-receptions, and
other incidents involving a number of actors, are effectively represented in dumb-show. The Temple at Jerusalem forms the background of the stage, and various countries are represented by the
royal thrones set up in front of it.

The author is a Christian and a German, but neither a fanatical
Christian, nor a fanatical German. In the second part of the play
Antichrist appears ; but the poet does not, as we might expect,
follow Church tradition, and represent him as the incarnation of evil,
as a less refined dramatist would most certainly have done. The

hypocrites, who prepare the way for Antichrist, begin their work by complaining of the secular power of the Bishops, a proof that the poet considers the Bishops as the pillars of the Church, and contemplates the world from the standpoint of the loyal imperial prelates.

The poet has shown great skill in handling his subject-matter. Though in essential respects he adheres to tradition, he allows himself great freedom in the development of his theme ; there is no exaggeration, and the characterisation of the figures introduced is very successful. This artistic and patriotic author is entirely dominated by the ideas of Frederick Barbarossa and his Chancellor; the Pope does not appear at all in the poem, or at least only in the train of the Church, which is itself supposed to be under the protection of the Emperor.

The revival of national feeling under Frederick Barbarossa, which gave new aims to German chivalry, secured also to German poetry the active sympathy of the nobility. The chivalrous poetry of the Middle High-German classical period might trace its origin back to the sixth decade of the twelfth century, when the Emperor conquered the Lombards, and caused Charlemagne to be canonised. The Emperor then conquered the enemies who wished to clip the wings of German poetry, and thereby opened a way for the ideals of a more refined secular life.

LADY WORLD.

At the beginning of the thirteenth century there lived in Franconia a knight called Wirent of Grafenberg, the author of a romance which became widely popular. A few decades after his death the following story was related of him, a story which one of his successors in the poetic art, Conrad of Würzburg. turned into smooth Middle High-German verse.

Wirent von Grafenberg was keenly desirous of outward distinction. He possessed everything that could make a man liked and admired. He was handsome, brilliant, and well educated, foremost in the chase, a good musician, and a favourite with ladies, whom he was always ready to serve. If a tournament took place, however far off, he would ride thither, to fight for the reward of love. Love filled all his thoughts. One day he was sitting in his chamber with a love-romance in his hand, to while away the time till evening, when a lady suddenly appeared to him, more beautiful than any living woman, more beautiful than Venus or Pallas; her beauty shone so brightly that the whole room was lighted up. She was gorgeously arrayed, and wore a crown on her head. Wirent, pale with alarm, sprang up and welcomed her. 'Be not frightened' said she; 'I am the lady for whose sake you have so often risked your life, whose faithful servant you were, whose praise was ever on your lips. You have flourished like a green branch in various paths of merit. I am now come to bring you your reward.'

Her speech sounds strange to the noble knight, who has never seen her, and yet is told that he has served her. 'Pardon, noble lady,' he exclaims, 'if I have served you, I know not of it; but tell me who you are.' 'Willingly,' answers she; 'you need not be ashamed of being my servant. Emperors, kings, counts, freemen, dukes, all serve me. I fear no one but God, Who alone is mightier than I. My name is—the World. You shall have the reward you have so long desired: behold it!' With these words she turned her back upon him, which was covered with snakes, toads, and adders, with sores and boils, full of flies and worms. A loathsome smell filled the room, her rich silken robe looked grey as ashes—and so she vanished from him.

But the knight learnt from the vision that the soul suffers injury in the service of this world. He left wife and child, took the cross, fought against the heathen, did penance, and won eternal bliss.

I have told this realistic story for the sake of its symbolical value. It bears the clerical stamp of its source, and probably originated in some monastery, where the poet Wirent was a known character, whose life seemed well fitted to point a moral. The Hostility of attitude of the clergy towards the chivalry and poetry the clergy of Middle High-German times is clearly seen in this to Chivalry. work. They condemned the whole spirit of chivalry as a base service of the world, whose reward would be eternal damnation. They represented all worldly ideals under the type of Lady World. And this figure was also introduced into plastic art; we find Lady World represented, according to the descrip-

tion of Conrad of Würzburg, on the porches of the cathedrals at
Worms and Basle.

It had not always been thus. It was a monk, Ekkehard, who in
the tenth century clothed an old heroic legend in Latin verse. It
was a monk who in the eleventh century wrote the romance of
Rudlieb. The chief care of St. Gotthard, on undertaking the charge
of a new monastery, was that his Horace and Cicero's Letters
should be sent after him. In those days there was no breach
between the children of God and the children of the world, or at
least it was not considered frivolous for a man to occupy himself
with secular literature. But in the course of the eleventh century
all this was changed. There came a revival of eccle- **Revived**
siastical power, at first encouraged by the Emperors, **influence of**
but afterwards directed against them. Side by side **the Church.**
with the struggle of the Popes against the Emperors, we have that
of the clergy against chivalry; the ideals of knighthood were condemned as mere pride and worldliness, and an attempt was made
to enlist the warlike instincts of the age in the service of the
Church. Man, it was said, should be a vassal of God, and should
fight all his life against sin and the devil. These clerical zealots
would hear nothing of the study of heathen classics. They opposed
secular poetry, and they denied all hope of future bliss to professed
poets, to the minstrels and wandering clerks. They condemned epic
poetry as a tissue of lies, classic songs and love lyrics as immoral.
The ideas of the ninth century revived. Sermons and spiritual
poetry were to set bounds to the encroachments of the powerful
lay spirit, and to supplant secular literature.

The preachers depicted minutely all the various sins in turn.
They painted heaven in the most glowing and attrac- **Sermons.**
tive colours, and hell in the blackest and most terrible.
Their style of rhetoric, consisting chiefly in piled-up analogies, was
adopted by the poets, and produced a special school of imaginative
writing.

The religious epic drew its materials from the Old and
New Testaments. Its chief biblical themes were the events
related in Genesis, the earliest history of the children of Israel, the
story of the heroine Judith, the lives of John the Baptist and

of Christ, and the Last Judgment. To these we must add the
enormous wealth of sacred legends, forming a complete Christian
heroic cycle, and running through the whole scale from harmless
pious tales to exciting sensational romances. But the heroism
which these legends celebrate is always the heroism of suffering
and renunciation, and the ideal of humility is contrasted with the
self-reliance of chivalry. Even the party leaders of the day, such
as Archbishop Anno of Cologne, were celebrated in poetry as
saints. Even the popular history of the empire was narrated
from a clerical point of view in the 'Kaiserchronik,' and used
as a weapon of controversy against the legendary creations of
German heroic song. The 'Kaiserchronik' gives more prominence
The 'Kaiser- to papal affairs than to imperial, and makes us realise
  chronik.' the absolute predominance of the Church after the
unfortunate termination of the quarrel about investiture. This
first German history in German is a poetical medley in which,
along with genuine history and much pious and patriotic feeling,
we find well-rounded tales, frequently in praise of good women.

The religious   The religious epic poetry of the time offers examples
epic of the   of all styles; it is diffuse and wordy, or short and sketchy,
11th century. moralising or amusing, and sometimes even inclining
to comedy. Its chief charm lies in the inability of its pious and
naïve authors to conceal their personal feelings. Thus, in describing the crucifixion and entombment of Christ, the author apostro-
phises one after another Mary Magdalene, Mary the Mother of
Jesus, Joseph of Arimathea and Nicodemus. 'Oh, thou good
Joseph,' he exclaims, ' had I lived then, how willingly would I have
helped thee to take our Lord from the cross, and bury him ! And
thou, Nicodemus, why could I not show thee some kindness, as a
reward for thy faithfulness ? '

Most of the clerical poets are personally unknown to us. They
do not give their names or aspire to posthumous fame, their
poetry being to them a work of devotion. Quite by chance we have
some record of a nun Ava, who died in Austria in 1127. She had
The nun Ava, been married before she retired from the world, and
  died 1127. had two sons. They were most likely theologians, for
they helped her in procuring the materials for her three religious

poems. In these she describes, with a woman's unpractised hand,
the seven gifts of the Spirit communicated to men, the appearance
of Antichrist at the end of the world, and the Last Judgment. She
is the first woman known to us by name, who wrote in German
verse.

Other religious authors sought to express the intellectual and
æsthetic instincts of the time in various instructive com- Religious
positions.   But we may well doubt whether these poetry of the
works found much acceptance in wider circles. What 11th century.
interest could be felt in rhymed geographies and astronomies,
rhymed compendia of theology, or treatises on the sacred number
seven? They could only appeal to an already awakened interest, and
certainly not attract the alienated lay spirit. The priests assumed a
more dangerous, but equally uncompromising tone when they tried
to arouse class-hatred in the hearts of the people, and openly
declared in their sermons that the knights were robbers, or when
they threatened the unjust nobles with the wrath of God, which
should throw down their castles, and against which their high walls
could be no defence.

The most effective weapon for breaking the secular spirit, for
persuading the nobles to retire from the world, for encouraging
pious works and rich donations, in the interests of the Church,
was the constant harping upon death, the future life, and the
punishment which awaited sinners. The traditional forms of confession were versified, and thus repentant sinners were furnished
with fixed models for the expression of their feelings. But where
a great character, that had lived in the midst of the world, was
through painful experiences forced back upon itself and the thought
of eternity, such an one would find other and more forcible
accents in which to preach the renunciation of earthly joys, and
to display the Medusa head of death to a society steeped in luxury
and enjoyment.   One poet at least of great talents did arise, who
seems to have passed through these experiences, and whose writings
reflected the struggle against secularism. This was Heinrich
Heinrich von Mölk, the Juvenal of Chivalry, the earliest von Mölk,
German satirist, and among indignant satirists one circa 1160.
of the greatest and most bitter to be found in German literature.

He seems to have lived about 1160, as a lay-brother in Mölk on the Danube. His former chivalrous life sometimes betrays itself. He still practises the duty of gallantry to noble ladies, whom he exempts from his unsparing satire. He does not condescend to conceal the corruption of the clergy, as loyalty to his order might seem to require. One poem in particular, which he left un-finished, treats especially of the life of the priests. An earlier poem, his principal work, begins with a somewhat informal introduction, i.e. a satire on all classes, in which bitter truths are told to clergy and laity, to princes and knights, to merchants and peasants. After this he turns to his real subject, the contemplation of death. This poem shows artistic sequence, a well-matured plan, a wealth of motives, a variety in treatment of the same subject, such as we find in few mediæval poems. The poet illustrates the misery of life by the story of a prince who is harassed by the struggle after honour and power, and the fear of disloyalty and treason. To show the hideousness of death, he leads a wife to the bier of her husband, and reminds her of all the joy and pleasure of life, whilst pointing in contrast to the fearful disfigurement of the corpse, which he describes with merciless realism. To make the terrors of death most powerful in their effect on the imagination, he conjures up the ghost of a father, who has to describe to his son the torments which he is enduring. It is in these dramatic scenes that the poet reaches the height of his power. The strongest human feelings are thus powerfully set forth in threefold gradation : the happiness of a high social position, the affection which binds man and wife, the love which unites father and son. Heinrich von Mölk's rhetoric is most powerful, and he does not avoid the strongest expressions or shrink from the ghastly, in order to gain an influence over hardened souls. He unites all the qualities which secure to the impassioned preacher and the bitter satirist such power over men's minds. The most effective things which could be said in the struggle between the clergy and the world flowed from his pen.

And what is the result of the whole poetic struggle, which, beginning at the year 1060, lasted more than a century, and which so passionately opposed the spirit of chivalry? Was the power of

chivalry broken? was its sphere narrowed? and could those few
men of the world who embraced the monastic life offer anything
as a compensation for that secular life which was ever increasing
in luxury and strength?

The clerical poets and their guides in church politics did not
follow any preconceived plan, and yet their actions give Ultimate
us from the first the impression of being based on such a triumph of
plan. It seems as if they knew that violent onslaught the secular
alone would not succeed; if they terrified men with spirit.
threats of hell, they must also win them by hopes of heaven; if
they required renunciation of the world, they must hold out the
grace of God as compensation; if they wished to alienate the minds
of maidens from earthly love, they must show them Christ in his
heavenly glory as the bridegroom of the soul; if they wished to draw
away the knights from the homage of earthly women, they must
direct their devotion to the Queen of heaven; if the pleasures of the
world were to be looked on as the work of the devil, the ideal joys
of the next life must be painted in an alluring manner. But for this
purpose only earthly colours were at their disposal. Though they
might give a spiritual interpretation to the Song of Solomon, still
the listener, charmed by its beauty, could only hear in it the tones
of the old Hebrew Love Song. From the eleventh century German
hymns and narrative poems were dedicated to the Virgin Mary,
but their original sublime earnestness gradually disappeared. The
Virgin, who was at first drawn almost like a nun, becomes more
and more like an earthly queen, whose court is furnished with all
the luxuries of the day. She is the type of the enamoured soul,
which longs for the moment of union with God. The clerical poet
is no longer the inspired preacher, but the elegant Abbé, who addresses himself to a spoilt female audience, and provides them with
an easy piety. Religious sentimentality is none the less sentimental
because it derives its material from religion. Instead of faith, confession and penance breaking into the realm of Lady World and
overthrowing her power, the slavish spirits of the world have, on the
contrary, forced their way into the Church, and made it a scene of
revelry. In one word, the hundred years' struggle between the
clergy and the world has resulted in the triumph of the world.

It is true that many ideas and customs of religious and ascetic origin, such as the meditations on death and the transitoriness of the world, the Church ordinances and ceremonies, and the Christian ideal of humanity, were transferred as necessary elements into the knightly life. The outward religious consecration was everywhere present. But the delight in combats and tournaments, the importance attached to honour and earthly renown, the joy in the beauties of nature and the pleasures and refinements of life—all these were by no means weakened, but rather increased in power and influence.

Where the service of art is invoked it soon gains the upper hand. Religious poetry proved one of the strongest solvents of the strict traditions of the Church. It set up Nature by the side of God as a power equally entitled to honour. More thoughtful spirits, who were not satisfied with the elegant piety of the world, were led on to unorthodox paths.

A short poetical fragment of this period affords us a glimpse of a soul which has struggled through despair to new conviction. The poet describes his inward development in the form of a parable. He accuses the heart, the seat of the passions, as the source of all evil. He has so large a heart that it would have been enough for a thousand people. When he was born, his heart had already taken the oath of allegiance to the world; he did not know this, and followed its counsel. He became subject to the devil, and perceived, when too late, that his heart was leading him to death. He wished to retire from the world, but it held him by a thousand artifices, its poisonous sweetness bound him hand and foot and kept him so close a prisoner that he had no hope of escape. He prayed to all the saints, but none would take pity on him and the heavenly hosts gave him up. At last he was entirely overcome by despair. He believed himself predestined to eternal death, and ceased to pray. But unhoped-for salvation came to him. A mighty lord bade him be of good courage, for he would relieve his distress and heal his wounds and leave no scar. Here the poem breaks off. Doubtless God himself came to the sinner's rescue, and perhaps the Bible was laid before his despairing eyes, and some comforting word of

Poetical fragment, 'Comfort in Despair.'

Christ's solved his difficulties. And since he praises voluntary
poverty, he probably employed his wealth in works of mercy, and
found rest for his soul in self-renunciation and poverty. But the
man whom the saints did not help could not have become an
ordinary anchorite. He must rather have been a gentle priest of
humanity, who, like the old philosophers, kept aloof from men without hating them, and enjoyed the happiness of needing nothing.

But the Church had in store for those whom the world could not
satisfy another resource besides the cell of the monk,—a far more
agreeable means of salvation, the one which was chosen by Wirent
von Grafenberg, as we saw in the beginning of this section—namely,
the Crusades.

THE CRUSADES.

In the eleventh century a sudden impetus was given to the pilgrimages to Jerusalem. In the eighth century we hear of only six, in
the ninth of twelve, in the tenth of sixteen such pilgrimages, but in the
eleventh century their numbers reached 117. They are, more than
anything else, an evidence of the more ideal tendency of the religious
feelings of the times, a witness to the spirit of religious self-sacrifice, a
proof of a quickened imagination, which desired to see   Motives
for itself the scenes of our Lord's sufferings and death.   which
But apart from the religious motive, the Crusaders were   prompted
actuated by other interests, love of adventure, thirst for   the Crusades.
knowledge and a desire to see the world, in fact the motives which
incite us to travel. In the time of the Carlovingian Renaissance
German monks travelled to Rome, to search for the remains of
classical antiquity and to collect Roman inscriptions. They soon
extended their travels to Constantinople, where artistic industry
still followed classical traditions, and a gorgeous court displayed its
marvellous wealth. And beyond Constantinople lay the Wonder-
land of the East, the home of strange monsters, half-human races
and other marvels according to mediæval geography and natural
history, and containing, they thought, the site of the original Paradise.

It was a master-stroke of papal policy to enlist in its service by
means of the Crusades all the love of adventure pent up in the

West, all the curiosity and belief in miracles so common in the middle ages. The authority of the papacy was immeasurably strengthened by the Crusades. The fertile brain of Gregory the Seventh originated the idea, his successor gave it life, and the Norman lords, the born friends of all adventure, were foremost among those who carried it into effect.

In the year 1064 some of the German spiritual princes had under-
Pilgrimage taken a pilgrimage, in which all Europe joined. They
of 1064. had to go through hard fighting before reaching their goal, and of the 7000 who set out only 2000 returned. The First Crusade, set afoot in 1095, was chiefly undertaken by French knights. But the news of victory excited men's minds in Germany also, and in the year 1100 many Germans, particularly from Bavaria, took the cross, most of them to perish unknown. From the year 1147 the German kings and emperors assumed the leadership of the crusading armies, Conrad III as the slave of the Church, Frederick I as the rival of Church authority, Frederick II as the enemy of the Pope. These three Emperors represent three stages in the development of religious thought and of the relation between Church and State. Many renowned German princes took part in these and other crusades; many renowned knights, known to us as German poets, joined the holy armies, and, from the eleventh century onwards, we can often prove or conjecture a connection between German poetry and these pilgrimages.

The spirit of the pilgrimage of 1064 is fully expressed in a Song written shortly before by a priest, Ezzo of Bamberg, at the command of his bishop, and set to music by another priest, Willo, also of
Song by   Bamberg. It is one of the most important religious
Ezzo of   poems of the time, and called forth a special school of
Bamberg.   poetry. In the midst of the German a Latin verse is occasionally introduced. It embraces the whole biblical story in twenty-eight stanzas, and introduces much popular theology, while preserving, on the whole, the tone of a hymn. Christ's life and miracles form the centre of the poem. The poet leads us on with great solemnity from the darkness of primitive times to the brilliant heights of future bliss. He gives the favourite spiritual interpretation to the deliverance of the Israelites from Egypt; Pharaoh is the

devil, our old enemy, who wishes to keep us out of our inheritance, but our leader is so mighty that under his guidance we shall win the promised land. The holy Cross is thus apostrophized, ' Oh, blessed Cross, thou art the best of all trees, thy branches bore the heavenly burden, the holy blood watered thee, thy fruit is sweet and good, it has redeemed the human race. Oh, Cross of the Saviour, thou art our mast, this world is the sea, God the Lord steers us, good works are the ropes, faith is the sail, the Holy Ghost is the wind, leading us on the right way—heaven is the home where we shall land, thanks be to God.' The song seems written on purpose to be sung on pilgrimage, and to give utterance to the feelings of the crusaders. The Cross ever before them as a holy symbol, the sea voyage, the combats on the way to a far off holy land—all this must have had a specially close and pathetic signifi- cance for those who were really on the road to Palestine, and who desired to deliver the holy land from the Paynim.

Williram's prose translation and paraphrase of the Song of Solo- mon, dating from about the same time as Ezzo's hymn, faithfully reproduced the rich imagery of the original, and displayed to the reader the splendour of an Oriental court. This theme was adopted by the minstrels, who dedicated special songs of praise to King Solomon, and represented him as a pattern for Christian princes. Like Williram and his prede- cessors, they regarded Solomon as typical of Christ, interpreted his bride as the Church, and the pillars of his throne as the bishops. In the lighter strain of the rabbinical legend they described him as the ' wise king ' to whom the spirits were subject and who built the temple by supernatural power. They laid hold of an old tradi- tion which told of his contest with Marcolfus or Morold, in which proverb was matched against proverb, and the king's lofty ideal was contrasted with Morold's baser view of life. These two characters furnished them with the materials for an amusing love romance in the jesting style of the tenth century, in which Morold appeared as the bold accomplice of King Solomon. Jerusalem and the surrounding country thus became a universally recognised theatre for romantic deeds.

(margin note) Williram's paraphrase of the Song of Solomon.

(margin note) Popular romance, ' Solomon and Morold.'

But it was not till 1125 that a poetry arose with real power to kindle the crusading spirit. This poetry may have influenced the crusade of 1147, preached by Bernard of Clairvaux. Exploits allied to those of the Crusaders engaged the attention of two priests, Konrad and Lamprecht ; the one described Roland's struggles with the Saracens, the other the Oriental campaigns of Alexander. Both were forerunners of the poetry of chivalry, but both were in opposition to the national heroic poetry. Both sought to avail themselves of the idealism of chivalry for clerical purposes. They are the first poets, known by name, who made French works accessible to a German public. Both translations are in the style of the popular poetry of the time, and neither reveals a strong poetic individuality.

Konrad translated the French national epic, the 'Chanson de Roland,' the most celebrated poem of Christian chivalry. It treats of Charlemagne's expedition to Spain, of the death of Roland through the treachery of Ganelon, of Charlemagne's revenge on the Moors, and the punishment of the traitor. This poem now rouses in France the same patriotic feelings as seventy years ago the Nibelungen-Lied did in Germany ; but the German priest of the twelfth century naturally looked upon it from a different point of view. The subject seemed to him to belong to the history of his fatherland, while it was at the same time half legendary in character; the first would please the German, the second pleased the priest. The great emperor was no longer remembered in German popular poetry, and in the recollection of the nation he survived only as a lawgiver and impartial judge, while his deeds and his heroes were forgotten. Through the medium of the French 'Chanson de Roland' his memory was revived, and to the imagination of Frederick Barbarossa he appeared once more as an ideal of political wisdom. The work of Konrad, which was begun in 1130, at the court of the Guelph Duke, Henry the Proud, produced a great effect. It long continued to be read, and underwent successive alterations to suit the change of taste, till about the year 1300, when it was incorporated, with other stories of the same cycle, in a bulky Carlovingian poem, the 'Carlmeinet.' The legend of the 'Chanson de Roland' was the production of a rude age, and reflects all the harsh-

Marginal note: Konrad's 'Rolands-lied,' circa 1130.

ness and intolerance of the Carlovingian epoch. Konrad makes
the pathos of the religious struggle the leading idea of his poem.
He strengthened the piety of the original without thereby increasing
its artistic value. All outward events become more indistinct in
Konrad's rendering, while the speeches reflecting feelings are much
elaborated. He describes battles and combats less graphically than
the French poet, but he has cut down exaggerations, and has raised
the moral tone of the whole and added many beautiful and impressive sayings. Much of his imagery must have been borrowed from
the popular poetry.

While Konrad lays special stress on the religious feelings which
were excited by the crusades, the bigotry, the hatred of Islam and
the delight of fighting against the false prophet Mahomet, his
colleague Lamprecht, on the contrary, represents the secular feelings
which found vent in Oriental expeditions. The work of Konrad
deals with an obscure and barbarous age, while that of Lamprecht
breathes the spirit of the most refined Alexandrian culture. Lamprecht translated the French 'Song of Alexander' by *Lamprecht's
Alexander of Besançon; a poem which traced its origin *Alexander-
through various steps to a life of the Macedonian king,   lied.'*
written at Alexandria, a kind of ancient historical romance. After
the short story of Alexander's youth the author relates his great
and successful campaigns. Then follow the legendary wonders of
the East, whither Alexander's victorious career carries him. He is
even said to have penetrated as far as Paradise, but not to have
been permitted to enter there.

If the 'Rolandslied' encouraged intolerance, the 'Alexanderlied,'
on the contrary, breathes a thoroughly humane spirit. In the
former, Franks and Saracens are opposed to each other as merciless
and cruel enemies; in the latter, the Greek shows chivalrous respect
to the Persian, and foe is merciful to foe. The poem is written in
a sympathetic spirit, and although the author's object is to glorify
Alexander, yet his heart is also moved by the grief of the vanquished Persians. Whatever may have been the private feelings
of the priest Lamprecht, his poem ranks among those works of the
tenth and eleventh centuries which were written in imitation of
classical models, and were rather allied than opposed to the secular

spirit. The seriousness of historical biography is modified; great deeds are interwoven with tender episodes, and a most charming idyll is introduced into the life of the great conqueror in the story of the flower-fairies with whom Alexander and his heroes spend three months of happiness in the spring time. This and other adventures, some of them very childish, are related by the king in a letter to his mother Olympias and his teacher Aristotle. Even a Circe is not wanting in this land of magic, nor prophecies concerning the future, so that we are involuntarily reminded of Odysseus and his narrative to the Phæacians.

Most of the Oriental and crusading poems might be compared Shorter epics with the Odyssey. The twelfth century did not pro-of the 12th duce any classical Odysseys of real importance, but it century. furnished several smaller epics, many of which survived long in popular tradition. Such were 'King Rother,' 'Duke Ernst,' 'St. Brandan,' 'Solomon and Morold,' 'King Orendel,' and 'St. Oswald.' Lamprecht had many successors among the wandering gleemen. These poets of the people also borrowed much from Latin and French sources, but they handled their originals with greater boldness and less pedantry than their classical colleagues. They were Style of the not mere servile imitators of foreign models, but ven-gleemen. tured on original composition, finding ready materials either in the heroic legends, or in the later historical traditions, or in the latest news from Palestine. They were very fond of well-known themes, such as the banished hero, or the wooing and abduction of the bride, and they laid the scene of their poems either in Constantinople or in Jerusalem. Their tone is either profane, or else pious to absurdity. In fact they seize on every opportunity for exaggeration. They revel in large numbers, they aim throughout at realistic effects, and they miss no chance of a joke. They delight in placing their hero in danger of his life, and then, before setting him free, they make an artificial pause and ask for a drink. Their style of narration is lively, if not so hurried as that of their predecessors of the tenth century. They do not care about variety, and in similar situations they employ the same words. They repeat incidents, and often, under pretence of having made a mistake, they break off suddenly and begin the story all over again, so

that their audience may pass through the thrilling scenes once
more. But with all this carelessness of style, their epic technique
has a certain merit; the course of the narrative is not hindered
by long descriptions, and the progress is everywhere merry and
rapid.

'König Rother' and 'Herzog Ernst' are works of a higher stamp
than the rest. Their authors are of higher rank, and
move in better society. The author of 'König Rother'
turned to the heroic legends for his story, while the
author of 'Herzog Ernst' enlarged on an historical
subject which we have already noticed as having been treated by
the journalistic poets[1]. The former is well acquainted with Constantinople; he deals in anecdotes of the crusade of the year 1100,
and, like the priests Lamprecht and Konrad, he prepared the way
for the second Crusade. The latter endeavoured to bring the Holy
Land within the German horizon, and prepared the way for the
third Crusade. Both these poets introduce us to the highest sphere
of earthly rank. In drawing his King Rother, the poet probably
had before his eyes the Norman Count Roger of Sicily, the most
celebrated man of his time, as a German chronicler calls him; but
he represents him as living in earlier times, makes him the grand-
father of Charlemagne, and the head of the German empire. The
author of the second poem chose the stepson of an emperor as
his hero. Both poets probably wrote in Bavaria and for Bavarians.
The former must have written after the recognition of the power of
Duke Henry the Proud by the Emperor Lothar. The latter most
probably worked at the Court of Henry the Lion, and introduces
incidents drawn from the Crusade of this Prince (1172). By
silently contrasting Duke Ernst and Duke Henry he helped to
bring about the defection of his master from the Emperor.

The following is the plot of 'Herzog Ernst.' Ernst is ruler over
Bavaria. His mother, Adelheid, becomes the second wife of the Emperor Otto. The Emperor adopts the duke as his son,
and makes him his confidential adviser. But envy and
calumny soon sow dissension, and Ernst, at length reduced to despair, and enraged to the utmost against his enemy, the

*'König
Rother' and
'Herzog
Ernst.'*

*Story of
'Herzog
Ernst.'*

[1] P. 56.

Count Palatine Henry, kills him in presence of the Emperor, declaring that he would have slain his stepfather also, had he been in
his power. After this highly dramatic scene Ernst takes refuge in
flight; he is laid under the ban of the empire, and his country
is invaded. After five years' resistance, he takes the cross, goes
through wonderful adventures, makes offerings at the Holy Sepulchre, and fights in Jerusalem against the heathen. He returns
and first makes himself known to his mother, and then, in the
Cathedral at Bamberg, he falls during service at the Emperor's
feet, who pardons him without knowing who he is. In all his
vicissitudes, a friend and companion of his youth, Count Wetzel,
remains faithful to him. The lighter emotions of love are hardly
touched upon in this poem. Only once is a maiden introduced,
such as usually meet the heroes of legend, and excite their affection.
Duke Ernst does indeed save a captive maiden from her oppressors,
but she is left dead in his arms.

Two historical traitors to the imperial power are united in the
Historical person of the legendary Duke Ernst—i. e. Ludolf, the
basis of the son of Otto the Great, and Duke Ernst of Suabia,
legend. stepson of Conrad II. Even in the song of the
eleventh century the hero was doubtless represented as being put
under the ban of the empire, and perhaps as leaving the country.
The poet of the twelfth century uses this incident in order to ascribe
to him a crusade and many fabulous adventures in the style of the
Alexanderlied. In the thirteenth century two great Middle High-
German poems treated this same subject, which ended by circulat-
ing as a ballad and popular romance.

Side by side with this tale of the wanderings of a German prince
'St. Bran- may be placed a poem relating the travels of the monk
dan.' St. Brandan, which brings again before us the fame of
the Irish monks. Brandan reads of a subterranean world, where it
is day whilst we have night. Vexed at the improbability of this
story he burns the book, and as a punishment has to experience
much stranger things than this on a long sea-voyage. He has
terrific encounters with devils, and many episodes of a farcical
character are introduced, such as that of the monk who had stolen
a bridle, or of Brandan's coat falling into the sea.

The story of 'King Orendel' reminds us yet more vividly of the
Odyssey. It must have been founded on some song , King Oren-
containing ancient mythological matter. With the del,' 12th
ancient Germans Orendel was the genius of navi- century.
gation, a personification of favourable weather. In late autumn
Orendel suffers shipwreck, and becomes subject to an Ice-giant,
Master Ise. He is cast naked on the shore, and covers his nakedness, like Ulysses, with a bough. By slave's service he earns a
grey coat, in which he returns unrecognised in the spring-time
to his own country. And after he has, like Ulysses, conquered the
suitors who besiege his wife, he is received by her with joy. In the
minstrel ballad of the twelfth century which has come down to us,
Orendel's wife is transported to Jerusalem and made the daughter
of King David. The Knights Templars serve and protect her ;
she takes part armed in the conflict with the heathen, like a
Walküre or Amazon. Though she receives Orendel as one well
known and long expected, yet when he suffered shipwreck he was
on a crusade and knew nothing about her. He now becomes King
of Jerusalem, and when the city falls, in his absence, into the hands
of the heathen, he recovers it by the help of his wife. The poet
has made a 'Gerusalemme Liberata' out of the mythological
legend. He knows the names of a few places in Palestine, and
also a little about the state of the kingdom after the capture of the
Holy City by Saladin in 1187. His intention doubtless was to
comfort the mourning Christians with a hope of its recovery. He
trusts implicitly in Divine help : as soon as his hero is in danger,
the Virgin Mary prays to her Son for him, and angels hasten to
help him. The author thus gains a 'deus ex machinâ,' such as
a Greek or Roman epic poet could avail himself of. He also appeals
thereby to pious minds, and by making the grey coat of Orendel
typical of the seamless coat of Christ, he gives to his work quite the
character of a sacred legend. But he is not of a pious disposition
himself. He makes no sharp distinction between Christians and
heathen, and never leads his readers into the world of spiritual
experience. In this respect the author of ' St. Oswald' St. Oswald.
fully resembles him. The Crusade which he describes
is also really a journey in quest of a bride. The talking raven of

the tale is a half-miraculous, half-comic element. A heathen maiden is carried off by fraud; the pursuers are defeated, killed, raised from the dead, and baptized. But we look in vain here for the seriousness, not to say the religious pathos of the 'Rolandslied.' The Priest Konrad stands alone in this respect. The gleemen sought only to amuse their audience by stories of the East, and of the struggle with the Paynim, and cared little to edify them. The supremacy of 'Lady World' was not broken by the Crusades, on the contrary, they placed new weapons in the hands of her servants; and so also the moral result of the Crusades, their influence on the spirit of chivalry, consisted only in the destruction of intolerant bigotry and the reconciliation of those who formerly were foes.

The Crusades, though they sprang from intolerance, resulted in an increase of toleration. Though they seemed to express a triumph of the Papacy, yet they proved in the end prejudicial to its interests. It was wise of Frederick Barbarossa to make the deliverance of Jerusalem one of his objects, and thus assert in this direction the supremacy of the empire. In theory Palestine, like all other countries of the earth, was under his protection.

The Latin play of Antichrist, which we have mentioned, had already set forth this idea, and even in wider spheres men were accustomed to look upon the power of the emperor as universal. 'Count Ru- An authentic proof of this is afforded us in a German dolf,' 1170. poem, 'Count Rudolf,' written in 1170, which at the same time gives us a clear idea of the hostile and friendly relations between Christians and heathen in the kingdom of Jerusalem. Count Rudolf, the hero of the poem, is a Christian Coriolanus. Having quarrelled with his brethren in the faith, he joins the heathen, in order to fight with them against the Christians. Probably the Count, tired and purified by many sufferings, returned at last to the ranks of the faithful. I say probably, because this beautiful tale, like so many others that especially excite our interest, is only preserved to us in fragments. Poems reflecting real life and choosing their materials from contemporary history found little acceptance with a mediæval public, which preferred tales of a phantastic and marvellous character. Hence, copies of poems like 'Count

Rudolf' were seldom multiplied, and it is only by a happy chance that fragments of them have come down to posterity. What remains of 'Count Rudolf' is throughout free from the over-refinement of later chivalrous romances. It is plain human life which is pictured to us, free from the artificialities of convention. The narrative flows on simply and clearly, yet at times the personal sympathy of the poet breaks out. Sometimes he shows his enthusiasm for his hero, and thanks those who are kindly disposed to him; sometimes he utters his own feelings in weighty language, and expresses his hatred of faithless coun-sellors or his admiration of noble women. In the course of the story he gives vent, in a naive manner, to his Imperial imperial leanings. The King of Jerusalem wishes to leanings of introduce imperial ceremonial and magnificence at his the author. court, fancying himself on an equal footing with the emperor; Count Rudolf, who understands such matters, is to aid him in the arrangements. But Rudolf begins to laugh and says, 'If you usurp imperial customs, it may be the worse for you; the emperor has no equal, your whole land would be forfeited.' The dominion of the German Emperor is thus tacitly extended to Jerusalem, and it is assumed that a word from him would be enough to destroy the whole fabric of usurpation. And yet it is only a question of harmless ceremonial.

But the time soon came when the German-Roman emperor really seemed to have extended his dominion to Extension of Jerusalem. On the 18th of March, 1229, the excom- the Imperial municated emperor, Frederick II, took a golden power. crown from the high altar of the Holy Sepulchre, and placed it on his head. A German poet, Meister Freidank, who had joined the emperor's army, described in short epigrams the condition of things at Acre. 'There is no difference,' he says, 'between Christian, Jews, and heathens at Acre.' And the honest Swabian seems not to have felt quite at his ease in this inter-national throng. Frederick's whole Oriental policy was founded on the idea of the possibility of peaceable intercourse between Christians and Mohammedans, and this policy was only the prac-tical outcome of that religious toleration which had for some time exercised such a beneficial influence on the minds of Europe. We shall find this spirit of toleration still more strongly expressed later on in some of the chivalrous poets, in Wolfram von Eschenbach, Walther von der Vogelweide, and Freidank.

In fact, Middle High-German poetry in its most famous representatives is, like our modern classic literature, founded on the principle of toleration. And in the thirteenth as in the nineteenth century, the rise of fanaticism and persecution betokened the decay of literature.

Signs of the same liberal spirit are not wanting in the science of this epoch. The classic period of the Middle Ages reverenced Aristotle as a profound thinker, but most of his works remained unexplored till Frederick II caused Jewish scholars to translate the Translation Arabic texts of Aristotle with their Arabic commenof Aristotle. taries into Latin, and thus opened these treasures to Western science. To the Arabs belongs the literary merit of the work, the Jews were the instruments, the Christian emperor originated the scheme. The adherents of all three religions worked together to breathe fresh life into the greatest philosopher of antiquity.

Frederick II stands at the head of the political and scientific Frederick II. movements of his time. He gave to politics the model of a state organized according to modern ideas; he endowed science with the Latin version of Aristotle; he united in himself the most vigorous features of that Italic-Norman life in the midst of which he grew up. Perhaps nowhere does the modern German experience so overpowering a feeling of the nearness of the spirit of mediæval Imperialism, as when he finds himself in the sombre landscape of Palermo, at the foot of the beautiful Monte Pellegrino, and pictures to his imagination the half Saracenic court of Frederick II, and then stands beside the two gloomy but magnificent coffins in the Cathedral of the Sicilian capital, only separated by a slab of porphyry from the earthly remains of Henry VI and his great son.

Frederick II was the last great champion of the temporal power against mediæval sacerdotalism. He seemed almost a supernatural being in the eyes of the Italian people. They would not believe that he was really dead, and their disbelief spread to Germany. False Fredericks appeared, and when these passed away the idea soon became current that he would come again at the head of a large army to reform the degenerate church. Till then he was supposed to sleep in the Kiffhäuser, or some other mountain. There he sits at a stone table, and his beard has grown to his feet. If any one approaches him, he asks whether the ravens are still flying round the mountain. If they are, he must sleep another hundred years. It was not till much later that the sleeping emperor was supposed to be Frederick Barbarossa, and not till this century that he came to be regarded as a symbol of the vanished dominion of the German people.

CHAPTER V.

In the history of German civilisation we notice from early times a difference between the Rhine provinces and South **Part played in literature** Germany on the one hand, and the Lowlands of **by the** Germany, particularly the territory of the Saxons, **various dis-** on the other. Lower Saxony had been one of the **tricts of Germany.** earliest homes of the Germans, whereas the Rhineland and South Germany were won from the Celts and Romans in later times. The traces of the older civilisation in these parts were never quite obliterated, and exercised a good influence on the conquerors. It was by their own free will that the Germans carried some elements of this civilisation to the North; while in the West and South they simply yielded to an irresistible influence due not only to the past and therefore temporary, but rendered permanent, as it would seem, by their geographical surroundings. Romanic culture continued to radiate from France and Italy to West and South Germany. The French influence asserted itself almost uninterruptedly, while the Italian influence was more fitful in its operation. In the end we can distinguish three districts in Germany clearly marked out from each other by their leading characteristics:—the Rhine, Lower Saxony, and Austria, i. e. Upper and Lower Austria, with Styria, Carinthia, and Tyrol. In Bavaria, and later on in Thuringia, we observe a kind of compromise in which these differences become reconciled and neutralised.

When the Carlovingians wished to create a Christian literature, Lower Saxony was drawn almost by force into the movement. But the 'Heliand' remained a solitary achievement. During the Carlovingian Renaissance German poetry, as a branch of written literature, almost entirely vanished. We do not even know at

what time alliteration—which certainly continued longer in Lower Saxony than elsewhere—finally gave place to rhyme. But the popular poetry, handed down by oral tradition, did not entirely disappear. The heroic songs, whilst retreating further and further from the Rhine and South Germany, found a refuge The hero-
in Lower Saxony, though only among the middle legends in
and lower classes. The Saxon national legends were, Saxony.
in consequence, almost entirely forgotten, and their place was taken by the Gothic-Frankish hero-legends. The Germanic heroes, banished from the castles, took refuge in the huts of the peasants, there to wait for the time when they might emerge from obscurity, and assume once more their place of honour. But during this time of banishment the legends underwent some modification. The achievements of those Saxons who had restored the empire in the tenth century reflected fresh glory on these old hero-legends. The redoubtable Gothic king, Ermanarich, was transformed first into a king of the Germans reigning in North Germany, and afterwards into a Roman emperor. The Italian campaigns revived the memory of Theodoric the Great, the Dietrich von Bern (Verona) of later Middle High-German poetry; and when the German soldier gazed in wonder at vast buildings like the amphitheatre at Verona, or the Castle of St. Angelo in Rome, he thought he saw before him a work of that Dietrich who, in olden times, had reigned so gloriously over the Amelungen, for the name of the Goths was forgotten and replaced by that of their royal family. The German legends and songs spread to foreign countries—to Denmark, Russia, Poland, Bavaria, Hungary, and Italy, and the wandering Saxon minstrel learned the legends of other lands, and wove the tales of foreign heroes into German song.

THE REVIVAL OF THE HEROIC POETRY.

French influence is not perceptible in German popular poetry until the eleventh century, the time of the rise of chivalry. At that period the Lower Rhine began to play an important part in German poetry. The gleeman of the Rhine learned from his Saxon brother how some of his poetic material had come to him from France by way of the Netherlands. The

Rhenish gleeman also had at his command the whole mass of
Lower Saxon legends and songs.   And it was not

Poetry of
the gleemen.

only up the Rhine that he wandered; even in Upper
Bavaria we find traces of his presence, while from Holland he
brought back the legend of Gudrun.

The German knight found food for his romantic aspirations in
the old heroic ideals set before him by the gleemen.   And not the
knights only, but the bishops too, cared sometimes to listen to the

Conflict be-
tween the
clergy and
the gleemen.

stories of the Nibelungen and the Amelungen.   But, as
we have seen, a clerical reaction set in, which sought to
destroy the activity of the gleemen throughout the whole
of South and West Germany, and to undermine the
power of a secular code of morals founded on honour and self-
respect.   The result was very different in different parts.   On the
Rhine, and in Allemania and Thuringia, the clergy succeeded in
supplanting the German heroes by the champions of the faith,
the destroyers of the heathen and the Crusaders.   The French
influence, represented at first by clerical poets like Lamprecht and
Konrad, also exercised its power on the gleemen.

The Austrian provinces, however, retained their independence.
The Austrian clerical poets being stricter, treated purely religious
subjects only, and in consequence could not hold their own against
the gleemen.   And in Bavaria, as we noticed before, these opposing
forces were reconciled.   There, gleemen and clerical poets were
equally welcome.   They sang of Gudrun, King Rother, and the
dying Roland, and the Kaiserchronik is likewise of Bavarian origin.

Heroic poetry reached its zenith in Austria and Bavaria.   There
those immortal epics arose which, about the close of the

Heroic
poetry in
Austria,
Bavaria, and
Lower
Saxony.

twelfth century, were fortunately rescued from the acci-
dents of oral transmission, and written down on parchment.   But in Lower Saxony the gleeman remained, as
a rule, sole master of the poetic art, and was content
merely to transmit his songs by word of mouth.   It was
only occasionally that a Saxon knight or priest appeared as a poet.
The whole treasure of the Low German heroic poetry of that time
would have been entirely lost to us, had not a learned Norwegian
of the thirteenth century, who took an interest in these songs and

legends, written down their substance, grouping them round the character of Dietrich von Bern, and thus forming them into a Prose Romance or Saga. This work, entitled the 'Thidrekssaga,' gives us some idea of what the Saxon songs must have been. As a rule they continued the style of the journalistic minstrel poetry, which prevailed in the tenth century: i. e. concise narrative, delighting in incident, striving after bold effects, shrinking from no coarseness, and lacking any deeper insight into human character or moral problems. Now again, as in the sixth century, the German heroic legends penetrated to the North, not only through this Norwegian Saga, but also through the living popular songs. There are Danish and Faro songs based on Low German ones which have been lost, and the Faro songs are to this day sung as an accompaniment to the dance on those far off islands.

The 'Thidrekssaga,' 13th century.

In Bavaria and Austria the development of the heroic song took another course. It gained more epic breadth and fulness of detail, while its rivalry with the clerical poetry wrought some change in its subject matter. The priest had the advantage of knowing Latin, as well as of being familiar with history. Armed with these he attacked the heroic legends, and found it easy to prove that Attila and Theodoric, the legendary Dietrich and Etzel, were not contemporaries, thus bringing the veracity of the gleemen into suspicion. The charge was a serious one, for all narrative poetry was expected to be true history. The result was that the gleeman made false appeals to fictitious historical authorities, and so rendered himself really liable to the charges of falsehood made against him.

Influence of clerical criticism on heroic poetry in Austria and Bavaria.

There is another kind of criticism, which we cannot so clearly trace, but which must also have been applied to these legends. The Nibelungen legend originally contained a number of mythical elements alike repugnant to Christian beliefs and to the comparative enlightenment of the twelfth century. The giants, dwarfs, and dragons, the fabulous elements in the story of Siegfried's youth and in the nature of Brünhild, were as much as possible

Removal or modification of mythical elements.

eliminated. The legend was thus made more perfect, being freed from superhuman elements. All the mythological elements were kept in the background, and it is evident that they did not excite so much interest as the more strictly historical portions, connected with well-known localities.

The legend must also have been submitted to moral censorship, Improved for all features that could possibly give offence to moral tone. refined feminine feeling were expunged, hardly to the extent perhaps which modern taste might demand, but we must remember that those were times of greater simplicity than ours.

In the oldest version of the legend there is a close connection between Siegfried and Brünhild. He has awakened her from her magic sleep, she has initiated him in hidden wisdom, and they have sworn to be true to one another. But a draught of oblivion given him by Kriemhild's mother makes him faithless; he marries Kriemhild, and helps her brother Gunther to win Brünhild for himself. But Brünhild has not forgotten the injury, and has her revenge. She drives the faithless but still loved Siegfried to destruction, and dies with him. Later times evidently took offence at Siegfried's relation to the two women. The later version of the legend omits almost all mention of his earlier connection with Brünhild, and seeks another foundation for those incidents which the story could not afford to lose. Thus the moral purity of the young ill-fated hero remained untarnished.

Kriemhild as the avenger of Siegfried is horrible, for her own brothers are her victims; and this formed such an essential part of the legend that it could not well be altered. In the Saxon tradition Kriemhild, when she sees that two of her brothers have fallen, thrusts a torch into their mouths to find out if they are really dead. According to another tradition, she strikes off with her own hand the heads of the two who lie bound before her. But the South German form of the legend rightly expunged such barbarities, and made another person the victim of Kriemhild's unnatural deeds. Here again a more refined moral feeling has raised the poetry to a higher level.

Among all the subjects of heroic legend, that which is pre-

served to us in the Nibelungenlied seems to have held the
highest place. It excited the strongest clerical op-   **Superiority**
position; it formed the greatest pride of the minstrel,   **of the**
and was in favour in the highest circles. The   **Nibelungen**
lofty tone of the Nibelungenlied in its original   **legend.**
form indicates that it was addressed to a highly cultured audience;
and the exact knowledge which it displays of Lower Austrian
localities renders it probable that the poems about Siegfried and
the Burgundians were first recited at the court of Vienna. For,
towards the end of the twelfth century, it was no longer the custom to
sing poetical narrations, but to declaim them or read them out.

Few of the other heroic legendary poems maintained the high
moral and æsthetic level of the Nibelungenlied. The   **Decay of**
sympathy of refined society was withdrawn from these   **heroic poetry**
poems in the thirteenth century, when French in-   **in the 13th**
fluence penetrated even to the valleys of the Alps.   **century.**
And as soon as the popular poems began to be adapted for a
lower audience, they lost their purity and serious tone. Authors
wished to maintain the popularity of these poems by foolish con-
cessions to fashion; they strove after realistic effects; they seized
on a few rags of chivalry, and decked the old heroes with them,
but only to their degradation.

Still, if we consider the leading ideas of these poems, there
reigns in all of them a high moral tone. The leading characters
in their salient features recur in the most various poems, and we
easily perceive that in these characters we have moral ideals
bequeathed from days long past, that the situations in which they
are placed are thoroughly out of keeping with chivalry, and
that all knightly elements, and even Christianity itself, are as
a rule a mere outside varnish that has not penetrated very deep.
So faithful was tradition, and so true the instinct which guided
the opposition of the clergy to the heroic poems.

The heroic legends grew up in the time of the migration of
races and in the Merovingian period, and it was the   **History and**
last of these two epochs that exercised the best in-   **character of**
fluence on them. The kings who appear in the   **the heroic**
popular poems resemble the Merovingians and the   **legends.**

H

Amals rather than the Hohenstaufen and Guelphs. The state is supposed to be the property of the whole royal family. Important acts of government are only carried out with the consent of the friends of the blood royal, and the fiction of blood-relationship is extended to nearly all those surrounding the throne. Honoured and faithful ministers guide the young princes, and rule the kingdom with power and wisdom. Throughout their lives they are looked upon as counsellors of authority, and their opinion is willingly listened to. The king is surrounded by a train of companions in arms, who are always ready to sacrifice themselves for him, while he in his turn bestows gifts on them with a liberal hand, and frees them from prison and distress, even at risk of his own life. The financial resources of the kingdom are represented under the idea of a vast and inexhaustible treasure. Precious weapons are handed down from father to son, and acquire a fateful import in bold deeds and hideous crimes. Even women demand that bloodshed should be avenged, and vengeance does not stop short of total destruction.

Ludwig Uhland has rightly divided all the various characters of **Conception of character in the heroic poetry.** the heroic legends into two groups ; the loyal and the disloyal. The duty of liberality is connected with loyalty, and avarice is a sign of disloyalty. Self-sacrifice, the root of all virtues, first appears within the family circle, then in the society at court, and in companionship in arms. As the lord and his vassals are bound together by a general bond, so the vassals are often connected with each other by some peculiar tie, and afford beautiful examples of heroic friendship. Over and above the duties imposed by natural ties, or by alliances expressly agreed upon, it is esteemed honourable and glorious for a warrior to relieve distress in strangers and to aid the oppressed. Action is free, so far as it does not conflict with a warrior's code of honour.

Violated faith amongst relations is the chief cause of all the complications of the heroic legends. When two parties are once on a footing of enmity their friends often find themselves in a dilemma. Loyalty to. a friend entails determined treachery to an enemy; loyalty to one who has been basely murdered leads to treacherous revenge on all his living enemies; the duties of a vassal come into conflict with family duties, and a marriage often becomes the source of a feud. The woman who was to form a connecting link between two houses suffers by her twofold position, and whilst trying to fulfil her conflicting duties, the flame of her shortsighted passion may become a firebrand destroying both houses. The spirit of chivalrous self-sacrifice, which instead of deriving a brutal pleasure from warfare, regarded it as a high and honourable calling, breathed a new life into the old heroes. They were typical examples of a noble secular life, a life of fighting and of many duties. A fervent enthusiasm for the profession of arms inspires every line of the Middle High-German heroic poems. The men are always described with solemn emphasis as heroes, warriors, swordsmen, and knights.

Though the heroic poetry remained on the whole true to its origin, still it underwent some modification in the *Gradual* course of centuries. New characters were admitted *modification* who bear witness to this influence of the times. Side *of the hero* by side with the dignity and nobility of the chief *legends.* characters we perceive in some of the subordinate ones the coarse minstrel humour of the tenth century, which loudly applauded a Kuno Kurzibold. In Wolfhart, nephew of the old Hildebrand, with his violent disposition and boundless love of fighting, his bloodthirstiness, his loud voice and rough jokes, and his aversion to the society of refined women, we recognise the earlier and far from ideal type of warrior. The courtly dignity of the chief cook had already been humorously treated in the older Latin poems, and Rumold, the chief cook in the Nibelungenlied, is a representative of unimaginative common sense : he advises the Burgundians, when about to march against Attila, to 'stay at home and earn their bread honestly.' So also the union of the warrior and the musician in the noble fiddler Volker von Alzei had probably at first a humorous significance; but as soon as the position of the minstrels was raised, and they were admitted in Bavaria and Austria into good society, this character was also idealised. After the middle of the twelfth century the knights began to write love-poems, to set them to music, and to sing them. Thus there were undoubtedly many instances of the union of the professions of arms and of minstrelsy in the same individual.

All this poetry is anonymous. The few names known to us **German** belong to a comparatively late time, and the works **heroic poems** connected with them are of no great value. In the **anonymous.** best period of Middle High-German poetry we must be contented with the poems themselves, without the name of the author. We must respect the voluntary obscurity in which these poets modestly hid themselves. They had no desire for literary fame and did not wish their names to be handed down to posterity; they willingly retired behind those heroes in whose favour they wished to enlist the sympathies of their hearers. This concealment of the author's identity is in harmony with the impersonal style of the poems themselves. The epic popular poet of the end of the twelfth century sometimes speaks in his own person, but it is merely a form of speech. He advances his personal reflections as if they were generally received opinions, and they often serve to foreshadow the future course of events. Nor do these poets allow themselves originality in depicting characters, things, and events. Throughout the different poems the same types of character are adhered to, for in this respect, as well as in their literary style, the authors bow to tradition.

The heroic poems of the Middle High-German epoch, like the **Style of** popular epics of Merovingian times, are full of **the heroic** conventional phrases and ideas, out of respect to **poems.** which the poet is content to forego all personal originality. We do not find in these poems the grandeur and pictorial breadth of Homeric description; on the contrary, the style is throughout perfectly simple. The heroes and heroines are characterised by such epithets as brave, bold, beautiful; sometimes these are emphasised into very brave, bold as the storm, wonderfully beautiful; sometimes they denote the leading characteristic of the person to whom they are applied, as when Rüdiger is called the generous, Eckhart the faithful, Hagen the cruel. The descriptive element is confined to the most ordinary epithets; such expressions as a white hand, a red mouth, bright eyes, yellow hair, are perpetually recurring. There are no detailed poetical similes, and the poet's imagination never goes beyond the very simplest comparisons, as, for instance, of the colour of young cheeks to the roses, of the rude love of fighting to the wild boar, of a malicious disposition to a wolf. Every mood has its conventional outward demeanour: the afflicted man sits silently upon a stone, and the man who has formed a resolution speaks not a word until he has carried it out. A downcast eye betokens dejection, an upward glance joy, silent contemplation inquiry, while turning pale and then red denotes a rapid change of mood. In the same manner remarks about stature, garments, and weapons are only made from a few fixed points of view. All the occupations of hero-life are reduced to conventional formulas, and though so many means are at the poet's command for the poetic glorification of battle, yet the popular epic writers seem only to have aimed at giving powerful expression to its most horrible aspects. So too the various localities in which different events take place are seldom more than vaguely indicated. In fact, the poet never concentrates all his powers upon one point, and hardly ever goes into detail. In this respect, as in others, the style of the German popular epics is inferior to the ideal narrator, Homer.

THE NIBELUNGENLIED.

From the earliest times the Germans used the falcon in hunting and in their poetry the fighting, hunting falcon served as the emblem of a youthful hero. Flashing eyes reminded the mediæval poet of falcons' eyes, and a noble lady of the twelfth century who has won the love of a man expresses this in poetry by saying that she has tamed a falcon. So too, in the opening of the Nibelungenlied, we read how Kriemhild dreamt in her girlhood of a falcon which she had spent many a day in taming, but to her lasting sorrow two eagles tore it to pieces before her eyes. This dream of gloomy foreboding foreshadows the events related in the first half of the poem. Siegfried is the falcon, his brother-in-law Gunther and Gunther's vassal Hagen are the eagles who tear him to pieces, and Kriemhild weeps for him and will not be comforted. The carrying out of her horrible revenge forms the subject of the second part. She gives her hand in marriage to the king of the Huns, and invites the murderers to a feast, which she turns into a massacre. With wooing and betrothal the tale opens, with murder and fire it closes, very like in this to the legend of the siege of Troy. But the Nibelungenlied does not merely consist of certain episodes selected from the legend, but exhausts the whole of the legendary material, thereby attaining a higher degree of unity than the Iliad.

The closeness with which this poem links a crime and its punishment is characteristic of an ideal world, such as the spirit of a nation · yet in its youth dreams of and desires. The heroes of the Iliad, on

Inequalities of the Nibelungen-lied. the contrary, with their naive selfishness are nearer the level of ordinary humanity. But notwithstanding the outward and inward completeness of the legend, the merit of the poem, as in the Iliad, varies in different parts; and these differences are much greater than in the Iliad. Side by side with the most beautiful scenes we meet with dull and sometimes even grotesque passages, through which we painfully make our way. Whilst the best parts—if we leave the difference of style out of consideration—may fairly compare with the noblest flowers of Homeric poetry, we can hardly venture to mention the name of Homer in connection with the inferior ones. This Middle High-German Epic is like an old church, in the building of which many architects have successively taken part, some of whom have scrupulously adhered to the original designs of their predecessors, while others have arbitrarily followed their own devices; little minds have added paintings, scrolls, and side-wings, and Time has thrown over the whole the grey veil of age, so that the general impression is a noble one; yet severer criticism will reject the excrescences, explore the architectural history, distinguish in it the work of various hands, assigning to each master his own, before judgment can be passed on the artistic design and execution of the whole.

Karl Lachmann attempted the work of restoring the Nibelungenlied and analysing its various elements, and accomplished the task, not indeed faultlessly, yet on the whole correctly. He has pointed out later interpolations, which hide the original sequence of the story, and has divided the narrative which remains after the removal of these accretions into twenty songs, Lachmann's some of which are connected, while others embody criticism of isolated incidents of the legend.   Some of them, but the Poem. certainly only a few, may be by the same author.   Small as is the scope left for poetical individuality to show itself in the Middle High-German heroic poetry, yet we recognise in most of these songs such differences in conception, treatment, and style, as point to separate authorship.   The whole may have been finished in about twenty years, from 1190–1210.

Lachmann's theory has indeed been contested.   Many students still believe that the poem, as we have it, was the work Single or of one hand; but on this hypothesis no one has suc- divided ceeded in explaining the strange contradictions which Authorship pervade the work, parts of which show the highest of the Poem. art, while the rest is valueless.   Even those who believe in the single authorship of the poem must acknowledge that the poet derived the substance of his work from older lays (for the heroic legends till about the end of the twelfth century existed only in the form of lays orally handed down), and that the internal disparities are explained by the various songs made use of by the author. But a careful examination of these inequalities and contradictions convinces us that the theory of single authorship is untenable. The author of the Nibelungenlied cannot be known.   Perhaps even a final revision of the poem never took place, and instead of speaking of a poet we can only speak of the man who first had the songs written down in a book.

In the beginning of the twelfth century there existed a song about Kriemhild's disloyalty to her brothers.   Perhaps it related in a shorter form all that is now included in the second part of our poem.   The desire for greater epic detail may have led to the separate treatment of single incidents, but this would always be done with reference to a former whole, and the single poems could therefore later on be the more easily re-united as episodes in a whole. In the same way the songs of the first part may have grown out of an older shorter ballad, certain incidents of which invited separate treatment. But much in this part is new and without any older source, so that here the poet was guided by his imagination only.

The first song, which opens with Kriemhild's foreboding dreams, **The** narrates the coming of Siegfried to Worms; we are **First Song.** told of his father King Siegmund, of his home in Xanten, of his beauty, his strength, and his chivalrous exploits. He hears of Kriemhild's beauty and coyness, and when urged to seek a wife, he declares that he will have none other than Kriemhild. The opposition of his parents, their fear of Kriemhild's brothers, Gunther and Gernot and their vassals, especially Hagen, only urge him on. He thinks at first of winning her by force, yet resolves to ride with only a small number of followers to the land of the Burgundians. Clad in magnificent armour, he and his companions excite general attention at Worms. But Siegfried ill rewards the friendly reception which is given him; he declares his intention of acquiring the Burgundian empire by force of arms, yet is pacified on being offered a share in the kingdom. He remains with the Burgundians, and the song closes with a peaceful joust between Siegfried and his hosts, in which Siegfried always proves superior. Throughout this song every word and action of Siegfried's is instinct with the boldness and impetuosity of youth. Without elaborate enumeration of his exploits, and using only the simplest means of description, the poet succeeds in impressing on us that Siegfried is a true hero. Hagen, who is represented as gloomy and terrible, is made prominent from the first, as being next in importance to Siegfried. Each of the Burgundians is graphically characterised, and untold dramatic force is thus given to their interview with Siegfried. It would take more words to describe the beauties of this poem than the poet used to accomplish his task. His power of depicting character and developing incident is quite remarkable. But the original intention of the hero to woo and win Kriemhild seems to be quite forgotten by the end of the poem. The author of this song probably left his work uncompleted, and must have certainly planned a very different continuation of the poem from that which we now find in the subsequent songs.

The second song is very trivial. The poet devotes all his
energies to extolling his hero Siegfried. He makes   **The**
him wage a successful war for Gunther against the **Second Song.**
Saxons and Danes, and take both of the hostile kings prisoners
with his own hand.

After this, the third song describes a feast, at which Siegfried
sees Kriemhild for the first time and immediately falls   **The**
deeply in love with her. There is no mention here of **Third Song.**
Kriemhild's coyness. On the contrary, she is at once attracted by
the young knight, who for his part does not dare to think of
winning her, but confines himself to exchanging tender glances
with her and secretly pressing her hand. The freshness and
innocence of first love are gracefully and tenderly described, but
without any particular originality.

The fourth song, on the contrary, is very powerful. It tells of the
wooing of Brünhild, the Amazon-Queen of Isenstein   **The**
far over the sea. The man who would win Brünhild's **Fourth Song.**
affection must conquer her in single combat, and lose his head if he
fails. Siegfried promises to win her for Gunther, on condition
that Gunther should grant him Kriemhild's hand in return. This
Gunther promises to do. Siegfried takes with him a cloak which
renders him invisible, the 'Tarnkappe,' of which he had stripped
the dwarf Alberich, and thus disguised he fights with Brünhild in
Gunther's place, and conquers her. We must suppose that he has
seen her before, for he alone knows the way to her country, and
she at once greets him by name and asks him what he wants.
He answers that he is Gunther's vassal, and is come with his lord
to woo her. The story is excellently told, with strange, almost
naive clearness of detail as regards the outward incidents. The
poet repeatedly impresses upon his hearers the fact that Siegfried
made use of secret arts, that *he* fought and not Gunther, and
that Brünhild and her followers believed that Gunther was the
victor; but he does nothing to bring out the characters, the
motives, the feelings of the actors, only meaning us to watch with
interest how Gunther will overcome the danger into which he has
entered.

A weak continuation of this fourth song gives a detailed but uninteresting account of the return of Siegfried as a messenger to Worms and of Brünhild's reception there, and at the end just touches on the marriage of Siegfried and Kriemhild.

The fifth song shows us the two couples at the wedding-feast.

The Fifth Song. Brünhild weeps because Gunther's sister has been given to a man who is only a vassal, and the King comforts her by promising an explanation in the future. But Brünhild's dark character reveals itself still further; Gunther must fight again with her, and again Siegfried in his ' Tarnkappe ' must aid him to overcome Brünhild, whose ring and girdle he carries off and gives to Kriemhild. The poet does not conceal his disapproval of this action, and remarks, ' He regretted it later.' Taking the work as a whole, it makes an unfavourable impression that Gunther should three times in succession be in need of help, and unable to do anything without Siegfried : firstly, in the Saxon war, secondly, at the wooing of Brünhild, and again here for the third time.

The sixth song, treating of the quarrel between the two Queens,

The Sixth Song. brings us nearer to the tragic *dénouement.* We learn that Siegfried is ruler over the land of the Nibelungen in Norway, and is the possessor of vast treasure. He and his wife accept an invitation from Gunther and Brünhild to come to Worms. One evening, when the two Queens are sitting together and watching the knightly games, the quarrel begins with Kriemhild's foolishly exaggerated praise of her husband. Brünhild thereupon tries to play the sovereign and treat her sister-in-law as the wife of a vassal. The latter at length shows Brünhild's ring and girdle, and Siegfried incurs suspicion as having boasted that he had overcome this terrible woman. Brünhild complains to her husband, whereupon Siegfried, with manly honesty, protests his innocence, blames the quarrelsome speeches of the women, and strictly forbids Kriemhild to carry on the quarrel. The narrative, which drags rather at the beginning of this song, becomes gradually more rapid and dramatic, and Siegfried's concluding speech is highly characteristic.

The author of the seventh song is filled with moral indignation

The Seventh Song. against Hagen, who in the previous poem had already shown a hankering after the treasure of the Nibelungen. Now Brünhild's sorrow moves him to take vengeance on Siegfried. Gunther here shows much moral weakness in being so easily talked over. A new war against the Saxons is proclaimed, and for the fourth time Gunther is in need of assistance, while Siegfried is ready to help and eager for battle. Hagen pays a farewell visit to Kriemhild, and with striking guilelessness she reveals to him Siegfried's secret, in order that he may protect him: when Siegfried had killed the dragon and was bathing himself in its blood, a lime-leaf had fallen between his shoulders, and there alone he was vulnerable. Kriemhild resolves, by Hagen's advice, to mark his garment in the dangerous place with a small silken cross. As soon as Hagen on the following morning sees the cross, he sends pretended messengers of peace from the Saxon King, and the campaign is changed into a hunting-party. The evident stratagem, the weakness of the King, the artfulness of his counsellor, the unsuspecting innocence of the young couple, are somewhat childishly represented by the poet. We do not feel ourselves in a world of reality.

But in the following song, in the narrative of the hunt and of Siegfried's death, German popular poetry reaches its highest perfection. Here we find the same capacity The Eighth Song. for indirect characterisation as in the first song, which this one, however, transcends in many respects: in the tragic nature of the subject, the loftiness of the style, the depth of the conception, the greater breadth of the narrative. We are again attracted by the impetuous character of Siegfried, who appears full of life and boyish spirits. Being very thirsty he exclaims: 'They ought to have brought me mules laden with mead and spiced wine, or else to have transferred the meeting-place nearer to the Rhine.' Hagen knows of a spring close at hand, and challenges Siegfried to race him thither, and Siegfried willingly agrees. With naive self-confidence he runs in armour, while Hagen and Gunther run in their shirts. Still he comes in first, but waits for Gunther to drink before him. Then while Siegfried is bending down to drink, Hagen takes away his weapons and hurls his own spear at his back through the silken cross. Siegfried has only retained his shield, and with it he throws the murderer to the ground; but then he turns pale, and sinks down exhausted among the flowers. He reproaches Hagen and Gunther, reminds them of his services and of his loyalty, and then turns his dying thoughts to Kriemhild, to his son and his father. And says the poet, 'The flowers all around were drenched with blood where he wrestled with death.' They lay the body on a shield, and as soon as it is dark, they take it across the Rhine.

The joyous opening and the tragic close of this song produce a most powerful effect on the reader, and show the very highest poetic art. The poet not only gives a clear idea of the events, but also of the locality in which they took place. It is not only Siegfried whom he clearly characterises, but also Gunther and Hagen, and he manages throughout to maintain an attitude of impartiality.

The ninth song, Siegfried's funeral, forms a worthy continuation

The Ninth Song. of the eighth, and is deeply affecting. Hagen is not content with the mere deed of horror, but carries his hatred so far as to choose the most painful way of communicating to Kriemhild the death of her husband, and have the corpse laid by night at her door. By this device the poet enhances our pity for the heroine in her overwhelming affliction. The first touching scene in this song is where Kriemhild, going to early mass in the grey dawn, sinks down in despair over Siegfried's body on the threshold. The second is where Siegmund, the old father, is awakened from sleep with the dreadful news. Yet a third equally touching is where Kriemhild causes the coffin, which had been already shut, to be opened again, and raises with her white hands the beautiful head of the dead and kisses it once more. Kriemhild's character is drawn with great skill, and, despite her love and intense grief, she is represented as so far mistress of herself that she is able to infer from the undented shield that her darling has been murdered; forthwith, instead of giving herself up to sorrow, she meditates active revenge. More prudent than the men, she restrains Siegmund and his adherents from hasty steps which, in view of the enemy's superior strength, would be utterly futile. In a word, instead of the coy girl, or the impressionable maiden, or the foolishly boasting woman, we have here for the first time the Kriemhild of the second part, the Kriemhild of revenge, energetic, resolute, and circumspect.

In the tenth song, which is one of the poorest, she appears quite different, weak and imprudent. How un- **The** natural it is that she should neglect her child in **Tenth Song.** order to remain in Worms, and lament over the dead with her youngest brother Giselher. The Nibelungen treasure is brought to Worms, and Hagen sinks it in the Rhine. The poet of this song seems again inspired with hatred of Hagen, but he also excites in his readers feelings of dislike and almost of contempt for Kriemhild and her brothers.

The songs of the second part differ less from each other in point of artistic merit than those of the first part. **The** Throughout there are more characters in action at **Second Part.** the same time. The poets describe in great detail the court of the Burgundian princes and that of Etzel, King of the Huns, scenes of richer and fuller life than have yet been depicted. In the first part it often seems as if the world were empty, save for a few heroes for whose benefit it was created. In the second part we are terribly impressed by the fact that the hatred and revenge of one woman may lead to the destruction of thousands.

The author of the eleventh song, 'Etzel's Wooing of Kriemhild,' has represented the Queen as a resigned mourning **The** widow, and we watch the idea of revenge only gradu- **Eleventh** ally arising in her mind. **Song.**

The twelfth song, 'Etzel and Kriemhild's Marriage,' gives us a grand picture of the throng of princes and nations at **The** Etzel's court, and it is particularly mentioned that there **Twelfth** was peaceable intercourse between Christians and **Song.** heathens. The poet seems here to notice with patriotic pride that, at her marriage feast at Vienna, Kriemhild was surrounded by riches and power such as she had never enjoyed at Siegfried's side.

In the thirteenth song Kriemhild's brothers are invited to the court of Etzel, to the country of the Huns. The poet **The** does not conceal Kriemhild's evil intentions, and **Thirteenth** contrasts her hidden malice with Etzel's honest plea- **Song.** sure at finding his invitation accepted. But still, it is the outward

course of events which interests the poet most, and he thinks a
great deal of courtly speech, which makes men outwardly similar
without destroying the deeper differences of character.

The fourteenth song differs in character from the other songs of
the second part, which are generally confined to a
purely human sphere, without trenching on the supernatural. Dreams, forebodings, prophecies, and mythological beings surround the grim central figure, Hagen. There
are many omens of the approaching tragedy, and Hagen's
undaunted courage, which resolves to struggle against it, stands
out in strong relief. The song describes in full but two scenes:
the morning of the departure from Worms, and the crossing of the
swollen Danube. Hagen, we learn, would have opposed the
journey had not Gernot reproached him with cowardice; then he
at once consented. We see a wild energy in every word and
action of Hagen's. He knows the way, he rides at the head of the
party, and is a comfort and help to the Nibelungen, as the
Burgundians are here for the first time called. Some mermaids
whom he sees bathing in the Danube warn him again of the fate
which he and his companions are riding to meet. ' Return while
it is time,' they cry, ' for he who rides into Etzel's land must die.'
But this does not make Hagen waver even for a moment. The
warning must not come from him, since Gernot accused him
of cowardice. The mermaids direct him to a ferry, and Hagen,
after having killed the ferryman for his hesitation, rows the boat up
stream to where the Burgundians are waiting, and himself ferries
the whole host across the river. Then, just as they are about
to march, he calls to them all, both knights and squires, ' A
direful woe I announce to you; we shall never return home to the
Burgundian land.'

The character of this man Hagen is grandly drawn, and he
excites our sympathy by his undaunted courage and resolution, and
by his loyalty as a vassal. But there is something weird about
his supernatural prowess, his readiness to kill and to lie, and his
striving to hide all evil omens until the Rubicon is passed, when
with fiendish pleasure he mercilessly prophesies sure destruction
to all. Yet in the scene with the mermaids the poet ventures to

The Fourteenth Song.

represent him as subject to human weakness, easily deceived, and outwitted; this mingling of opposite · traits shows great skill on the part of the author, and his poem, though it moves rapidly and is generally drawn in broad lines, is yet full of life-like touches.

The gloominess of this song is relieved by the bright sunshine of the following one, which describes the sojourn of the Burgundians in Pöchlarn with the Margrave Rüdiger. The poet tells us in an easy and graceful style of the wealth and festivities which there surround them. The first greeting kiss of Hagen inspires the young Markgräfin with terror. The minstrel Volker displays his convivial talents. Rüdiger's daughter is betrothed to Giselher, and at parting there is a general giving of presents, and soon the first warning comes through Dietrich · von Bern, who rides to meet the Burgundians.

The Fifteenth Song.

Two different songs have been preserved to us narrating the reception of the Burgundians by Kriemhild. Both make particular mention of the heroic friendship between Hagen and Volker, who inspire the Huns with great awe. The first of these songs is rather rude; its author takes part against Kriemhild, and makes his heroes bandy rough words with one another. But he also gives us one touching scene: the Burgundians are betaking themselves with heavy hearts to rest, when Hagen comforts them and Volker takes his fiddle and makes their hearts glad with his loud melody, then playing more softly he lulls them to sleep. After this he again seizes his shield and stands on guard with Hagen outside, and his helmet shines through the night and frightens away the stealthily approaching Huns. The author of the second song must have been acquainted with the preceding one, for he is offended by the feeling displayed therein against Kriemhild, and by the bad manners of Hagen and Volker, nor does he care like his rival poet to caricature the cowardice of the Huns. He makes the sequence of events clearer, and diminishes the individual guilt of his characters by representing their actions as forced upon them by stress of circumstances or by a conflict of noble motives. At the same time the mainspring of the approaching tragedy is made

The Sixteenth and Seventeenth Songs.

to lie in the fated chain of events through which the past avenges itself.

The last three songs deal with the outbreak of hostilities, the beginning and end of the massacre; they describe thronged conflicts in which single heroes distinguish themselves: for instance in the eighteenth song Dankwart, Hagen's brother, and in the nineteenth Iring of Denmark.

The last three Songs.

But the twentieth song, 'der Nibelungen Noth' (i. e. the last straits and destruction of the Burgundians), surpasses all the others, being the most powerful portraiture of action and character produced by Middle High-German heroic poetry. The catastrophe of the tragedy is worked out with true poetic feeling, the tragic horror of the whole being redeemed by incidents of noble heroism or true pathos. The poet differs from many of his fellow-workers in attributing to these old heroes some gentler sentiments, such as a longing for peace. Throughout he hints at means of escape, by which the wholesale slaughter of the enemy might have been avoided. But in vain! The passions of men are always too strong, and draw them on to destruction.

The Twentieth Song.

The song opens on a midsummer evening, when the Burgundians issue from the building in which they are imprisoned and demand reconciliation and peace. But Etzel refuses, for they have slain his child and many of his relations, and the wrong which they have done must be avenged. The heroes then request a fight in open field, but Kriemhild dissuades the Hunnish knights from granting this request, and demands instead the surrender of Hagen. The kings, however, are true to their vassal. The Burgundians are then driven into the house, which is set on fire all round, and tortured by the heat they drink blood by Hagen's advice. The following morning there is more fighting, and 1200 Huns are slain. Rüdiger comes and sees the misery; Etzel and Kriemhild require him to take part in the fight, which, after a hard inward struggle, he resolves to do. Giselher thinks that Rüdiger is bringing peace, and breathes more freely. Rüdiger then speaks to Gunther, Gernot, and Giselher in words full of sympathy and sorrow. Just as he is going into the fight, Hagen calls to him and begs for his shield, which Rüdiger gives him, touching even his grim nature by such an act of kindness. Gernot and Rüdiger fall by each other's hands, the latter being killed with his own sword which he had given to King Gernot in Pöchlarn.

The news of Rüdiger's death is told to King Dietrich, who had held aloof from the fight. He sends old Hildebrand, escorted by the whole host of the Goths, to learn how it happened. Sharp words arise between Volker and the wild Goth warrior Wolfhart; from words they come to blows, and all the heroes who meet there, except Gunther, Hagen, and Hildebrand, fall in the strife; Hildebrand flees before Hagen's sword-strokes and returns to his master with the dreadful tidings. The poet gives a touch of powerful tragic irony in making the king of the Goths lament for Rüdiger while Hildebrand stands before him with news of a still greater woe. On learning of the loss of all his followers Dietrich breaks out into bitter lamentations over his fate and over each of the fallen. He then sets out to subdue Hagen and Gunther, whom he vanquishes and leads in chains before Kriemhild, after exacting from the latter a promise to spare them. She demands that Hagen should give up the stolen Nibelungen-treasure, and when he replies that he has sworn not to give it up as long as one of his masters still lives, she has Gunther slain, and brings his head to Hagen. 'It has come to pass as I thought,' says he; 'no one now knows where the treasure is save God and myself, and from thee, thou she-devil, it shall for ever be hidden.' Then, remembering Siegfried, Kriemhild draws his sword, which Hagen has on, out of the sheath, swings it high with both hands, and strikes off the warrior's head—to the horror of Etzel and the anger of Hildebrand, who springs forward and kills her. The king's feast had ended in woe, as joy always at last turns to sorrow (*Als ie diu liebe leide ze aller jungiste gît*).

The author of this last song has, with great art, gathered together once more all the elements of the tragedy. The poem is full of allusions to the preceding events, and recapitulates the leading incidents of the whole legend. In the composition of his work the poet has strictly adhered to a preconceived plan, according to which a large part of the story is told indirectly in messages and narrations, and this is specially the case where the

I

deeds to be related are so extraordinary that they would naturally create a strong impression and lead to exaggeration. Nor is it unintentional on the part of the poet that his narrative towards its close becomes meagre and sparing of detail, for he probably reckoned on having aroused in his readers so lively an interest in his main plot that they would not care to dwell on all the minor circumstances.

The characters in this twentieth song stand out each with a well-marked individuality, which finds its appropriate setting and natural outward expression in the events related. Gunther is

The characters in the twentieth Song. shown in a more favourable light than in the other songs. He appears as a true king, resolute, kind, and dignified. His brother Gernot is more hasty, and his love of fighting is not restrained by his sense of dignity.

There is something touching in the bright and hopeful character of the third brother, the youthful Giselher, while in contrast with him we have the realist Volker who destroys the youth's illusions. Hagen, Volker's companion in arms, does not appear half so barbarous and unfeeling as in the former songs. It is only after Volker's death, and when he is brought before Kriemhild, that he becomes the 'grim' Hagen and fully reveals his unbending and terrible nature. The poet felt rightly that Etzel must be pre-eminent over the rest of the Huns, but he does not give him this pre-eminence throughout. As for Kriemhild, he does not reveal much of her inmost character; he neither describes her with abhorrence nor excuses her, but represents her simply as was necessary for his purpose, as the instrument of woe. He lingers with sympathy, however, over the character of the Margrave Rüdiger, who shows his generous nature even on his way to death. In the poet's delineation of the Margrave we can trace the influence of the clerical poetry, with its absorption in the inner life and in questions of guilt and innocence; thanks to that influence the poet was able to conceive and create the character of a hero, on whom is laid a heavy burden of conflicting duties. On the one hand are his friends to whom he had shown hospitality, on the other, his king who had made him rich and his queen to whom he had sworn implicit obedience in Worms. The struggle of conscience is fully described, yet without any direct psychological analysis. In his distress the hero turns to God for counsel and guidance, and most probably it was the opinion of the poet that God would wish a man's duty as a vassal to take precedence of all his other duties. Among the Goths many names are mentioned, but only three characters are drawn with much individuality: the impetuous Wolfhart, the old and somewhat enfeebled Hildebrand, who in a most important crisis by no means shows the prudence of age, and the splendid figure of Dietrich von Bern, noble and temperate, with that moral strength which those win who bear nobly some great and enduring sorrow. His grief for Rüdiger becomes of fatal import to himself; while he is lamenting, the foolish step is taken, and his heroes go with Hildebrand to their destruction. His lament over the fallen shows us the whole nature of the man: 'And are all my followers dead? then God has forgotten me, poor Dietrich.' The banished man feels the whole extent of the misfortune which pursues him. His fate is summed up in these words: 'I was a powerful, great, and rich king.' He knows not who will now help him to win back his land, and regrets that sorrow has not power to kill.

The poet gives us no hope that Dietrich's fate may be mitigated, and that happiness may again spring up somewhere under his powerful rule. He says particularly that he knows nothing more but that the fallen were lamented. No brighter future is in store for Etzel, Dietrich, or Hildebrand as they stand by the grave of all their hopes.

DIETRICH VON BERN.

Another poem is generally attached to the Nibelungenlied, being connected with it by its subject. It is called 'The Lament,' and consists chiefly of an enumeration of the fallen 'Die Klage.' at their interment, and of lamentations over their past glory. But it contains one beautiful and impressive scene: the seven remaining squires of Rüdiger bring his war-horse and robe of battle to Pöchlarn, and when interrogated by the women, they try to conceal the truth, as they have been straitly charged to do; but

the women have been already warned by bad dreams, and now
their presentiment of evil becomes stronger, their enquiries more
searching, till one of the squires can no longer restrain his tears;
then all the messengers begin to weep and the terrible foreboding
is turned to certainty.

The same poem tells how Dietrich took leave of Etzel and set
out with old Hildebrand for his home. But we do not hear what
awaits him there, or what he intends to do, and it is only the
Saxon legends which afford us a satisfactory explanation, and give us at length a picture of peace after the
long-continued din and tumult of battle. According
to the Saxon legends, as we know them through the Norwegian
Thidrekssaga (cf. p. 95), Dietrich has to flee before Ermenrich (who
in the legends had long taken the place of the historical Odoacer) and
takes refuge with the Huns. He is again defeated by Ermenrich
at the battle of Ravenna. Hadubrand, Hildebrand's son, grows up
at Ermenrich's court, and becomes ruler of Verona. As soon
as Hildebrand and Dietrich return to their country, they hear that
Ermenrich is dead and that the traitor Sibich, who had incited him
to all his misdeeds, is his successor. Hildebrand fights with his own
son Hadubrand, whom he recognises; but he hides his name from
Hadubrand and conquers him, without killing him. The gentler
feelings of this later age shrank from the tragical conclusion of the
older song, and turned the deep moral conflict in the father's soul,
which was the grandest feature of the old Hildebrandslied, into
a mere hero's freak with a moral purpose. In this later version
of the story the old man merely wishes to show the young one that
he is still the stronger, and thus gives a wholesome lesson to the
arrogance of youth.

Later on Hadubrand leads his whole host to join the returning
King Dietrich; Sibich is defeated and Dietrich is crowned in
Rome, where he reigned long, and performed many new deeds
of valour. At length one day, in his zeal for hunting, he mounted
a black horse, which bore him away so fast that no one could follow
him, and since that time nothing more has been heard of him.

There are many High-German poems extant which glorify
Dietrich and give us incidents out of his early life. They

Marginal note: Saxon legends of Dietrich.

turn him into a fashionable hero in the style of the chivalrous
romances, and attribute to him marvellous adven-   High-
tures with dwarfs, giants, and dragons. They make   German
heathens oppose him, whom he afterwards converts   poems about
to Christianity. They either say that he rode out from   Dietrich.
Verona and found his enemies in the mountains of Tyrol, or they
adhere to the historical legends and describe his flight to the Huns
and his conflicts with Ermenrich. But we cannot gain from these
poems a connected sketch of Dietrich's fortunes, and their value as
poetry is small, with the exception of the account of the battle of
Ravenna and the song of Albhart's death.

In the former, side by side with a wild chaos of combats, often
very coarsely described, we have the touching episode   The song
of Etzel's sons, who accompany Dietrich and Rüdiger   of the
to the war and are killed by Wittich. With them   Battle of
falls their companion-in-arms, Diether, King Dietrich's   Ravenna.
young brother. Dietrich on hearing the news is transported with
wild grief, and follows up the murderer in mad pursuit till he disappears in the waves of the sea, where a mermaid protects him. After
Ravenna has been taken, Rüdiger rides back with the evil tidings
to the land of the Huns. Queen Helche, the mother of the
murdered princes, is going into the garden to enjoy the beautiful
flowers, when she sees two horses with empty blood-stained saddles
galloping up to the palace; they seem to her like those on
which her sons rode to Verona. Rüdiger can no more hide the
terrible truth, and a touching scene ensues when the queen in
her transports of grief recalls the picture of her sons, as they were
wont to wake her in the morning and to fondle her with their white
hands. 'That is all over now,' she exclaims, and imprecates
a curse on Dietrich; but she is more reconciled on hearing how
he mourned for her sons, and that he had himself lost a brother.
The closing scene is sublime and touching; Dietrich tells the news
to Etzel, and the latter, conquering his sorrow, folds him in his arms
and declares him free from all blame.

The tone of the second poem, 'Albhart's death,' is equally
mournful. Albhart, Wolfhart's brother, a young and bold hero
is keeping an outpost alone; he overthrows a troop of eighty

men, and even forces the tried warrior Wittich to yield, but
The Song of generously spares the life of his conquered and de-
Albhart's fenceless foe. Then Heime comes to Wittich's aid,
death. and by Wittich's suggestion, they both, contrary to all
knightly honour, fall on the brave youth and kill him. This
poem has a direct moral purpose and enforces the principles of
honour and loyalty. At the same time, for subtle contrast of
characters and reflection of the same in action, as well as for
dignified and detailed narrative, the poem will bear comparison
with the better parts of the Nibelungen-Epic.

Throughout all these songs Dietrich appears as the most humane
Character of heroes, just as in the account of Kriemhild's revenge
of Dietrich. he abstains from fighting until incited to it by his great
losses. He is never eager for combat, but needs the strongest
moral impulses to rouse him to fight. When once aroused, however, he shows great valour.   •

The same characteristics are attributed to Dietrich in two poems
'Biterolf' entitled 'Biterolf' and the 'Rosengarten,' which de-
and the scribe his fights with Siegfried. In both these works
'Rosen- the characters of the legend are evidently taken as
garten.' typical of the countries to which they belong. Both
describe a tournament which takes place at Worms, in which the
Rhenish heroes, Gunther, Hagen, Siegfried and others, measure
their strength against the heroes of South-East Germany—Hildebrand, Wolfhart, Dietrich, and others. Both songs favour the latter
group of heroes, and claim that the countries once ruled over
by Theodoric the Great are equal or superior to the Rhenish
provinces in the profession of arms. Perhaps the authors sought
to console themselves in poetry for the fact that in reality it was
quite the opposite; for warlike and peaceful culture really spread
from the Rhine to South-East Germany, and thus the South-East
German might occasionally be made painfully conscious of his
inferiority. This local jealousy gave birth to the story of Siegfried
having once been vanquished in single combat by Dietrich von
Bern. In 'Biterolf' the struggle is still left undecided, and the
poem only brings together a great number of heroes and exhibits
rich pictures of chivalrous life. But the 'Rosengarten,' a work

which attained great popularity after the second half of the thirteenth
century and was freely altered and revised, repre- The 'Rosen-
sents King Dietrich as completely victorious. The garten.'
poem aims at a popular, realistic, and comic style of narrative, and
returns to the sensationalism which, though long abandoned by the
more refined poets, had never ceased to be in vogue with the lower
class of minstrels. The poet takes special pleasure in the somewhat coarse character of Hildebrand's brother, the monk Ilsan,
who is brought out of the monastery to take part in Dietrich's
procession to Kriemhild's 'rose-garden' at Worms. A very late
tradition says that Dietrich killed Siegfried in the fight in the
Rosengarten at Worms, and that Kriemhild's revenge was directed
against Dietrich's house.

In the mist of such errors and vague traditions the heroic
legends gradually disappeared during the fifteenth
century from the field of literature. But as late Disappear-
                                                    ance of the
as the sixteenth century three songs were printed   heroic
which show that the tradition of certain important   legends,
                                                    15th century.
incidents in the national heroic poetry had not even
then entirely died out. These three songs are: the Siegfriedslied,
the later Hildebrandslied, and the song of Ermenrich's death.

The Siegfriedslied, or the 'Hürnen Seifried,' tells us more
about the hero's youth than we learn from the   The
Nibelungenlied. It tells how the maiden Kriemhild 'Hürnen
was carried off by a dragon, but was rescued by 'the Seifried.'
proud youth Seifried,' and contains allusions to important points in
the Nibelungen legend, to the treasure, to Siegfried's death by
Hagen's hand and to the great slaughter in the land of the Huns.
In 1557 Hans Sachs made a tragedy out of this story, and the
same song was also the nucleus of a popular prose romance,
while in one local tradition Seifried lived on under the name of
Säufritz.

The later Hildebrandslied follows in its general outline the
Saxon form of the story mentioned at the beginning The 'later
of this section. Here too Hildebrand knows with   Hilde-
whom he is fighting, but seems to look upon single brandslied.'
combat as a peculiarly agreeable way of meeting his son again, and

only reveals himself after he has vanquished him. The poem ends with a cheerful picture of family-life, showing us father, mother, and son at supper.

The song of Ermenrich's death gives the legend in a much-
'**Ermenrich's** obscured form. Dietrich himself, at the head of
Tod.' eleven companions, appears before King Ermenrich and questions him about the new gallows which he has had built; he then suddenly draws ' a sword of gold so red ' and strikes off the tyrant's head. Thus Dietrich or Theodoric, the great king of the Goths, appears for the last time before the German people in the peculiar character of a Brutus. For the space of a thousand years or more after his death his praises had never ceased to be sung in German poetry. But the contrast which is dwelt on in this poem between rude tyranny and mild government, the former being represented by Ermanarich, the latter by Theodoric the Great, must have found expression in early Gothic songs. We shall notice the same contrast later on among the Franks.

ORTNIT AND WOLFDIETRICH.

The German hero-legends possess a certain element of reality, in so far as they are always connected with fixed localities; but the scene of the legends is often shifted from a desire to give them more local colouring, and this often gave rise to great confusion. Thus the Lower Saxon traditions have transferred Attila's home and the death-struggle of the Nibelungen to Soest. 'Bern' is generally understood to mean Verona, but sometimes Bonn. The most curious geographical changes of this sort are found in the legend of ' Ortnit and Wolfdietrich.'

The heathen Vandals, as we know, worshipped a pair of divine
Local brothers, who (according to a clever conjecture of Karl
variants of Müllenhoff) lived on in songs after the downfall
the legend of the national religion as two Vandal kings, named
of Ortnit and the Hartunge. These brothers are united by the
Wolfdie-
trich. tenderest affection, and when one of them, Hartnit
or Ortnit, is slain, like the Greek Kastor, by an enemy's hand, the survivor avenges him, like Pollux, and marries

his widow. In the middle ages the Vandals were confused with the Wends and Eastern Slavs, and thus it happened that the Lower Saxons, who were well acquainted with Russia through their commerce, transferred the home of these Hartunge to Nogarden (Novgorod). The South-Germans, on the contrary, being less acquainted with those northern lands, supposed Nogarden to be the Italian Garda, on the lake of that name; thus in the South-German versions of the legend Ortnit became a ruler over Lombardy and Italy and an emperor of Rome. But the second Hartung, Ortnit's brother, is called in South-German poems 'Wolfdietrich;' and through this name the old Vandal Myth was blended with one of the most modern additions to heroic song, namely, with an historical legend, drawn directly from   Historical the history of the royal house of the Merovingians, elements in and based on the adventures of Theodoric and Theo- the legend. debert, the son and grandson of Clovis. These two princes seem to have lived on in poetry as 'Hugdietrich' and 'Wolfdietrich.' Hugdietrich, like the Merovingian Theodoric, shrinks from no crime, while Wolfdietrich, like the Merovingian Theodebert, is a pattern of virtue and an object of special providence. After the death of his father, his elder brothers wish to drive him from the throne; but he is supported by his loyal vassals, and ends by being as victorious over his brothers as was the historical Theodebert over his grasping uncles. Hugdietrich is in this legend represented as a heathen, and Wolfdietrich as a Christian, who is protected in all dangers by his baptismal robe. Tyranny and justice, faithlessness and loyalty are contrasted; a cruel and criminal race gives place to a milder and better one, and Christianity is represented as bound up with moral goodness. The Merovingian prince Theodebert's distress after his father's death takes in this legend the form of a long banishment from home; and he is probably called 'Wolf' because in Old German law this word designated a banished man. In later times, when the significance of the name had been forgotten, its use was accounted for by a story of how the wolves had spared Wolfdietrich when he was a child, or how they had carried him away to their cave.

The legends of the twelfth and thirteenth centuries represent him as coming during his exile to Garda, avenging the death of King Ortnit and marrying his widow.   But to complete the geographical confusion Hugdietrich and Wolfdietrich are made out to be Greeks, reigning over Greece and living at Constantinople.   Thus the legend raised the Merovingian princes to the Byzantine throne. The Middle High-German poems in which these widely circulated legends were embodied did not ever attain the rank of classics.

The Epic of Ortnit, like the Crusading poems of the twelfth

Epic of Ortnit.   century, supplemented a tradition which had become very meagre.   It must have been composed before the Crusade of Frederick II, about the year 1225, but it seems rather to warn against than to encourage the expedition.   For Ortnit is also made to undertake a Crusade, but his struggle with the heathen involves terrible sacrifices.   Ortnit wins a beautiful heathen maiden, but her father remains hostile to him and has a dragon brought to Trient, which devastates the land and even devours the Emperor himself.

At least four different versions of the story of Wolfdietrich were

Story of 'Wolfdie- trich.'   written during the thirteenth century.   His adventures during his banishment were constantly being added to, the effects being rendered more striking and a considerably larger space assigned to supernatural and marvellous elements.   It is to be regretted that of the poets who treated this subject the best left his work incomplete.   He, more than the rest, grasps the leading types of character which figure in the legend.   It is true that, instead of putting Hugdietrich's unscrupulosity in the right light, he lays all the blame on his evil counsellor Saben; but he has done his best to give a worthy rendering of the devotion existing between Wolfdietrich and his tutor Berchtung.

The following is a short outline of the story as this poet tells it. Berchtung has been commanded by Hugdietrich to kill the boy Wolfdietrich; he is only persuaded to undertake the task by the strongest threats, and seeks by force to stifle the pity in his breast. The child has been taken away from the side of its sleeping mother in the cold night, and calls out shivering in Berchtung's arms : ' Mother, cover me up ;' to which the old man answers with forced

harshness: 'What do I care if you shiver.' In the morning, when
the sun breaks through the clouds, the child forgets the cold and
plays unsuspiciously with the rings on the armour of the man who
is to murder him. Berchtung cannot reconcile himself to the
murderous deed and returns his sword to its sheath. The child
plays in the meadows alone, yet fearlessly, the whole day till night
comes on, while Berchtung hides in the bushes and watches it. By
moonlight wolves appear, but instead of hurting the child they lie
down around it and allow it to play with them. Then the old
man perceives that Divine Providence is watching over the child,
and resolves to spare it. He afterwards suffers imprisonment for
its sake, for the same king who commanded him to slay it now
accuses him of the deed, and stands abashed when his own guilt
comes to light. The boy's deliverer now becomes his tutor, and
many years later, after the old king's death, he and his sixteen sons
fight for their beloved master Wolfdietrich against his elder brother
and the treacherous Saben who wish to keep him out of his
inheritance. After the battle only ten of Berchtung's sixteen sons
remain alive, but still his loyalty is not shaken. These ten with
their father now form Wolfdietrich's whole army. He is afterwards
besieged in their castle, is obliged to leave them, and goes into
exile; still he prays for their safety in distress, and in happiness
considers it his most sacred duty to help them; and with the fulfilment of this duty the narrative of his deeds terminates.

The relation between Wolfdietrich and Berchtung is to some
extent a repetition of that between Dietrich von Bern and the old
Hildebrand. Theodebert, the historical original of Wolfdietrich,
did in fact show himself a faithful friend and would not carry out
the murderous command of his father, but himself warned the intended victim, who was his godchild, of his impending fate; he
persuaded him to flee, and when he returned after the death of
the cruel king, received him with open arms, gave him rich presents
and re-instated him in his possessions. In the legend prince and
vassal have, as it were, changed their parts; still, the kind of
loyalty represented in the poem was not unknown in the epoch in
which the legend arose. In this legend, as in that of the Nibelungen, loyalty is the inspiring principle of the drama.

HILDE AND GUDRUN.

The Epic of Gudrun is again a song in praise of loyalty, and, like
Epic of the legend of Wolfdietrich, it stretches over two genera-
Gudrun. tions, and tells us the story of the loves of both mother
and daughter. Here too we notice, though not strongly accentuated,
a certain change of manners between the two generations. The
principles of education have changed: where the mother trembled
the daughter can act freely; where the former had to submit the latter
follows the prompting of her own heart. In the first story fear
and disloyalty are produced by sternness; in the second love and
loyalty are called forth by kindness. But the same heathens fight
for the daughter, who helped to woo and win the mother.
Geographically and historically the scene is the same in both
cases; the epoch of the Norman sea-faring expeditions seems
to be that which the poet had in his mind, as is evinced
by the incidents of the poem. For instance, invasions always
come from the sea, and castles and towns on the coast are suddenly surprised and taken. Pursuers and pursued often meet on
islands.

A Moorish king, Siegfried, who is introduced in an episode of
Historical this poem as fighting in Friesland, reminds us of a
element Norman leader of the same name who conducted the
in the great siege of Paris in the years 885 and 886, and
legend. lost his life in an attack on the Frisians in the autumn
of 887. In the time of the Crusades the heathen Normans were
often confused with the Saracens and Moors. But the real story
of the poem is in some respects older, in others later than this.

The story of 'Gudrun' is most probably based on an old myth
Mythical reflecting the continuous conflict between day and
element. night; but the myth is here made entirely human
in its interest and all supernatural elements are discarded. It
becomes one of the many legends, all so similar to each other,
narrating the abduction of a woman. A girl's parents refuse her
suitors; then follow abduction, pursuit, fighting, peace, and marriage. And here again, as in the romance of Rudlieb, the story

was made to embrace the lives not only of the parents but of the children. Thus the fair Hilde, who was the centre of the old mythical story, has a daughter Gudrun, whose youth repeats many of the chief incidents already related about her mother.

The story attained its fullest development in the Netherlands, probably in the eleventh century; it was then con- *Various* nected with Normandy, and so brought into relation with *versions of* contemporary history and interests. It became a lead- *the story.* ing epic theme, and gained in popularity in proportion as love grew to be the exclusive topic of poetry. The story was known in Bavaria before the year 1100, and was treated in a celebrated poem not preserved to us, but referred to by the clerical poets of the twelfth century. About the year 1210 a poet of remarkable *Best version* talent made it his theme. His work, like the songs of *made in* the Nibelungen epic, was afterwards much added to *Bavaria,* by other poets, and we have it in this enlarged form *circa 1210.* in a late manuscript. Many critics have busied themselves in removing these excrescences, and amongst them Karl Müllenhoff takes the foremost rank.

The author of 'Gudrun' has treated his subject in two songs, the first of which narrates the wooing of Hilde, while the *Division* second, which is somewhat longer, tells the history *into two* of Gudrun. It was traditional to divide the story into *songs.* two halves, nor did the poet venture to depart from the tradition, but actually took advantage of the perplexing repetition of incidents to produce the most charming poetic effects, by frequently bringing the two parts into direct contrast with each other. The song about Hilde is a prologue, the song of Gudrun's distress and delivery being the kernel of the poem. The former leaves us in a cheerful mood; the latter becomes more and more gloomy, and in fact almost tragic. A fearful crime receives its punishment, but we are not allowed to see the happiness which lies beyond.

The wild king Hagen of Ireland has all the suitors of his daughter Hilde slain. King Hettel of Denmark nevertheless resolves to sue for her hand. He sends out for this purpose three of his vassals, Wate, Frute, and Horand, who succeed in concealing from Hilde's father the real purpose of their mission, and having First song, gained the consent of the maiden carry her off by 'Story of stratagem. On reaching Denmark, Hettel receives Hilde.' them on the shore; but the ships of the pursuers are already seen approaching, and their arrival suggests to the poet some grand and picturesque scenes, such as we shall frequently meet with in the course of his narrative. Hagen springs from his ship, and after wading to the shore through a shower of arrows, engages the terrible Wate in unequal combat till he is rescued from his peril by Hettel at Hilde's entreaty. After this Hettel, desiring a cessation of arms, takes off his helmet; the fighting hosts greet this sign of peace with loud acclamations, whereupon the wild Irish king no longer resists. Finally, Hilde, led by Horand and Frute, timidly approaches her father, conscious of her wrong-doing, and we see how love at length triumphs in the old man's heart and disposes him to kindness. He leads away his daughter from the battle-field, and at the end of the song we see him sitting at home again with her mother and declaring himself quite satisfied with Hilde's lot. This succession of exciting incidents, graphically described, is compressed into about sixty lines.

In the beginning of the second song, Hettel and Hilde haughtily Second song, refuse the suit of Hartmut of Normandy for the 'Story of hand of their daughter Gudrun, on the ground that Gudrun.' he is not her equal in birth. Neither will they receive Herwig von Seeland as a son-in-law, and, enraged at this insult, Herwig declares war. His knightly courage in the battle wins the heart of Gudrun, who is watching the fight; she separates the fighters and is betrothed to Herwig. Soon afterwards, while Hettel is helping his future son-in-law against Siegfried, the Moorish king, Gudrun is carried off by Hartmut and his father Ludwig. Hettel and Herwig hear of this in time to pursue and overtake them ; but Hettel falls by Ludwig's hand in the battle on the Wülpensand, and the robbers escape unperceived in the night, taking the women with them. For seven years Gudrun has to endure the greatest humiliation and cruelty at the hands of Hartmut's mother Gerlind, who is enraged at Gudrun's refusal to marry her son, and makes her perform the most menial tasks.

Gudrun submits, but in a defiant manner, and constantly broods on revenge. At length the hour of deliverance comes. Her brother Ortwin, her betrothed Herwig, and the old heroes Wate, Frute, and Horand approach with a large army; the enemies meet in a fearful battle, which the poet describes in the most graphic way. Ludwig falls, and his son Hartmut is just yielding under the strokes of the infuriated Wate, when his sister Ortrun, who has shown kindness to Gudrun in her banishment, entreats her to save her brother's life. Gudrun's cry from the battlements reaches Herwig in the midst of the fight, and at his own peril he averts the mortal blow from Hartmut. Hartmut is taken prisoner, and Herwig and Gudrun are at length united.

The key-note of the Nibelungenlied, as we have already noticed, is that joy is turned into sorrow; but in Gudrun it is Character of the interweaving of joy and sorrow, the conflict of the poem. emotions which seems to have specially attracted the poet. Three times in the poem the warlike passion of the men is restrained at the entreaty of the women, whose moral feeling they feel bound to respect. Three times a woman interferes as peacemaker; first, Hilde sends out Hettel to protect her father from Wate; secondly, Gudrun separates Hettel and Herwig; thirdly, Gudrun sends Herwig to protect Hartmut from Wate. These three incidents all form important turning-points in the narrative; and in the second case, where Herwig's bravery excites Gudrun's admiration and love, though he is an enemy, the poet expressly mentions the conflict of emotions in her breast; the new feeling, he says, was both 'pleasant and painful to her' (*lieb und leid*). And again, in their first secret interview after their long separation, when he finds her in the deepest humiliation and begins to hope that he may set her free, then, in the midst of their kisses and embraces and their talk of what they have experienced and suffered, they feel glad and sorry (*lieb und leid*).

It is only by such slight allusions as these that the poet enters the realm of feelings at all, and he never attempts to describe them in detail. By means of the simplest words he produces the most masterly effects. His character-drawing is far removed from that

exaggerated idealization which gains the applause of the multitude;
he was too great an artist to condescend to such means. His
Character of Gudrun, far from being the perfect type of feminine
Gudrun.   gentleness, is rather hard. Even from her first appearance in the battle between Herwig and Hettel, we are led to feel
that hers is an unbending character. She declares her feelings without any maidenly bashfulness and succeeds in carrying out her will.
With passionate and irresistible entreaties she persuades her father
to help her lover against the Moorish king; and when her father's
absence brings misfortune upon her, she shows great fortitude, shedding no tear, and making no lament. Her demeanour towards
Ludwig, towards Hartmut and his mother Gerlind, her tormentor, is
always cold and distant, and she never loses her royal dignity. She
fulfils every command in a defiant manner, and all the while dreams
of revenge.

In a highly poetic scene the author describes how, while washing
clothes on the sea-shore, she hears the consoling news of the approach of her friends. In this scene alone the poet admits the
supernatural, and uses the device of a talking bird, like the raven
in the epic of 'St. Oswald' (cf. p. 87). He has succeeded in
imparting to Gudrun's repeated questions about her beloved
ones and the bird's answers a peculiar melancholy and expectant
tone, full of lyric tenderness and reminding one of later popular
ballads.

The meeting with Herwig and Ortwin the next morning on the
shore turns the hope of speedy delivery into certainty. And then
the whole force of Gudrun's passion breaks loose in a manner
which the poet renders almost offensive. He seems determined to
be true here even at the expense of beauty. Gudrun at once
throws down the clothes which she was to wash, and lets them be
carried away by the tide. She meets the threats of Gerlind with
counter-threats, and declares herself ready to become Hartmut's
bride. She assumes all the rights of the future queen, and excites
the courtiers to emulate each other in her service. She has food
and drink brought to her, and then having shut herself up in her
bed-chamber with the other women who had been carried away
from home with her, she drinks with them, laughs at their sadness

and reveals to them the prospect of deliverance on the morrow.
And when in the thick of the fight next day the kind-hearted
Ortrun prays Gudrun to help her brother, it is only after passionate
and heart-rending appeals that Gudrun yields to her request.   And
though she protects Ortrun, yet, when her humbled enemy Gerlind
entreats for mercy, Gudrun only gives her mocking words, and
stands by while Wate, inexorable as fate, puts an effectual end to
her supplications.   It is in the midst of slaughter that Gudrun
finds her lover again.   Compared with an ideal character such as
Berchtung in ' Wolfdietrich,' Gudrun produces the impression of a
powerful portrait.   Her character may owe some of its coarser
elements to the time and the locality in which it first arose.   And
this thirteenth-century poet, being himself a manly and vigorous
nature in an almost effeminate age, was probably for this very
reason attracted by the legend, and only toned it down so far that
the mingling of tender and powerful elements might produce the
effect of a study from real life.

The other characters, too, are not merely black or white.   Even
Gerlind is not a pure she-devil ; her cruelty to Gudrun springs
from pride in her house, which Gudrun despises, and   Other
from love to her son, whom Gudrun scorns.   Her   characters
daughter Ortrun, on the contrary, is kind and loveable, in the poem.
and hardly ever appears on the scene without tears or entreaties.
Hildeburg, Gudrun's maid, who voluntarily shares Gudrun's deepest
humiliation, retains her fear of Gerlind till the last, and thus forms
a contrast to her mistress.   In these secondary characters feminine
weakness prevails.   Even Hilde is not free from it ; she fears her
father, and his tyranny leads her into cunning and deception.
Her haughty family pride, which leads her to reject all her
daughter's suitors just as her father had done in her own case,
brings about the catastrophe.   In the defence of the castle against
Ludwig and Hartmut she shows greater wisdom than the soldiers
around her.   In the midst of her sorrow at the death of Hettel
her mind is occupied with the thought of revenge, which she
carries out deliberately at the right time.   Hilde's strength of
will is inherited by her daughter Gudrun, and it enables her to
endure her misery with fortitude.

Hagen is an uncouth barbarian, clumsy, naively conceited, but good-natured at bottom, and the poet has drawn his character with much humour. The Danes turn him to ridicule, although they stand in awe of him; he is powerless against intelligence, for his only weapon is brute strength. The Danish heroes who come to ask Hilde in marriage for their King Hettel, have each their special sphere of activity : Wate works by force, Frute by cunning, Horand by art. Wate is the wild, desperate warrior whose very appearance inspires terror. Frute, who on the expedition to Ireland is disguised as a merchant, otherwise appears but little in the poem. Horand is the German Orpheus, whose singing makes all creatures listen to him.

Hettel seems to have been drawn as a contrast to Hagen, and corresponds to the idea of royal dignity such as we find it in the Nibelungenlied. He does not wish to excite fear but affection in his subjects. He allows his daughter great freedom, and grants her wishes. His son Ortwin is an attractive picture of a youth full of noble affection for his parents and his sister.

As we have contrasted Hagen and Hettel, the tyrannical and the considerate father, so we may also contrast Hartmut and Herwig, the despised and the favoured lover. The latter always acts according to his own judgment, and works energetically and perseveringly towards the end which he has in view. He intends to gain Gudrun by force, and thereby he wins her heart. He fulfils her ideal of what a knight should look like, and his character corresponds to his outward appearance. But he too is not the conventional ideal of the invincible hero. He cannot over-throw the Moorish King without assistance, and in the final battle we are told that Ludwig pressed him so hard that his vassals had to hew a way out for him. Then he looks up at once to the battlements of the castle to note whether Gudrun has seen his distress, for if she has, he thinks she may reproach him with it when they are married. There is a delicious *naïveté* in this little matrimonial scene which the poet brings before our eyes in the midst of the tumult of battle. He is not afraid of injuring his hero in our esteem by this humorous sally.

In contrast with Herwig, Hartmut is weak and easily led by his

mother Gerlind. It is she who advises him to woo Gudrun, and he
follows her, in opposition to the wiser counsel of his experienced
father. He does not approve of the cruel indignities by which
Gerlind tries to force Gudrun into loving him, but he is too weak
to offer any resistance. There is something ignoble in his whole
conduct towards Gudrun; he attacks her father's country when it is
undefended, he threatens to use force against Gudrun, and yet expects affection from the woman whom he has thus threatened. Yet
both Hartmut and his father are by no means drawn by the poet
in a wholly unfavourable light. In Normandy, in his own castle,
Hartmut approaches the captive Gudrun with tender words only,
and treats her with wise forbearance, so that some pity is aroused
in us for this constantly rejected lover. And in the final battle
Hartmut excites our admiration: he rides at the head of his
troop, resplendent as an emperor, and performs deeds of great
valour. The two rival lovers do not encounter each other; on
the contrary, Herwig becomes Hartmut's deliverer. This incident,
which so greatly raises our opinion of Gudrun's lover, is related in the simplest manner, without any endeavour to produce
a sensation.

King Ludwig of Normandy not only shows extraordinary
bravery, but also great wisdom. He kills Hettel, and Herwig has
to be rescued from his fury by his vassals. He foresees all the evil
which will result from Hartmut's wooing of Gudrun. He employs
stratagem where it would be most useful. He is rather rough and
sometimes most insulting in his language; but he too lets his wife
have her own way, so that the ambitious Gerlind appears throughout as the moving force, which brings sorrow and distress on
Hettel's house and on her own.

The poet has formed a clear idea in his own mind of all these
characters, and he succeeds in bringing them vividly   The poet's
before his readers; but he very rarely allows us a   style.
glance into their feelings. Herwig alone has a short monologue. Dialogue is often used, but always in order to tell the
reader things which it is necessary for him to know, but which the
poet does not wish to narrate directly. He also leaves much to
the reader's imagination; his narrative demands full attention, yet,

in spite of his brevity, he is never obscure. He does not neglect
to describe personal appearance, but he is careful not to weary
us by detailing the attire of each of his characters. It is only in
certain important moments, when the excited imagination longs
to see everything in detail, that he describes appearance and clothing, thus completing the illusion and making us feel as though
transported into the very midst of the events. He never indulges
in long descriptions of external nature, but he sometimes produces beautiful effects in a very few words. For instance, he tells
us that Wate, when meditating an attack, communed with the
clear night, the air being pure and the moon shining full. So,
too, he mentions that the morning-star had risen high when in the
dawn one of Gudrun's maidens saw from the window helmets
and shields glittering, and soon the whole landscape was shining
with them.

The poem of 'Gudrun' has been too often called the German
Odyssey, and this name has aroused expectations

Comparison
of 'Gudrun'
with the
Odyssey.
which are not satisfied by reading the epic. The
subject indeed afforded opportunity for something
'marine and insular' (*Meer- und Inselhaftes*) in its
treatment, to use Goethe's expression. But this South-German
poet was not well acquainted with the sea, and so perhaps did well
in not entering more fully into the subject of sea-voyages and
storms. Again, the fabulous element of the Odyssey would here
have seemed entirely out of place. Thirdly, in 'Gudrun,' far more
than in the Odyssey, it is the hostilities of nations which absorb
the interest of the reader; the fate of the chief characters is bound
up with the issue of battles and sieges.

The many-sidedness of the author has imparted great variety to
the poem. It is the most important production in

Special
merits of
the poem.
that class of Middle High-German poetry which was
based on native tradition; and it is the only one in
which a great poet set himself to treat the whole of an epic subject
from beginning to end in one poem, while at the same time paying
careful attention to details. The poets of the Nibelungenlied,
being under the influence of the separate songs in which alone the
subject was known to them, only dealt with single portions of the

story. But the author of Gudrun freed himself from the song-form,
and yet at the same time turned it to account to spare himself
transitional passages, to avoid the repetition of secondary incidents,
and to make the whole more connected. The beginning of the
poem is slight and sketchy, and it is only after Gudrun's imprisonment that the narrative becomes fuller; the poet thus attains
dramatic concentration without giving up any of the advantages
of the epic. He has throughout imparted grandeur and originality
to the legend, which had become rather trivial in certain parts.
But for this very reason his work never attained the wide-spread
popularity of the Nibelungenlied. It was not readily adopted
by the people, for it had not that same local hold on South
Germany which, for instance, Siegfried had in Worms, or Rüdiger
in Pöchlarn, or the Huns in Hungary. Hence the fame and
popularity of the poem were by no means commensurate with its
intrinsic merit.

The conciseness of the narrative in 'Gudrun' afforded the
minstrels an irresistible opportunity for supplements
and additions, and an enormous number of such
additions have accumulated round the original poem.
Their main object was, as in the Nibelungenlied, to devote more
attention to the manners and customs of chivalry, to describe court-
festivals, clothes, tournaments, and generally to introduce detailed
description of circumstances and things. Though the author himself
despised these outward considerations, yet he had much in common
with the true essence of chivalrous life as seen in its noblest representatives. The Minnesang furnished him with some suggestions,
and his true place is by the side of Wolfram von Eschenbach
(cp. chap. vi. § 3). Wolfram, the greatest of the chivalric
epic poets, has among his contemporaries no one more closely
related to him in mind and art than the unknown author of
'Gudrun.' Both avoid the prolixity so common at the time; both
have the same rugged sincerity, humour, and manliness. In both,
the culture of the nobility, which stood under French influence, is
mingled with the best that could be accomplished by the national
art of the minstrels. Though the proportion of these two elements
is different in each of these two poets, yet each had an interest in

[margin note: Later addi-tions to 'Gudrun.']

both spheres. And yet a third, a lyric poet, is connected with these two epic poets through the same union of the chivalrous and popular elements, I mean, Walther von der Vogelweide (cp. chap. vii. § 1). Gudrun, Wolfram, and Walther are the three culminating points of Middle High-German poetry.

CHAPTER VI.

THE EPICS OF CHIVALRY.

THE twelfth century is marked far and wide in the literature of
the world by the prevalence of love-songs and love-romances. In
Persia Nisami sang the fates of Medschnun and Leila, **Prevalence**
of Khosru and Schirin. In Provence the Troubadours **of love-**
originated those forms of love-songs which were after- **poems in the**
wards adopted by the Romanic and Germanic nations. **12th century.**
Northern France produced a rich harvest of romances of chivalry
and love, derived in part from Celtic sources. The German
knights followed the example of their French companions in arms,
and, inspired by Frederick Barbarossa's glorious deeds, began themselves to cultivate the art of poetry. They borrowed from the
Provençal as well as from Northern French ; they cultivated both
lyric and epic poetry, and advanced gradually from simple popular
songs to artistic imitations of foreign models. They imitated the
French in relating stories of famous lovers ; they endeavoured to
realise in their lives what had delighted them in romance, and their
lyric poetry was in turn inspired by their own varied love-
experiences.

The three pairs of lovers who were first received into the favour
of the German poets of this period, were : Flore and Blancheflur,
Tristan and Isolde, Aeneas and Dido.

'Flore and Blancheflur' means ' Flower and Whiteflower,' and
perhaps the story of these two lovers was originally **' Flore and**
a fairy-tale of the loves of two flowers, like the rose **Blancheflur.'**
and the lily. Flowers and love are indissolubly connected ; the
blossoming of the flowers brings joy to the lover's heart ; he likens

the colour of his lady's face to roses and lilies, and mediæval poetry loves to tell how two flowers, entwining themselves together, grow out of the graves of devoted lovers, who in life could not be united.

Flore and Blancheflur are two children who are devoted to each other, and notwithstanding all difficulties are united at last. Blancheflur is born among heathens, being the daughter of a Christian taken prisoner in war. Flore, the son of the heathen king, born on the same day, loves her and wins her love. Blancheflur is sold to Babylon, and is to marry the Sultan, who keeps her shut up in a tower. But Flore follows her, bribes her keeper, and is carried into her tower entirely hidden in a basket of flowers. They are discovered together and condemned to die. Flore, having a magic ring which can protect him from death, offers it to his beloved, but she refuses to accept it, so they throw it away **German** and resolve to die together. This devotion touches the **poem on this** tyrant's heart, and the pair are pardoned and at length **subject,** united. This poem was translated from the French, **circa 1170.** about 1170, by a poet of the lower Rhineland, who told the story with the simplicity which it demands in order to produce the right effect. Unfortunately, only portions of his work have come down to us.

Tristan and Isolde were introduced into German literature about **Eilhard von** the same time by a knight called Eilhard von **Oberge's** Oberge, who came from the neighbourhood of Hildes-**'Tristan and** heim, and appears to have written at the Court **Isolde.'** of the Guelph prince, Henry the Lion (1139–1195). His work, perhaps more than any other, became an ideal of chivalrous life. It contained everything that could fire the knightly imagination, for its main theme was a passionate attachment leading to many tragic complications, while it also furnished descriptions of battles and single combats, faithful pictures of real life, of chivalrous education and refined manners, together with fabulous elements, such as a conflict with a dragon and a powerful love potion. The book is a complete biography of an ideal hero, to whose lot fell all that the world can yield of honour, fame, and happiness, but also of bitter sorrow.

But Flore and Blancheflur, Tristan and Isolde, were soon forced
to retire in favour of a third pair of lovers; it was Aeneas and
Dido who were to usher in the classical period of chivalrous poetry
in Germany. The two former stories were later on treated afresh
in a new and more perfect style, and the pioneers who had first
sung of Flore and Blancheflur, of Tristan and Isolde in the German
tongue were forgotten or despised. They were entirely eclipsed by
Heinrich von Veldeke, who introduced the Aeneid into German
literature, and who, in the thirteenth century, was looked upon
as the father of chivalrous poetry. His more renowned followers
bore witness to his merits, saying that he had planted on German
soil the tree from whose branches they plucked the blossoms of
their poetry.

HEINRICH VON VELDEKE.

Heinrich von Veldeke was born in the neighbourhood of
Mastricht, and was in the service of the Counts of Looz and
Rineck, who were also Burgraves of Mainz. He was most
probably in Mainz during Whitsuntide in the year   Great
1184, when Frederick Barbarossa bestowed knight-   imperial
hood on his sons Henry and Frederick, and held a   festival at
feast which displayed to all Europe the magnificence   Mains, 1184.
of the imperial German court. Nearly seventy thousand knights
were assembled in the Rheingau, and were accommodated in a
city of tents and wooden sheds. Latin, German, and French
poets, as well as the historians of the period, are full of the glories
of this gathering.

Poetry itself must have derived much benefit from the friendly
intercourse of German and French knights on that festal occasion.
Hardly twenty years had passed since the German nobility had
begun themselves to write poetry; it therefore still had for them
all the charm of novelty, and must no doubt have been one of the
ornaments of this feast. It was then probably that the Crown-
Prince Henry sang those love-songs which bear his name, or
ordered them to be composed by some of the wandering gleemen.

Then, if not earlier, the bright joyous songs of Heinrich von
Veldeke must have been brought to the notice of the South-

German poets, and he may then have personally set forth those new laws of poetic diction, which he was anxious to see established. He had finished his Aeneid a short time before, and had a new secret to impart to his brother poets, namely, the discovery of pure rhyme.

The rhyme of the ninth century, the rhyme of Otfried and his colleagues, was mere assonance. Even the religious poets of the eleventh century at first employed a perfectly free assonance, which **Pure rhyme** in the course of the twelfth century gradually ap- **introduced** proached nearer to pure rhyme, without ever perfectly **by Heinrich** attaining it. The honour of having made the last **von Veldeke.** step in this direction was attributed by his contemporaries to Veldeke, and history has adopted their statement. That they should have prized so highly a mere technical improvement shows how much they thought of perfect form, of which pure rhyme is a symbol. At the same time Veldeke's language was not even pure Middle High-German; he used his native dialect, though perhaps with some modifications. But the knights of the Lower Rhine and of the Belgian provinces were considered the most cultivated in Germany, so much so that, as far as the borders of Austria, people who wished to affect an air of refinement mingled Flemish phrases in their conversation. Thus Veldeke was armed with a certain authority owing to his birthplace, when he joined the knightly company which had gathered round the Emperor at Mainz. His opinion was received, it appears, without opposition, and his example exerted an influence in and around Mainz; in Thuringia he founded a regular school of poetry, in what was then called Allemannia Hartmann von Aue followed in his steps, and in Bavaria the great Wolfram von Eschenbach called him his master and lamented his early death.

Veldeke had already written a Legend of St. Servatius, which excited no attention; he then wrote his Aeneid, and at once became famous. The names of Rome and Troy had not yet lost their magic power. Chivalry was supposed to have begun at Troy, and the ancient Roman empire was now in German hands. The founder of Rome was, according to Virgil, descended from the Trojan Aeneas, and Virgil, who had sung Aeneas' adventures, was looked upon in the Middle Ages as a prophet of Christ.

But Veldeke did not found his Aeneid on that of Virgil, though
he appeals to his authority, but on a French rendering   Veldeke's
of the Latin poet. He had already begun it about the   'Aeneid,'
year 1175, and sent what was finished to a Countess   completed
of Cleves. On the lady's marriage with the Land-   1184.
grave Ludwig of Thuringia the manuscript was stolen from her by
a certain Count Heinrich, who took it to Thuringia, evidently
meaning to enjoy it with his friends. This incident is an evidence
of the great interest which nobles took at that time in German
poetry. It was not till nine years later that the poet got back his
work in Thuringia, and completed it there under the patronage
of the Count Palatine of Saxony, afterwards Landgrave Hermann
of Thuringia. This cultured prince, at whose court Wolfram von
Eschenbach and Walther von der Vogelweide afterwards met, first
comes before our notice as the patron of Veldeke.

Veldeke, like his predecessors the authors of ' Flore' and 'Tristan,'
and like his successors, Hartmann von Aue, Gottfried   His French
von Strassburg and many others, was a translator from original.
the French. These poets all followed in the steps of the priests
Lambrecht and Konrad. They had little to do with the invention
of their stories, as little as, or even less than the authors of
the Nibelungenlied, and much less than the older gleemen, the
authors of the Oriental and Crusading poems. These chivalrous
epic poets were as faithful to their French authorities as the poets
of the Nibelungenlied were to the traditional form of the legend.
The chivalrous poets only show originality in their lyric songs ; as
romance-writers they are mostly translators. Their individuality
only appears in the choice of their story and in their method of
treating it. But they are not faithful translators in our sense of the
word, for they do not care to reproduce a foreign work in its own
style and with its own peculiar characteristics ; they are rather, to
borrow an expression of Goethe's, ' parodying translators,' trying
to replace the foreign fruit by a substitute which has grown on
their native soil. In this the German chivalrous poets only
followed the method of the French writers who were their models.

The old French writers, however, were far bolder in their treatment of foreign works than their German translators. Veldeke is

more faithful to his French original than the latter is to Virgil. The
Character of French author expanded the six lines which Virgil
Veldeke's devotes to Lavinia into fourteen hundred, and thus
poem. made a complete romance out of this episode. Veldeke never ventured on such bold changes as this; for the most
part he only expanded still further those portions of the story in
which outward events and marvellous incidents were kept in the
background, so as to give more scope, on the one hand, to the
expression of feelings, and on the other to the description of
weapons, costumes, and such like. The chief points of interest to
these aristocratic poets were the feelings of men and the luxuries
with which they could surround themselves; their own pride and
their own love of luxury could thus find utterance. Veldeke
briefly passes over the story of Laokoon, the destruction of Troy,
the death of Priam and the flight of Aeneas, but misses no word
of the loves and sorrows of Dido. He omits the marvellous
elements, so far as they were connected with ancient mythology; he
omits almost all pictures of ancient manners, all antiquarian or
topographical details, in fact everything that appeals to the interest
in vanished times and places. He also leaves out a number of
classical allegories, such as the description of Fortuna or of Fama,
or of the gates of the lower world, which the French author had
taken a certain delight in translating. On the other hand, the
German has outdone the Frenchman in his description of the
Sibyl and Cerberus, of whom he makes most terrible monsters.

But on the whole we must confess that Veldeke's individuality
Veldeke's hardly appears at all in his Aeneid, and it is only
songs. from his songs and proverbs that we learn anything
about his character. In them he appears as a simple-hearted,
merry individual, who worships cheerfulness and abhors discontent,
and enjoys the simple pleasures of life with a grateful enthusiasm.
He praises love, the spring, and the song of birds. He says that
the song of the birds and the trees in blossom fill his heart with
such gladness, that he is even comforted at parting with his lady-
love, whence we gather that his grief at leaving her is not very
deep. He is always ready with humorous touches. Thus, after
he has offended the lady of his heart, he is yet in the humour

to write a song in which he makes her scold him roundly. His style is lively and his imagery clear and effective.

In Thuringia Veldeke found a successor in the lyric poet Heinrich von Morungen, whose songs have at times quite Heinrich von a modern ring about them. He, too, is graphic in Morungen. style and full of imagination, though his ideas and similes often repeat themselves; at the same time he is witty, like a true follower of the Troubadours. Morungen has drawn on ancient mythology more than any other Minnesänger, and this may be attributed to the atmosphere in which he grew up; Veldeke's Aeneid Classical had more influence in Thuringia than anywhere else. Influence due In Thuringia a certain Biterolf composed a Song of to Veldeke's Alexander, which has not been preserved to us. Aeneid. Herbort von Fritzlar, a 'learned scholar' as he calls himself, wrote, at the instance of the Landgrave Hermann, a 'War of Troy,' as a kind of introduction to the Aeneid. Albrecht von Halberstadt, a divine of Jechaburg, began in 1210 tb translate Ovid's Metamorphoses. While Herbort's work is again based on a French author, Albrecht returned directly to the original. Thus the Epic poets of the Augustan era were revived to new honour, and even of Homer some shadow at least was conjured up.

Benoit de Sainte More, the French narrator of the Trojan war, did not derive his materials from Homer, but from very late and doubtful sources. He introduced the whole legend of the Argonauts into his poem, and enlivened the narrative of the many combats round Troy by the episode of Troilus and Briseida ; this story was very popular in the Middle Ages, and was treated by various poets, amongst others by Chaucer ; it was finally immortalised by Shakespeare in his 'Troilus and Cressida.' In introducing pairs of lovers like Aeneas and Lavinia, or Troilus and Briseida, the French romance writers of the Middle Ages paid homage to the prevailing taste of their time, just as in a later era Corneille and Schiller thought it necessary to satisfy the sentimental readers of their days by introducing love passages into heroic tragedy.

Herbort von Fritzlar considerably curtailed the garrulous Benoit, so much so that his narrative sometimes becomes a little obscure. He asserts his own individuality far more than Veldeke did. He is rather coarse, and delights in scenes of horror and murder, in Herbort von imprecations and abusive language. He pays little Fritzlar's heed to artistic form, but he has clearly realised the War of Troy. story to himself. Instead of directly describing Medea's attire, he transfers description into action, and shows her to us fetching her toilet accessories, parting her hair and plaiting her tresses. Herbort describes every little circumstance so minutely that it becomes ludicrous. For instance, he tells us that Jason kissed Medea at parting once, twice, thrice, and would have kissed her oftener, but her mouth was wet with her tears. The description of the death of Paris is most poetical. The lamentations over the beautiful youth, slain in the spring-time, breathe the tone of genuine grief, and the dull brooding sorrow of his mother Hecuba is especially well described.

From the moral point of view too, Herbort asserts his independence. He purposely omits, as against his conscience, the praise which the French author bestowed on King Pelias, for he thinks that all the good qualities that the sun ever shone on cannot supply the place of honesty, which the king is totally wanting in. He likewise tries to bring the conduct of the Trojan and Greek heroes more into harmony with the feelings of honour demanded by chivalry. He makes Achilles kill Hector in open combat, not, as in the French tale, by treacherously seizing on a favourable moment. Again, it is not Achilles himself who drags about the body of Troilus, but some inferior person specially introduced by the poet ; and the gentle words which Achilles speaks to the dying Hector are likewise due to the imagination of the German author. Either naively or purposely, we cannot say which, Herbort has introduced into the narrative ideas of German popular belief, and even Christian sentiments and German customs and legal forms.

Albrecht von Halber- In this his example was followed by Albrecht von stadt's trans- Halberstadt, who tried to spare his readers everything lation of that would be strange to them. In the introduction Ovid. to his translation of Ovid Albrecht thinks it necessary to inform them that there was a time in which men worshipped idols, and that the stories he was going to tell belonged to that time. He introduces into his rendering of Ovid ideas of

chivalrous life and conventional rules of propriety which are sometimes most absurdly out of place. Thus the Princess Europa,
when carried off by the bull, does not forget in her distress to
gather up her royal robes out of the water. In telling the story of
the grief of Niobe, the poet mentions that she forgot feminine
propriety so far as to run. He seeks to deprive mythology of all
its peculiar strangeness, and calls nymphs simply ' Wasserfrauen,'
and dryads ' Waldfrauen,' while the Furies receive the names of
' Herzeleid ' (heart-sorrow), ' Vergessenheit' (oblivion), and ' Wahn-
sinn ' (madness). Albrecht delights in describing such things as
the quiet of the woods or a hidden spring in a cool shady dell.
He relates, with great feeling, the solitary thoughts and dreams of
the maiden Thisbe, as she waits and longs for her lover in the
bright moonlight, and her sorrow afterwards when she calls on
the birds of the wood and the wood itself with its grass and foliage
to join in her lamentations.

The impression produced on us by all these poets and their
disciples is decidedly a pleasing one. They never entirely lose
sight of reality as known to them, and they avoid what is abso-
lutely fantastic. They transport us, if not into the midst of ancient
ideas, yet at least on to ancient soil. But in the twelfth and thirteenth centuries, with the one exception of the Aeneid, this remote
world of antiquity never gained general favour. At the same time
graphic representations of contemporary life were also little cared
for, otherwise one excellent poem of this period would have found
more popularity and called forth more imitation than appears to
have been the case. It is a poem which probably *Poetical*
appeared at Mainz as a first-fruit of Veldeke's in- *fragment,*
fluence, and which describes a love adventure of the *' Moris von*
French poet Maurice de Craon. The framework is *Craon.'*
somewhat out of proportion to the central theme; the poem begins
with a history of chivalry, telling how it was handed down from the
Greeks to the Romans, how it decayed under Nero, and finally
revived in France, whence it was transplanted also to other countries. The real story only begins after this lengthy introduction.

Maurice de Craon is in love with a Countess of Beaumont, who
promises him her favour, if he will arrange a tournament, for she

has never seen one. He agrees, and causes a ship to be constructed, which is set up within the lists before the castle of the
Countess, and from which he rides forth to the combat. The lady
afterwards neglects to keep an appointed tryst with her lover, which
reveals to him her coldness of heart, and he ends by abjuring her
service and advising her to devote herself a little more to her
husband. The lady feels guilty, dejected, and humiliated. On a
summer morning early, being unable to sleep for sorrow, she gets
up and goes to a bower on the castle walls. She stands alone at the
window, and rests her cheek on her white hand, and listens to the
song of the nightingale. One of her maidens, who is her confidante,
joins her, and to her the lady for the first time opens her heart,
and laments her misery and her spoilt life. Here the poem ends.
It is throughout fresh and original, and breathes all the early delight in chivalrous life and chivalrous poetry. The strange mixture
of narrative and reflections, of amusement and moralising does not
offend us. Certain requisite features and adornments of the love-
ròmance are introduced as a matter of course, conventional situations such as are presupposed in lyric poetry and described in the
epic. The influence of Eilhard von Oberge and Heinrich von Veldeke cannot be mistaken, but the unknown poet of this little tale
gives us more pleasure than the authors of those diffuse poems.
He also shows greater epic talent, for his narrative is more concise
and animated, he prefers narration to description, and describes
things, where necessary, in a cursory manner.

　　Towards the end of this poem the author laments the poverty of
the German language, which, he says, throws great difficulties in
the way of the poet. Perhaps it was this lament which called forth
'Legend of　an answer from some patriot in the 'Legend of
Pilatus.'　Pilatus' which appeared about this time in the same
district of the middle Rhine. In this legend Pilate's father is made
a King of Mainz, and he himself is said to have killed his brothers
and gone to Rome. After this he slew Paynus, conquered the
land of Pontus, and was summoned by Herod to oppress the Jews.
This Paynus was the son of a French king, but the Romans did
not venture to punish his murderer, because they were more afraid
of the Germans than of the French. There is here a direct con-

trast between this writer and the author of 'Moriz von Craon,' who
upheld the Romans and French, as the sole patterns of perfect
chivalry. And the polemical purpose of the poem is made still more
clear in its opening words; the poet begins by referring to the
fact that it had been said of the German language, that its rough-
ness was but little suited to poetry; but, he continues, the language
must be handled like steel, which becomes pliant on the anvil, and
care and labour must be bestowed on it. And so this poet sets
himself to his work with modest confidence and patriotic zeal.

In these poems connected with Mainz, which very probably
owed their origin to the grand court-festival there in 1184, we stand
at the very source of German chivalrous poetry. These earlier
poems may seem to some readers to possess a freshness which
they miss in the more classical later works. The steel of which
the author of 'Pilatus' speaks was far from flexible enough for the
writers of the end of the twelfth century. It was beaten out again
and again, and at length refined to a degree which may excite our
admiration, but which betrays more artificiality than real art.

HARTMANN VON AUE AND GOTTFRIED VON STRASSBURG.

Among the great German dynastic families of the twelfth century
the Guelphs were probably the first who gave strong
support to German poetry, and thus paved the way
for the literary culture of the nobles. Next to the
Guelphs, from about the eighth decade of the century,
Landgrave Hermann of Thuringia and the Austrian
princes of the house of Babenberg distinguished themselves most
as patrons of poetry. *Patrons of poetry among German princes of the 12th century.*

The influence of the Hohenstaufen is less apparent, and yet
their accession to power was an important event for German
poetry. Their vassals, inhabiting numerous castles on both sides
of the Upper Rhine, formed the nucleus of Alemannic chivalry.
The court of the Hohenstaufen was the centre of life for the whole
South-West of Germany. Alsace, Switzerland, and Swabia, terri-
tories of early civilization and of great political influence, developed considerable literary activity. The minstrels were probably
well received there throughout the twelfth century; the only one

L

whom we know by name, a certain Heinrich der Glichezare, made translations from the French at the commission of an Alsatian nobleman, and in this way produced the oldest German poem on Reineke Fuchs. This would seem to point to a taste for comic subjects, but fashion often changes quickly, and the great poets of the classical period belonging to the Upper Rhine, Friedrich von Hausen, Reinmar von Hagenau, and Gottfried von Strassburg, are distinguished by their lofty seriousness. The circle of the Hohenstaufen nobility supplied all the conditions for producing poetry like that of the troubadours, and no territory was more fitted to become the German Provence than the Upper Rhine. There too, as in the province of Lan-

German lyric guedoc, lyric poetry seems at first to have prepon-
poetry of the derated, but the bold individuality, the passion of the
12th century. troubadours were wanting. The Rhenish poets do not make their poetry reflect their own feuds and hatreds, their active and varied life. They lay aside their armour when they approach the Muse, and their lyre, like Anacreon's, breathes only tones of love. But it is not love, the consuming passion, which they describe, nor even thoughtless love bent on careless enjoyment; their love-poetry consists for the most part of clever conversations on the subject of love. The lyric poem became in their hands an elaborate form of courtship full of languishing entreaties and flatteries, in which there was less of the language of the heart than of the play of wit, less of real feeling than of intellectual subtlety. Refinement and culture were sought after at the expense of all the sensuous elements of poetry. Enjoyment of spring and of the song of birds, or lamentation over the fading foliage or the cold of winter, were now considered trivial. These poets lack vivid colouring in describing either joy or sorrow, and their utterances are toned down to suit the conventions of a society where strong feelings are considered objectionable in a poet, and he is only expected to be interesting.

The chief representatives of this kind of lyric poetry are Friedrich von Hausen and Reinmar von Hagenau.

. Friedrich von Hausen, one of the most renowned knights of his time, belonged to the circle of Frederick Barbarossa. He went with him to Italy and afterwards to the East, where he was killed by a fall from his horse six months before the Emperor's own death (May 6, 1190). From Italy he sends forth his love-com- **Friedrich** plaints across the mountains. The Crusade, he says, **von Hausen.** has produced a conflict between his heart and his body; his body wishes to fight the heathen, but his heart is devoted to a lady from whom it cannot bear to part. In an epigram he threatens with eternal perdition those who have taken the cross and yet have not joined in the Crusade, and he warns the ladies to withhold their favour from such dastards. He commends to God's protection the friends whom he leaves for God's sake. But in general there is little of real life reflected in his poetry. He delights in painting strange contrasts and possibilities, and in astonishing his hearers by unexpected incidents. The highest level of his art is shown in the monologue of a lady who cannot make up her mind whether she will grant or deny her affection to her lover. She weighs the pros and cons, she wavers from one resolve to another and dares not follow her own wishes, and yet at length she cannot help doing so, and love triumphs.

Reinmar von Hagenau continued Friedrich von Hausen's manner and even exaggerated it. He delights in antithesis **Reinmar von** and in the description of joys which are not his, **Hagenau.** but which he ardently longs for. He is gentler and more sentimental than his predecessor, and love seems to form the only interest of his life. The most trifling incidents are spun out by him with the greatest art, but to very weariness. His eternal lamentations only excited ridicule; people asked how old his lady-love might be, as he had sung her praises so long. But nothing could shake his seriousness, and he made a virtue of his necessity by exalting the torments of love to the level of a new principle of morality. We see throughout that Reinmar is only following the fashion and flattering the taste of noble ladies, who were interested by his melancholy, love-lorn appearance. There are a few notes in Reinmar's songs which are really the utterance of a tender poetical soul, and as such move us to joy or sorrow; but the greater part of his poetry is evidently an artificial product, and hence is wanting in truth and genuine feeling. We may admire its construction, but we miss the warmth which we expect in lyric poetry.

The Swabian poet, Hartmann von Aue, was somewhat younger
Hartmann von Aue, circa 1200. than Reinmar, and wrote chiefly in the last decade of
the twelfth and the first years of the thirteenth century.
He was an honest amiable man, who took life easily and
preserved his cheerfulness to the end. He had been through the
school-training of the time, and had learnt the fundamental principles
of the clerical view of life without their having any serious influence
on his own lighthearted secular life. It is true that occasionally in
his poems he preaches a retreat from the world and refers to the
transient nature of all earthly happiness; he also took part in the
Crusade of 1197, and gave utterance in some of his songs to fitting
sentiments in connection with it; but in his principal works he
exalts the ideals of chivalry: courage and love. Hartmann expressly requires that a man should serve two masters, the World
and God. He does not attempt to conceal the opposition of these
two powers, but effects a compromise between them.

Hartmann's lyric poems are more fresh and vigorous, more manly,
too, than Reinmar's. We see him at first as an unhappy and
rejected lover, but he afterwards finds happiness in a second love.
Sad moods are only transitory with him, and his real character
is cheerful and contented.

Hartmann's two poetical love-letters, or 'Büchlein' as they
His two 'Büchlein.' were then called, show a great deal of pleasant
wit and *naïveté*. The first of them again betrays
his clerical education. It is an argument between the body
and the heart, closely resembling in character those Latin poems
in dialogue ('*Streitgedichte*') so popular in the Middle Ages, in
which body and soul were made to utter reproaches against each
other. The poet's Body complains of his miserable and unsuccess-
ful love, but his Heart highly esteems the ideal resignation, the virtue
which love calls forth, and the honour which it brings. The
Dialogue begins by solemnly defining the respective positions of the
opponents, and then passes on to short alternate speeches of great
dramatic power and subtlety. The two enemies are finally reconciled, and promise to be good friends, and the Heart gives a magic
receipt by which happiness and love can be won: the herbs generosity, modesty, and humility must be mixed with truth and con-

stancy, with chastity and true manliness, and poured into a vessel, i.e. into a heart free from hatred; those who carry this mixture about with them will surely find happiness. The tone of Hartmann's second 'Büchlein' is more serious and passionate. The poet gives vent to despairing lamentations over the sufferings that spring from love and over his separation from his beloved, which he thinks will drive him mad. But even here he finds comfort in the thought of the faithfulness which will at length bring true lovers together.

God and the World, the Heart and the Body, quiet resignation and endless longing, the higher and the lower elements of human nature,—contrasts such as these and the means of their reconciliation run through all Hartmann's works, and also influenced him in the choice of his epic themes.

The legend of 'St. Gregory' calls its hero, even in the title, the 'good sinner.' The poet was apparently at- Legend of tracted by this legend of an innocent man who un- St. Gregory. wittingly fell into a great crime. He welcomed a story which presented the most extreme contrasts, a decided secular life and as decided a life of penance, and in addition to this the most rapid transitions from happiness to misery and from misery again to happiness. Gregory is the Oedipus of the Middle Ages, who has unwittingly married his mother, but this terrible tragedy here ends in a reconciliation. Gregory endures severe penance, being fastened by his own wish to a lonely rock in the sea, where he lives miraculously for seventeen years, nourished only by the water which trickles down the rock. Repentance and penance turn the sinner into a saint; Gregory is made Pope, and finds his mother again.

Hartmann's 'Gregory' was founded on a French poem; his 'Armer Heinrich,' which is now his best-known 'Der arme work, was based on a Latin story which, however, Heinrich.' probably only furnished him with the bare outline, leaving him free scope for exerting his epic talent. 'Poor Henry' is a kind of Job, a man of noble birth, rich, handsome, and beloved, who is suddenly visited by God with the terrible affliction of leprosy, and who can only be cured by the life blood of a young maiden who is willing to die for him. The daughter of a peasant, to whose house he has retired in his despair, resolves to sacrifice her life for him. Heinrich accepts her offer, and the knife which is to kill her is already whetted, when a better feeling rises in his breast and he refuses to take upon himself the guilt of her death, resolving to resign himself to the will of God. This resignation saves him; he recovers and marries the maiden, the difference in rank proving no obstacle to their union.

Besides the legend of 'St. Gregory' and the pious tale of 'Poor Henry,' Hartmann wrote two romances, 'Ereck' and 'Iwein.' The former was written before 'St. Gregory,' the latter after 'Poor Henry.' Both treat of the contrast between heroism and love, between devotion to the duties of a knight and indolent enjoyment of domestic happiness.

Knight Ereck is in danger of becoming effeminate (*sich zu 'ver-liegen'*) by the side of his beloved Enite. He sinks in public opinion, the knights and squires around him are discontented, and Enite herself is unhappy about it. Her husband who overhears her lamentations, compels her to confess the cause of her grief, and is from that moment roused from his sloth. He starts alone with her to seek for adventures, but being angry with her punishes her by repeated instances of foolish tyranny, till at length her faithful constancy, which repeatedly saves his life, and her unfailing patience and humility soften him and win his love anew.

'Ereck.'

The knight Iwein wins a beautiful woman for his wife, but shunning effeminacy he leaves her and sets out on adventures. He fails to return at the appointed time and thus trifles away her affection. This drives him to madness, from which he is only cured by a wonderful salve. He then sets free a lion, who thenceforward devotes itself to him as companion and helper. Under the title of the Knight with the Lion, Iwein, who has concealed his own name, gains fresh renown. Under this title he meets his lady again and wins her anew by cunning.

'Iwein.'

Both these knights, Ereck and Iwein, belong to King Arthur's famous Round Table. 'Ereck' was Hartmann's earliest work, and had a great success, becoming at once the model of narrative poetry to many less distinguished poets. Through his 'Ereck' Hartmann von Aue introduced the Arthur-romances into German literature.

The 'Arthur-romances' form a special class of mediæval epic poetry. King Arthur himself occupies but an insig- The 'Arthur-nificant place in them; he is only the centre round romances.' which the stories are grouped, just as Charlemagne was the centre for another cycle of tales. The chief heroes of these romances belong to Arthur's court and are members of his Round Table, and the Arthur-romances narrate their love-adventures and knightly deeds. A high conception of manly duty is the fundamental idea of the Arthur-romances, but this ideal is sometimes rendered weak and even absurd through one-sided exaggeration. The knight of Arthur's court travels through the world like Theseus or Perseus, as a protector of the weak and a destroyer of the monsters who threaten life and peace. He is compassionate and generous, sacrifices himself for the good of others, and is kept back by no danger, however great. In return it is but fair that the hero should be rewarded in this life for his deeds, that he should win the heart of the lady whom he frees from danger, and that she should at the same time, perhaps, bring him power and wealth. The knights themselves are faithful companions in arms, ready to come to each other's aid in any distress. But these knights of mediæval romance too often court danger without any purpose, and only in order to boast before their companions of what they have endured. And as the danger often becomes utterly improbable, and every horror is conjured up that an excited imagination can dream of, we often lose all belief not only in the actual, but also in the symbolical truth of the narrative. Knowing for certain that the hero will not be finally vanquished, we cannot long keep up a feeling of suspense. The poetry touches us more closely where the threatened danger comes from within, when we fear that two lovers who have quarrelled will not be reconciled, that injury will not be forgiven or despotic tyranny longer endured, when we see the hero driven to despair or madness. These poets love to appeal to the pity of their readers. The subjects are often well chosen and interesting, but the development of the story is spoilt by improbability or exaggerated idealization.

The Arthur-romances allow women a great part in influencing the destinies of men, but they never describe love-adventures with the lifelike details which we noticed in ' Moriz von Craon.' Great freedom of manners seems taken for granted, but this freedom never rises above the level of frivolity, either through the influence of strong passion or noble devotion.

Meaningless adventures and meaningless love-making characterise the decline of the Arthur-romances, and there is hardly a work in this widely developed class of literature that is free from these

Characters of the Arthur-romances. blemishes. We must not, therefore, expect to find in the Arthur-romances any rich development of character. The men never get beyond the Theseus-ideal, and the possible variations in this ideal are but few. The general type of hero, without fear and without reproach, is seen in the Knight Gawein or Gawan, the nephew of King Arthur and the friend of Iwein and Parzival. One figure alone is brought forward as a complete contrast in character to all the rest, the Knight Kei, Seneschal of Arthur's court. He is the Thersites of the Round Table, impudent, malicious, boastful, and at the same time always unfortunate in the combats into which he rushes. Even the women are all reduced more or less to the same type through this system of vague idealisation. They are all lovely, all objects to be coveted, all gifted in conversation; there is no apparent difference between maiden and wife, or between mistress and maid.

King Arthur had already been introduced into literature in the

Geoffrey of Monmouth's Chronicle, 12th century. first half of the twelfth century. The British chronicle of Geoffrey, Archdeacon of Monmouth, written in Latin, first proclaimed his fame to the world. It told how King Arthur, the ruler of Britain, had subdued the Saxons and Germans, how he conquered Ireland, Iceland, Norway, and Gaul, and how his knights became an example for distinguished warriors in the most distant parts of the earth. Even a Roman army under Lucius Tiberius was said to have succumbed to his power. But he was mortally wounded in a civil war, and died in 542 A.D. It is not strange that Geoffrey's contemporaries should have accused him of falsehood, but his bold forgery of history was at all events in part based on Breton tradition. The Bretons told many stories about their wonderful King Arthur who was still alive somewhere, and would come again to restore greatness to his people. The Breton popular poetry showed great fertility in the second half of the twelfth century, and the popular epics of Brittany were eagerly taken up by the French minstrels. Romances, both in prose and poetry, were founded on these minstrel-poems, and Celtic traditions, myths and stories, thus found their way into European literature. This was the case with the tale of Tristan and Isolde, with the Arthur-romances, and probably with the story of the Holy Grail and of Parzival.

Chrestien of Troyes was the first French poet of culture who treated the Arthurian legends. He was one of the most important poets of the twelfth century, and was patronised and encouraged by the Flemish court. He immortalised Ereck and Enite and the Knight with the Lion in his brilliant romances, and Hartmann von Aue made these romances accessible to the German public. For Hartmann also was but a translator like Veldeke, and kept his own individuality in the background. Still, we find in his epics many slight but characteristic departures from the original, and the differences, such as they are, seem to spring from greater refinement and better taste. The Frenchman is reckless in his wish to represent everything graphically, and when he wishes to produce a strong effect he has no regard for the dignity of his subject. He makes one knight say, he would rather have a tooth drawn than relate a certain story. Another knight hacks a piece off the cheek of a giant, the size of a cutlet. Hartmann avoids all such expressions. Chrestien at dinner gives us the full *menu*, while Hartmann replaces it by generalities. Chrestien jestingly remarks that women can only aid a warrior by their prayers, for they have no other weapon. Hartmann replaces the jest by the gallant remark that 'God is so noble that He cannot refuse the petition of so many beautiful lips.' Chrestien introduces religious forms and ceremonies wherever it seems convenient, but he also allows himself occasional

Hartmann translated from Chrestien of Troyes.

Differences between Chrestien and Hartmann.

attacks on the clergy. The latter Hartmann omits entirely, and replaces Chrestien's admixture of prayers and religious forms by a vague
devotion to God, who appears as a helper in time of need. Probably
the direct introduction of religious acts in a romance seemed to him
blasphemous. Hartmann again is of a much more sentimental
nature than Chrestien. In Chrestien's work Iwein and Gawein are
merely fellow-soldiers and boon-companions, but Hartmann thus
characterises their friendship: 'They bore each other's joys and
sorrows.' Chrestien endows his women only with grace of demeanour
and language ; Hartmann makes goodness of heart and gentleness
their chief ornaments. The Frenchman occasionally speaks in
a derogatory tone of women; the German would never think of
doing so. With Hartmann all is courtesy, consideration, kindness,
and modesty. In short, the Frenchman is natural and therefore
interesting, the German conventional and monotonous. The
characters of the Frenchman are meant to amuse, those of the
German to serve as ideals of life. Chrestien is a true exponent
of Gallic humour, of the much renowned 'gaîté gauloise.'
There is no more pleasant occupation than to read his 'Ereck.'
The cheerful radiance of the chivalrous life is diffused over the
whole of it. Chrestien revels in his story and tries to make
it as interesting and amusing as possible, not even shrinking from
rudeness and coarseness where it suits his purpose. Hartmann, on
the contrary, treats his characters with a kind of religious veneration, and adorns them with all virtues and excellencies. He avoids
all realism, and, like the translators of the twelfth century, pays
special attention to the development of the inner life. Outward
incidents are kept in the background, but their influence on men,
and the feelings and utterances of the latter are brought into
prominence. The chief events of the story are intended to excite
a gentle emotion in the reader.

All these characteristics of Hartmann's poetry are in harmony
with the literary traditions of the chivalrous poets of
the Upper Rhine. His colourless measured style
belongs to the school of Friedrich von Hausen and Reinmar von
Hagenau. In conduct as in style he favours grace, refinement,
and uniform polish. His 'Ereck' still shows some youthful imper-

Hartmann's style.

fections, but 'Iwein' is a really classical work, marvellously fluent in language, and remarkable for its perfect finish and pleasing variety. The work begun by Eilhard von Oberge and his contemporaries, and carried on by Heinrich von Veldeke, reached its culminating point in Hartmann von Aue. These chivalrous poets had to acquire afresh that ease and breadth of style which epic poetry demands, and which, after having been neglected by the minstrels of the tenth, had only been partially recovered by the clerical poets and minstrels since the eleventh century. Where the minstrel of the tenth century rushed on hurriedly, the chivalrous epic poet of the twelfth century lingered to contemplate ; the former laughed at his heroes, the latter looked up to them with admiration.

The bold style of the earlier epics acquired breadth and adornment in the hands of the chivalrous poets, and acquired them to a higher degree than was ever attained by the great popular epics of the same period. This was partly owing to difference of form. The verse-form employed in the popular epics required that the thought should be completed with each stanza. Hence the narrative would naturally proceed rapidly from one incident to another and have something about it akin to the ballad. The usual form adopted in the chivalrous epics, on the contrary, is that of short couplets, not divided into verses, and somewhat similar in character to the alliterative 'Long-verses' of the old Germanic epics. These continuous rhymed couplets allowed a liberty of style almost approaching that of prose. The verses of the popular epic would naturally be sung, while with the rhymed couplets this would be impossible. The style of the popular epic has something declamatory about it, while the tone of the chivalrous epic is that of refined conversation. But the chivalrous epic only slowly freed itself from the style of the popular epic, and we can clearly trace the development of this process.

Style of the chivalrous and popular Epics compared.

Eilhard von Oberge's style is still closely akin to that of the minstrels. He gives us descriptions of battles expressed in the traditional realistic formulae, and though he shows many traces of humour, yet he often adopts the conventional pathetic tone and employs many set forms of

Eilhard's style.

expression. His style is unequal and abrupt and lacks anima-
tion, and he observes no restraints in his choice of language.
On the other hand we find him employing many foreign words
which had been introduced into aristocratic society, and attaching great importance to a due observance of etiquette. He
also makes attempts to describe externals, such as weapons
and garments, and constantly introduces monologues to reveal
the feelings and thoughts of his characetrs, while in dialogue
he employs the short dramatic colloquy, in which question and
answer follow rapidly, like blow on blow. By these devices,
chiefly borrowed from the French epics, he distinguished himself
from the popular poets and prepared the way for his greater
chivalrous colleagues.

In Veldeke, too, the popular element has not quite disappeared.
Veldeke's When praising the sword which Vulcan sends to
style. Aeneas, he compares it with three famous swords of
German hero-legend, and declares it to have been harder and sharper
than any of these. Veldeke still has much in common with Eilhard,
but his poetry has less of set formulas and traditional similes than
Eilhard's, and he is also superior to him in pure rhyme and skilful
syntax. Veldeke went much further in psychological analysis than
any of his predecessors, French or German, and his poetry also
gave much greater scope to description.

In his 'Ereck' Hartmann von Aue carried description to the
Hartmann's extreme of absurdity. His description of Enite's
style. horse occupies about five hundred lines. In 'Iwein'
he laid aside this bad habit, and this later poem is a model of epic
style. Situations and habits of life are fully described, but never
so as to become wearisome and always in connection with the
main action. Battles are no longer pictured in set formulas, but
with due regard to their special characteristics. But the representation of the inner life is always the chief interest with
Hartmann. While 'Ereck' still showed at times a want of
refinement, 'Iwein,' on the contrary, is a model of good
taste and elegance. Again, while in 'Ereck' the diction is
rough and unequal, in 'Iwein' the language has attained the
highest level of perfection, and readily fulfils all that the poet

demands of it. The narrative is smooth and flowing, and all exaggeration is avoided. 'How clear and pure,' exclaims a contemporary of Hartmann's, 'are his crystal words. Gently they approach you and glide into your soul.'

This contemporary was Gottfried von Strassburg, the author of the famous epic poem 'Tristan and Isolde.' His   Gottfried admiration of Hartmann betrays itself repeatedly in   von Strass-his own poems, for he emulates him and tries to   burg. excel him. But where Hartmann hit on the right medium, Gottfried exaggerated, and what with Hartmann is perfection of style becomes with Gottfried mannerism.

Gottfried was a man of genius and a great artist, but he was a virtuoso in style, and carried polish and elegance   Character-to extremes; he exaggerated intellectual subtlety, and   istics of his delighted in antithesis and conceits of language. His   poetry. sense of metrical harmony was less delicate than Hartmann's, and his periods, admirable as they are, show less freedom and more effort at rounding and finish than the easy-flowing sentences of his predecessor. He had all Hartmann's delicacy without his simplicity. Gottfried is rhetorical, and overlays his narrative with a network of reflections. He is fond of obtruding his own personality and opinions upon his readers, and he strives after originality. He seems never to have written a love-song himself, and he mocks at the trivial laments of the Minnesingers. He declines to describe a festival or a tournament, because it has been done so often by others, but he gives in detail the best manner of dressing a hunted stag, because this was something new, and also gave him an opportunity for displaying his knowledge of the technical expressions involved, and of their etymology. He is generally careful not to weary us with the description of garments and outward appearances, but yet he occasionally goes further into these details than the author of 'Iwein' and further than the rules of epic poetry would allow.

Notwithstanding Gottfried's efforts after originality, he had no other artistic means at his disposal than those which he had inherited from Hartmann and the French poets, and he had as little power as Hartmann of inventing a story. He borrowed his

'Tristan and Isolde' from a French poem, which he followed
French source of Gottfried's 'Tristan.' almost slavishly, even where he would have done better to differ from it. The actual poem which he made use of is lost, and we only know it from abbreviations. Since the time when Eilhard von Oberge had written his poem of 'Tristan and Isolde' after a French model, new poets in France had taken up the story afresh, and refined its incidents. Gottfried's work was far superior to Eilhard's, with which he was acquainted, both through the greater perfection of his French original and also through the greater perfection of his own style. No French treatment of the story, as far as we know, **Superiority of Gottfried's 'Tristan' poem.** has attained to the artistic perfection of Gottfried's 'Tristan;' it was reserved for a German to give a classical form to this famous mediæval legend, which in human interest and life-like characters far surpasses the Arthur-romances. Gottfried's refined diction, his flowing language and rich imagery, were admirably adapted for the description of an overpowering passion and its destructive effect on character. The irresistible force of love is symbolised in the legend by a powerful love-potion. While German heroic poetry of the twelfth century freed itself as much as possible from fabulous elements, the Celtic stories which were introduced into German literature from France again revived a whole world of marvels. The enlightenment of the earlier period gave place to a romantic delight in the super-natural and improbable. By means of a magic potion Tristan **Legend of Tristan and Isolde.** becomes for ever attached to Isolde. The love which thus arises is an overruling passion, triumphing over the greatest difficulties, and asserting itself in defence of right and law. It leads to deceit and immorality, and yet from a certain point of view it is a moral power, for though an egoistic passion it yet goes contrary to egoism. Such a passion makes a man endure all the agonies of longing and the most terrible dangers without flinching, and developes in him all the energy of devotion and self-sacrifice. It makes him bad, but never vulgar. But love is not the exclusive theme of the legend or of Gottfried's poem; it also presents us with a glorious picture of chivalry in its first bloom. The hero first appears at the court of his uncle Mark

in Cornwall as a charming clever boy, who wins all hearts. He has perfect manners, and is an excellent chessplayer, huntsman, musician, and poet. In a word, he is ' höfisch' (chivalrous) through and through. After being dubbed a knight by Mark, he avenges his father's death on Morgan of Brittany. He then conquers Morold of Ireland, and thus frees Cornwall from a humiliating poll-tax. He kills a dragon in Ireland, makes peace between that country and Cornwall, and wins the Irish Princess Isolde the Fair for his uncle. But on board the vessel which is conducting the bride to her future home, Tristan and Isolde, through an unfortunate accident, drink the love-potion meant for Isolde and Mark. The mischief cannot be counteracted, and their passionate love makes them faithless to Mark, and gradually corrupts all who are connected with them. Tristan flies to the continent, enters military service, becomes acquainted with a second Isolde, Isolde the White-handed, and marries her; but he cannot forget the fair Queen of Cornwall, he visits her again and so makes the second Isolde miserable. Being wounded in some adventure he secretly summons his beloved to come and cure him. But his plans are frustrated by Isolde the Whitehanded, and Mark's wife dies on Tristan's dead body.

This is the complete story, but Gottfried's poem breaks off suddenly in the midst of the sophistic monologue in which Tristan resolves to marry; the completion of the work is said to have been prevented by the poet's death, about the year 1210.

The original intention of the legend seems to have been to show how noble knighthood may be ruined by passion; but Gottfried von Strassburg and his predecessors did not give this interpretation to the story. The German poet selected the theme with a distinct object. In all probability he was not Gottfried's a nobleman by birth, but wished to make himself reasons for appear as aristocratic as possible. He must have choosing this received a careful education, for he borrows from the subject. classical writers, especially from Ovid, who has written so much of love, and when he takes a very high flight he introduces classical mythology. He is well acquainted with French, but he parades his knowledge of it till it becomes wearisome, and even goes so far as to

speak of his fatherland only as Allemagne, 'Almanje.' He adopts
as gospel the easy-going, tolerant view of life held by the nobility,
defending it with the inexorable logic of a fanatical apostle, and
actually declaring that without love no one can possess either
virtue or honour. He recognises no bounds for the desires of
men, except the public .opinion of refined society, which for its
part allows everything that does not create a painful sensation.
There is no hint of any higher code of morals than this. Hartmann had already spoken of the gallantry of God, which makes
him grant the requests of beautiful women; but Gottfried's God
even helps Isolde the Fair, in deceiving her husband, and in
falsifying the ordeal by Divine judgment. Gottfried is not content
with describing passion faithfully, but he takes the part of the
guilty lovers against the outwitted King Mark. All charms are
heaped upon Tristan and Isolde, and the King is made to appear
mean and contemptible in various ways.

The fact that the author is evidently writing with a purpose in
Defects of view, i.e. that of defending the chivalrous philosophy
Gottfried's of life even in its utmost extremes, introduces an ele-
poem. ment of stiffness into this otherwise sensational narrative. Moreover the author cannot free himself from that tendency
to personify abstract qualities, which is one of the characteristics
of the chivalrous epics, and this tendency often betrays him into
artificial conceits. For instance, Tristan is armed for the fight, not
like Aeneas, by Vulcan, but by Magnanimity, Goodness, Reason,
and Culture. Again, in describing the woody Grotto of Love where
Tristan and Isolde live for a time in banishment, Gottfried not
only paints each detail, but makes each bear some reference to
love; in this he resembles the mediæval commentators on the
Bible, who not only took the words of the text literally, but also
gave them an allegorical meaning.

In his attitude towards questions of literary art too, Gottfried
Gottfried's appears as a conscious theorist, who wishes to enforce
criticisms of his opinions. In one often-mentioned passage of his
his contem- poem he drops the thread of his narrative to enter
poraries. on an argument with his poetical contemporaries, and
set forth his own principles of art; he is describing the ceremony of

dubbing Tristan a knight, when he suddenly stops to declare that he does not mean to emulate his predecessors in the description of the feast, and then goes on to speak not only of the epic poets who preceded him, but also of the lyric poets, who have nothing to do with the matter. The characteristic sketches which he draws of them are certainly most brilliant, and furnish   Gottfried's the finest examples of the intellectual acuteness and criticism of delicate touches which could at that time be ap- contempo-plied in literary criticism. He mentions with admira- rary poets. tion Hartmann von Aue, Blicker von Steinach, (only known to us by a couple of songs,) Heinrich von Veldeke, Reinmar von Hagenau and Walther von der Vogelweide. On the other hand, he speaks in terms of the strongest disapproval of an unnamed writer, whom he compares to a conjuror or a juggler, a man who seeks out dark sayings, and who ought to send out an interpreter with each of his tales. Gottfried, for his part, will only adjudge poetic laurels to the writer whose diction is smooth as a level plain, which a man of simple understanding can traverse without stumbling.

This unnamed writer was, doubtless, Wolfram von Eschenbach, and it does not surprise us that Gottfried should have disapproved of him. While the four epic poets, Eilhard von Oberge, Heinrich von Veldeke, Hartmann von Aue, and Gottfried von Strassburg form a complete series, embracing the four decades from 1170 to 1210, and marking a constant progress towards clearness and grace of diction, Wolfram stands quite apart from them—a man with a totally different ideal of life and art, and with a breadth and depth of insight far beyond anything which Gottfried could conceive.

WOLFRAM VON ESCHENBACH.

The sentence passed by Gottfried on Wolfram did not express the general opinion of the time, nor does it correspond with the verdict of posterity. Wolfram was, without doubt, the greatest German poet of the Middle Ages, and was also recognised as such. 'No lay-mouth ever spake better,' said a poet of the time, who gazed with wonder on the rising star of Wolfram's genius, and succeeding centuries concurred in his judgment. According to the opinion of his countrymen Wolfram surpassed all secular writers, and was only inferior to the Bible and to the great religious teachers. And indeed, he seems distinguished from all other writers, for all that he says bears the stamp of a marked indivi-.duality. Still, many of the characteristics of his writing may be traced to older sources.

Wolfram came from Bavaria, and, true to the literary tradition of this country, he united in himself chivalrous and popular, secular and clerical elements. While Hart-mann sought to keep as far as possible from the style of the national epics, and thus became more and more careful in the choice of his words, more and more rigid in his diction, Wolfram, on the contrary, adhered in many respects to the older popular manner. He was probably about the same age as Hartmann, though he made his first attempt in epic poetry some ten years later. He may have already formed his taste on Eilhard, Veldeke and celebrated French poets like Chrestien of Troyes, before he got to know Hartmann's ' Ereck.' He refers to events in the heroic legends, and does not scorn him-self to adopt the naively extravagant manner in which the old songs extolled the virtues of their heroes. He possesses the gift of humour, and succeeds in establishing a lively sympathy between himself and his audience. His mastery of language far exceeds anything attained by any of his contemporaries, but he exercises no restraint in the use of this power ; he is like a wild torrent, which will not flow gently or tolerate a narrow bed. He had no regular education, being unable even to read or write, and he did not wish himself to be counted among the poets. ' I was born to the profession of arms,' he proudly asserts. His rhymes are some-times bad, his style bears no traces of artistic rhetoric, and his syntax is simply the natural flow of ordinary speech. His metre is too confined for the wealth of thoughts which crowd in upon him, and he has not learned to disentangle them and place them clearly before the reader. But, after all, the striving after elegance and refinement too often crushes natural feeling, and Wolfram, while indifferent to elegance, had the courage to be true to his own feelings. He says straight out what he thinks, and is not scrupulously anxious to avoid everything which could offend delicate ears. He teases ladies for their weaknesses, where others only worship them, but he also draws them true to life, where others only idealise. The Bavarians were, according to the opinion of the Allemannic knights, behindhand in the customs of chivalry, but this had the advantage of making them feel less strongly the despotic power of etiquette. In the works of the Allemannic poets, Hartmann and Gottfried, we only see the world from the windows of an elegant drawing-room; when reading the writings of the Bavarian Wolfram we are in the open air, in the woods and on the mountains. Wolfram's poetry is the more real of the two and therefore appeals more to our sympathy.

While Hartmann in translating Chrestien of Troyes carefully omitted all touches of humour, as being out of place, Wolfram, on the contrary, seems to have adopted the humorous boldness of poets like Chrestien, and made full use of it to suit his own taste. **His humour.** Good-natured humour is always at his command, and he often makes somewhat outrageous use of it in his desire to represent things clearly, for, like Chrestien, he has no sense of what is fitting to the dignity of his subject. He boldly compares the slender figure of a beautiful lady to a hare stretched on the spit, or to an ant, and likens the hair of an ugly but learned woman to the bristles on a pig's back. He says of a knight who is weeping for joy : ' His eyes would be of no good as a cistern, for they did not hold the water.' Here he borders on bad taste, and there are some instances even worse than these. Like Chrestien, he wishes at all costs to pourtray vividly, and he does it with incomparable freshness. Wolfram is not afraid, like Gottfried, of vieing with his predecessors in the description of tournaments, combats and festi- **His freshness and originality.** vals, for he possesses that poetic power which lends a new charm to what has been heard already a hundred times. Everything in his poetry breathes, acts, moves ; the powers of the mind, the forces of nature, and even lifeless objects assume personality and action. Wolfram prefers to draw his metaphors and similes from chivalrous life, but all that comes within his horizon also serves him for the purpose. Wolfram enters more into details than Hartmann and

Gottfried, and is, in consequence, more true to nature. In this respect again he resembles Chrestien, while he differs from Chrestien's German translator. Wolfram describes in full the vain endeavours made to heal the wound of King Amfortas, and for this he receives a disparaging side-glance from Gottfried, who observes, in describing the healing of Tristan, that he does not care to take his words from the apothecary's shop.

Wolfram is not purely objective as an epic poet; his works show us not only the puppets, but the mind which is guiding them. Still, it is not often that he speaks in his own person; as a rule, we see through the eyes of his heroes, and feel what they feel. We gain an idea of the scenery from their speeches and actions, and it is mostly by what they say and do that their characters are made known to us. We soon see that the poet does not bind himself to any fixed method of narration, but is guided everywhere by his natural tact, and, at least in the years of his mature power, he never becomes diffuse, or wearisome.

Wolfram von Eschenbach is the last great poet in universal His illite-   literature who was without the elements of literary rateness.   culture, and he is, perhaps, the only one with whom this defect was not due to the general condition of education at the time. Like the popular poets, who developed their memories to such perfection that they could easily remember several thousand verses, Wolfram treasured up in his memory, as material on which to exercise his art, all such learning in the way of poetry, theology, astronomy, geography, and natural history as was accessible in his age to a layman, who only knew German and a little French. His poetry also reveals much tender observation of the life around him, —chivalrous, sporting, social, or domestic.

Instead of reading and writing, Wolfram had to be read to and to dictate. But his very illiterateness gave him an incomparable force and independence. Reading always lays certain shackles on the imagination, and, moreover, in the Middle Ages the clergy were the only teachers of the art. Wolfram, never having gone through this training, retained his natural independence of mind. He bears no traces of clerical instruction, and his soul was never confined by a strait jacket.

Wolfram's epics contain more of his own experiences than Hartmann's do of his.　His native place, Eschenbach, **His life.**
was in the northern province of Bavaria, south-east
of Ansbach, and close to it lay Abenberg, Wassertrüdingen, Nörd-
lingen and Dollnstein, all of them places mentioned in his poems,
and well known at the present day.　He was often hospitably entertained at the castle of Heitstein in the Bavarian Forest, and he
sings the praises of its mistress, the Margravine of Vohburg, sister of
Duke Ludwig of Bavaria, who lived there till 1204.　He paid long
and frequent visits to the Landgrave Hermann of Thuringia, whom
he likewise sometimes mentions in his works.　But his home was
at Wildenberg, probably what is now Wehlenberg, near Ansbach.
There he lived with his wife and child in humble circumstances,
which, however, did not embitter him, as is shown by his frequent
jests at his poverty.

Those of his songs which we possess are sometimes hopeful,
sometimes impatient in tone.　In others, which have been lost, we
know that he gave vent to his anger with an unfaithful woman, for
he acknowledges, in a later poem, that he went too far in his reproaches, though even then he does not lay aside all bitterness.
He wrote four ballad-like poems, belonging to the **Wolfram's**
class called 'Tagelieder,' or 'Tageweisen' poems, which **'Tagelieder.'**
described the parting of two lovers in the morning, such as Shakspeare represents in his ' Romeo and Juliet.'　These ' Tagelieder '
were suggested by the watchman's songs, so common in Provençal
poetry.　In these songs the watchman announces the dawn, and
warns the lovers to part ; thus an occasion is afforded to the poet of
describing passionate attachment intensified by the pain of parting.
In Germany, these songs at first assumed the somewhat conventional
form of a duet between the lovers.　Wolfram followed the Provençal
form more closely ; he retained the character of the watchman, and
infused into these songs such a glow of passion, such truth and
earnestness, that he stands forth as the greatest master in this kind
of poetry.　But there is one poem in which, instead of telling the
tale of illicit love, he praises the happiness of marriage; perhaps
this song was written at the time when he founded his own
household.

Wolfram, like Gottfried von Strassburg, knew and loved gay secular life, but he was not wholly given up to it, and did not think it the summit of all happiness; nor was his soul, like Hartmann von Aue's, divided into a worldly and a spiritual portion, which existed side by side in seldom disturbed tranquillity. Wolfram was convinced of the insufficiency of worldly wisdom, and sought the eternal beyond the temporal. At the same time, he was by no means an ascetic after the church's own heart, for he had his own independent opinions, though his nature was deeply religious. His 'Parzival' two great epics, 'Parzival' and 'Willehalm,' both **and 'Wille-** have a religious vein running through them. In **halm.'** ' Parzival,' Wolfram borrowed from French poems of Celtic origin, while 'Willehalm' is derived from French national poetry. 'Parzival' contains supernatural elements, such as we noticed in the Arthur-legends and in 'Tristan,' while 'Willehalm,' on the contrary, has an historical basis. Both poems treat of the relations between Christians and heathens, and besides this, 'Parzival' contains still deeper religious ideas of a distinctly original character.

The poem of ' Parzival' presents to us a Christian and a heathen **Tolerant** as brothers. In the story of the life of Parzival's **views ex-** father, Gahmuret, we are introduced to a state of things **pressed in** in which Christians and heathens have learnt to toler- **' Parzival.'** ate, and even to esteem and respect each other, as was really the case in Spain; heathens of rank speak French, chivalry and homage to women reign as in the West, and knightly service forms a link between the two different religions. Gahmuret, a Christian prince of Anjou, is in the service of the caliph of Bagdad, the heathen pope, as Wolfram explains. He becomes famous among the Saracens, and is not ashamed to marry a Moorish lady, Belakane, whose noble and pure character seems to him to make up for her not being a Christian. But seized with a longing for knightly adventures, he soon afterwards makes the difference of religions a pretence for accusing her of unfaithfulness. He forsakes her, wins the hand of Queen Herzeloide at a tournament in the land of Valois, and marries her, though not without a sense of the injustice which he is doing to his heathen wife. His duty to

the caliph calls him back to the East, and he falls in battle. Parzival is Herzeloide's son; but Belakane also had a son, Feirefiss by
name, of whose existence Parzival learns for the first time later on,
in a very important moment of his life. Towards the end of the
poem he meets this brother in the hardest combat which he has
ever fought. Parzival's sword breaks asunder, and, but for the noble
forbearance of the heathen, he would have been lost. But at this
point, the two brothers recognise each other, and Feirefiss shows
loyalty equal to that of any Christian, though, as the poet remarks,
it was through Christ that loyalty came into the world. Out of love
to a Christian woman Feirefiss is at length baptized, and he carries
Christianity to India, spreading it however only by peaceable means.

These relations with heathendom form, as it were, a framework
to the story of Parzival, but the central point of interest
in the poem is the Holy Grail, on which the whole fate   The Grail.
of the hero depends. The Grail is an object of ancient legend
transformed into a religious symbol. The word 'Grail' (Latin
Gradalis) originally signified a large, deep dish, with several divisions,
in which various sorts of food could be served up at once. The
Grail of the legend was originally a kind of magic dish, which offered
at all times an excellent meal. According to a religious version of
the story, the Grail is said to have served as a dish at the Lord's
Supper, and then to have been used by Joseph of Arimathea to catch
the blood from the Saviour's side. With Wolfram, the Grail is made
of one precious stone which, like the black stone of the Kaaba at
Mecca, originally fell from Heaven. At first the angels watched and
guarded it; afterwards, the care of it was transferred to a religious
order of knights, the 'Templeisen.' It is a symbol of salvation and of
eternal life; whoever sees it cannot die, and remains always young.
The place where it is kept is called 'Munsalväsche' (mont sauvage)
in Wolfram's poem, originally, perhaps, *Mons Salvationis*, 'mountain
of salvation.' No man can, by his own power, penetrate into the district that surrounds this mountain. Those who may serve the Grail
are called by a summons which appears in writing on the vessel itself.
Those who are chosen must renounce earthly love, for its king alone
may be wedded, whose rule extends over the whole earth. The
brotherhood of the Grail comprises men and women, knights and

squires, priests and laymen. They need take no thought of what they shall eat and drink, for the Grail yields sustenance for all.

Thus the Grail gathers around itself a brotherhood unprejudiced against the Church, but still independent of it. The idea is clearly that of an order of knighthood, and the 'Templeisen' of the poem were suggested by the Knights Templars, though, of course, those knights were not surrounded by so much mystery, nor was their superior an earthly sovereign. The Knights of the Grail, such as Wolfram represented them, could have no exact counterpart in real life.

Parzival is destined to the dignity of becoming the sovereign of this chosen order. He at last finds salvation, although he has been guilty of many sins, for these sins have been committed in ignorance, like those of Saint Gregory in Hartmann's poem. But while Gregory atones for his fault by undergoing a long course of penance prescribed by religion, Parzival's purification, on the contrary, is accomplished simply by a change of disposition, without the services of religion. But there is a still greater difference than this between the attitude of the two poets. Hartmann von Aue says in the prologue to his 'Gregory,' that there is only one sin which cannot be put away by repentance, namely, unbelief and doubt, which inevitably lead to damnation. Wolfram's epic, on the contrary, begins with the assertion that doubt does indeed hurt the soul, but that if the doubter be of undaunted courage, he may still attain salvation; heaven and hell both have hold over such an one, and it depends on himself alone whether he will rescue his soul. Only wavering and weakness of character lead necessarily to eternal death, while, on the other hand, steadfast endeavour must secure salvation. We have here the leading idea of Wolfram's poem. Like Goethe, in 'Faust,' he gives a secular answer to the question: who can be saved? Goethe says: 'He who continually aspires and strives' ('Wer immer strebend sich bemüht.') Wolfram says: 'The steadfast and true man' ('Der Stete und der Treue.') These two answers sound different, but they are really closely akin. Faithfulness to his wife and to the Grail, steadfast striving to realise his ideal in public and private life, combined with recovered trust in God, constitute Parzival's saving faith.

Marginal note: Difference between Wolfram's and Hartmann's views.

Wolfram's Parzival passes through darkness and despair, and finally rises chastened to the highest level of per- Story of fection. His mother, wishing to withdraw her son 'Parzival.' from his natural career, lets him grow up in the solitude of a wood, without any knowledge of knighthood ; but a chance meeting with some knights, and their reference to King Arthur, is enough to make Parzival's chivalrous bent declare itself. He goes out into the world, and breaks his mother's heart, for she dies the moment that he vanishes from her sight. Unaware that he is guilty of having caused his mother's death, Parzival enters with boldness and self-reliance on his new life. He is dressed in motley, and following too literally the precepts given him by his mother, he excites the ridicule of those whom he meets, but soon proves himself a dangerous opponent. He next arrives at Arthur's court. Ignorant of his kith and kin, and unacquainted with the laws of knightly honour, he kills one of his relations, and then plunders the body. From the knight Gurnemanz he learns, for the first time, what is becoming for a knight in fighting and in peace, and amongst other things, Gurnemanz warns him against useless questions. After this, Parzival comes to the rescue of Queen Condwiramurs of Pelrapeire, and makes her his wife. He leaves her, however, to go and seek adventures, wishing also to find his mother again. He comes to the mountain of the Grail, where he is splendidly entertained. He sees there much that is strange and magnificent: the King Amfortas lying on a sick-bed, a bleeding lance brought in, at the sight of which all break into lamentations. He receives a present of a sword from Amfortas, accompanied by an allusion to the King's misfortune, yet he does not ask the meaning of what he sees, and has no enquiry of sympathy for his kind host. His natural warm-heartedness has been crushed by the conventional precepts of propriety inculcated by the knight Gurnemanz, precepts which, in his innocence, he follows as literally as he had formerly followed the instructions of his mother. Parzival's conduct is a satire on knightly breeding and knightly manners, designed to show their inadequacy. The simple enquiry of human sympathy, which was expected from him, would, according to the decree of the Grail, have cured Amfortas and have rewarded the enquirer with the sovereignty of the

Grail; but instead of this he quits the castle in disgrace. And just as Arthur has received him as a member of the Round Table, and his secular knighthood has thus attained its highest glory, the messenger of the Grail appears and rebukes him for his fault. Parzival, however, repudiates the charge, and stung by this open disgrace he renounces his allegiance to God; for, he argues, if there were a divine power, it would not have let this shame come upon him. God may punish him, if it pleases Him! Henceforth the thought of his wife alone shall inspire him in the battle, for from God he expects no further help. He seeks the Grail, and longs to see it again and win it. For five years he thus wanders about, till on a Good Friday he meets a pilgrim-knight, who bids him examine himself, and directs him to a pious layman, the hermit Trevrizent, who first enlightens him about the true nature of God and the nature of the Grail. From Trevrizent the hero learns humility and submission to the dispensations of Providence. He is freed from the burden of his sins, and leaves the hermit as an altered man. Trust in God henceforth guides all his actions. His fight with Gawan symbolises the triumph of the higher spiritual chivalry over mere secular knighthood. He is now summoned to the Grail, makes the enquiry which he had formerly neglected, enters on the sovereignty, and is again united to Condwiramurs and his two sons.

The story, at least in its later parts, has really two heroes, though we are made to feel throughout that Parzival is the chief hero. When he is withdrawn from our eyes, to sojourn for a time with the knight Trevrizent, the stage is occupied by another figure, the knight Gawan, the type of secular chivalry, whose adventures for a time absorb the poet's attention.

It is only by the introduction of Gawan that the poem becomes a complete picture of chivalrous life. The contrast between children of God and children of the world is typified in Parzival and Gawan. Parzival is serious, while Gawan is frivolous; Parzival is faithful to his wife, while Gawan passes quickly from one love to another. Around Parzival are grouped serious characters, like Gurnemanz, the pilgrim-knight, and Trevrizent, faithful and pure women, like his devoted mother, Herzeloide, his fair cousin, Sigune, and his loving

Contrast between Parzival and Gawan.

wife, Condwiramurs. Gawan, on the contrary, is not only surrounded by all the legendary marvels of the Arthur romances,
but is also the centre of a purely worldly and somewhat questionable society; his companions, however, like himself, pass through
a kind of purification. The women with whom he associates,—the
charming young girl Obilot, the coy Obie, who is at length conquered by love, the strong-charactered Antikonie, the alluring
coquette Orgeluse, the enthusiastic and emotional Itonie, Gawan's
sister,—all of them represent the conventional requirements of
society with regard to women; at the same time, the poet's respect for
women keeps him from making any of these characters unpleasing.
Parzival and his friends on the one hand, and Gawan and his
associates on the other, represent two hemispheres of the world of
chivalry, a higher and a lower form of knighthood. The Arthur-
romances and ' Tristan ' only show us one of these hemispheres, but
Wolfram introduces both, and fills each with a succession of
characteristic figures, far removed from the vague ideals of a
Hartmann von Aue. But Parzival and Gawan are friends, and
although the poet gives the palm to the former, yet he has no
intention of condemning the latter. He may have found the
material for both in his own breast. He distinguishes between
a higher and a lower knighthood, but knighthood in general is
to him the only form of life worth living.

In 'Parzival' an illiterate German has immortalized the deepest
ideas of European chivalry. Wolfram's 'Parzival,' **Wolfram's**
like Gottfried's ' Tristan,' is the classical form of the **poem com-**
story in mediæval literature. And Wolfram counted **pared with**
among his predecessors in the same field no less **Chrestien's.**
a man than Chrestien of Troyes. The French poet had told
Parzival's story as far as his sojourn with Trevrizent, and had
described Gawan's adventures down to a short time before the
combat with Parzival, had told them too in the same order, and
with so much similarity, on the whole, that we cannot help thinking
that Wolfram must have been acquainted with Chrestien's romance,
in some form or other.

But Chrestien's 'Perceval' is, perhaps, his weakest work, and it
is probable that his talents were, in any case, not adequate to the

subject. Wolfram is superior to the French poet in all points. · He surpasses him in depth of thought and also in artistic power. Wolfram shows much more skill in developing and connecting the incidents in his poem, and he also draws his characters much more sympathetically than Chrestien, and is more successful in gaining our sympathy for them. The Grail too gains much more significance in Wolfram's treatment of it; Wolfram alone makes it clear to us that Parzival has neglected an enquiry of sympathy, that his feelings of humanity were appealed to in vain. Again, how powerfully Wolfram depicts the sudden breaking in of evil upon the brilliant circle of the Round Table! How clearly he brings before us the condition of Parzival's soul, when relapsing into a state of defiance towards God! In Chrestien's poem, on the contrary, the hero merely announces his intention of learning what he had formerly neglected to ask concerning the Grail, and it is only afterwards that he tells the hermit, that for five years he had neither loved God nor believed in Him. The hermit gives him, for the improvement of his soul, external precepts about prayer and attending church, in strong contrast with the profound and serious considerations which Wolfram puts into his mouth in this connection. Wolfram has treated the story with the free, bold hand of an artist, filling it with beauty and life. He is a true painter of humanity, like Shakspeare; a poet of tolerance and reconciliation, like Goethe.

Wolfram had become so attached to the characters in 'Parzival' that he could not break from them. He was especially attracted by the character of Sigune, the youthful widow, whom Parzival meets on his first sallying forth into the world, and who appears again at several momentous periods of his life, instructing, reproving, and comforting, and is at length found by Parzival lying dead on the coffin of the man she loved. As Wolfram had painted her sorrow, so he also wished to paint her love. For this he chose a form closely akin to the popular ballad, namely, stanzas describing separate episodes, interspersed with allusions to the whole story. He sought to approximate his style still more to that of the national epics, borrowing certain characteristics from them and laying aside his jocularity.

These songs of Wolfram are generally called ' Titurel,' because
the first begins with Titurel, the sovereign of the Grail,   'Titurel.'
and the great-grandfather of Sigune and Parzival.
But the real subject even of this first song is the childish love of
Sigune and Schionatulander, which is charmingly pictured in conversations between the two children, imitating the speech of their
elders, and in their confessions to their trusted teachers, those of
Schionatulander to Gahmuret, and of Sigune to Herzeloide.   Gahmuret and Herzeloide approve of their affections, only it is looked
upon as a matter of course that the young hero must first earn
Sigune's love by brave deeds.   The second song gives us the story
of Sigune's foolish wish, which drove her lover to his destruction.
Schionatulander has caught a hunting-dog in the wood, but it
escapes before Sigune can finish reading the inscription on his
splendid leash.   Schionatulander, at her command, must pursue the
animal through bush and briar, but all in vain.   Then he is sent out
again, love being the prize of his success, and this, as the poet says,
is the beginning of his misfortunes.   He loses his life in the foolish
quest, and Sigune may now mourn for him all her life long.   The
despotic etiquette of that time avenges itself on Sigune as on
Parzival.   If the little lady believes that she may require anything
from her devoted knight, this is just as foolish as when Parzival
thinks that he must ask no questions.   While Hartmann von Aue,
as we have seen, is anxious to bow in all things before the courtly
ideal of propriety, Wolfram von Eschenbach protests against it,
here and in ' Parzival,' in the name of humanity.   Here again, the
fact that Bavaria was backward in chivalrous education was an
advantage to him as a poet.

The same humane sentiment appears in Wolfram's second
important work, ' Willehalm,' and here again it is   'Wille-
arrayed on the side of religious toleration.   Willehalm   halm.'
is Saint William, Count William of Aquitaine, who, in the year
793, fought against the Saracens between Carcasonne and Nar-
bonne, and though defeated, yet succeeded in checking the advance
of the enemy.   French songs celebrated this battle and the life of
the hero with many legendary adornments.   They told how he
carried off a heathen woman, who received in baptism the name

of Giburg; how he fought at Aliscans against her father and her former husband; how after the battle he sought assistance from King Louis, and was victorious in a new battle, in which Renouart ('Rennewart' in Wolfram), specially distinguished himself. Renouart is a heathen prince, Willehalm's brother-in-law, who has lived undiscovered at the royal court as scullion, and who, after performing valiant deeds in this battle with a huge bar of iron, finally consents to be baptized.

We possess the French original of Wolfram's story, or at least **French poem on the same subject.** a poem very closely related to it. He has not handled it with the same freedom and success as he did the story of Parzival, for he has made the long descriptions of battle still longer, and the diffuse speeches still more diffuse; but he has toned down barbaric deeds of violence, and has moderated the all too martial tone. He has introduced his tolerant views of heathendom into a legend which owed its fame to religious fanaticism, and into a poem which formed a pendant to the Chanson de Roland.

In 'Willehalm,' as in 'Parzival,' we see Christians and heathens **Story of 'Wille-halm.'** bound together by a family tie. The fair heathen Giburg is the cause of the fight, like the Greek Helena. Her father, her former heathen husband, and her son by her first marriage, are all opposed in the field to the Christian who has carried her off. And Giburg, 'the holy woman,' as the poet calls her, is far from having entirely broken with her past life. She acknowledges that Tybald, her first husband, was free from all blemish, and she exhorts the Christians to spare the heathen, who are God's creatures as much as themselves; all heathens, she says, cannot be damned, for were not Adam, Eve, Noah and the three Magi heathens? Giburg is only expressing Wolfram's own view of the heathen. He thinks it a **Comparison with the French poem.** great sin to slaughter them like cattle, for they have never heard of Christianity. Unlike his French original, he endeavours throughout to represent the heathen in a noble light, and, as a contrast to their ferocity in battle, he introduces many palliating instances of generosity and refinement. In the French poem, Willehalm answers an insulting speech of his heathen step-son with the assertion that all heathens are dogs, and that whoever kills one of them destroys a devil; Wolfram's Willehalm, on the contrary, receives the taunting words in silence, and avoids fighting with the son of his own wife. In Wolfram's poem, Giburg's father only makes war on his daughter because the caliph and the heathen priests require it; he would rather, if it only depended on him, have died for her.

In the French poem the heathen Rennewart is a greedy, drunken, stupid giant, who serves as a butt for the rough jokes of his com-rades, and rewards them with a good beating in return. But Wolfram draws him in a far nobler light, and if he had not done so we should grudge this rough warrior the charming king's daughter, who, in the legend, becomes his bride. Many other instances might be quoted in which Wolfram has improved on the French poet.

Love plays but a small part in this serious poem, but Wolfram has beautifully represented in Willehalm and Giburg the faithful devotion of husband and wife. There is one especially charming scene, which describes how Willehalm returns home despairing and exhausted from the battle, and Giburg takes off his armour, binds up his wounds, and grants him a moment's rest in her arms; then he lays his head on her breast and falls asleep, while she gives herself up to prayers and lamentations, and her tears flow down on the sleeper's face. But when he wakes, he speaks words of comfort and encouragement to her.

In 'Willehalm,' as in 'Parzival,' Wolfram has given a religious colouring to chivalry. He even mentions that the Christians signed themselves with the cross before the battle, an incident of which there is no trace in the French original. There is a great resem-blance between Wolfram's 'Willehalm' and the crusading poems of the twelfth century. It was no wonder that the knights of the Teutonic Order esteemed this poem more than any other.

The poem is incomplete. The last thing narrated is how Wille-halm provided for a worthy burial to the fallen heathen, **Death of** according to their own rites. Soon after dictating **Wolfram,** Willehalm's noble words, the poet himself probably **circa 1220.** died. Wolfram is thought to have died in 1220, when he must have been close upon sixty years old. In 'Willehalm' we seem to trace a failing of power. He probably began it before 1216, and worked at 'Parzival' chiefly during the first decade of the thirteenth century. Wolfram was buried in the Frauenkirche at Eschenbach, and as late as the year 1608, a citizen of Nürnberg, Hans Wilhelm Kress, could still read on the tombstone the inscription: 'Hie ligt der streng Ritter herr Wolfram von Eschenbach ein Meister Singer.'

Wolfram's grave.

Successors of the Great Chivalrous Poets.

The master-works of chivalrous epic poetry appeared in quick succession between 1190 and 1220, in the following order: Hartmann's 'Ereck,' 'St. Gregory,' 'Armer Heinrich' and 'Iwein,' the first part of 'Parzival,' Gottfried's 'Tristan,' the second part of 'Parzival,' and Wolfram's 'Willehalm.' Side by side with the greater minds smaller geniuses successfully established their claims. The division between the religious and the secular view of life, which was so marked in the eleventh and twelfth centuries, had gradually disappeared, and among the poets of this period it is impossible to infer from the rank or position of the writer what the tendency of his poetry will be. The knight Hartmann composes a sacred legend, the knight Wolfram has religious aims, the burgher Gottfried is a pure child of the world. The Swiss Ulrich von Zetzikon, the author of a frivolous Arthurian Romance, 'Lanzelet,' was a priest at Lommis, in Thurgau. He imitated Hartmann's 'Ereck,' but adhered more closely than Hartmann to the popular style. The Austrian knight Konrad von Fussesbrunnen applied the new art of chivalrous poetry to the charming idyll of the childhood of Christ, as told in the apocryphal gospels. The Franconian knight, Wirent von Grafenberg, who imitated, first Hartmann, and then Wolfram, tried in his 'Wigalois' to introduce a religious element into the Arthurian romance, and made the chief enemy of the hero a heathen, and the hero himself a kind of Crusader. The Austrian Stricker a man of the bourgeois class, wrote many fables tales, and farces, and composed an Arthurian romance, 'Daniel von Blumenthal,' in which the love ad-

Ulrich von Zedzikon and Konrad von Fussesbrunnen.

Wirent von Grafenberg.

Stricker.

ventures occupy a secondary position, and the descriptions of fighting preponderate; he also turned the 'Rolandslied' into smooth, elegant verse. Unlike Stricker, the some- Konrad what worldly poets Konrad Fleck and Ulrich von Fleck and dem Türlin were of noble birth. Konrad Fleck of Ulrich von Allemannia related the story of the child-love of Flor dem Türlin. and Blancheflur, dwelling specially, in true German spirit, on their faithfulness to each other, and showing as strict regard for etiquette as Hartmann. Ulrich von dem Türlin, a Carinthian, wrote a long and somewhat dreary epic, entitled 'The Crown of Adventures' ('Der Abenteuer Krone'), and thereby introduced the Arthurian romance into the South-East districts of Germany. His coarse and realistic style bears witness to the lower level of chivalrous culture in the circles for which he wrote. All these poets follow the example of the great masters in choosing some foreign Characteris- original for the basis of their works; most of them turn tics of these French poems into German couplets, and think that later poets. what they are telling is true history. In the thirteenth century, however, many poets followed in the steps of the old minstrels, who in their stories of King Rother, Morold, Orendel, St. Oswald, allowed their imagination to get the better of tradition. They appeal to some book which they pretend to have found in an out-of-the-way place, and seek by this device to secure the desired authority for their works, for palpable inventions would have found no audience at that time. They thus really followed their own inspirations without being able to free themselves entirely from the spell of tradition. They mainly exercised their invention in new combinations of approved ideas and incidents, drawn chiefly from the Arthurian legends, but also from the heroic poetry, from 'Parzival' and from other poems. The name of the hero often shows what poem has served as their model. 'Daniel von Blumenthal' finds a successor in 'Garel vom blühenden Thal.' Wigalois is replaced by Wigamur, the knight with the lion by the knight with the eagle, or even the knight with the goat. Elements derived from the Arthurian Romances were introduced into the heroic legends; the institution of the Round Table was attributed to Apollonius of Tyre, a hero of Greek romance. Eastern subjects connected with the crusades,

N

elopements, and conversions of the heathen were again revived, and the marvels of 'Herzog Ernst' were combined with the marvels of Celtic legends.

But the reality of everyday life also began to assert its claims and history gained new favour. The twelfth-century poem of 'Graf Rudolf,' which connected romantic incidents with real Historical events in the history of the kingdom of Jerusalem, romances. found imitation in a series of semi-historical romances. The scene of these romances is generally laid in some well-known part of Europe or Asia, and they either describe real historical incidents, or narrate the deeds of valour and marvellous adventures of the fabled ancestors of some German reigning family. The style of narrative in these romances is sometimes very realistic, and all the incidents seem to reflect conditions of contemporary life.

The newly awakened historical interest showed itself in yet another direction. There was a greater demand for historical information, such as had been supplied by the 'Kaiserchronik.' Chronicles. The 'Kaiserchronik' itself was continued down to 1250, to Rudolph von Habsburg. Alexander the Great and the Trojan war found new historians, and several universal chronicles appeared which began by versifying the Old Testament, then advanced to the New, and arrived by great bounds at Charlemagne or Frederick II. Many rhymed chronicles were also produced, narrating in German verse the history of convents, towns, or provinces, dry records of fact as a rule, but sometimes showing real Ottokar's epic talent. In this class of literature the palm belongs to Meister Ottokar of Styria, who relates the History of Germany. fortunes of Germany in the latter half of the thirteenth and beginning of the fourteenth century from the political standpoint of a Styrian noble, and delights us by an astonishing wealth of information. He has great powers of narrative, and writes with still greater art. In this respect he is certainly one of the greatest German historians. He applied to the writing of history the art of narrative, which had been developed in the chivalrous epics. The knowledge of the inner life of men which had been gained through the introspective poetry of the

chivalrous classical period, the power of drawing character or revealing it in characteristic actions, was here applied to the writing
of history.   Thanks to the realistic tendencies of this later period,
we gain from this history many welcome details of manners, costumes, and ways of life.   The Bavarian plain-spokenness, which had
already shown itself in the satirical writings of the twelfth century,
imparts great vigour to the descriptions.   We see that the knightly
taste for tournaments and festivals still continued, and that the service of women still exerted its ennobling influence.   Ottokar and
many of these later poets are fond of appealing to the genius of
Wolfram and Gottfried, and wishing that these poets could come
to their aid when they are in difficulties; but if placed side by
side with such great masters these lesser writers would be totally
eclipsed.

   The poems of Wolfram and Gottfried furnished much work for
their successors, for ' Tristan ' and ' Willehalm,' as we have noticed,
were both left unfinished.   Two poets tried their hand at a continuation of 'Tristan,' the better of the two, as late as 1300.   A conclusion
was added to ' Willehalm,' and also an introduction narrating the
carrying off of Giburg, the former being borrowed from a French
source, and the latter due to the author's imagination.   Gottfried's
In general Gottfried's school pursued the old conscien-   and
tious method of seeking some authority for what they   Wolfram's
wrote, so as not to seem to be telling anything untrue.   disciples.
Wolfram's disciples on the contrary gave free rein to their imagination.
Gottfried's school flourished in Allemannia, while Wolfram found
his followers in Bavaria.   Gottfried's successors aimed at elegance
and clearness, which however often degenerated into trivial verbosity; Wolfram's disciples strove to be intellectual and thoughtful,
and easily became obscure and affected.   Gottfried's school produced poets who were something more than mere imitators, such
as Rudolf von Ems and Konrad von Würzburg; Wolfram's
disciples preferred to conceal themselves behind their great master
and speak in his name.   But while Gottfried's fame declined with
the decline of that elegant culture which was his chief characteristic,
Wolfram's reputation lived on, partly owing to the fact that the
bad qualities of his successors, who were confounded with himself,

appealed to the taste of a period which could no longer appreciate the true worth of this great poet.

Rudolf von Ems and Konrad von Würzburg are far from
Rudolf von Ems and Konrad von Würzburg. adopting the purely worldly principles of their master. Both have something honest and sterling about them, the knight Rudolf still more than the bourgeois Konrad. Each again formed a school of his own, setting an example to lesser poets, and doing good service to German literature in preserving the tradition of cultivated form and refined language.

The object of Rudolf von Ems seems to be rather to instruct
Rudolf's 'Guter Gerhard.' and edify than to entertain. His 'Guter Gerhard,' which preaches self-sacrifice and humility, is the story of a merchant of Cologne, who ransoms Christian prisoners from the heathen and refuses the Crown of England.
His 'Barlaam and Josaphat.' His 'Barlaam and Josaphat' inculcates renunciation of the world and voluntary poverty. It is the story of an Indian prince Josaphat, who is converted to Christianity by the hermit Barlaam, resists all temptations, gives up his throne, and himself turns hermit[1]. His 'Wilhelm von Or-
Works of history. lens' is a realistic semi-historical romance of the kind described above. His 'Alexander,' his lost 'Trojan War,' his 'Universal Chronicle,' which he only brought down as far as Solomon, are records of profane and sacred history.

Rudolf probably began to write about the year 1225; he was somehow connected with the champions of the Hohenstaufen party in Germany, and his universal chronicle is dedicated to Konrad IV, in whose train he went to Italy, where he died between 1251 and 1254.

Konrad von Würzburg went by Strasburg to Basle, where he
Konrad von Würzburg's 'Frau Welt,' circa 1250. married and settled, and where he died in 1287, at the same time as his wife and daughters, probably from some epidemic. He probably began his literary career about the middle of the thirteenth century with that poem of 'Lady World,' which we have already mentioned,

---

[1] This story really originated in India, and contains in fact the narrative of the life of Buddha.

whose hero was Wirent von Grafenberg. (Cf. p. 72.) Gottfried's influence on him is not very marked. Konrad was gifted with great fluency, and he generally worked up his poetic material in a rather mechanical fashion. His poetry is full of empty padding, there is no end to the long descriptions and speeches, and it is only here and there that we are pleased by a good simile or a well-described situation. Konrad's culture must have been acquired in some monastery-school. He related in verse some of those German legends of which the eleventh and twelfth **His German** centuries produced so many in Latin, (cf. pp. 84–88,) **legends.** the stories of Otto with the beard, of the Swan-knight, and of the devoted friends Engelhart and Dietrich. But at Basle he also wrote sacred legends at the commission of nobles **The** and burghers, and in the 'Goldene Schmiede' he put **'Goldene** forth his highest powers to sing the praises of the **Schmiede.'** Virgin Mary. Out of all the fantastic images and epithets which pious worship of the mother of God and curious enquiry about the mystery of the Incarnation had piled up for centuries, Konrad, like a skilful goldsmith, as the title of his work implies, has made a sparkling crown for the head of the queen of heaven. His 'Partonopier und Meliur,' on the contrary, is a **'Partono-** true French romance, full of tournaments, conflicts with **pier und** the heathen, and tender love-scenes, the best of which **Meliur.'** reminds us of Cupid and Psyche. Lastly, he too was haunted by the mediæval ghost of the Iliad, which we have already noticed as a characteristic of the Middle Ages, and concocted a poem on the Trojan war, drawn from Benoit de St. More and various classical sources ; death prevented him from finishing this work, which was continued by a later poet to the length of nearly 50,000 lines. Konrad also wrote lyrical poems, mostly **Lyrical** roundelays, in which he displayed a marvellous power **poems.** of rhyming. The thoughts embodied in these poems are for the most part very trivial, and they contain hardly any of the poet's personal experiences. Konrad repeatedly tells us that the times are unfavourable to poetry, and that the patronage which the art required was declining. · And he could give us no stronger proof of this than his own actual endeavour to make clear

to an unappreciative audience the utility of the poetic art. Poetry,
he says, benefits the ear, the heart, the tongue ; it sounds pleasant
to the ear, it lends courtly breeding to the heart, and imparts eloquence to the tongue. He himself would sing like the nightingale,
'Klage der even if no one listened to him. His 'Complaint of
Kunst.' Art,' which deals with the same subject, is written as
an allegory—a form of poetry which recurs again and again in later
literature, and which found favour even as late as the sixteenth
century. The poet is led by Imagination to a beautiful spot in a
wood, which he describes in charming language. There he finds
a gathering of noble ladies : Justice, who wears the crown, Truth,
Mercy, Loyalty, Steadfastness, Generosity, Honour, Modesty, and
Chastity, in fact all the cardinal virtues of chivalry. Lady Art
appears before Justice in a torn robe ; she has been struck by the
arrow of Poverty, and brings a complaint against Generosity for
having withdrawn her aid from true Art. After a long discussion
the accusation is of course found to be just, and everyone is exhorted to lend their support to true Art.

Rudolf and Konrad stand, both intellectually and artistically, on
The later a far lower level than their chosen master, Gottfried.
'Titurel' by Another poem of this period, a later ' Titurel,' which
Albrecht. for a long time was taken for a work of Wolfram von
Eschenbach's, is equally inferior to the work of the real Wolfram.
In this uninteresting epic, full of single combats, wars, tournaments,
and sea-voyages, the songs of Wolfram's 'Titurel' have been
worked up and enlarged into a complete history of Schionatulander
and Sigune. The object of the writer is evidently to complete
Wolfram's Parzival ; all that is merely hinted at there is here
carried out in detail ; the race of the Grail-sovereigns is traced
back to Troy, the position of the Grail-castle is fixed in Spain, and
the Grail itself is finally transported to India. The author speaks
as though he were Wolfram himself ; at the same time he does not
really wish to be taken for Wolfram, for he makes no secret of the
fact that the materials which he uses were fifty years old. His
real name was Albrecht, he had relations with Duke Ludwig the
Stern, and wrote between 1260 and 1270. He knew his Wolfram
well, and was not shy of decking himself in his master's feathers. But

he also appeals to Homer, Aristotle, Hippocrates, and Avicenna, and he is really well acquainted with many secular and religious writings to which he refers. He is a very learned man, and loves to display his learning. He ranks the priestly order the highest of all, but immediately after them he places the scholars, then the men of high nobility, and far below these the knights. He is a faithful and enthusiastic servant of the church, and makes his heroes and heroines pray to the Virgin Mary, fast, confess, seek indulgence and found monasteries, become hermits, monks and nuns, spread Christianity by fire and sword, and generally increase the power of the hierarchy. Albrecht condemns and despises the savage, mad heathen and the barbarian Greeks, who, according to him, worship cattle. And this poet actually ventures to speak in the name of Wolfram, who could not read or write, who prided himself on his knighthood, who spoke so kindly of the heathen, who made his Parzival attain salvation only through inward conversion, and in whose works there appears no trace of Mariolatry! But the pious and intolerant spirit of Albrecht's work recommended it to the clergy, while the fighting and interludes of love found favour with the knights; the obscurity and vagueness of style were taken for depth of thought, and thus the success of the poem was assured.

At the end of Wolfram's 'Parzival' a slight allusion is made to the history of Parzival's son Loherangrin, who was carried by a swan to Antwerp, where he landed and became the husband of the much-admired princess of Brabant, on the condition that she should never ask who he was; but she breaks the agreement, and he is therefore obliged to depart; the swan with its boat comes to fetch him, and takes him home again to the Grail. The author of the later 'Titurel' also mentions Loherangrin, and tells of his second marriage and his death. Konrad von Würzburg treats the same legend in his 'Schwanritter,' but without naming the knight, and without introducing any connection with the Grail. In a Bavarian poem, written before the year 1290, a detailed history of Loherangrin or Lohengrin is put in the mouth of Wolfram von Eschenbach himself. In this poem Lohengrin is made to fight with Friedrich von Telramund in the presence of

Legend of Lohengrin.

Bavarian poem on the subject, before 1290.

King Henry I, for the possession of Elsa of Brabant. He takes
part in the Hungarian wars of this prince, fights against
the Saracens, and after his return to the Grail, the poem gives us a
short sketch of German history down to Henry II; the historical
tendency and the everlasting theme of the Crusades here too assert
their power. The treatment is realistic, and the poem reflects the
spirit of Wolfram rather than that of the later Titurel. It was enlarged by subsequent additions, like a popular ballad, and was later
on entirely remodelled under the name of 'Lorengel.'

Wolfram's influence can be traced still further in Bavaria.
Hadamar Hadamar von Laber, a Bavarian, wrote, about the
von Laber's year 1340, an allegory called 'Die Jagd,' which en-
allegory, joyed great popularity and was repeatedly imitated.
'Die Jagd.' The 'Chase' which he describes is courtship, and his
heart is the dog which leads him on the track of the game. Joy,
constancy, faithfulness, desire, and other emotions of the mind are
likewise represented as dogs, and thus under the image of a chase
a little romance is unfolded before us. Though the idea may seem
strange to us, and though its childish ingenuity may appeal but
little to our more critical taste, yet we must acknowledge that there
is a breath of Wolfram's freshness throughout the poem, and that
the author shows love of nature, reverence for women, and independence of mind. An older sportsman directs the young huntsman
towards the things which are eternal, but the youth answers in words
something like these: 'I should like to set myself free from the
world, if I had only the favour of the one woman whose love seems
to me the highest happiness.' The secular view of life here shines
out once more in a noble light, in contrast with the general decay
of the refined manners and lofty sentiments embodied in the
chivalrous epics.

Clerical intolerance was beginning to make its appearance even
Revival of in Wolfram's own school. The Bavarian priests were
clerical not idle, and their influence is clearly discernible, for
influence. instance, in a long epic in praise of St. George, written
Religious about this time by a knightly imitator of Wolfram. In
poems.
Austria various religious poems appeared about the
year 1300, while in Allemannia Konrad's sacred legends and praises

of the Virgin were much copied. A knight of the Teutonic order, Hugo von Langenstein, narrated the history of the martyrdom of St. Martina (1293) in a poem of nearly 33,000 lines; the life of the Virgin was also a favourite subject. In central Germany, a writer influenced by the example of Rudolf von Ems made two great collections of sacred legends in verse, extending over several thousand lines, and an imitator of Konrad von Würzburg wrote a life of St. Elizabeth and a poem on the Redemption. Yet a third writer from this district related the Assumption of the Virgin, and warned men against worldly love, exhorting them to devote their affections entirely to the Queen of Heaven : this noble lady, he says, will not require them to write dance-songs for her or to risk their lives in tournament. In Cologne too the writing of sacred legends was much cultivated, and a leading citizen of Magdeburg, Bruno von Schonebeck, translated the Song of Solomon in the year 1276. Finally, in Prussia the Teutonic knights, besides recording the deeds of their order, made many verse and prose translations from the Bible.

If we include under the title of artistic epics, as contrasted with popular epics, all those narrative poems which are not based on national tradition, on early German legends, then we may say that the Middle High-German artistic epic begins in the eleventh century with the poetical paraphrase of the first book of Moses, and ends about 1350 with the Chronicle of the Teutonic order by Nicolas of Jeroschin, with Henry of Munich's Universal Chronicle, and the 'Alexandreis' of the Austrian Seifried. Period of Middle High-German Artistic Epics, circa 1050-1350.

The movement began with the clergy, was carried on by the minstrels, and the knights were its classical representatives. But the clergy and the mechanical poets akin to the old minstrels, come again into prominence at the close of this period. The aristocratic names which we begin to meet with in German literature about the year 1170 become rarer after 1250, and then their bearers generally appear only as writers of sacred legends. About the year 1200 a few great poets succeeded in developing a truly individual style of writing; their successors Summary.

borrowed, now from one, now from the other of these great writers whatever suited them, and even this eclecticism was better than the crude and mechanical manufacture of verses which set in about the year 1300. Artistic poetry had been developed from the sermon, and the biblical and sacred legendary poetry of this later period was tending more and more to return to the style of the sermon. The movement had started from religious and didactic subjects, and to these subjects it returned again.

CHAPTER VII.

'Good morrow to both bad and good,' sang Walther von der
Vogelweide, referring to the guests assembled at the Court of
Landgrave Hermann of Thuringia. Wolfram von Eschenbach
laments the same mixture of company at this court, and another
time Walther exclaims, 'Let anyone with sensitive ears avoid
the court of Thuringia, for crowds are always passing **Poetry at**
in and out there by day and night, and it is a wonder **the court of**
that any man keeps his hearing amid such a din.' **Landgrave**
Walther repeatedly praises the generous hospitality **Hermann of**
of the Landgrave, and says : 'If a cart-load of wine **Thuringia.**
cost a thousand pounds, he would allow no knight's goblet to
stand empty.'

Though this hospitality was not very discriminating, yet the
best might profit by it; Walther and Wolfram enjoyed it, as did
Heinrich von Veldeke before them. It was at the commission
of Landgrave Hermann that Herbert von Fritzlar wrote his
'Trojan War,' and Wolfram von Eschenbach his **The 'Wart-**
'Willehalm.' We still possess love-songs written by **burg-krieg.'**
Hermann's son-in-law, Duke Henry of Anhalt; yet another love-
poet, the so-called 'virtuous writer,' appears in Hermann's immediate circle, and we may be sure that the popular singers were
not absent. The Thuringian Court stands in the first rank of
those which have at various times patronised German poetry.
The poem of the 'Wartburg-krieg,' describing a contest among a
number of poets, shows clearly that the glorious times when Landgrave Hermann held his court on the Wartburg and patronised

singers, were treasured up in the memory of later popular poets. In this poem Heinrich von Ofterdingen, a writer whose works are unknown to us, is made to praise the Duke of Austria as the first among princes. The 'virtuous writer' opposes him, giving the first place to the Landgrave. Wolfram von Eschenbach also declares in the Landgrave's favour, and Walther von der Vogelweide does the same in so artful a manner that Ofterdingen is apparently conquered.

The strange poem which bears the title of the 'Wartburg-krieg' is composed of the most various elements, the Bavarian poem of 'Lohengrin' even being one of its appendages; it was not written merely in praise of Hermann of Thuringia, but chiefly to glorify Wolfram von Eschenbach, and it proves to us how the fame of this great poet lived on among the wandering gleemen. The magician Klinschor of Wolfram's 'Parzival,' with whom Gawan comes into contact, is transformed in the 'Wartburg-krieg,' under the name of Klingsor of Hungary, into a contemporary of Wolfram's, a necromancer and astronomer, in reality a representative of clerical book-learning. He propounds riddles, which Wolfram easily guesses, and he calls hell to his aid, but Wolfram easily vanquishes the Devil. The simple layman defeats the learned clerk.

The poem of the 'Wartburg-krieg' still takes up a hostile position towards the Church, and attacks the covetousness of the clergy. But in its style we notice the same learned obscurity which characterised so many of Wolfram's followers, and which soon assumed a clerical colouring, as we have already seen in the later 'Titurel.'

The sounds of feasting had long since died away at the court of Thuringia. The days of Landgrave Hermann were followed by those of his daughter-in-law, St. Elizabeth. Knightly games, Poetry again dancing, and entertaining, were succeeded by fasting, assumes a mortification, and works of mercy. Wolfram, the religious friend of the heathen, was followed by Konrad of character. Marburg, the condemner of heretics. The preacher took the place of the gleeman, as we shall see in the lyric and didactic poetry which we are now about to consider.

We have noticed the first blossoming of the 'Minnesang,' the troubadour-poetry of Germany, on the Lower Rhine and in Thuringia, and have become acquainted with the lyric poets, Heinrich von Veldeke and Heinrich von Morungen, Friedrich von Hausen and Reinmar von Hagenau. The art of the troubadours spread from the Rhine down the Danube, from Swabia to Bavaria and Austria. Wolfram von Eschenbach had Bavarian predecessors in the domain of love-poetry. But Austria carried off the palm, for it was there that the greatest lyric poet of the Middle Ages learnt his art. Walther von der Vogelweide was of noble birth, and yet a wandering singer; he was a follower of Reinmar von Hagenau, and at the same time a disciple of the best among the gleemen; he wrote the most charming love-songs and also serious religious poetry. He was a chivalrous poet and at the same time a popular successor of the Latin poets of the twelfth century, a successor of the Arch-poet in his patriotic struggle against the encroachments of the papacy and the abuses of the Church.

The 'Minne-sang' on the LowerRhine, the Upper Rhine, and in Bavaria and Austria.

WALTHER VON DER VOGELWEIDE.

On the 12th of November, 1203, a travelling bishop, stopping at Zeisselmauer on the Danube, gave a sum of money to the singer Walther von der Vogelweide to buy him a fur coat. In the year 1215, an Italian canon, Thomasin von Zirclaria, who himself made some attempts in German poetry, accused Walther von der Vogelweide of leading the people astray, of befooling thousands by one of his poems, and making them disobedient to God and to the commands of the Pope.

Walther was only a wandering gleeman, yet his voice was heard far and wide through Germany. He was considered a powerful enemy, and his friendship was probably much sought after. He lived at a time when poetry was a great force, and his songs flew through the world like a pamphlet which everyone reads, or like an eloquent speech printed by all the newspapers. Walther was probably born in Austria, and found a patron in Duke Friedrich the

Walther, a wandering gleeman.

Catholic, of the house of Babenberg. When his protector died
in Palestine, in 1198, Walther left Vienna and tried his fortune as
a political singer. He was singer to Philip of Swabia, to Otto IV,
and Frederick II; we can trace the course of his life from 1198 to
Walther 1227, and his poetical career began at the latest in 1187.
a political His songs celebrated important events in German his-
poet. tory. We cannot fairly criticise his change of political
opinions and his transference of allegiance from one emperor to
another; for at this distance of years, we have no means of estimat-
ing the motives and actions of men in those times of civil war, when
each party only fought for the upper hand. Personal advantage
was no doubt a powerful motive in Walther's case. In those
simple times men did not mind openly acknowledging egoistical
interests, and Walther evidently feels no shame in begging for
presents and reminding people of their promises to him, while
he also thankfully acknowledges the favours he has received.
Walther's heart's desire was to have a home of his own. He
His wander- had relations not only with the Emperors, but with
ing life. many German princes, having been a visitor at the
courts of Austria, Thuringia, Meissen, Bavaria, Carinthia, and
Aquileja; he had travelled from the Seine to the Mur, from the Po
to the Trave, but nowhere could he find a fixed dwelling-place;
not one of these princes and patrons gave him a home, and the
greatest lyric poet of the time was long condemned to be a
vagabond and a beggar. At length the emperor Frederick II
satisfied his desire, and gave him a small fief, probably in Würzburg. The poor fellow cannot restrain his joy at this, and
exclaims in one of his poems: ' I have a fief, hearken all the world,
I have a fief!'

This wandering minstrel who gained his livelihood, and that
but a meagre one, by the favour of his patrons, may, under the
pressure of necessity, have changed his party, if that simply meant
changing his patron, but he never changed his principles. He
was always a good patriot, a religious man, and an enemy of
the Pope. He loved and admired his country and has sung its
praises in a celebrated poem. No other country, he says, has
pleased him so much; German manners surpass all others; the

men are well educated, the women are like angels. 'Let him
who seeks virtue and pure love,' he exclaims, 'come   Walther's
to our country: much joy is there; oh, may I long   patriotism.
live in it!' True, he was not able to retain throughout his
life this happy view of the world around him; evil years came,
years in which chivalry decayed in Germany, and the poet might
well ask himself whether his life was all a dream, whether everything that he had held sacred and true had been really but a
delusion. Yet, even in the touching elegy where he expresses
his grief at the change in his fatherland, it is still the enthusiastic
patriot whose voice we hear, and his grief flows from his love.
His sorrow for his country is combined with pious sentiment, and
his heart is set on a journey to the Holy Land. There was an older
German poet, unknown to us by name, who, like Walther, lamented
his wretchedness, longed for a home of his own, praised his patrons
and at the same time confessed his personal faults; this poet
afterwards took to exhorting his contemporaries, sang about all
the sacred subjects of Christian doctrine, and quite adopted the
religious view of the world. In later life Walther's poetry likewise
assumed a religious colouring, and he wrote, in solemn measures,
a declaration of his faith and a confession of his sins; he sang of
the Holy Trinity, of the Virgin Mary and of Christ's   Religious
crucifixion; declared all men fools who did not seek   and didactic
temporal happiness and eternal salvation from the   character of
Virgin and her Son, and discouraged as vain all   his later
speculations about the nature of God. He implores   poetry.
the blessing of heaven in a morning-prayer full of childish piety.
Walther is far removed from the frivolity of the Arch-poet. He
wrote special poems in reproof of intemperance, and with true
moral seriousness he insisted upon a right medium in all things.
He who conquers himself seems to him the true hero, for such
an one has really overcome a lion and a giant. A man's character must be firm as a stone, in loyalty smooth and straight
like an arrow. Walther attacks the double-tongued, the liars
and deceivers. He knows the value of friendship, and esteems it
higher than relationship; 'let the smile of a friend,' he says, 'be true
and without falseness, clear as the evening glow which prophesies

a fine morrow.' Walther specially notes that the striving after gold and riches, as well as extreme wealth or extreme poverty, exercises a demoralising effect on a man. In his old age he exerted his influence to forward the Crusade of Frederick II, and wrote pious marching-songs for the army. He turned from earthly to heavenly love, and took leave of Lady World whom he had served so long.

But all his piety does not prevent his looking at things from a free human stand-point, and distinguishing Christianity itself from its official representatives. This homeless roving singer is an enlightened apostle of humanity and toleration; he knows **His liberal** and declares that death makes master and servant **views.** equal, and that Christians, Jews, and heathens serve one and the same God. He scorns the belief in dreams, demands liberal education, tells princes their duties, and vindicates the **His hostility** rights of the German people against papal preten- **to the** sions. He ascribes the Civil War then raging in **Papacy.** Germany to papal machinations, and calls the pope the new Judas, characterising him as a servant of the devil, who wishes to deliver over all Christendom to his master. He reminds him of the curse which he as Pope had pronounced against all the emperor's enemies at his coronation, and says he had thereby cursed himself. Walther opposes any interference of the clergy at all in secular affairs, and quotes in reference to this Christ's words about the tribute-money: 'Render to Cæsar the things that are Cæsar's, and to God the things that are God's.' He considers the secular power of the pope a poison which has entered into the Church; 'Christendom,' he says, 'lies in the hospital, and waits in vain for a healing drink from Rome. The Pope himself increases infidelity, for he leads the clergy by the devil's rein; they are full of vices, they do not practise what they preach, and he who is a Christian in words only, not in deeds, is really half a heathen.'

All those poems of Walther's which refer to public affairs, **Walther's** or express his own principles, are generally called **'Sprüche.'** 'Sprüche' (sayings, proverbs). They are all short and easy to remember, songs of one verse, probably accompanied by a pleasing and easy melody, so that they could wander from mouth to mouth like an anecdote or an epigram. They are as interesting as a fable, as pregnant as a proverb, and often entirely calculated for popular effect. Many of these 'Sprüche' may be reduced to one leading proposition, which is sometimes contained in the opening line, sometimes to be inferred at the close; a few furnish a short illustration of the main statement. A 'Spruch' written in favour of the election of Philip of Swabia as emperor gradually works up to the final challenge to the German people: 'Place then the crown on Philip's head.' Walther wishes to express his thought in the most graphic form, and in doing this he does not mind exaggeration. Inward moods are expressed by outward symptoms; instead of saying, 'I was grieved,' Walther says: 'My haughty crane's steps changed into dragging peacock's steps, I let my head hang down to my knees.' A general truth is, if possible, brought home to us in a concrete instance, and many similar experiences are reduced to one typical form. As an instance of the former we may mention the 'Spruch' beginning: 'Ich sass auf einem Steine.'

Some of the 'Sprüche' are purely narrative, as, for instance, the one on King Philip's Christmas feast at Magdeburg; or the story may be told for the sake of its symbolic meaning, as in the case of Christ and the tribute-money. But in many of them only the opening lines are narrative, in order to give the poem a more popular character, as in the one mentioned above, 'Ich sass auf einem Steine,' or, 'Ich hört' ein Wasser rauschen,' or, 'König Constantin der gab so viel.' Sometimes the narrative element is combined with the dramatic, as in the poem: 'Ich hörte fern in einer Zelle lauten Jammerruf,' where Walther puts his complaint about the pope into the mouth of a holy hermit. Great dramatic effect is also attained by Walther's manner of directly addressing the emperor, the pope, the princes and other persons, or even lifeless objects. In one poem he addresses Lady World, while in another he attacks the 'gift-staves,' in which Innocent III. caused money to be collected for the Crusade; 'Say on, Sir Stick,' he exclaims, 'hath the pope sent thee hither to make him rich and to plunder the Germans?' The gist of this 'Spruch' is given in

the conclusion: 'Sir Stick, thou art 'sent hither for an evil purpose, to seek out foolish men and women in Germany.' But
Walther's boldest attempt at dramatizing is seen in the poem where
he dares to introduce the pope in the midst of his Italian subjects,
laughing and scoffing at the Germans, and boasting of his shrewd
policy: 'I have put two Germans under one crown, so that
they may devastate the land. Meanwhile, we can fill our coffers.'
Bitter hatred dictated this 'Spruch,' and a more stirring epigram
was probably never written. Here the people's poet becomes in
truth the people's leader, or the people's misleader, according to
the words of the Italian canon quoted above. The gleeman here
becomes the demagogue.

In his 'Sprüche' Walther followed in the steps of the gleemen,
while he wielded a power attained by no popular singer before
or since. But in his love-lyrics it is the knight who is speaking
throughout. Some of the qualities, however, which distinguish him
in his 'Sprüche' appear again, as far as the subject and the
artistic form will allow, in his lyrics. He is lively, realistic, and
plain-spoken, sometimes even to excess; he introduces narrative
and dramatic effects, and proves himself in all these respects a true
son of the Bavarian stock.

In Austria and Bavaria, the Minnesang of the nobles sprang
from the popular love-songs. Even at the present
day the inhabitants of the Bavarian and Austrian
highlands are distinguished by their gift of bold improvisation in song, and we may look upon this as
an inheritance from older times. Love-songs are
a universal heritage, and if conveyed in a happy
simile, or a pregnant expression, they may continue to live for
centuries. 'Thou art mine, I am thine;' this thought is common
to all poetry, and we find it expressed with a pretty simile in
a short German popular lyric of the twelfth century:

> 'Du bist mîn, ich bin dîn:
> Des solt du gewis sîn.
> Du bist beslozzen
> In minem herzen,
> Verlorn ist daz slüzzelin:
> Du muost immer drinne sîn.'

Margin note: Popular character of the Minne-sang in Austria and Bavaria.

The German popular love-ditties were wafted into the castles of the nobles. The unnoticed impromptu jests of an earlier time were, in the twelfth century, developed into short songs, which the newly-awakened artistic consciousness of the aristocracy admired and appropriated.

About the end of the twelfth century a knight called Küren- berg, from the neighbourhood of Linz on the Danube; Ritter von invented a four-lined stanza of easy construction, Kürenberg. which became the fashionable form for improvised verses, and remained for a long time in such favour on the banks of the Danube, that it was even adopted by the writers of the Nibelungen songs.

Later on, a Burggraf of Regensburg sang similar simple songs in kindred forms of verse. These are the only names Burggraf von of lyric poets known to us in this early period; little Regensburg. has been preserved from this spring-tide of the national Minne- sang, but the little which we have ranks among the best produc- tions of mediæval lyric poetry; even in the present day the simple words appeal forcibly to our hearts, and the conventional forms of chivalrous intercourse prove no hindrance to our appre- ciation.

Woman's love is represented in these early poems as quite different in character from man's. The social supre- The early macy of noble women is not yet recognised, and the Minne- man woos with proud self-respect: 'I will share joy singers. and sorrow with thee; so long as I live thou shall remain dear to me, for I would not wish thee to love a bad man.' Another refuses himself to a woman who desired his love. A third warns his mis- tress, whom he loves secretly, to hide her real self from the world like a star in the clouds, and to pretend to let her eyes rest favour- ably on others. A fourth boasts of his triumphs: 'Women,' says he, 'are as easily tamed as falcons.' Sometimes a lady is introduced by a slight description, and then made to express her sentiments, as in the poem attributed to Dietmar von Aist, beginning: 'Es stuont ein frouwe alleine, Und warte über heide.' In another song a lady tells how she tamed a falcon, but he flew away from her and now wears other chains. Love of nature is interwoven with the tender passion; the joy of summer is not thought complete without the lover's presence, and his love is compared to the rose.

In these early lyrics the women are tender, devoted, and anxious; they alone know the sorrows and the tears of love. But all this was changed as French influence gradually **Triumph of French influence in the later Minnesongs.** asserted itself in life and poetry. Even in the Austrian songs mentioned above, the spies, the eavesdroppers (*merker*) are beginning to appear as the enemies of all lovers, and secret love is already praised as the only true love; Tristan and Isolde became more and more the type of all true lovers, and the relation between women and men, such as we find it in these older songs, soon became inverted. In the later Minnesongs it is the women who are proud and the men who must languish. The women have gained the upper hand, and the relation of a lover to his lady is like that of a vassal to his lord: he must serve her, and though he looks for a reward for his service, yet it is but seldom that he receives the smallest favour at her hand. Love gained in moral purity, but love-poetry lost its life and freshness, and became monotonous and affected, as in Reinmar von Hagenau's compositions (see p. 147). But Bavaria and Austria never quite followed the fashion of the day; in these countries popular tradition still asserted its power. Wolfram's 'Tagelieder' with their epic and dramatic elements and their ballad-like character, are closely related to certain popular forms of song. The Austrian Dietmar von **Dietmar von Aist.** Aist in his songs does at least sue for the hand of the lady, towards whom he assumes the attitude of a servant. He says he is subject to her control as the ship is to the hand of the steersman ; his feelings are more sensitive than hers, or at least he pretends that they are ; he cannot sleep at night, and thinks he must die of love. But his wooing never remains unrewarded; the women all long for him, each grudges him to the other, and he seems to be a veritable Don Juan, hurrying from one conquest to another.

At the time when Dietmar flourished, Walther must have begun to write, and Reinmar von Hagenau must have already come to

Austria. Reinmar found a friendly reception at the court of Vienna, and wrote a beautiful poem there on the death of Duke Leopold V (1194) in the form of a lament put into the mouth of the dead prince's widow. Reinmar exercised a visible influence on Walther; in his clever conversational poetry Walther is following in Reinmar's steps. But though there are some con- necting links between them, the difference between the two is also very apparent. Exaggerated feeling was little in harmony with the healthy common sense and cheerful wit of the Austrians. When Reinmar spoke of cherishing his long, sweet love-sorrow like a tender plant, he is sure to have excited ridicule in Austria. And though Walther follows Reinmar's example in many points, though he says he does not weary of long and fruitless wooing, though he calls love a sweet distress and a treasure-house of all virtues, yet he would never think of regarding the sorrow of love as its highest glory. Reinmar writes : ' I am suing for that which comprises all joys that a man can ever have in this world—namely a woman ;' but Walther is not so absorbed in the service of women; for him the world has other joys and duties besides. In one passage he directly ridiculed Reinmar's sentimentality and the exaggerated ingenuity of his style. Reinmar wishes to exalt his lady above all others ; Walther, on the contrary, says quite candidly to his beloved: ' Perhaps others are better, but you are good.' He does not wish to force the virtues of his lady upon anyone's attention; let everyone praise his own, or as he himself expresses it : ' If I praise here, let him praise there.'

Comparison between Reinmar von Hagenau and Walther von der Vogelweide.

Reinmar's songs evince no feeling for nature ; he never hails the spring or mourns over the winter. ' I have other things to do than to lament over flowers,' he says. Walther, on the contrary, without ever connecting nature and love in the conventional way, has repeatedly sung of the various seasons in a manner always fresh and original. He introduces some human interest into his picture of spring, and shows us girls playing at ball in the street. One of the most charming of his spring-songs is his praise of May ('Muget ir schowen waz dem meien wunders ist beschert?'). Another poem of his

Walther's feeling for nature.

\

describes how the flowers peer up from the grass on a summer's morning and smile at the rising sun; but fairer than all the glories of spring, says the poet, is a beautiful woman.

Reinmar is one of those poets who impoverish their poetry by their one-sided taste; Walther's lyrics, on the contrary, are more rich and varied than those of any other Middle High-German poet. Walther stands in the same relation to Reinmar as Wolfram von Eschenbach does to Gottfried von Strassburg. Gottfried was also prevented by his conventionalism from doing full justice to his subject; but Walther and Wolfram appropriated the whole wealth of their predecessors, and were always successful in putting a new stamp on the old gold, or in giving it a new setting. According to Walther's own testimony, Reinmar seems to have felt the same enmity towards him as Gottfried did towards Wolfram. And as Wolfram put his adversary to shame by his generous praises of him, so Walther too sang a dirge for Reinmar, which for truthfulness, sincerity, justice, and earnest feeling ranks among his grandest compositions.

How close the connection may have been between Walther and Wolfram we cannot say; at all events they were acquainted with each other, and recognised each other's merits. Each quotes from the other's works, and Walther has written a 'Tagelied' in Wolfram's manner. Walther, like Wolfram, is full of a noble self-respect both in life and love. He speaks quite openly of his 'rich art,' and constantly dwells on the fact that he gives others pleasure by his songs, that no one can praise a lady better than he, and that her fame depends on his praise. But Walther's writings have not the splendour, the rich imagery, the ever fresh originality of his Bavarian countryman. His love-poems contain many thoughts and incidents which we also meet with in Friedrich von Hausen, Reinmar, and others. He is also indirectly a disciple of the troubadours, and we can seldom or never discover in his writings with certainty where tradition ends, and independent development begins.

Many of Walther's poems show no striking originality, but his peculiar talent is seen at once in such a poem as that where he narrates a dialogue between a knight and his lady, a regular tournament of words; or that in which he represents Fortune distributing her gifts, but persistently turning her back on him. He seizes on the old idea that the body is the garment of the man, and turns it to account in praising his lady. He has never seen a more beautiful robe than hers : wisdom and good fortune are embroidered upon it.

Friedrich von Hausen in his earliest and shortest song tells of the happiness of love which he has enjoyed in a dream, and reproaches his waking eyes for robbing him of it. One of Walther's poems also describes how, in a dream, he met a girl going to the dance, and presented her with a wreath, how she granted him happiness, and how since then he has sought her everywhere. This whole poem was evidently meant to be sung to dancing.

The incident of a girl telling of a secret meeting with her lover had also been turned to account by earlier poets : but Walther's song, 'Unter der Linde an der Heide,' stands alone in its *naïveté*, grace, and roguish fun. We are almost inclined to declare it the most beautiful song in the whole poetry of the Minnesingers, so full is it of life and variety.

Walther everywhere gives us dramatic situation and action. He contrasts favourably with Petrarch, who, though he took so much trouble to hand down the beauty of his Laura to posterity, yet never gets beyond a tedious enumeration of her charms. Petrarch never gives us a clear portrait of his lady; but Walther's 'red lips with their loving smile' ('der rothe Mund der so minniglich lachet') at once bring a picture before us. Walther is sparing in statements about the outward appearance of the ladies of whom he sings, and prefers to show them us engaged in action, or in some particular situation : getting out of the bath, or going to church; or he shows us a noble lady in full dress, going with her suite into society, and only now and then casting a modest glance around her. Walther knows how to introduce into such descriptions that grace which he prizes higher than beauty.

Throughout all his poems it is Walther's realism and power of graphic description that charm us. But his special talent lies in imaginative treatment. He pictures the outer world in the most vivid way, and invests it with a peculiar charm; at the same time he also clothes spiritual states with the appearance of the visible world, and thus imparts to his reflections a poetical and tangible body. The life of the soul, however, is grasped by him through reflection only. The whole world of sentiment was a country un-discovered by the poetry of the Middle Ages, and described only from a distance. Inward states and phases of the soul are analysed here and there, both in lyric and epic poetry, and the epic poetry in particular possesses splendid expressions for translating them into real action; a few of the Nibelungen songs, 'Gudrun' and Wolfram von Eschenbach attain the highest excellence in this respect. Walther possesses the same talent, but he is seldom able to grant us a direct glance into his own soul. If he does some-times move us by his simple words, like those old Austrian lyrics, yet he soon passes into reflections, which appeal pleasantly to the intellect, but do not move the heart.

Germany has no lyric poet before Goethe who can be compared with Walther, and among the mediæval lyric poets of other coun-tries he yields the palm to none. The lyric poetry of *Walther's superiority to Petrarch.* the Middle Ages has been chiefly represented to later times by Petrarch. Petrarch was the successor of the Troubadours, and the authority which they had formerly enjoyed passed over, in the opinion of the Renaissance, to this scholar-poet. Yet Walther deserved much more than Petrarch to exercise his influence on posterity, and continue to live in future ages. How great is Walther's variety, compared with the mono-tony of Petrarch! Petrarch collects the richest ornaments from Mythology, from antique and mediæval love-poetry, and fits them carefully together like mosaic, to form new pictures; but his conceits quickly pall upon us. Walther, on the contrary, is almost as simple in his manner as the Middle High-German popular epics; he only adorns his poetry with that which nature offers in all times and places: bright blossoms, and green branches, things which *Walther's character.* never grow old. And the best thing which he gives us is himself: a man such as one would desire for a friend, transparently sincere in his whole character, a gentle, serious, and strong soul, with a bright lovable manner, rejoicing with them that rejoice, weeping with them that weep, inclined from childhood to be hopeful, unwavering in his lofty aspirations, fresh and cheerful even in want, thankful in happiness, gloomy only in his old age, and this with some cause, for the spring and summer of the Minnesang were past, and Walther felt the coming autumn.

Minnesang and Meistersang.

A beautiful monument was raised in the fourteenth century to the German Minnesang. A manuscript, now in Paris, and which was probably prepared originally in Switzerland, contains the songs of 140 German poets from the twelfth to the fourteenth centuries. At the head of the collection stand the two Minnesingers of the house of Hohenstaufen, Henry VI and Conrad the Younger, i.e. Conradin. The kings are followed by the higher and lower nobility, and these in turn by the bourgeois poets. Nearly every poet has a picture; these pictures are of course not authentic portraits, but they give us a succession of scenes drawn from the life of chivalry: pictures of war and tender domestic scenes, pictures of love-incidents and of all the varied interests of chivalrous life. Heinrich von Veldeke is sitting on a grassy mound, with the birds gathered round him and flowers blossoming at his feet. Friedrich von Hausen is in a boat and pointing to a sheet of paper which is floating on the waves, doubtless his greeting to his lady. Walther von der Vogelweide is sitting upon a stone, deep in thought, in accordance with the description in one of his songs ('Ich sass auf einem Steine'). Wolfram von Eschenbach stands fully armed with closed visor, by the side of his saddled horse, as if on the point of mounting.

Unfortunately the manuscript gives no melodies. It has thus only preserved one half of that art by which the Minnesingers exercised such a strong influence on their contemporaries. For all these poems used to be sung; they appeared from the first before the public together with a melody, generally composed by the poet himself. Many of Walther's 'Sprüche'

[margin notes: Paris manuscript of Minnesongs. / Minnesongs always accompanied by a melody.]

consisting only of one verse had the same melody, and some poets always made use of one particular melody. But in songs of many verses, the tune, which was repeated from verse to. verse, was generally used for one song only, and thus every new song implied a new melody. But it was not only the melody,

Great but also the metrical construction of the verse which **variety** was different in each song. Middle High-German **of metrical** lyric poetry possessed a variety of metrical forms **forms.** and artifices of rhyming quite unknown to modern poetry. The power of metrical and musical invention was seen in its highest development in the form of poetry called a 'Leich,' in which various forms of verse and melody succeed each other. The 'Leich' is the show-piece of the Minnesang; at first it was always serious and solemn, later on it sometimes assumed a gay and frivolous character.

The songs of some Minnesingers, when read in succession, seem to form a little romance, but we learn little of the actual incidents which gave rise to the poems. One poet alone, the Styrian knight Ulrich von Lichtenstein, has written down the story of his romance, and in so doing has given us a picture of the brilliant life of chivalry. But with this one exception, we learn more of what that life must have been from the paintings of the Paris manuscript than from the poems which it contains.

Ulrich von Ulrich's 'Frauendienst' (Service of Ladies) contains **Lichten-** the history of his love experiences, while his 'Frauen- **stein's 'Frau-** buch' sets forth the causes of the decay of chivalry. **endienst'** Ulrich's poems are inserted in his 'Frauendienst' **and 'Frauen-** wherever they originated in the course of his love. **buch.'** From 1222 to 1255 he gives us a candid record of his wooing and mourning, his hopes and disappointments, but he is carefully silent about his happiness. He was a superficial man of the world, who enumerates the following as the five greatest sources of joy to a man : beautiful women, good food, fine horses, rich clothing, and a beautiful ornament on the helmet. He has served two ladies, and there was no folly which he was not capable of performing for their sakes. He was a slave to those conventional laws of society against which Wolfram rebelled. The romance

of Tristan and Isolde was the model on which he expressly based
his actions, and by making himself a Tristan he thought to win
an Isolde. Thus, because Tristan once appeared among lepers,
Ulrich also mixes in their company. Every wish or hint of his
lady's was a command to him; when she remarked that his
mouth did not please her, he had it operated on to give it a
better shape, and he mentions many other follies of the same
kind which he committed. In spite of his devotion Ulrich was
continually getting the worst of it, and once even his life was
endangered. But nothing daunts him, and the smallest token
of his lady's favour consoles him for the worst trick that has
been played upon him. For one lady he undertakes an expedition
through the land as Lady Venus, and measures his strength with
all the knights whom he meets on the way. For another he
travels through the land as King Arthur. And all these follies
are committed by a married man, the father of several children.
We learn quite by the way of the existence of his family,
and the fact somewhat surprises us, for he has said not a word
about his marriage; that had nothing to do with his ' Service of
Ladies.'

Though the style of the memoirs themselves is not remarkable,
some of the poems which are introduced are very beautiful; they
show tenderness of thought, melody, flowing diction, and great
facility in difficult arts of rhyming. But nothing else comes up
to the beauty of this one stanza :—

> In dem Walde süsse Töne
> Singen kleine Vögelein ;
> An der Heide Blumen schöne
> Blühen in des Maien Schein.
> Also blüht mein hoher Muth
> Wenn er denkt an deren Güte,
> Die mir reich macht mein Gemüthe
> Wie der Traum den Armen thut.

Walther, as we noticed, was fond of comparisons between
the appearances of nature and human feelings, and Ulrich's
Minnesongs may be considered an echo of Walther's love-
lyrics.

The connection with the great master of mediæval lyric poetry

is still closer in Minnesingers like Ulrich von Singenberg, Rubin,
Ulrich von Singenberg, and Rubin. and others; and Reinmar von Zweter is his worthiest successor as a writer of 'Sprüche.' Reinmar was born on the Rhine, and grew up in Austria; he lived at the Austrian, Bohemian, and Danish courts. Between 1230 and 1250 he discussed in one special form of **Reinmar von Zweter.** 'Spruch' almost all the problems of life, treating them all with great seriousness and in a graphic and concise style. He wrote riddles, stories (*Lügenmärchen*), short fables, and tales, like the minstrels before Walther. He praises marriage and the moral power of love, and compares a beautiful woman to the Grail, saying that he who wishes to win her must be pure as the guardian of the Grail. He laments the decay of chivalrous culture, the worldliness of the monasteries, the increase of drunkenness and dice-playing, the degeneration of the tournaments, which were no longer chivalrous (*ritterlich*), but brutal (*rinderlich*), injuring the body and endangering the life of those who took part in them..

The Minnesang in its first beginnings had shown a strong tendency to follow French models, but in its further development there are no visible traces of Western influence. Walther did not directly follow any Provençal or Northern French models, and though his Minnesang indirectly owed its origin to these, yet he preserved his loyalty to the national poetry, not only in his ' Sprüche,' but also in his love-lyrics. Such a poem as the graceful dance-song mentioned above, in which he describes his pleasant dream, directly resembles in character the popular dance-songs which were in vogue in Bavaria and Austria. Walther in this poem **Neidhart von Reuenthal, beginning of 13th century.** pointed out the path which was afterwards pursued by the Bavarian knight Neidhart von Reuenthal. But it seems that Walther did not approve of Neidhart's new departure, for we find him lamenting that a form of poetry which was of peasant origin had found much favour at the great courts, and had driven away the right kind of song. Perhaps along with the rustic dance-songs, rough and noisy country-dances may have been introduced, which supplanted the refined merriment of the golden age of chivalry. Neidhart von Reuenthal lived at the Bavarian and Austrian courts till 1240, and became known to the German public about the second decade of the thirteenth century. He wrote no true Minnesongs, i.e. poems courting the favour of some noble lady; his characteristic works were dance-songs, which with their brightness and humour, and, as we may doubtless add, with their attractive tunes, made their **His dance-**way all over Germany, in the same manner as the **songs.** valses of Strauss and Lanner have done in our own century. These dance-songs fall into two quite separate groups: Summer-songs for dances in the open air, and Winter-songs for dances in the house. The former are more dramatic, the latter more epic in character. The Summer-songs open with a description of spring, and an invitation to merriment, to a dance under the linden-tree or to a game of ball in the street, and this is generally followed by a dialogue. In the Winter-songs the lament about winter is succeeded by a short anecdote, usually of a satirical character. In many of these songs Neidhart appears in person in intercourse with the peasants. The dialogues in the spring-songs are very charming, and these songs are most probably based on popular dance-songs of similar construction and with similar motives. Sometimes two girls converse together and open their hearts to each other. Generally the song is in the form of a dialogue between mother and daughter; the girl wishes to go to the dance and the mother warns her against its dangers, and even tries to prevent her by force from going; or it is the old mother who is seized with a passion for dancing, and the daughter tries in vain to dissuade her from her folly. In all these songs it is the girl who longs and pines, while the knight is a happy lover, as in the old Austrian improvised songs.

The Winter-songs, on the contrary, are written in the sighing and languishing tone of the later Minnesongs. In them the knight is unhappy and scorned, and the peasant-girl, whom he woos, lets him languish. Whereas in the Summer-songs the knight is superior to the peasants, here it is the peasants who get the better of the knight. The knight revenges himself by ridicule and by satirical stories, in which he either calls up events of the past summer, and alludes to the rough fun of the dance, or scoffs at the quarrels and fightings of the peasants, at their hatred of the knights or their luxury in dress. These satirical elements may have been imitated from the popular lampoons which the peasants were wont to use as weapons against each

Enmity between Neidhart and the peasants. other. Neidhart's poetic attacks were answered by rustic poets in the same tone. The enmity between them is quite serious, for Neidhart's songs are really an expression of the hostility between the rich and insolent peasant-class in Austria and Bavaria, and the poor nobles, who grudged them their luxury. As far as the sixteenth century Neidhart lived on in popular poetry and in the memory of the Germans as the enemy of the peasants, now victorious over his adversaries, now duped by them. His style of writing was much imitated. Even in his own poems there is a great deal of coarse fun, and in the end this whole class of poetry owed its extinction to its entire absorption in grossness.

Tannhäuser. Bavarian productiveness in the province of the Minnesang was not exhausted in Neidhart's poetry. The Bavarian district also produced the poet Tannhäuser, a member of the Salzburg family of Tannhusen, and ·a thoroughly original character.

Tannhäuser led a wandering life from about 1240 to 1270, staying at the Bavarian, Austrian, and other courts, and even · visiting Eastern lands in the course of his travels. He scoffs at the service of love, by making fun of the impossible things

Humorous character of his poetry. which ladies require of their lovers. His lady, he says, will be gracious to him, if he will divert the course of the Rhine, so that it shall not flow past Coblentz, if he will bring her sand from the lake in which the sun goes to rest, if he will deprive the moon of its light, if he can fly like a starling, can use up a thousand spears, if he will fetch her the salamander out of the fire—and so on. Tannhäuser, like many humourists, produces his effects by heaping up analogous expressions in a lively flow of bombastic language; and, like other humourists, he uses the opportunity to display his wide knowledge and reading. Sometimes he introduces numbers of foreign words to designate common things, apparently meaning to ridicule the German affectation of everything foreign. He is most delicious in those passages where he allows us a glimpse into the wretched state of his own affairs, and tells us how Sir Want (*Mangel*), Sir Donothing (*Schaffenichts*), and Sir Seldomrich (*Seltenreich*), are continual inmates of his house; how his property has been mortgaged for the sake of beautiful women, good wine, dainty food, and a bath twice a week. He is charming, too, when he pretends to be making riddles, which are, however, only meant as nonsense, or finally in his 'Tanzleiche,' where he relates love-adventures as though they were his own experiences, and then invites people to the dance till a string of his fiddle breaks, which is the usual ending to the poem.

Ulrich von Lichtenstein had practically reduced the service of ladies to an absurdity; Neidhart brought it down to the peasants, and Tannhäuser turned it to ridicule. Each one of these poets was instrumental in bringing about the decay of the pure Minnesang. And in fact, in Austria and Bavaria the genuine Minnesang hardly maintained itself till the end of the thirteenth century; a love-poet like Hadamar von Laber no longer made use of this form of poetry. The Allemannic poets remained faithful to it a little longer. Henry, the unfortunate son of Frederick II, who lost his life in a rebellion against his father, gathered round him at his court in Swabia, about the year 1230, a circle of young and gay nobles, amongst whom Burkard von Hohenfels and Gottfried von Neifen were distinguished as poets. Their writings betray the influence of Neidhart and of the popular poetry. Both of them frequently introduce the popular device of a refrain. They not only wrote popular dance-songs, but Neifen also imitated the popular cradle-song, and the short ballad, as far as it dealt with matters of love.

Burkard von Hohenfels and Gottfried von Neifen.

Other poets, especially those from Switzerland and Alsace, introduce us to the circle of Rudolf von Habsburg. Many of them were in the army with which he set out to invade Austria. One of these was Steimar of Thurgau, who wrote on till 1294,

and composed beautiful and serious Minnesongs in simple
and almost popular forms. But his practical na-
Steimar. ture did not feel quite at home in the ideal
sphere of the Minnesong. In one poem, for instance, which
begins quite seriously, he suddenly permits himself this absurd
simile : 'My heart moves up and down like a pig in a sack,
and it is wilder than a dragon through its wish to fly to my
beloved.' The state of things which he describes soon became
wearisome to the poet, and he gave up his hopeless languish-
ings. He changed his tone, and wrote a song in praise of
autumn and also an eating and drinking song, in which he
calls upon the host to produce fish, geese, fowls, swine, sausages,
peacocks, and foreign wines, and himself prepares to devour a
large goose at a sitting. Like Neidhart and others, he seeks
out a peasant-sweetheart, whom he woos by presents of clothes.
He introduced the old form of the 'Tagelied' into the sphere of
rustic life.

Thus in Allemannia, as in Bavaria and Austria, the refined
Minnesang gave place to a coarser kind of lyric poetry. But the
sentimental song of the old conventional type continued to exist
Werner till the beginning of the fourteenth century. One of
von the last of the Allemannic Minnesingers was Werner
Homberg. von Homberg, Henry the Seventh's general in Italy,
and one of the most celebrated swordsmen of his time. He died
in 1320, whilst besieging Genoa, at the early age of thirty-six.

Meanwhile the Minnesang had spread over a wide territory in
the North, but poetry in general did not reap much advantage
Princely from this. German Minnesongs were written by
Minne- King Wenzel of Bohemia, a son of that Ottokar who
singers. succumbed before the arms of Rudolf von Habsburg.
Margrave Otto IV of Brandenburg (1266–1308), Duke Henry IV
of Breslau (1270–1292), and Prince Wizlaw of Rügen (1320
–1325), all of them princes reigning on old Slavonic soil,
were not merely patrons of the poetic art, but also themselves Minnesingers. Of these Wizlaw was the best. He wrote
'Sprüche' and love-songs in a fresh and jovial style, and
his praise of Autumn and its gifts reminds us of Steimar.

But by the beginning of the fourteenth century all this poetic activity had died away in the North as elsewhere. **Decay** The practice of the poetic art by nobles became **of the** more and more rare, the service of ladies decayed, **Minnesang** and the wooing of the one beloved lady gave place **towards** to a bare praise of women in general. Secular lyrics **the 13th** retired into the background; religious hymns and **century.** pedantic Spruch-poetry became more and more predominant in the course of the thirteenth century; the Minnesang was transformed into Meistersang.

The ordinary gleemen, the 'Gumpelmänner,' mechanical poets who travelled about like journeymen of a trade, and who were ready to write either eulogies or censures to order, **Poetry** greatly increased in number during the course of the **becomes** thirteenth century; and this increase is a strong proof **increasingly** of the growing power of that popular poetry, whose **popular.** influence we have already pointed out in the history of the Minnesang.

But above these gleemen there was a class of wandering singers of a somewhat higher rank, more educated and with more claims to respect; they called themselves 'Masters,' and **The** later on 'Mastersingers.' These poets had received **Master-** school instruction; they sought admittance at the **singers.** princely courts, and in fact carried on the tradition of that lyric poetry which had been developed by Walther von der Vogelweide and his predecessors. The actual tunes of some of their poems have been preserved to us, and the traditions of their art, together with its technical terms, were treasured up by the later Mastersingers. Thus we learn, for instance, that a compound stanza was made up of two equal parts, called 'Stollen,' and one unequal part, the 'Abgesang' (descant); and from the music which has been preserved to us, we see that the 'descant' often led back into the melody of the 'Stollen,' so that the whole construction coincided in a remarkable manner with the form of our Sonata. One of these singers called Marner tried **Marner.** his hand at all the various forms of German lyrics, and excelled besides in the art of writing Latin poetry. He

P

belonged to the school of Walther von der Vogelweide, and was at the same time a follower of the Arch-poet. His poetical career lasted forty or fifty years; he continued to write till about 1270, and composed Minnesongs, 'Tagelieder,' dance-songs and 'Sprüche' in great variety, including fables, stories (*Lügenmärchen*), riddles, prayers, songs in praise of the Virgin, and political poems; besides these, he also used to recite songs taken from the heroic legends, and he complains that the public will listen to nothing else.

Unfortunately the wealth and variety of the early Master-singers was not continued in their successors; we notice their power visibly declining, their sympathy with public life diminishing, and religious subjects coming more and more to the fore in their poems. They parade their learning, and think they show depth of thought in being enigmatical and obscure. It was among these later singers that the poem of the 'Wartburg-krieg' was produced. One of these 'Masters,' the celebrated Heinrich von Meissen, called 'Frauenlob,' occupies much the same

Heinrich von Meissen, called 'Frauenlob.' position in lyric poetry as that held by Albrecht von Scharfenberg, the author of the later 'Titurel,' in the province of the epic. From about 1270, Frauenlob led a wandering life, roving over the whole of Germany; but after 1311 he permanently settled in Mainz, where he died in 1318. He had a poetic contest with the worthy Mastersinger Regenbogen, on a subject which had been already debated by Walther von der Vogelweide, namely, the question whether 'Weib' (wife) or 'Frau' (lady) be the more honourable title for women. Walther had declared himself in favour of 'Weib;' 'Wife must always be the highest title for a woman,' he says. Regenbogen also defended the word 'Weib,' while Frauenlob decided for 'Frau,' and hence derived his nickname. Frauenlob pays the deepest homage to the Virgin Mary, and sings her praises with much display of bombastic obscurity. He is puffed up with conceit, and speaks in a disparaging tone of the older poets. But both he and all the other Masters contemporary with him only worked on the old stock of poetic material, and did not do anything to increase the store. Almost all of them lament the decay of morals, the disturbed times, the decline of

art, the stinginess of the nobles; Rudolf von Habsburg is especially attacked for his meanness. Almost all of them are jealous
of their fellow-poets, with whom they have to share the favour or
disfavour of the public. Only two of these early ' Masters ' deserve
to be singled out from the rest: the ' wild Alexander,' a South-
German poet, and Hadlaub of Zürich, who lived about the year 1300.

The wild Alexander wrote a song containing a charming picture
of childhood, drawn as though from memory in some- Der wilde
what indistinct outlines. It describes children play- Alexander.
ing in the woods till evening and being warned by an old wood-
man to go home before nightfall.

Johann Hadlaub was a Minnesinger from the bourgeois class.
Probably he did not lead a wandering life, and in this Johann
respect he occupies a somewhat peculiar position Hadlaub.
among the other lyric poets of this period. The same applies to
a few schoolmasters, who also contributed to the store of Middle
High-German lyric poetry. Hadlaub is a disciple of Steimar,
and repeats his master's scurrilous comparison of a beating heart
to a pig in a sack. He narrated a rustic love-adventure, and wrote
autumn feast-songs, but he also composed conventional Minnesongs, ' Tagelieder,' and ' Leiche.' His realism is turned to good account in his descriptions of nature and love. He introduces human
figures into his descriptions of scenery, and shows us for instance
in the summer a group of beautiful ladies walking in an orchard,
and blushing with womanly modesty when gazed at by young men.
He compares the troubles of love with the troubles of hard-working
men like charcoal-burners and carters. Hadlaub tells us more of
his own personal experiences in his songs than any other Minnesänger. Even as a child, we learn, he had loved a His
little girl, who however would have nothing to say to love-poems.
him, but continually flouted him, to his great distress. Once she
bit his hand, but her bite, he says, was so tender, womanly, and
gentle, that he was sorry the feeling of it passed away so soon.
Another time, being urged to give him a keepsake, she threw her
needle-case at him, and he seized it with sweet eagerness, but it
was taken from him and returned to her, and she was made to give
it him again in a friendly manner. In later years his pains still

remained unrewarded; when his lady perceived him, she would get up and go away. Once, he tells us, he saw her fondling and kissing a child, and when she had gone he drew the child towards him and embraced it as she had embraced it, and kissed it in the place where she had kissed it.

In one particular song Hadlaub praises Herr Rüdiger Maness

Hadlaub's praise of Rüdiger Maness. of Zürich, and his son, because they would not let the Minnesang perish, and collected books of songs with great zeal. This collecting-mania probably affected other people also about this time; men clearly felt that they were at the end of a brilliant epoch of poetry, and to their desire to preserve its achievements we owe such precious monuments as the Paris Manuscript described at the beginning of this section. Hadlaub's words to Rüdiger Maness would supply a fitting motto for that work:

'Sang ist ein sô gar edlez guot.'

Didactic Poetry, Satires, and Tales.

Not far from Ansbach, in the country of Wolfram von Eschenbach and Wirent von Grafenberg, there lived, in the begin-

'The Winsbeke.' ning of the thirteenth century, a certain Herr von Windsbach, who was called the 'Winsbeke.' He was an aristocrat like many another, an average man like Hartmann von Aue, pious, and yet devoted to all the interests of chivalry. He was the only nobleman of the Middle High-German period who tried his hand at didactic poetry. He chose for this purpose the old form of counsels given by a father to his son; the father is a knight, and in fifty-six stanzas the whole system of the chivalrous morality is expounded in elegant language with pleasing illustrations, and in an idealizing and generalizing style.

The father begins with a warning against the world and its illusions; he recommends his son to honour the clergy, but only for the selfish reason that they dispense the last Sacraments; what he chiefly enjoins on his son is really service of the world, namely, worship of women and deeds of arms. The Winsbeke, like all the moralists of the time, declares noble birth to be worthless, if virtue is not added to it. And he condemns in strong terms the effeminate spirit ('das Verliegen') which would prefer a life of ease and luxury to one of action and endurance.

This poem shows us what ideal aspirations filled the hearts of the German knights. The distinctly moral colouring which characterizes German chivalry may have been due in part to the influence of the Church, but some of the chivalrous ideals were not only independent of the Church, but even opposed to its teaching. How, for instance, could the service of women have found a place in the system of Church-morality? The golden period of chivalry in the twelfth and thirteenth centuries is one of the most ideal epochs known to us in history. All the romances reflect to some extent the chivalrous ideal, and many of the chivalrous epic poets directly express their views upon it; they also place general maxims at the beginning of their works, which contain, as it were, the moral of the story which follows. But the task of elaborating a system of chivalrous ethics, and of writing poems of merely didactic import was left, as a rule, to the clergy and the bourgeois-poets, who introduced more or less fragments of Church-morality and dogma, till at last these elements once more gained the preponderance. These poets did not write in stanzas as the Winsbeke and even Walther had done in their didactic poems, but employed the continuous rhyming couplets of the chivalrous epics, a form of verse which of all the Middle High-German metres is the nearest approaching to prose.

Moral character of German chivalry.

Loyalty, honour, moderation, generosity, steadfastness—these were the virtues chiefly developed by chivalry and strengthened by the chivalrous poetry.

The virtues of chivalry.

Loyalty had regained its ancient glory and dignity through the revival of the heroic poetry. Loyalty bound the vassal to his feudal lord, and the relation of a lover to his lady was in many respects a similar tie.

The idea of Honour is a reflection of the power of public opinion, and so great was this power that we find men of a religious turn of mind warning the knights not to forget in their anxiety about honour the care of their soul's salvation. Not only universal respect, but universal love was considered a worthy object of aspiration. 'Thou shalt make thyself beloved' is one of the oldest commandments of chivalrous morality.

One particular song of the twelfth century strongly recommends Moderation (*Mâze*). This virtue, however, had its questionable sides, for much that was immoral was allowed to pass, if it was done with moderation, that is to say, if public scandal was avoided. Generosity (*Milde*) included all humane duties, care of the 'Der Wilde sick, compassion for the poor and the unprotected. Mann,' 12th A poet of the Lower Rhine, who lived in the twelfth century. century, and was called the 'Wild Man,' wrote, in this spirit of generosity, against avarice. Another, the Thuringian Werner chaplain, Werner von Elmendorf, derived the duty of von generosity from the unequal division of this world's Elmendorf. goods. The same Werner sketched a system of morals based, not on the Bible, but on the heathen classics, the Roman philosophers and poets. There is little trace in him of any specifically Christian feeling. The spirit of the chivalrous virtue of moderation pervades his whole work, and it is chivalrous society that he has in his mind throughout. He argues against the sentimentality of love, the 'stupid Minne,' as he calls it, not an enemy of worldly pleasure, but as an enemy of unreason and exaggeration.

To be free from passion, not over-elated by prosperity nor reduced to despair by misfortune, and to be just in all things—all this is included by Werner in the virtue of Steadfastness (*Staete*). Steadfastness is what we should call strength of character, persistence Thomasin in what is good. This virtue was elaborately anaof lysed by the Italian Thomasin of Zirclaria, canon Zirclaria's of Aquileja, in his 'Italian Guest,' a work of nearly 'Welscher 15,000 lines; it is the result of much learned study, Gast.' is carefully provided with a preface and a table of contents, and divided into ten books, which were written in ten months between 1216 and 1217. Thomasin, like Werner von Elmendorf, draws chiefly from the ancient writers, and from those Mediæval writers who base their statements on the authority of Cicero, Plato, and Aristotle. But he does not go beyond the essential principles of chivalrous morality, and he starts with a discussion not only on morality but on etiquette, which he places almost on an equal level with morality. It is not enough for him that a woman should do right, she must also be able to behave herself becomingly and to converse well ; if she has intellect and knowledge besides, she is not to show it. Thomasin gives a number of precepts about the fitting demeanour of knights and ladies, some of which are most absurd. A lady, he says, should not take large steps in walking nor look round often. A maiden should only speak when she is questioned, and even a married woman should not speak much, and never converse while she is eating. A knight should not ride while a lady is walking, and should not gallop up to her so as to frighten her ; in speaking he should keep his hands still, and at table he should never eat his bread before the first course has been served up, nor look over the rim of his cup while drinking. Thomasin recommends people to choose some noble character as their model, and to mould themselves after that pattern. Gawein, Ereck, Iwein, Arthur, Charlemagne, Alexander, Tristan, and Parzival are held up as models to young men, while the women are advised to imitate Andromache, Enite, Penelope, and Blanche-flur. The author has no prejudice against the chivalrous epics ; he only regrets that they contain so many lies, and he considers them as essentially more suited for those of riper years.

[margin: Thomasin's precepts of etiquette.]

Thomasin throughout draws his materials not only from books, but from his own independent knowledge of life. He always speaks of things, not in a vague and general manner, but as a man thoroughly acquainted with the world, who also has at his command effective illustrations and a style not indeed elegant but powerful. We follow him with pleasure, and do not tire in reading him. He and Freidank are the classics of Middle High-German didactic poetry ; but Freidank's work was far more popular.

Freidank was a wandering gleeman, probably from Swabia, who went with Frederick II to Palestine, but did not enjoy it at all (cf. p. 89). He called his work ' Beschei-denheit,' which then meant something like ' practical common-sense.' This book is closely connected with the popular didactic poetry. Freidank had a perfect treasure of proverbs at his disposal, and knew how to express his individual views in such

[margin: Freidank's Bescheidenheit.]

characteristic and pregnant language that they seem like sayings handed down from old times.

Freidank, like Walther von der Vogelweide, was an enthusiastic Imperialist and an enemy of the princes, whose great power undermined the glory of the Empire. He extends to the clergy the same indulgence as the Winsbeke had done, but he makes a sharp onslaught on the Papacy: St. Peter, he says, received from God the charge of feeding His sheep, not of shearing them, yet all treasures go to Rome and never return thence. The question of indulgences also occupies his attention, and he recommends with bitter irony that the man who wishes to commit a murder in the coming year should seek indulgence for it already in this year. Freidank only recognises three ranks in society: Peasants, knights, and clergy; only these three, he says, were founded by God; the fourth, the trading-class, whom he calls ' usurers,' were created by the Devil. The opposition to the rising middle-class could not be more strongly expressed than it is here. Freidank, though not of noble birth, looks on things entirely from an aristocratic point of view, and he knows the fashionable world as well as, or even better than, any of the Minnesingers. His remarks about women are most refined, and would do honour to Hartmann von Aue. The word ' Frau,' he says, comes from 'Freude' (delight); women are the delight of all lands. Their power is enormous; they have had an influence in everything that has happened in the world; they never let themselves be quite seen through, but they wish to read the soul of man; and he who understands their excellences must acknowledge that they are better than men.

His Imperialism and hostility to the Papacy.

His dislike of the middle-class.

His respect for women.

Serious teaching is the real object both of Freidank and of Thomasin in their writings. Didactic poetry is, however, closely connected both with the satire and the tale. Didactic poems and satires are both off-shoots of the sermon; the most scathing satire was written in the form of penitential sermons, and satirical sketches of character were inserted in purely didactic poems. The fable is didactic and epic at the same time; fables about men

Connection between didactic poetry and satires and tales.

were added to those about animals, and passed by an imperceptible transition either into the serious tale or the farce. Satire is generally the school for broad and realistic description, and the broad and the comic are closely allied. Farce and comic satire appeal to the widest circles ; every man likes to laugh, and hence the laughable is always popular.

Fables, tales, and farces were written by the minstrels during the tenth and eleventh centuries, and this inferior class of poetry probably continued to exist even when, at the beginning of the twelfth century, the nobler branches of literature came to the front. The ancient tradition **Fables, tales, and farces, 10th to 14th century.** of fable-writing was never entirely broken off. The tale was at all times an international form of literature, and this was especially the case in the tenth and eleventh centuries, through the Latin poetry which then held sway all over Europe. In the twelfth and thirteenth centuries there was a great increase from Oriental sources of new material for tales, brought to Europe by Spanish and Italian Jews. Indian tales, which had been transferred to Persian, and thence to Arabic, now passed into Hebrew and Latin, and from thence into the various European languages.

In Germany itself we find that the districts in which the popular epic flourished, and in which lyric poetry retained or regained its popular character, namely Austria and Bavaria, were also the classic lands of satire, tale, and farce. In the twelfth century Austria produced the powerful satirist, Heinrich von Mölk[1], and his views lived on in clerical circles **Heinrich von Mölk.** during the thirteenth century. In Bavaria at the same period, we find an old minstrel, a forerunner of Walther von der Vogelweide, writing short fables confined to didactic purposes, as Lessing did some centuries later. Austria produced Stricker, **Stricker.** the most important name among German mediæval story-tellers ; we have already become acquainted with him as an epic poet, and one of the later followers of the classical chivalrous poets. The tale, as Stricker treats it, stands on a level with the fable and the parable, and belongs to the class of what was called in mediæval German the 'Bîspell,' that is a 'Spel,'

---

[1] Cp. chap. iv. p. 76.

a tale, with a double meaning (Modern German ' *Beispiel,*' example).
These tales narrate a single occurrence typical of many similar
ones.   Stricker generally, but not always, adds a moral to his tales,
and often extends this moral beyond all reasonable limits.   He, too,
brings the didactic purpose as much as possible into prominence,
and his views are strictly clerical and pious.   His strict views did
His 'Pfaffe not, however, hinder him from writing ' Priest Amis,'
Amis.' the story of a clerical swindler, a hawker of false relics
and pretended miracle-worker.   Stricker also wrote a series of satires
bewailing the decay of chivalry, and giving a dreadful description
of the moral corruption of the aristocracy.   The Austrian nobles
are compared to a glutton, who has been surfeited, and in consequence of this becomes temperate ; thus, says Stricker, formerly
Austrian lords could not get enough of German song, and singers
streamed to Austria from all parts, till there were so many that the
lords had too much of it, and would give nothing more.   Now no
one cares about fiddling, singing, and reciting ; only rude and unseemly words are prized, and good ones are disdained.   Politically,
too, the poet is opposed to the nobility ; he takes the side of the rebel
peasants, praises the emperor as the defence of the weak and
poor, and accuses the nobility of trying to injure him in every
way.

The complaints about the decay of chivalry are continued till the
Satires   end of the thirteenth century.   The fifteen satires
attributed   falsely attributed to a certain Seifried Helbling, and
to Seifried written in Austria between 1280 and 1300, deal with
Helbling,   the same subject.   The author complains that he who
1280-1300.
now visits court-feasts may hear the courtiers around
him speaking of cattle and of the corn and wine-trade.   The chivalry
of depredation increased ; the lesser nobles saw themselves menaced
by the great clans on the one hand, and by the rising peasant and
'Meier   bourgeois-class on the other. ' Farmer Helmbrecht,' a
Helmbrecht,' Bavarian village-tale by Werner the Gardener, describes
by Werner   the aspirations of the peasant-class in a ' Beispiel,' with
von Gärtner. a moral pointed at those who are not contented with the
rank in which they are placed.   The young Helmbrecht is an ambitious peasant's son, just such a youth as Neidhart loved to scoff at ; he

wishes above all things to shine at court, and, in defiance of his father's warning, he joins the train of a robber-knight. After a year he shows himself at home in his new glory, and the old and the young generation are thus brought into characteristic contrast. The father, who in his youth had also had the opportunity of observing chivalrous life, when sent with cheese and eggs to the castle, tells of knightly jousts, of seemly dances accompanied by song and fiddle, of the reading aloud of heroic poems. The son, on the contrary, only knows of drinking and coarse talk, lying, deceiving, and scolding. He answers his father's warnings with rough threats. His sister follows him secretly; he wishes to marry her to his comrade Lämmerschling, and it is during the wedding that the catastrophe takes place; the judge comes with the beadles and destroys the nest of robbers. Young Helmbrecht has his eyes put out, is driven home, and hanged by the peasants.

The increasing rudeness of manners soon began to make itself felt in the tales of this period. A Tyrolese poem, for instance, called 'The bad wife,' introduces us to a poor ill-treated husband, who describes his own misfortunes, compares himself to the holy martyrs, and appeals to public sympathy. The conjugal battle-scenes, in which he regularly comes off the worst, are most graphically described. The wife feels herself so superior to her husband that she threatens to take him under her arm and carry him off to Vienna.

Tyrolese poem, 'Das üble Weib.'

Vienna is the first great city which plays a part as such in German poetry. Already in the Nibelungenlied we find Vienna occupying a place of honour. The Austrian satires make us more intimately acquainted with the town-life of Vienna; they introduce us, for instance, to a public bath, or show us the foreigner besieged on his arrival by the minstrels, who offer themselves for any service. The Viennese burgher Enenkel sketched in bad verses a graphic picture of the happy times of the Babenberger, and wrote a universal chronicle, more amusing than instructive, in which anecdote and farce reign supreme. Humorous tales about the Viennese became a favourite form of literature. The 'Wiener Meerfahrt' (Sea-

Satires on town-life.

Enenkel.

voyage of the Viennese), belongs to this class. A number of
The 'Wiener carousing Viennese burghers imagine in their drunken-
Meerfahrt.' ness that they are going on a pilgrimage to Accho,
and are in the midst of a storm, which they think is the fault of
one of their companions who has drunk himself under the table;
they throw the wretched man out of the window so that he breaks
his arms and legs. The next morning they are not half sober
enough to recognise the mischief they have done, and it is only
after they have had a good sleep that repentance comes over them.

Another of these Austrian tales, ' Der Weinschwelg' (the carouse),
describes in detail the drinking-feats of a tremendous toper, who
resolves not to move from his seat as long as there is wine in the
cask before him.

This literature of tales is spread over the whole of Middle and
South Germany during the thirteenth century, and is quite inexhaustible. The poets treat their materials with more or less
talent and skill. The moral at the end was soon dropped.
Faithfulness and unfaithfulness are the chief subjects of these tales,
and we find in them not only frivolity and coarseness, but also
instances of generous self-sacrifice and noble feeling.

No genuine didactic poem had been written since the time of
the Winsbeke, Thomasin, and Freidank. A fellow-countryman
of the Winsbeke, called Hugo von Trimberg, took up this form
of writing. Hugo was a schoolmaster in a suburb of Bamberg,
had a numerous family, and was poor and weighed down with
cares. Nevertheless he managed to collect a library of two
hundred volumes, and himself wrote twelve works, eight in
German and four in Latin. His Latin writings show a rare
amount of reading; of his German works the ' Renner' is the
Hugo von only one preserved to us. Hugo wrote this long
Trimberg's poem in 1300, when about sixty years of age, and
' Renner,' continued adding to it till 1313. His definite pur-
1300. pose in writing it was to produce a theory of morals.
Where he cannot treat the subject exhaustively he refers us to
St. Bernard, Gregory, Ambrose, Augustine, Jerome, or John Chry-
sostome. He wishes by his work to render a service to those
who do not understand the writings of these fathers of the Church.

Hugo is a preacher, preaching in rhymed couplets, but he does not follow any fixed plan in writing. He starts, like Dante in his 'Inferno' and 'Purgatorio,' from the basis of the seven deadly sins recognised in the ecclesiastical system of morality; but he does not adhere to this, and towards the end he forsakes all system. His point of view throughout is that of Church-teaching, but this does not hinder him from criticizing the clergy and the Papacy. In this respect he resembles Freidank, from whom he has borrowed much, but he is far removed from Freidank's liberal views. He assigns a very low position to women, he is hostile to the higher classes, and he attacks the chivalrous epics as being full of lies and dangerous to piety. He reproaches Konrad von Würzburg for his too great refinement of language; 'the learned,' he says, 'may praise him, but the laity do not understand him.' Hugo's style, which is racy and forcible, and scorns all finer charms, seems to have been all that the public demanded in this period of literature.

In tracing the chief sins through the various ranks of society, and attacking them all in turn, Hugo was adopting an old form of writing; satires on all classes, or moral precepts for all ranks were a favourite form of poetry in the Middle Ages. In the second half of the thirteenth century a Dominican of Lombardy, called Jacobus a Cessolis, invented a very happy form for this class of literature, by connecting it with the game of chess; he went through all the pieces of the game in a succession of sermons, and thus sketched living **Jacobus a Cessolis' 'Chess-poems.'** portraits of a king and queen, of councillors, knights, craftsmen, and agriculturists, holding up to each class its various duties. Not less than four German translations in verse of this work were made between 1300 and 1375: two in Allemannia, one in Central Germany, and one in Dorpat.

About the year 1300 a Dominican monk, Ulrich Boner of Bern, produced the oldest German Fable-book; it was written for a wealthy Bernese citizen, and was called **Ulrich Boner's 'Edelstein.'** the 'Jewel.' It is a collection of a hundred fables, well told, and each provided with a popular moral; the frequent proverbial form given to these morals reminds one of the less important parts of Freidank's 'Bescheidenheit.' Ulrich, like Hugo von Trimberg, makes a conscious effort to adapt his work to the general level of intelligence, and blames those who skilfully combine their words and preach high wisdom which they themselves do not understand; doubtless Boner was here thinking of Mastersingers like Frauenlob. Thomasin, Freidank, and Hugo von Trimberg only occasionally wrote in fables; with Stricker the fable hardly differs from the tale, but with Boner it appears for the first time in German literature as an independent branch of writing reduced to a fixed form. There is a decided poverty in Boner's moral sayings; if he turns his gaze on the inner nature of man, he can only see its coarsest features, and he never gets beyond the well-known rudiments of Church morality, which the clergy had preached for centuries. But his aspirations are very modest, and his narratives as well as his teaching please us by their gentle humour and a certain simple grace. Hugo

Hugo von Trimberg and Dante. von Trimberg had put forth higher claims. He wished to draw a picture of the actual world, and by rebuke to lead men towards the Christian ideal.

Hugo attempted what Dante has accomplished; and whilst Hugo thought to win the multitude by his intentionally commonplace language, Dante, with his depth of thought, has won the centuries.

THE MENDICANT ORDERS.

Dante's 'Divina Commedia' helped to lay the foundation for a united Italian nationality; the classical achievements of Middle High-German poetry did the same for Germany.

Development of a united German nationality. Whilst the power of the Emperor and of the Empire continued to decay, whilst politically the nation was becoming more and more divided, the various sections of the people were being drawn closer together by common ties. National feeling took the place of

Tendency towards Middle High-German as the literary dialect, circa 1200. clan-feeling, and language and law tended towards unity. About the year 1200 Germany had no recognised literary language, but we may say that the whole of the written language of Germany was gravitating towards Middle High-German, which was represented in its purest form in Allemannia.

Whilst in the sphere of language South Germany triumphed over the North, in the province of law, on the contrary, the South was indebted to the North. About the year 1220 the Saxon law was reduced to writing under the name of the 'Sachsenspiegel' by the sheriff, Eike von Repkow, from the neighbourhood of Magdeburg; this record furnished in 1275 the foundation for the 'Schwabenspiegel,' a South German code, which claimed to represent the common law of Germany, and did in fact obtain over a wide area. *Supremacy of North-German Law. The 'Sachsenspiegel' and the 'Schwabenspiegel.'*

But while the beneficial effects of a flourishing literature were thus gradually revealing themselves, the literature itself, namely Middle High-German poetry, was becoming extinct. In the course of the thirteenth century we have had to note a decline in all the branches of literature— in the popular epic, in the chivalrous epic, in the Minnesang, and in the Didactic poem; about 1225 Walther von der Vogelweide perceived clearly the change which had set in; by 1300 the revolution was virtually accomplished. It had become inevitable that beauty should yield up her sceptre to piety, desire of knowledge, and love of amusement. *Decay of Middle High-German poetry.*

This painful change was not due to any inner necessity; it was not the natural senility and decay of Middle High-German poetry; that poetry had not by any means exhausted its resources, and might have borne fruit yet in many directions. Middle High-German poetry did not decay from within, but was deprived of light and air from without; the old enemy of secular poetry, the German clergy, commenced with redoubled power a new attack, which was this time successful and decisive for a long period. *This decay due to the influence of the clergy.*

The struggle between the Empire and the Papacy in the eleventh and twelfth centuries had, as we have already seen, exerted its influence on German poetry; the Crusades had been reflected in it, and the successful expeditions of Frederick the First had indirectly been the means of calling chivalrous poetry into life ; the idealism of the imperial policy was reflected in the idealism of German poetry.

But the practical ideal of life set up in Middle High-German poetry
was also of advantage to the practical age which followed on the
decay of the imperial power. The force which was formerly ex-
pended in the Crusades or the Italian campaigns could also be
exercised on the coasts of the Baltic. The empire was not the
nation, and the decline of the Hohenstaufen took place in a period
of immense national aspiration. The German nation now showed
Expansion　a talent for expanding its power and extending its
of Germany. sphere, such as it had never manifested before, even
in the time of the migrations or in the days of Charlemagne. The
influence of the chivalrous ideal was an important factor in the
steady colonisation of Brandenburg, Silesia, Pomerania, and Mecklenburg, in the achievements of the Teutonic Order of Knights, in
the peaceful conquests of Bohemia, in all the German enterprises
against Slavs, Prussians, and Esths. German towns, like Augsburg
and Nuremberg, became centres for the trade of the world, and acquired much of the power and splendour which before the Crusades
Rise of the　had belonged to Constantinople, in the same capacity.
commercial　Germany passed from agriculture to trade; German
spirit.　　commerce and German industry made marvellous
progress during the course of the thirteenth century, and in this
aspect, too, of the activity of the German citizen, we seem to trace
the influence of those virtues which Middle High-German poetry
so rigorously demanded—noble ambition, constancy, and perseverance, and that firmness of character which breaks all chains, and
clears away all hindrances.

But Middle High-German poetry itself reaped no advantage
from the national prosperity which it had contributed to bring
The practical　about. The whole social and political life now took
tendency of　a new direction. Everyone had to labour for himself.
the age　　The new political influence acquired by the princes
injurious to　called out their best qualities. Knighthood had to
poetry.　　struggle for its existence. Too much importance
was attached to practical activity, and no space was left for that
contemplative leisure which is the only atmosphere in which poetry
can flourish. Freidank was right in his complaint about usury and
the princes; poetry had now to yield before material interests. With

the fatal one-sidedness which we have noticed as characteristic of
the Germans, the nation plunged heart and soul into the new
movement. Even Frederick II was a merciless realist, and valued
science more than poetry. He welcomed poetry only where it
served as a political weapon; in rewarding Walther von der
Vogelweide he was rewarding the influential journalist who had
done him important services; but beyond that he did nothing for
poetry, whilst on the other hand he made Aristotle accessible to
Western science and himself wrote works on natural history.

But all this would only have deprived German poetry of its outward conditions of prosperity; its real spirit, its noblest ideas were
threatened by the hostility of the Church. Middle
High-German poetry had become, as we have often
had occasion to remark, an independent moral force.
It was tolerant in its spirit, and had declared through
Wolfram that unbelief could be expiated by a mere

*Heretical
tendencies in
Middle High-
German
poetry.*

change of views. In the Nibelungenlied it had inculcated the unchristian duty of revenge; in the Minnesingers it assigned a position to women which the Church could never yield to them; in the
chivalrous and popular epics it set up ideals of life utterly at vari-
ance with those represented in the lives of the Christian saints; in
Walther and Freidank's hands it assumed a directly hostile attitude
towards the Church and the Papacy. It was not only in Provence
that heresy went hand in hand with the secular poetry. In Germany too heretics acquired great influence; they gained the hearts
of the people, and composed hymns and songs which were taught
to children. A favourable political conjunction might have given
them as much power as they enjoyed in the South of France under
the protection of the nobility. During the quarrel between Innocent IV and Frederick II a German prince was on the point of
openly declaring himself in their favour, and it was only death that
prevented him from carrying out his intention. There might then
have been Albigensian wars in Germany also, and German poetry
would not have been inferior in merit to the sturdy polemical songs
of the Troubadours. But the armies, which were formerly at the
disposal of the Pope for spiritual warfare had become indolent.
The monasteries, which had produced the clerical poets of the

eleventh and twelfth centuries, were sunk in luxury. Even from
Worldliness their doors chivalrous poetry could not be kept away.
of the   One day a Rhenish Abbot, who was preaching to
monasteries. his monks, perceived that they were all comfortably
slumbering; he then raised his voice and cried: 'Hearken,
my brethren! here is a quite new and wonderful history: there
was once upon a time a king called Arthur'—at this they all started
up at once, and received from the preacher a fitting reproof. That
was about the year 1200. In 1291, there was at the monastery
of St. Gall no one who could write, but the Abbot tried his hand
at composing 'Tagelieder.'

Meanwhile the Church had long since brought new troops into
Rise of the the field, who were doing their work with victorious
Mendicant energy. The mendicant orders were beginning to
Orders.   appear already under Innocent III, and the popes
Dominicans
and Fran-   soon perceived what a useful instrument they might
ciscans,   be to them. About 1220 the Dominicans and Fran-
circa 1220. ciscans began to establish themselves in Germany.
Here, as elsewhere, they did not settle in solitary places, but in
the towns, and had a hand in all that was going on; as preachers
and confessors they strove to obtain entire dominion over men's
souls. The Dominicans were the more cultivated, the Franciscans the more popular. The latter began to be remarkable
as early as the thirteenth century for their popular preaching.
With the greatest zeal and ardour they commenced an onslaught
Religious   on the life of chivalry, and condemned everything
revival.   connected with it as sinful. The preachers specially
sought to gain an influence over the minds of women, and in this
they thoroughly succeeded. Their power soon made itself felt in
chivalrous circles; ladies began to despise finery, and to behave
themselves like nuns—'Instead of going with us to the dance,' so
the knights complained, 'we see you standing day and night in
church.'

The most powerful of all the Franciscan popular orators was
Brother   Brother Berthold of Regensburg, of whose sermons
Berthold.   we have numerous records in German and Latin.
As an orator he evinces the very qualities which we had occasion

to praise in the poets of the Bavarian race. As Walther used to excite the people by his songs, so Berthold now carried them away by his discourses ; this greatest preacher inherited the power of the greatest singer. Berthold's style, like Walther's, is naive and popular ; he too makes use of epic and dramatic devices, illustrating his teaching by stories, representing his audience as making objections to what he says, and passionately apostrophising those whom he is attacking, whether he thinks they are to be found among his audience or not. Like Walther he makes it easy for his listeners to follow him, for his language is graphic, his imagery vivid, and he knows how to excite breathless suspense ; he adheres strictly to the subject in hand, and carries out a clear system of subdivision in his sermons, carefully numbering each head of his discourse. He always seeks an external and sensuous basis on which to build up his spiritual teaching. For instance he speaks of ten pence which we owe to God, meaning thereby the ten commandments. Berthold, like Walther, has a strong love of nature ; he calls heaven and earth the Old and New Testament, the two books of religious instruction for the laity, and shows them repeatedly how these books should be read. Berthold too is an enemy of speculation, and warns his listeners against indulging in subtle enquiries about the mysteries of religion ; he speaks less of faith than of morality, and less of virtues than of vices. He easily glides into the satiric vein, but never into the comic. He scorns the course pursued by the indulgence-mongers, the pence-preachers, who loved to paint the sufferings of Christ with the most horrible details, shedding many tears at the same time, and thus moving their audience to weep. Berthold does not wish to touch but to terrify ; he wishes to excite terror and disgust of sin, and fear of punishment in hell. He was no great scholar ; he does not even quote the Bible correctly, and in morality he does not found his statements on accurate scholastic knowledge. But he has a thorough knowledge of life, and is well acquainted with the people whom he is addressing.

Berthold vehemently attacks the heretics, and thus bears witness to the wide influence which they exercised in Germany. Still more

[marginal notes:] Resemblance between Berthold and Walther.

Berthold's manner.

vehemently does he oppose the striving after wealth, and thereby
bears witness to the increase of material luxury and
the growth of the trading interest in this period.   He
His views.
attacks the minstrels, condemns dancing and tournaments, and
finds fault with that intermingling of morality and social convention
which was one of the characteristics of chivalry.   He protests
against the oppression of the weak by the powerful, and he acknowledges that it is as unlawful to kill a Jew as a Christian.
Nevertheless he is wont to introduce the Jews with the ornamental
epithet of 'stinking,' and he assures us that Jews, heathens, and
heretics will equally go to hell.

Berthold exalts the authority of the priest to an extraordinary
extent ; he says that if a priest passed by where Mary and all the
heavenly host were sitting, they would rise up before him.   He
places the Pope far above the Emperor, and asserts that the secular
dominion and authority are bestowed on the Emperor by the Pope.
He lived, in fact, in an age in which new glory was shed on the
priesthood, and when the authority of the Pope was more apparent
than the power of the Emperor.   He commenced his
activity as a popular orator in the year 1250, and continued it till his death on the 13th of December, 1272.
Berthold's career, 1250-1272.
Bavaria and Allemannia were the chief scenes of his labours, but he
also went down the Danube to Austria and Hungary, and northwards to Bohemia, Moravia, and Thuringia.   Everywhere thousands
of people flocked to hear him, and he had to preach in the open
air.   His audience was usually composed of citizens and country-
people, but he also penetrated into the castles of the great, and
succeeded even there in softening some hard hearts.   He is mentioned by several of the chroniclers, and he long continued to live
in the memory of the people ; there is not one of the German
mediæval poets of whom we have so many accounts as of this
mendicant monk ; his appearance was an historical event.

It would be an exaggeration to attribute to Berthold alone the
destruction of Middle High-German poetry ; but he is anyhow
the most striking figure among many similar men,
who zealously attacked that beautiful secular life
His great influence.
which was the source of Middle High-German poetry, and which had

already begun to be threatened from other quarters. We notice the influence of the sermon in the 'Spruch-poetry' and didactic poetry of this period; we see it converting the chivalrous epic into the saintly legend, trying to confine lyric poetry to sacred hymns, and only stopped in its advances by the invincible love of laughter and desire of amusement inherent in the masses of the people; and Berthold is the man to whose charge we may lay all this.

But it was not piety alone that spoilt the poetry of this later period; zeal for culture and thirst for knowledge *Increased* had also something to do with its decay. The chief *love of* representatives of learning in the thirteenth century *learning.* were the Dominicans. It was to their Order that Albert the Great belonged, a Swabian noble, who was Bishop of Regensburg from 1260–1262, and died at an advanced age in Cologne. *Albertus* He was a scholar of wide learning, and a most fertile *Magnus,* writer. He was the first really to introduce the re- *Bishop of* vived Aristotle into Western science, for the works of *Regens-* *burg.* that great philosopher were at first sternly repudiated by the Church. Albert drew up an abstract of the whole of the Aristotelian philosophy, and transformed it in ac- *His abstract* cordance with Church dogma. He set up Aristotle *of Aristotle.* as the great authority in natural science, so that he became in the opinion of the Middle Ages the forerunner of Christ in knowledge of nature. Albert laid the foundation for Western *Konrad von* natural science generally by his endeavour to sketch *Megenberg's* a complete picture of the universe. He also inspired *handbooks* *of natural* his order with an interest for natural observation, *history and* and although he himself wrote nothing in German, *astronomy,* yet his influence acted at least indirectly on Konrad *14th century.* von Megenberg, who in the fourteenth century compiled the first German hand-books of natural history and astronomy. Albert was also indirectly the means of inspiring a *Albert and* *Thomas* certain class of German theological literature, which *Aquinas,* was handed on in extracts and text-books down to *the fathers* the sixteenth and seventeenth centuries; this was *of German* *mysticism.* the literature of German mysticism. Albert and his still greater pupil, the Italian Thomas Aquinas, a Dominican like his master, furnished a considerable part of the thoughts embodied in the writings of Meister Eckard and the other German mystics, who were the first philosophers in the German language, and also belonged to the Dominican order.

The central idea of mysticism is the poetical conception of **Definition of** the soul as the bride of God. The glowing love-**mysticism.** yearnings of the Song of Solomon were interpreted in this sense, and mystic theology described the steps by which the soul could mount up to her heavenly bridegroom. Albert the Great asserts that the soul, by inward withdrawal from all earthly things, may become united in spirit with God. The Dominican, Meister Eckard, called this process the apotheosis of the soul, and sought to give it a psychological and speculative basis. Meister Eckard, the most gifted of the German mystics, **Meister** probably came from Thuringia; from 1304 he filled **Eckard.** several high offices in his order, and died in 1327 at Cologne. He and his associates created a German terminology for the abstract ideas of scholasticism. They set forth their views in sermons and treatises, but these did not come before the masses of the people, so that the sphere of their influence was in general restricted to the cloister. And even there they could only reckon on being understood if they succeeded in embodying their ideas in a concrete form, and in illustrating their thoughts by sensuous imagery. The imagery employed by the German mystics is generally noble and refined in character, seldom coarsely realistic. Mysticism has a bond of connection with poetry through the figurative style which it adopted for religious instruction ; and it not only influenced religious poetry, but also produced a number of prose-writings, through which the purest poetry shines. Eckard is the real philosopher among the mystics ; Tauler and Suso, his younger contemporaries and followers, never got beyond his sublime thoughts. No other of the mystics soared so high, or shared that bold attitude of mind which made Eckard go the length of saying: ' If it were possible that **Tauler and** God could turn from truth, I would cleave to the **Suso.** truth and forsake God.' Tauler is more practical, more bent on edifying than Eckard, and seeks to inspire his hearers with an active love of humanity.   Heinrich Suso is less a preacher than a man of letters, less of a theologian than of a lyric poet.   Eckard, it is true, sometimes reminds us, by his skilful dialectic, of certain representatives of the Minnesang, but Suso is simply a spiritual Minnesinger writing in prose.   He transfers the exact language of earthly love to heavenly devotion; he introduces descriptions of nature, and gives them a spiritual interpretation; he connects spring and love, winter and mourning; he compares women to flowers, and worldly-disposed people to roving falcons, and even goes so far as to introduce Lady Venus, and that 'master of loves,' Ovid, into his writings.   Suso is a sentimental and somewhat effeminate writer, and he assumes that his book will be read in the first place by women.   His life, which was written by a woman, is not a biography in our sense of the word, but contains memorable events in his spiritual life, which was of a very emotional character.   The book forms a religious pendant to Ulrich von Lichtenstein's secular love-memoirs.

Pious women played a great part in the whole movement of mysticism.   Mathilde von Magdeburg, who died about the year 1277, describes in her fragmentary reve- lations the marriage of the soul with its heavenly bridegroom; her language is exalted in tone and sometimes passes into rhyme.   She feels herself carried up to heaven, and imagines herself gazing into the future; she laments the corruption of the Church, and praises the Dominican order. Mathilde found a number of imitators, both in her lifetime and after her death.   In the fourteenth century visions became the fashion, and religious ecstacy was looked upon as the state of union with God.   If one nun had tasted the blessed rapture, none of her sisters would wish to be thought inferior to her.   One monastery rivalled another in this respect, and a record was kept of the visions seen in each; there was an interchange of spiritual experiences, and an active correspondence was kept up with the most prominent mystics, in addition to personal intercourse with them.

In Allemannia this movement proceeded side by side with the last efforts of the Minnesang.   It was in the writings of the

Female mystics. Mathilde von Magdeburg.

mystics and of their pious female worshippers that the chivalrous
spirit found its last refuge. There, and there only, did refinement
and a sense of form still survive. In this movement women
played as conspicuous a part as they had done in the golden days
of chivalry. Women with higher intellectual capacities, who had
formerly felt themselves happy in intercourse with the poets, now
retired to the seclusion of a convent or almshouse and joined in
company with sentimental priests in seeking after the Eternal.
Interpretations of the Song of Solomon heralded the commence-

Mysticism closes the period of the Minnesang. ment of the epoch of chivalrous love-poetry, and a
spiritual love-philosophy signalizes the end of the
period. And just as we noticed in the twelfth century, that when the clergy began to give a poetic
tinge to their piety, their writings lost their former
seriousness and devoutness, so too, in this later period, we shall
see that mysticism formed a stage of transition to an epoch which
was to make the most vehement attacks on the Roman clergy
and to limit their influence for ever.

Mystical theology often borders on pantheism, and it easily came
under the suspicion of heresy. Meister Eckard had to answer for

Rising opposition to the Papal power. his opinions before the Inquisition ; he had to make
a recantation, and some of his doctrines were con-
demned. The mendicant monks, once the most
faithful servants of the Pope, had now attained to such independent power that they could even turn against the Papacy.

In the reign of Ludwig the Bavarian (1314–1347) we actually
find the Franciscans ranged on the Emperor's side against the
Papacy. While Brother Berthold of Regensburg had made the
Emperor's authority dependent on the Pope, we find his brothers
of the same order at Munich attacking Papal omnipotence and in-
fallibility, attributing to the Emperor judicial power over a heretical
Pope, and beginning to discuss the boundaries of Church and State.
In literature also there are increased signs of an important change

Attacks on the clergy. towards the middle of the fourteenth century. The
attacks on the power of the clergy became more bitter,
the condemnation of the unholy lives and mental dishonesty of the
priests more vehement. A more decisive resistance was offered to

the Papal prohibitions of the Bible, which had been repeatedly
issued since 1229. There has been preserved to us a German
version of the Sunday Gospels and Epistles, with a preface in
which a layman defends himself against the 'highly learned priests,'
and boasts of having translated the Gospels into German; he also
says that he is preparing another work in defiance of the priests.

From 1308 to 1382 there lived in Strassburg a layman, Rulmann
Merswin by name; he was a merchant who had 　Rulmann
given up his business, and in middle life devoted 　Merswin.
himself to literature, though his works were not at first intended
for the public. He had been a penitent of Tauler's, but afterwards
left his confessor and sought his salvation independently. Rulmann
calls the clergy Pharisees and reproaches them with teaching things
that they could not prove from Holy Writ. On the other hand he
exalts the God-favoured laity, the true friends of God, who had
attained to union with Him, and recommends them as pastors and
spiritual fathers instead of the priests. The direct way to God, as
taught by the Mystics, became in Rulmann's hands a weapon against
sacerdotal authority. He went so far as to invent the character of
a lay mystic, whom he called the 'Friend of God in the Oberland,' and he made those around him believe in the reality of this
man. Rulmann's lay mystic receives many revelations from God,
and exercises a magic power over men's hearts; he is the leader
of a secret community and edifies his faithful followers by many
writings; he subjects a learned priest to his spiritual dominion, and
even exercises a personal influence over the Pope. Later on it
was thought that Tauler was referred to in the priest who had submitted himself to the friend of God instead of to God Himself. It
was also told of Meister Eckard that he had bowed in reverence
before a visionary woman, had envied her for her holiness and had
thankfully received her spiritual teaching. The religious independence of the laity could not have been carried further than this.

Rulmann's prose is diffuse and uninteresting, and full of wearisome repetitions owing to his lack of invention. 　His 'Buch
But one of his works, the 'Book of the Nine Rocks,' 　von den
is remarkable as reminding us in its plan of Dante's 　neun Felsen.'
immortal poem. It begins with a pessimistic picture of the world,

a satire on all classes, which corresponds to the Inferno; then the soul climbs up nine terraces one above the other, as Dante climbed up the mountain of Purgatory, and at the end we have a glimpse into the Holy of Holies, into the origin of things, where the soul is wedded to its Creator. Rulmann calls back to our mind the tolerant times of Walther and Wolfram when he denies that all Jews and Heathens are damned, and asserts that God loves some Jews and Heathens much better than many Christians. At the same time the poetic terms of mysticism are familiar to him, and he thus unites the dying strains of Middle High-German love-poetry with the first tones preluding the Reformation.

CHAPTER VIII.

In the year 1348, the fearful plague known as the Black Death broke over Europe, and for the space of two years **The Black** continued to ravage most of the German provinces. **Death, 1348.** Men were then seized with deep remorse for their sins, and began to do penance on their own account. Bands of excited people wandered from place to place, and read out what they declared to be a letter fallen from heaven, in which Jesus Christ Himself addressed the faithful, and did not spare the clergy. These people also scourged themselves in public, and one layman confessed another. Fear of Divine judgment made men more pious, but it did not reconcile them to the Church; the religious independence of the laity is as clearly expressed in the processions of the Flagellants as in the writings of Rulmann Merswin of Strassburg, which belong to about the same period.

In the same year 1348, the first German University was founded at Prague, and the basis was thus laid for the exist- **Foundation** ence of the learned classes in Germany. The Church, **of the first** thinking to strengthen its power by new bulwarks, **German** gave its blessing to the undertaking. But it was **University** possible also for the Universities to become enemies **at Prague,** to the Church. The scholars trained by the Uni- **1348.** versities entered the service of the ruling princes, and it was by co-operation of scholars and princes that the Reformation was accomplished.

The processions of the Flagellants and the foundation of the first German University stand as significant events at the entrance

of a period of 300 years, which extends to the peace of Westphalia
Character-   and includes all the religious and political move-
istics of the   ments preparatory to and consequent on the Refor-
period from   mation. Tolerance was not a characteristic of this
1348 to 1648.   epoch; it had its persecutions of the Jews, its Hussite
wars and its Thirty Years' War; it was only the powerless and
persecuted who taught that belief should not be forced upon any
one. The tendencies which in the course of the thirteenth century had undermined chivalrous life and destroyed Middle High-
German poetry, were now carried still further. Men had a super-
stitious respect for knowledge, although in the sixteenth century
popular wit gave birth to the saying which soon became current:
' Die Gelehrten, die Verkehrten ' (scholars are all crazy). German
industry and German trade experienced their greatest prosperity
and their deepest decadence during this period. Natural science
and industry together produced those discoveries which changed
the face of the world; the arts of engraving, wood-cutting and
printing were directly advantageous to intellectual life and to
literature. But the jealousy which already in the thirteenth
century reigned between the nobility and the bourgeois-classes,
now produced civil wars, and the egoism of the various parties
weakened the power of the whole nation. The position of
Germany with regard to foreign countries continued to decline
in importance from the fifteenth century onwards; the expansive
power of the German people was exhausted for the time being,
and the nation most powerful in arms of all Europe learnt to
tremble before Turks, French and Swedes, as it had once
trembled before Saracens, Normans and Magyars. In this vast
religious, scientific, warlike and material struggle, there was little
room left for poetry or for æsthetic interests in general. Only
the industrial arts could attain to any importance, and the achievements in this direction far surpassed the results attained in painting, sculpture and architecture. This whole period down to the
Decay of   seventeenth century did not produce a single poetical
poetry.   work which could even satisfy the most elementary
claims with regard to purity of form. Versification passed for
the most part into a mechanical counting of syllables or into

total irregularity, and even the language itself was barbarously mutilated. This period amassed vast quantities of poetic material, nor were new forms wanting in which the peculiar spirit of the age found expression; but the good material was treated in a bungling and careless fashion. Though dramatic spectacles found the greatest favour with the people, yet no plays of any permanent artistic value were produced. Humorous realism was most in sympathy with the taste of the times, yet these Aristophanic centuries, as they may well be called, brought forth no Aristophanes. The cultivated manners of the age of the Hohenstaufen had entirely passed away; formerly women had been worshipped as blessed saints, now they were burnt as witches, and all possible evil was said of them. In the preceding period great importance was attached to refined manners, and almost too great *Coarseness* sacrifices were made to the conventions of society. *of the age.* Now shamelessness reigned supreme; St. Grobianus (Grob=coarse) became the idol of the age, and the obscene Eulenspiegel its darling.

The study of the ancients was the only thing that could restore to the Germans the vanished sense of beauty. But no real improvement resulted from this quarter until the classical tendency in other modern literatures exerted its influence on Germany, until the examples of France, Italy, Spain, England, *Influence of* and Holland succeeded in awakening a Renaissance *the Renais-* in Germany also. Poetry then passed into the hands *sance very* of the scholars, who once more introduced purity *Germany.* and regularity into language and metre.

At the beginning of this period the lower classes became the audience for whom the poets wrote. In most of the towns which were centres of intellectual life the plebeians were in power, and thus it was they who naturally gave the tone to poetry. The popular song, the tale, the comic anecdote, but above all the drama, which exercised such an influence on the masses, now attained greater prominence. The nobility still re- *Poetry* mained faithful to the romance; and when in the *becomes* seventeenth century the aristocracy again began to *popular.* take an interest in poetry, the drama reaped no lasting benefit therefrom, but still continued to follow the taste of the people. The character of the masses, however, had changed; towards the close of the Middle Ages we find them increasingly frivolous, but after the Reformation increasingly serious. In earlier times they had laughed at the devil, in later times they regarded him with terror. It is the earlier and larger half of this epoch, the time from 1348 to 1517, which will occupy us in the present chapter.

RISE OF THE DRAMA.

The German drama owes its origin to the Middle High-German period, and here again legend leads us to the foot of the Wartburg and draws a vivid picture of the great power which dramatic spectacles then exercised over the minds of men. We possess an old German drama founded on the parable of the Wise and Foolish Virgins. The foolish ones are children of the world, who play and amuse themselves, thinking they will still be in time for the feast; but the Lord refuses them admission, and even Mary's intercession cannot move Him; they are carried off by devils, and break into heartrending lamentations.

Play of the Wise and Foolish Virgins, circa 1320.

The story is that this piece was represented at Eisenach in 1322 before the Landgrave, Frederick of Thuringia; when he saw that even Mary's efforts could not help the guilty, the Landgrave was filled with despair and anger, and said: 'What avails then the Christian faith? Will God not have mercy on us for the sake of Mary and all the saints?' And he went to the Wartburg and was unconscious for five days or more, and then was seized by a stroke, in consequence of which he kept his bed for three years and finally died, at the age of fifty-five.

Dramatic spectacles produced a deeper impression on the mind than could ever be attained by the sermon. The clergy knew this well, and therefore they cultivated the religious drama, till at last it became independent of their control and served more for amusement than for edification. So far as we know, the parables of the New Testament were seldom used as dramatic subjects before the Reformation. In the Old Testament, the

stories of Joseph in Egypt, of the Judgment of Solomon, and of
Susanna, were favourite subjects for plays. Sacred legends furnished the stories of Mary's Ascension, of the Finding of the
Cross, of St. Dorothy, St. Katharine, St. George and Theophilus;
Church history supplied the character of Pope Joan. But the
starting-point of all these plays, the origin of the
Christian drama, is to be traced to the dramatic   Origin of the
embellishment of the Church-festivals. Ancient and   Drama to be
found in the
simple ceremonies were developed into complete   Church-
dramatic representations. A manger behind the altar,   festivals.
a boy as an angel announcing the birth of Christ, other boys as
shepherds coming to adore at the manger,—these were the germs
of the Christmas-play, which in later elaborations extended from
the Messianic prophecies of the Old Testament to the massacre of
the Innocents, and ended with the heart-rending cries of the mothers
of Bethlehem. The Passion-plays arose from the custom of reading aloud, during Passion-week, the Gospel-accounts of the sufferings of Christ, and assigning to various persons the sayings and
dialogues occurring in the narrative; these Passion-plays usually
ended with the entombment. The Church-festival of Easter gave
rise to the Resurrection-plays. Tableaux vivants of the Creation,
the Fall, and the Redemption, were an adjunct of the procession
of Corpus Christi Day, and thus arose the Corpus Christi plays. ·

The Passion-plays and Easter-plays might be united into one,
and would then extend, perhaps, from the Baptism of Christ in
Jordan to the outpouring of the Holy Spirit. In the   Character
fifteenth century these plays often attained a length and Develop-
of 8000 rhymed lines; they went on for three or four   ment of the
days, and about 300 people were employed to take   religious
part in them. The oldest religious plays had been   Drama.
in Latin, but now only a few traditional Latin hymns reminded
people of their original form. At first the Church was the scene
of these representations, but later on the stage was set up in the
open air. While the earlier plays had many points of resemblance
with the opera, in the later ones predominance was given to
spoken dialogue, written in prose-like couplets. The dramatic
art was as imperfect as the scenic appliances. The stage, or

rather the play-ground round which the spectators gathered, was generally supposed to represent a plan of the city, or a map of the country; if the player passed from one corner to another, this might mean that he went into another house or journeyed into a foreign country. The actors had no entrances and exits; each had his fixed station, from which he advanced when taking part in the action, and to which he afterwards retired. Later on, scenic decoration was not totally wanting: a tree, a pillar, or a table was introduced, a garden was hedged in or a temple set up; heaven was represented by a scaffolding to which a ladder gave access, and in a distant corner the very jaws of hell were seen to yawn. But in the fifteenth century hell had still to be represented by a barrel; a barrel, too, was the pinnacle of the temple, and another barrel stood for the high mountain where Christ was tempted by Satan. Many years might elapse in a few moments without the ending of the act. Everything was represented in detail on the stage and there was no idea of concentration. The trouble of any dramatic exposition was most simply avoided by making each actor announce who he was. The dramatist treated his subject like an epic writer, and his work was merely a narrative in action.

Similar features may be traced in all these plays throughout the whole of Germany; like the Nibelungenlied, the story of the Wartburg-contest and other popular poems, they arrived at their present form through the elaboration of simple incidents and the collection of the same by the hands of various poets. None of these writers sought his own fame by his work, and few of their names are known to us. Not one of them felt any scruple in plundering his predecessors, or making literal transcriptions of epic poems. Truth in costume and accessories was as little an object with the mediæval dramatists as it was with the writer of the 'Heljand' or the artists of the fifteenth century; and indeed, the latter simply transferred to their canvas the impressions which they received from these religious spectacles. As the poets of the ninth century had blended feudal ideas with the life of Christ, so now a bourgeois conception prevailed, and Jerusalem became a mediæval German town in the imagination of German poets and painters.

The noblest poetic features which the Drama added to the Biblical narrative date from the twelfth and thirteenth centuries; that epoch, in which so much poetical sentiment prevailed, made its influence felt also in this sphere of literature. Mary Magdalene is the favourite figure of the dramatists of that period; she is represented as a child of the world, who is converted, and even in her sinful life her character is not without charm. Again, many touching traits were invented in connection with Christ's mother. For instance, in some of the Passion-plays, Judas has hardly put away the thirty pieces of silver when he is met by Mary, who calls him her dearest friend, and unsuspectingly confides her Son to his care. On the way to Calvary she hears the blows of the hammer with which Christ is being nailed to the cross. In her unceasing lamentations the pathetic and the horrible are closely mingled.

Religious drama in the 12th and 13th centuries.

As we advance in the fifteenth century the delight in comic characters becomes greater, and the audacity which would introduce them even into religious plays more marked. The Jews are the victims not only of hatred, but also of ridicule. Thus Judas is made to weigh the blood-money coin by coin. The watch at the grave are depicted as cowardly braggarts. The dealer from whom the three Marys buy spices had long been represented as a Jewish quack-doctor; in the later plays he receives the addition of a branded thief as his servant, and a quarrelsome woman as his wife, with whom he is constantly having fights. The race between Peter and John to the grave is also treated in a humorous spirit, and the later religious plays generally are full of coarse fun of this sort.

Coarse fun characteristic of the religious plays of the 15th century.

But it was the devil who was the privileged comic character and intriguant *par excellence* in the popular religious drama. His part was continually enlarged; the hosts of hell grew more numerous, the names of the devils more and more eccentric. Chosen representatives of the various classes are brought into the presence of Lucifer; there is the usurer, the monk, the witch, and the robber. Lucifer imposes a punishment on cheating cråftsmen, but a priest who has been dragged into hell is able to drive even the devil into

R

a corner by the vapour of incense and by his curses, and then
easily sets himself free. We see that the serious spirit of the early
Eisenach play had completely vanished.

The legend of Theophilus and that of Pope Joan were favourite
subjects of the religious drama. Theophilus is a priest who has
handed himself over into the power of the devil by a bond, in which
he renounces God and the Virgin Mary; afterwards, however, he is
moved by a sermon, and repents. The Virgin herself espouses
his cause, and succeeds in moving her Son to mercy, and in com-
pelling the devil to give up the bond. Pope Joan is an English
girl who goes to Paris disguised in man's clothes; accompanied by
a priest, her lover. She is made a doctor there and a Cardinal in
Rome, and finally rises to the Papacy. At last she is unmasked
with shame, and is received by the devils in hell, whence, however,
she is freed by the intercession of Mary and St. Nicholas. This
subject was treated by Theodorich Schernberg in his play, ' Frau
Jutta ' (1480).

At this time the devil also played an important part in German
farce. Old German comedy never attained to anything higher
than the farce. Bodily deformities, indecencies of all kinds, beat-
ings, scoldings and curses, comic surnames, speeches in foreign
languages, verbal misunderstandings, literal interpretations of figurative expressions, bombastic speeches—these were the means by
which the wit of this age satisfied the taste of a laughter-loving
audience.

The German religious drama is divided into very much the same
classes as the French; in this branch of literature also France set
the fashion, both in the general spirit and in the details of execution. Germany as well as France produced Mysteries, Moralities,
Mysteries or Farces, and Sotties. The Mysteries or Miracle-plays
Miracle were derived from the Old and New Testaments, or
plays. from sacred legend or history—for instance, from
the Trojan cycle of legends.

The Moralities included New Testament parables, disputations,
Moralities. (for instance between Synagogue and Church, or Life
and Death), and other pieces with allegorical characters or personified abstractions. The dance of Death which Hol-

bein has immortalised is the picture of a Morality-play, in which Death was made to fetch away the various ranks or periods of life one after another to the dance, and to hold a short dialogue with each.

The Farces, the real burlesques, were frequently written in the form of a legal trial; they mostly deal with questions of love and marriage, and the scene is generally laid in **Farces.** the present. But they also draw their materials from the Arthurian legends, from the poetry of the gleemen, and from that of Neidhart, or from classical, Italian and German tales. We meet with the heroes of the Rosengarten, with Dietrich von Bern, the dwarf-king Laurin, Solomon and Markolf (Morold), Aristotle and Phyllis, the Emperor and the Abbot (as in Bürger's ballad of that name).

The 'Sottie,' the clown-play, was acted on Carnival night, the day before the beginning of Lent. It originated in **Sotties,** processions of maskers. Young people used to go **Carnival-** dressed up from house to house and act little plays, **plays.** in return for which they expected hospitality to be shown them. In the simplest form of these plays each person merely recited a speech, in which he satirically characterized the class whom he typified. Lovers, women, rustics, penitents, and quack-doctors were favourite subjects for ridicule. Sometimes there is a central character round which the others are grouped; for instance, in one farce, one maiden makes fools of a number of men, while in another the foolish lovers all appear before Lady Venus. Dialogues might be introduced, and we even find traces sometimes of a definite plot, as, for instance, when one maiden is wooed by representatives of various classes, and ends by taking the clerk. All these farces are marked by a coarseness and indecency beyond all conception. This licence, which is often apologised for at the end of the piece, was a special feature of the Carnival.

But the German Carnival-play was not confined to Sotties. The four classes of drama enumerated above were not so strictly distinguished from each other in Germany as in France. The whole of the German secular Drama of the fifteenth century may be classed under the head of Carnival-plays. All the plays which

R 2

were not connected with the Church-festivals were probably represented on Shrove Tuesday, namely farces, moralities, and even the
secular Mysteries.   And we have evidence that even Biblical pieces,
like the judgment of Solomon, were acted on the last night of the
Carnival.   The terrible prophecy of Antichrist was treated in a comic
manner, and used to ridicule the clergy.   Antichrist was considered
as the lord of Shrove Tuesday.   Carnival and Lent were personified and made to bring accusations against each other; or various
classes would lament over Carnival-night, which leads them into
excesses that they afterwards regret.

The festival of Carnival-night was an institution of bourgeois ori-
gin, and it was in the great towns that it was most faithfully observed.
Moralities were produced, we know, from Reval on the Baltic, to
Basle ; Lübeck also preferred more serious plays for Carnival-night.
Nürnberg, on the contrary, seems to have been the centre of comic
revelry.   It is there alone that we can mention writers of Carnival-
plays by name, namely Hans Rosenblüt and Hans Folz.
Rosenblüt's real name seems to have been Schnep-
perer, and he was chief gunmaker of the town of
Nürnberg. Folz came from Worms, and was a surgeon and barber.
Both may be considered as forerunners of the celebrated shoe-
maker and Mastersinger (cf. chap. ix, § 4) Hans Sachs, who, like
them, lived in Nürnberg, and, like them, wrote many Carnival-plays,
Mastersongs, and serious or comic poems in short rhymed couplets.

In a few single farces the German drama of the fifteenth century
attained something approaching to a regular plot.   But it was the
German classical scholars who first gave the drama a stricter form.
They made the students at the Universities perform Roman
comedies, and they themselves wrote Latin plays.
The best of these, Reuchlin's 'Henno' (acted in
1497), is derived from a genuine French farce, 'Maître
Pathelin,' well known even at the present day; this farce in
turn owes its origin to the 'Masques' of Italian popular comedy.

Maître Pathelin, the lawyer, cheats a merchant about some cloth,
and succeeds by a trick in obtaining the acquittal of a shepherd
who has been justly accused by the same merchant; he advises

his client to answer nothing but *baa* to all questions put to him in court. But when Pathelin demands his fee, the shepherd again answers *baa* and runs away.

Reuchlin was not very successful in his treatment of the subject; he imitated Terence, and perhaps from his own knowledge of Italian comedy introduced the character of the soothsayer.   But, thanks to the good source from which the play is drawn, it stands far above the mass of Latin and German comedies even of the sixteenth century; it was translated by Hans Sachs, and there are two other translations or adaptations of it. Gottsched was not wrong, especially from the standpoint of his own achievements, in calling this play a masterpiece.

In the fifteenth century Roman comedy was revived in modern European literatures, and we meet with Plautus and Terence in German garb.   Unfortunately the first efforts in this direction remained also the best. Albrecht von Eyb (1420 to 1495), canon of Bamberg, Eichstädt, and Würzburg, translated two comedies of **Revival of Roman comedy in the 15th century.** Plautus (the 'Menaechmi' and 'Bacchides'); they did not appear till long after his death, and were then printed as an appendix to his 'Spiegel der Sitten' ('Mirror of Morals') in 1511. He wrote them in an easy flowing prose, gave German names to the heroes and **Albrecht von Eyb's translations from Plautus.** heroines of Plautus, and put German sentiments in the mouth of his Heinzes, Lutzes, and Barbes; he replaced the maxims and expressions of Plautus by German proverbs and popular illustrations, and thus Germanised these immortal old comedies.

But these promising beginnings led no further. Albrecht von Eyb had written an original prose-work on marriage, and dedicated it to the chief magistrate of Nürnberg; but neither as an original writer nor as a translator was his example followed by the play-writers of Nürnberg. The German drama retained its monotonous doggrel couplets, and was thus cut off from all natural freedom of speech, and from all the charms of an artistically constructed dialogue. But notwithstanding these and other imperfections the drama was the most influential form of poetry in the fourteenth and fifteenth centuries, and a certain tendency to dramatic treatment is noticeable in all branches of poetry at that period.

Songs and Ballads.

The bourgeois singers whom we first met with in the thirteenth century do not disappear even in the sterile times of the fourteenth and following centuries. They were the upholders of the poetic tradition. They practised song - making as a craft, and handed down the technical art of the Minnesang. They were professional

The later Master-singers. poets, and felt their importance as such. If a man came to a strange place, and claimed to be a poet, he was asked where he had learnt his art. And in order to bear the title of Master, a man had to produce certain fixed works in the traditional departments of lyric poetry.

A few of these Masters were still to be found at this period at the courts of princes; as Heinrich von Mügeln in the fourteenth, Michel Beheim in the fifteenth, and Jörg Grünwald in the sixteenth century. But these instances are rare, and in the sixteenth century all these poets had to give place to the court-musicians. For though they were artistic poets, they were not artistic musicians such as were now required; their songs were only for one voice, and the favour of the art-loving public was now exclusively given to part-songs.

In the towns the Mastersingers were better able to retain their power. In the middle of the fifteenth century Mainz and the Upper Rhine in general were held in honour as the last refuge of the ancient forms of song. These songs might only be written to the melodies of the earlier great masters, for all efforts after novelty in music were condemned. These degenerate successors of the great masters made a sacred principle out of their own incapacity. Against them there rose up the Moderns, who had some con-

Ancient and modern school of Meistersang. fidence in their own powers, and at least showed great activity in other provinces of literature. They wrote Carnival-plays, and handed on the stories of the hero-legends, treating them afresh in an abridged form, or enriching them with their own inventions. These writers, who gathered around the play-writer Hans Rosenblüt in Nürnberg, followed some handicraft beside their art. As the public at large

continued to take less and less interest in poetry, it became more
and more the private property of these worthy Mas-   Character-
ters, and received from them that dried-up form   istics of the
which lived on in certain parts of Germany down to   later
the present century.   The poetic art became in their   Meistersang.
hands a craft, organized into a guild like any other craft.   It was
these later Mastersingers who invented the strange idea of poetic
meetings, and also those extraordinary names of melodies, those
artificial tricks of metrical construction, which we meet with in
German poetry towards the close of the Middle Ages.   To them,
too, was due that intellectual barrenness of matter, that self-con-
tented revelling in the depths of didactic wisdom and in the im-
penetrable mysteries of faith.

Already in the fourteenth century these Masters began to com-
plain of the increasing usurpations of dilettantism.   Popular
'There lives,' says one of them, 'no peasant ever   poetry out-
so common, who does not pretend to be a singer.'   side the
Numerous evidences of the participation of the people   Meistersang.
in poetry at this period are to be found in many of the songs that
have been preserved to us, to which the names of the writers are
appended : a student, a scribe, a fisher, a miner, a baker's appren-
tice, a warrior bold, a rich peasant's son, three riders brave of
Augsburg, three maidens of Vienna, &c.   There may be many
fictitious authorships among them, but the fiction would not have
been possible without some basis of reality.   Noblemen, too, whom
we know by name, continued the tradition of the Minnesang; such
were Oswald von Wolkenstein, whose romantic life is like a fantastic poem, Hugo von Montfort, who had his songs set to music
by his servant, and a few others.   They too sometimes adopt
the so-called popular tone, and Oswald's poems have been included
among the popular songs.   But the real representatives of popular
lyric poetry, those who set the example for all the dilettanti, were the
common singers, the descendants of the 'Vagrants' of the twelfth
century, the 'Gumpelmänner,' of whom we hear so many complaints
in the thirteenth century, the 'Bänkelsänger' (ballad-   'Bänkel-
singers) of the sixteenth century, who did not shine   sänger.'
by their learning, but whose object was solely to find favour in the

widest circles. These singers played for dancing, and it was then The 'Volks- too that they sang those songs which are generally lieder.' known as the 'Volkslieder' (people's songs) of the fourteenth, fifteenth, and sixteenth centuries, and which were also sung in chorus by the dancers. There could hardly have existed a distinct line of separation between the Mastersingers and these ballad-singers; the Masters sometimes condescended to write simple poems, and probably it was just those lighter songs which they themselves considered inferior, that attained a wide popularity. And there is no other distinguishing mark by which the 'Volkslied' may be known, but wide dissemination and general favour.

The singers of the twelfth century were the descendants of the wandering clerks of the Archpoet's stamp, and it was through these Various minstrels that many of the forms developed by the Latin classes of the poetry of that time were adopted in the 'Volkslieder;' 'Volkslied.' such were the drinking-song, the 'Streitgedicht' (cf. p. 47), frivolous love-ballads, poetry mixing Latin and German, as in the song : 'In dulci jubilo, nun singet und seid froh,' part-songs, in which the singers enthusiastically praised their free, wandering life, and thus incited other classes to the same self-exaltation. The *répertoire* of these singers further comprised what were called 'Priameln' (short epigrammatic poems on all subjects), and 'Lügen-lieder' (lying songs), as well as riddles, fables, and parables, and songs of praise or censure with allusions to public and private life.

In the 'Volkslied,' as in the fable, animals, plants, and even inani-General mate objects, are endowed with speech. Parables and character- a parabolic form of expression are also very common. istics of the Now, as in the twelfth century, we find a lady speak-'Volkslied.' ing of her lover under the symbol of a falcon; and the lover who must part from his beloved, describes himself as an owlet who has tumbled from the branch where he used to rest. The 'Volkslieder' are full of this kind of figurative language.

From the earliest times the gleemen or popular singers had been the patrons of comic poetry; and the comic elements of the 'Volkslied,' like those of the Carnival-play, are closely related to the poetry of Neidhart, and the satires of the thirteenth century. The leading features of Neidhart's dance-songs, coquettish girls, clumsy peasants, strings of bad names, women's quarrels—all lived on in the 'Volkslieder.' In them, as in Tannhäuser's poems, we meet with parodies of the Minnesang, descriptions of domestic misery, names of comic import, as *Seldomsober*, *Beat-the-guest*, and others of the same sort. The praises of autumn and the eating-songs, where the host is called and the various dishes are ordered, remind us of the Minnesinger Steimar. This class of songs received a strange addition in the songs for the feast of the Michaelmas-goose. In fact everything in the Minnesang, which owed its origin to the gleemen, or was written in the popular tone, meets us again in the 'Volkslieder.' We find the refrain, the announcement of the seasons, the same epic and dramatic elements, and the same pic- Connection between the Volkslie- der and the Minnesang. torial and graphic tendency. The parting-songs (*Scheidelieder*) of the Minnesingers received a rich after-growth in these later popular songs, and it was only in them that a breath of Walther's poetry still lingered; we even find his beautiful summer dance-song reproduced trait for trait, in later popular poems. But the popular singers also tried to appropriate some of those elements of the Minnesang which were derived from the French; they carried into wider spheres that colourless phrase the 'service' of the lover, as also the idea of envious and malicious tongues, the short alternating dialogue which owed its origin to the chivalrous epic, and above all the 'Tagelied.'

The women of these popular love-songs, are not mostly married women, as in the poems of the Minnesingers; they are, as a rule, young maidens, who are not only praised, Popular love-songs. but also turned to ridicule and blamed. The woes of love do not here arise from the capricious coyness of the fair one, but are called forth by parting, jealousy, or faithlessness. Feeling is stronger than in the Minnesang, and seeks accordingly for stronger modes of expression. The range of permitted subjects and recognised forms of expression is enlarged, and a wider scope is given to imagination. The 'Volkslieder' offer many instances of a very primitive form of poetry (cp. p. 5), namely a picture from nature in direct, sometimes in unconnected juxtaposition with an incident of human life; the following lines may serve as an instance :

> 'Three leaves upon a linden-tree, they flourished fair to see;
> The maiden blithely leapt and danced, her heart was full of glee.'

And we often find longer poems opening with such descriptions of nature as the following, revealing a whole landscape to our eyes in a few words :

> 'There stands a tree in yonder vale,'

or,

> 'There lies a town in Austrian land,'

or again,

> 'Up yonder on the mountain there stands a stately house.'

By this word 'yonder' the scene is at once brought immediately before our eyes. In other ways, too, these poets do their utmost to produce a vivid impression, and especially at the beginning of a poem. The song often opens with a question, an exclamation, an address, or a short sentence which takes us at once *in medias res.* It is also a favourite device to begin with the words, 'I heard,' or 'I know,' thus bringing the subject within the poet's own experience. These popular poets always draw with bold, sometimes with coarse strokes. Words of importance are repeated to make them more effective, and graphic realism is aimed at throughout. Much is left to the reader's imagination, and thus the connection between the various details of the song is often not apparent, though the general meaning may be quite intelligible, and every detail clear by itself; the song, 'Ich hört' ein Sichelein rauschen,' is a good instance of this.

This method of leaving much to the hearer's imagination is one of the most effective features in these popular songs. The sensuous is expressed, and the spiritual significance must be inferred. Lovers speak less of their feelings than of wreath or ring. Some songs reveal a whole human destiny in a short dramatic dialogue.

The striving after brevity, which is so marked a feature in the 'Volkslied,' caused a corresponding popularity of the Ballad, which in the Minnesang had been almost entirely confined to the one form of the 'Tagelied.' We know for certain that about the year 1360 shorter songs of three verses came into fashion. In the ninth and tenth centuries the heroic songs had shrunk in compass, in the twelfth and thirteenth they had again attained epic breadth, and now they were once more confined to narrower limits. The poems about Herzog Ernst, which had been expanded to 6000 rhymed lines, now sank to 819 stanzas (1068 lines), or even to 54 stanzas (648 lines), i. e. to a sixth or a tenth of their former extent. In the same manner, short narratives and poetic tales were now transformed into ballads written in stanzas. The story of the murdered lover whose heart is set before his lady to eat, already told by Konrad von Würzburg in rhymed couplets, now appears again in the popular ballads. The melancholy character of most of these ballads, and the fact that they most of them deal with matters of love, lead us to place their origin in the sentimental thirteenth century. Pyramus and Thisbe, Hero and Leander, were favourite stories. The 'Tagelied' was now made to embrace all the meetings of the lovers, from the first tryst down to the tragic ending, and many other new features and fresh incidents were introduced in the ballad-poetry of this period.

Ballads based on the heroic legends.

The names of four of the Minnesingers lived on in popular poetry. The first was Reinmar von Brennenberg, a Bavarian lyric poet, to whom is attributed the story of the lover's heart mentioned above. The second and third were Heinrich von Morungen and Gottfried von Neifen, whose names are preserved in the song of the noble Moringer, who returns from the East just in time to prevent his wife from contracting a second marriage with the young lord of Neifen; in this song two genuine stanzas of Walther von der Vogelweide are put into the mouth of the hero. The fourth Minnesinger, whose memory was preserved by the popular poetry, was Tannhäuser; a penitential poem attributed to him had been handed down together with his frivolous dance-songs, and this gave rise to a story that he had in later life bidden farewell to the world like Walther von der Vogelweide. This story suggested to one of the popular

Reminiscences of the Minnesingers in the later popular poetry.

poets the idea of introducing Tannhäuser's 'Farewell to Lady Venus,' and in giving an account of Tannhäuser's penance, he took the opportunity of inveighing, like Freidank, against the pope's cruelty and holding up the mercy of God in contrast. The pope has a dry staff in his hand, and declares to the penitent Tannhäuser: 'As little as this staff can bud, so little can you obtain God's mercy.' But on the third day the staff begins to bud; the pope sends out in search of Tannhäuser, but all in vain, for he has returned to the mountain of Lady Venus.

In the 'Volkslieder' it was no longer remembered that Brennenberg, Morungen, Neifen, and Tannhäuser were poets; but in preserving their names the 'Volkslied' was really looking back on **Summary of** its own classical period. The 'Volkslieder,' as we **the history** know them from the collections of the fifteenth and **of the** sixteenth centuries, are often faulty and inartistic; it **'Volkslieder.'** is quite clear that verses have been added, that phrases and incidents of various origin have been patched together, that good plans have been badly carried out; in short, that splendid material has been misused and handed down in a mutilated form. On the other hand, the little which is known to us of the popular lyric poetry of the twelfth and thirteenth centuries is not inferior to the Minnesang in correctness and perfection of form.

As the epic poetry of the gleemen attained its perfection in the Nibelungenlied, 'Gudrun,' and 'Albhart's death,' so, too, their lyric poetry probably reached its zenith about 1200, the period to which the popular poems of Walther von der Vogelweide belong. But during the thirteenth century we can hardly trace it except by its influence on the chivalrous poetry. It was only with the total decay of the latter, and the simultaneous rise of the lower classes in the towns, that the 'Volkslied' came into prominence. After the third decade of the fourteenth century the political poems, the so-called historical 'Volkslieder,' become more numerous; and Tilemann Elhem von Wolfhagen, the writer of the Limburg Chronicle, tells us of some popular songs that came into existence between 1350 and 1380. In the beginning of the fifteenth

century, the power of the popular songs was so great that they
exercised an influence on religious poetry. But soon afterwards
we meet with inferior songs, consisting only of well-worn phrases.
The political songs are generally descriptions of battles, seldom
more than very dry reports with lists of those who distinguished
themselves, and numerous details, which were of more interest
perhaps to the poet's immediate audience than they are to posterity.   Hatred and passion seldom attain artistic expression in the
'Volkslieder,' and there is hardly any trace of narrative-talent
which would bring the events vividly before us.   There is little
in this political poetry that rises above the level of rhymed prose.
The ballad, too, soon fell into neglect again, and the love-song
greatly deteriorated in the hands of the sober burghers of the
sixteenth century.   The ardour of passion seems damped, and
feelings are expressed in sententious and pedantic language;
the songs become more and more artificial and affected.   Here
too, prose gradually gained ground, till in the second half of
the sixteenth century romanic models began to assert their
power.

RHYMED COUPLETS.

The rhymed couplets of epic poetry were made to answer almost
all the purposes to which the stanzas of the singer had been
turned ever since the fourteenth century. Corresponding to the
love-song, we have the love-letter, which already, in the thirteenth
century, had begun to avail itself of this couplet-form. Political
subjects could be more effectively handled in this form than in
that of the stanza. Tales and farces, fables, satires, allegories,
and didactic poems remained faithful to these rhymed   Decline of
couplets, though they could not hinder the gradual   the epic.
encroachments of prose.   In the fifteenth century epic poetry
became well-nigh extinct, and had to give place to the prose
novel.

One single important epic appeared in Flanders, shortly before
the Reformation, and has since then continued to assert its place

in German literature : the epic of Reineke Fuchs. It is not
Flemish indeed an original poem; the Low-German provinces
Epic of drew their poetry almost entirely from foreign sources.
Reineke High-German and Dutch romantic tales were tran-
Fuchs. scribed into Low-German, and translations of Latin
fables were made in the same dialect. The predilection for poetry
about animals, together with that delight in law-processes which
we have already noticed in connection with the plays of this
period, rendered the story of Reineke Fuchs a specially attractive
theme ; the story could boast of a long history, and had already
once before this been introduced into Germany (cp. p. 146).

The Æsopian fable of the sick lion, who, on the advice of the
Origin of fox, is cured by a fresh wolf's skin, had come from
the story of India to Greece, had then passed to Italy, and from
Reynard thence, in the eighth century at the latest, to Ger-
the Fox. many. About 940 the story appears in a short Latin
epic, by a monk, in which he narrates, under the form of an
Latin ver- animal-fable, his flight from his monastery at Toul.
sion, 940. It was probably at the beginning of the twelfth century that the chief characters of the fable, the Wolf and the Fox,
acquired in Flanders their German names of ' Isengrim ' (he with
the iron visor) and 'Reinhart' (the very hard, invincible in cunning).
'Isengrimus' In 1148 Master Nivardus of Ghent completed his
in Flanders, Latin poem ' Isengrimus,' in which this fable ap-
1148. pears, enlarged by the addition of many others,
and thus raised to the rank of an epic. The monks were the
originators of the epics of animal-life ; they described their own life in
the fable of the Wolf turned monk, and made the fable of the lion's
illness into a satire of court-life. But the story of Reynard the
Fox was also seized on by the poets of the chivalrous period as
an excellent subject for epic treatment. In France it gained such
Heinrich der popularity that the Flemish word *renard* became
Glichezare's the general name for the fox there, instead of the
'Reinhart Old French word *goupil* (Latin *vulpes*). It was from
Fuchs,' 12th French sources that the Alsatian gleeman, Heinrich
century. der Glichezare, in the twelfth century, derived the
materials for his Middle High-German poem ' Reinhart Fuchs.' And

it was a French poem written by the priest, Pierre de St. Cloud, at the beginning of the thirteenth century, which was used by the Flemish poet Willem, as the basis for his Flemish poem 'Reinaert' (1250). This remarkable poem, which far excelled its French original, was remodelled and continued by an inferior poet about the year 1380; this later poem, again, was furnished with
Willem's
Flemish
poem
'Reinaert,'
1250.
a prose commentary in 1480, and a Low-German translation of it was printed and published at Lübeck in 1498. In 1544 Michael Beuther made a bad High-German version of the same poem, and in 1566 it was excellently translated into Latin by Hartmann Schopper. The interest in the story continued unabated till Goethe wrote his 'Reinecke Fuchs' in hexameters, and thus returned to some extent to the style of the tenth century.

Since Willem's work, the story of the sick lion no longer formed the centrē of the fable, which was devoted almost exclusively to the misdeeds of the fox, ending with his being outlawed. The poet who continued Willem's
Various
phases of
the story.
work altered the conclusion, and made the fox return again to court, and attain to new honours by his triumph over Isengrim in single combat. In the tenth century, the fable had glorified the sly, cruel fox, and made him come out triumphant; in Willem's work the requirements of justice are satisfied, and the evil doer is outlawed; but Willem's successor made him triumph again, an evidence that in the fourteenth century the moral standard had sunk again to what it had been in the tenth.

High-German poetry of this class produced no work coming up to the level of Reineke Fuchs, but, on the other hand, its productions show more of originality. A poem like Heinrich Wittenweiler's 'Ring' (fifteenth century), represents to a certain extent a new department of poetry. The satiric tale, after the style of 'Meier
Heinrich
Witten-
weiler's
'Ring,' 15th
century.
Helmbrecht,' has here advanced to the level of the burlesque epic. The story runs thus: A peasant wedding gives rise to a war between the two villages of Lappenhausen and Nissingen; both collect troops from all parts, and epic heroes such as Hildebrand and Dietrich von Bern, are represented as espousing one

side or the other; Lappenhausen is destroyed, the bridegroom Bertschi Triefnas alone escapes, and becomes a hermit in the Black Forest. Many of the scenes in this poem might easily be

Influence of the popular drama on other kinds of poetry.

transformed into short dramas, such as were in vogue at that time. Smaller poems, too, of satiric tendency were often written in the manner of Carnival-plays. Many allegorical poems of this period of the kind which we have already noticed among Konrad von Würz-

burg's writings (see p. 182) could, with little trouble, be turned into Moralities. Such are, for instance, the poems in which the author describes himself going out of a morning, and meeting with mytho-logical characters or personified virtues, from whom he learns maxims of trivial wisdom. There is a Swiss satire on all classes, written at the time of the Council of Constance (1414 to 1418), which

Swiss satire: 'Des Teufel's Netz,' circa 1415.

in its plan closely resembles a Morality-play; it is called 'The Devil's Net,' and is in the form of a dialogue between a hermit and the devil. The Swabian poet, Hermann von Sachsenheim, who died in the year

1458, wrote some poems of a semi-didactic character in which he

Hermann von Sachsen-heim's 'Spiegel' and 'Mohrin' (1453).

adopted the form of the legal trial so much in favour with the writers of Carnival-plays; in his 'Mirror,' written after 1451, the poet has to answer the charge of disloyalty before an allegorical character; in his 'Mohrin' (1453) Lady Venus accuses him before King Tannhäuser of inconstancy in love. Hermann

von Sachsenheim was a scholar who had been at the University and had received a special education in law.

Another South-German scholar, also a student of law, Dr. Sebastian Brand of Strassburg, sought to impart new life to the whole of popular didactic poetry. Brand studied and lived at Basle till 1501, when he was recalled to Strassburg, where he died

Sebastian Brand's 'Narren-schiff' (1494).

as town-clerk in 1521. He translated the moral maxims of Cato (a mediæval Latin poem), and a few subsequent moral writings, modernised Freidank's 'Bescheidenheit,' and himself wrote the 'Ship of Fools,' which was published in 1494. Through a Latin

translation, which appeared in 1497, this poem attained a European reputation. It is based on the plan of the Sottie, more especially of that form of farce in which many fools were grouped together in one framework. The idea of a number of fools going on board a ship had probably already been introduced in carnival amusements of the Upper and Lower Rhine, and certainly was not new to literature. About this time also moral picture-sheets were published, in which human vices were represented as figures in fool's dress. All that Brand did was to expand the rhyme which accompanied these woodcuts into a satire on various types of human character. There are over a hundred fools on the ship, which is sailing past 'Schlaraffenland' (land of idlers) to 'Narragonien' (Fool's land), and Sebastian Brand introduces them individually to the reader : there is the book-fool, the miser-fool, the fashion-fool, the spoiler of children, &c. Sometimes we seem completely transported into the Carnival-play, for instance, when the various fools describe themselves, or when Venus appears in their ranks and is represented on the accompanying wood-cut leading two fools and a monk in a leash; for Brand has added wood-cuts which take the place of the actual appearance in the drama, and are as much an integral part of the work as the text itself.

Similar in style to Brand's poem, but still more dramatic, is the Franciscan Thomas Murner's 'Exorcism of Fools;' here again we have a series of pictures of fools, with elucidatory verses to each picture. In other works of Murner's the fools are replaced by vagabonds and rogues. Murner had more poetical talent than Brand, in whose *Murner's 'Narren-beschwö-rung,' 1512.* writings the rhyme is the only thing to remind us of poetry. But while Murner used to throw off his works hastily, Brand worked most conscientiously and endeavoured to make his book a compendium of moral wisdom. Like some of the didactic poets of the twelfth and thirteenth centuries, he drew from the Bible and from the classical authors, turning extracts into easy German verse, and making use of the proverb-form when convenient. His writings, like Murner's, are uncouth in form, and show no idea of euphony or style. All the same, he fell in thoroughly with the taste of his contemporaries, and he is one of the most influential writers in earlier German literature.

While the spirit and the characters of the Carnival-play made their way into didactic poetry, the ideas of the Morality-play were reflected in the epic. The taste for serious epic poetry had not yet entirely died out. In Bavaria Wolfram von Eschenbach and his school were still held in high repute. A worshipper **Later imi-** of Wolfram, Püterich von Reicherzhausen, was a **tators of the** **chivalrous** zealous collector of Middle High-German chivalrous **poetry.** poetry, and about 1480 a Munich painter, Ulrich Fütrer, wrote at the bidding of Duke Albrecht IV a comprehensive cyclic work on the Round Table, the last echo of the chivalrous epic poetry. But the true representative of the **Maxi-** Middle High-German tradition in this period is the **milian I.** emperor Maximilian I (1493–1519), who in poetry as in real life deserves the honourable title of 'last of the knights.' **The 'Am-** He ordered the writing in Tyrol of the 'Ambraser **braser Hel-** Heldenbuch' (so called from the castle of Ambras in **denbuch.'** Tyrol, where it was long kept); this book is a collection of the best popular and chivalrous poems of the Middle High-German period, and the knowledge it affords us is quite inestimable. Maximilian also described his own life from various points of view; in the rhymed epic Theuerdank he narrated his personal experiences, in the 'Weisskunig,' a prose work, he gave the history of his wars, and in a Latin prose work, of which we have but uncertain record, he probably related the peaceful acts of his reign. **The 'Weiss-** In the 'Weisskunig' the emperor himself and the other **kunig.'** European sovereigns are called by the names of various colours, and thus concealed as it were behind a mask; this work **'Theuer-** did not appear in print till 1775. The 'Theuerdank,' **dank' (1517).** in the writing of which Maximilian's secretaries, Melchior Pfinzing and Marx Treizsauerwein took part, was published in 1517, and soon gained the favour of the German public. A number of incidents and adventures in Maximilian's life are here connected together by a thread of romantic narrative, full of allegorical figures. The noble hero Theuerdank, i.e. Maximilian, woos the queen Ehrenreich, which means that he strives after honour; he holds his own against the Evil Spirit, who comes to him in the guise of a learned doctor, and also successfully resists the Devil's captains, Fürwittig (*Vorwitz*, imprudence), Unfalo (*Unfall*, mischance), and Neidelhart (*Anfeindung*, enmity). The personifications in 'Theuerdank' remind us of a Morality-play, while the attacks of the Devil and his companions offer some points of resemblance even to a Passion-play: Theuerdank repels the Tempter very much in the same manner as Christ does.

'Theuerdank' is a somewhat strange last product of the chivalrous epic poetry. At the time when it was written, the poems of the Middle High-German period were endeavouring, through the means of printing, to assert their power once more in a world which had been totally transformed. But it was only the didactic poetry of that period, as represented in the Fable-writer Boner, in Hugo von Trimberg and Freidank, that found acceptance in these later times. 'Parzival' and the later 'Titurel' were printed in 1477, but not again after that. Of the heroes of the popular epics, only Ortnit and Wolfdietrich lived on in the collection of stories called the 'Heldenbuch.' With the sole exception of Neidhart's poems, the Minnesang had no interest for the general public of this period. The works of Hartmann and Gottfried disappeared from the horizon of the reader; 'Herzog Ernst,' on the contrary, together with Wirent von Grafenberg's 'Wigalois,' and Eilhard von Oberge's 'Tristan,' were preserved in their original freshness owing to the fact that in the fifteenth century they were turned into prose.

Revival of some Middle High-German poems.

The 'Heldenbuch.'

PROSE.

As early as the thirteenth century there existed a German prose romance, whose hero Lanzelet was one of the knights of Arthur's Round Table. But it was not till the fifteenth century that the prose-romance, the true novel, attained any real importance. The great literary activity in the province of the chivalrous epic ceased about 1350, and a new literary force then arose in the prose-romances, drawn from French, Italian, and Latin sources. They were first produced in

The Prose Romance, 15th century.

aristocratic circles, but became popular in the course of the six-
The 'Volks- teenth century, and have been preserved down to our
bücher.'   own time in cheap editions, which were sold in large
quantities at the annual fairs; owing to this fact they were usually
called 'people's books' (*Volksbücher*).

Many stories which had already been treated in verse now ap-
Favourite   peared in new prose-translations, often drawn from
characters of different sources. We meet again with Alexander the
the prose-   Great, Solomon and Markolf, Flore and Blancheflur,
romance.   Apollonius of Tyre and the seven Wise Masters.
The pair of devoted friends celebrated in chivalrous poetry under
the names of Amicus and Amelius, or Athis and Prophilias, or, as
in Konrad von Würzburg, Engelhard and Dietrich, come before us
in the prose-romances as Olivier and Arthur. The pair of much-
tried lovers, who are at length happily united, go by the names of
Pontus and Sidonia. The fairy woman, who is married to an
earthly man, and has to leave him again because he does not
simply trust her, is called Melusine. The legends of the Carlovingian princes supplied the material for the stories of 'Lother
and Maller,' and 'Valentine and Orson.' Hugh Capet appears
under the name of Hugh Schapler as a butcher's son, who gains
the throne by his bravery.

Fortunatus too, the possessor of the inexhaustible purse and of
Eastern   the wishing-cap which makes the wearer invisible, now
stories.   appears among the foreign heroes. The Indian collection of tales called 'Pantschatantra,' after going through many
Translations intermediate stages, finally passed into German as a
from   book of parables of the old sages. Boccaccio's 'Deca-
Boccaccio's
'Decame-   merone' found a translator, and the tales of Patient
rone.'   Griseldis, and of the unfortunate pair of lovers, Guis-
cardo and Ghismonda, excited the deepest sympathy. The excel-
'Euryalus   lent love-story of 'Euryalus and Lucretia,' by Æneas
and Lucre- Sylvius (afterwards Pope Pius II), was translated into
tia,' by Pope German and eagerly read; no German writer of the
Pius II.
   time possessed the talent for psychological analysis
displayed in this work. What the public desired, and what the
translators supplied them with, was thrilling incidents, amusement,

and suspense; style and skill in developing a story were considered quite an indifferent matter.

Among the translators noble ladies took the lead, such as Elisabeth of Lorraine, Countess of Nassau-Saarbrücken, and Eleanor of Scotland, wife of Duke Sigismund of Austria. The former translated 'Lother and Maller,' the latter 'Pontus and Sidonia.' And the other translators whom we know by name, the two doctors, Johannes Hartlieb and Heinrich Steinhöwel, the town-clerk, Nicholas von Wyle, the parish-priest, Antonius von Pforr, the Bernese statesman, Thüring von Ringoltingen, all worked, as we have evidence to show, on commission from noble patrons. Wilhelm Ziely, also a Bernese statesman, forms the only exception to this rule. It was in the Rhine-provinces and the neighbouring country—in the same district where Hartmann von Aue had introduced the Arthur-romance, and where the chivalrous epic had struck deepest roots—that the prose-romance was first cultivated. In form these prose-romances are far inferior to the classic masterpieces of Middle High-German poetry, but they will bear comparison with those great works in the lofty spirit of chivalry which animates them.

Translators.

By the side of these noble works, derived from foreign sources, it is somewhat humiliating to consider Germany's special contribution to the prose tales of the period preceding the Reformation, namely the stories centreing round the character of Till Eulenspiegel. These stories arose in the lowlands of North Germany, were favourably received in South Germany, and succeeded in effecting an entrance into the literatures of Holland, France, England, Denmark, and Poland. Eulenspiegel has become as celebrated a character as Reynard the Fox; and while the French word 'renard,' as we have already noticed, owed its origin to the German 'Reinhard,' the German 'Eulenspiegel' gave birth to the idea and the word of *espiègle*. It is probable that a man of the name of Eulenspiegel did really live in the fourteenth century, and that he was born in Kneitlingen near Brunswick, and was buried in Mölln, as is told in the history of his life, which was not written down till the year 1483, and was printed about 1500. But it is no longer possible to decide which

Stories of Till Eulenspiegel.

of the pranks attributed to him are really his own, and which are only put down to his name. He has become the centre for all those stories in which a man annoys his fellow-men without the slightest reason, but from mere delight in mischief. The stories of Till Eulenspiegel hold the same place among the romances of the fifteenth century that the Carnival-play does among the dramas. But while the civic Carnival-plays turned the peasants to ridicule, Eulenspiegel shows us, on the contrary, how a peasant might revenge himself on the town-people. Till Eulenspiegel is a vagabond of peasant origin,.who hires himself out to artisans and does them harm by literally carrying out, as rustics might do, commands which have been figuratively expressed. For instance, a shoemaker gives him the following instructions for cutting up the leather : 'Cut both small and large, as the shepherd's flock which he drives out of the village;' whereupon Eulenspiegel cuts up the leather into pigs, oxen. calves, and sheep. He does not confine his activity to artisans, but also plays pranks on princes and noblemen, clergy and scholars, and on all occasions indecency is his best weapon. The character of Eulenspiegel is an imperishable monument to that rustic cunning which cheats with all the appearance of simplicity, and glories in the power of rudeness.

All the works which we have named, romances and collections of farcical tales, cover but a small area of the prose-literature of the fifteenth century. The literature of sermons and treatises, of biblical translations and commentaries, could boast of a long pedigree. Since the days of Charlemagne the line had never been quite broken, and the nearer we approach to the Reformation the more we find original work in these branches taking the place of mere translations from the Latin. German juristic prose-writing dates from the thirteenth century, scientific prose-works from the fourteenth, while books on medicine and pharmacy go back still further. German prose-history began in the thirteenth century with the Saxon Universal Chronicle, and spread in the course of the fourteenth century to South Germany. In 1390 Jacob Twinger, of Königshofen near Strassburg, published the first edition of his important historical work, a chronicle of the

Other branches of prose literature in the 15th century.

History.

chief events of his time. In 1433 Eberhard Windeck, of Mainz, brought out his history of the Emperor Siegmund. All the great towns, Lübeck, Magdeburg, Breslau, Nürnberg, Augs-   Town-burg, Basle, and Berne, had each their own chronicle   chronicles. in German. If German versions were made of Latin historical works, it was only for the purpose 'of amusing and entertaining the laity;' the style of historical narrative in these translations became more graphic and full of detail ; stories and legends were inserted, and in fact we can trace everywhere the strong love of stories characteristic of this age, and the desire to give to history the form and completeness of the tale. Even the preacher had long since availed himself of the tale to illustrate moral   Sermons. truths in his sermons; this element, together with satire on public affairs and moral interpretations of various events of life, soon rendered the pulpit just as much a source of enter-tainment as the religious stage had long ago become.

The general predilection for the drama and for dramatic forms of writing is also visible in the prose-works of this The 'Acker-period. In the so-called 'Ackermann aus Böhmen,' mann aus a widower is made to express his feelings at the loss Böhmen.' of his wife in a prose-dialogue between himself and death, which attains a most dramatic ending in the final appeal of both to God for His judgment on the matter. This work was written by Johannes Ackermann of Saaz in Bohemia, in 1399, on the occa-sion of the death of his wife Margarethe. Though we cannot give it unqualified praise, yet it must be reckoned as one of the most original productions of mediæval literature ; the author shows wide culture and his prose is thoroughly artistic.

Unfortunately there was no further development of the artistic prose-dialogue during the fifteenth century. Niclas The prose-von Wyle translated some dialogues of Petrarch and dialogue. of the Swiss Renaissance-scholar Felix Hemmerlin; the flippant satirist Lucian found many imitators, and Ulrich von Hutten trans-lated his dialogues into German. But it was the anonymous pam-phlet-literature of the Reformation which really raised the German prose-dialogue to the rank of a recognised branch of literature. The introduction of the prose-dialogue into literature was due to the revival of classical learning, which also exercised a beneficial influence on the whole of German prose-writing, and introduced a more refined idea of life and of the arts.

The more serious branches of the new Renaissance literature **Niclas von** found favour in the same select circles which had **Wyle.** patronised the prose-romance. Niclas von Wyle made translations from the classical authors, and from Petrarch and Poggio; he also translated an epistle of Æneas Sylvius on the use of classical studies. In 1474 he wrote a work in praise of women, in which he enumerated all the blessings which the human race had received through them—a marked contrast to the satire on women which formed so favourite a feature of the popular literature of the period. Wyle's noble patrons were most ready to do all they could to advance learning, and two new universities, Freiburg and Tübingen, bore witness to their generosity in this respect. The women belonging to this educated circle also took an interest in the movement ; chief among them was the 'Lady of Austria,' as she was called in popular songs, Mathilda of Wittelsbach, sister of Frederick the Victorious, who married first Count Ludwig of Würtemberg, and secondly the Archduke Albert VI, ruler of the Austrian possessions on the Rhine; Mathilda had friendly and sympathetic relations with all the representatives of refined culture in Swabia and Bavaria. In the Palatinate itself the University and Court of Heidelberg were the head-quarters of the New Learning, or, as it is also called, Humanism; and till just before the Reformation, Greek, Roman, and Renaissance works were there translated into German and dedicated mostly to the young Counts Palatine.

THE NEW LEARNING, OR HUMANISM.

In 1348, as we have already said, the first German University **First** was founded at Prague by the Emperor Charles IV. **German Uni-** Both this university and the others which soon fol- **versities,** lowed it—Vienna in 1365, Heidelberg in 1386, Co- **14th century.** logne in 1388, Erfurt in 1392—were all foundations which owed their origin to clerical policy, or to princely or municipal ambition; they were imitations of the Paris University, from which most of them at first recruited their forces, and were not specially centres for the study of classical literature, and the development of a pure Latin style. Their merit lay rather in the transmission of traditional learning than in the advancement of knowledge generally. The subtleties of logic and the conflicts of philosophical parties were a good school for abstract thought, and for that art of disputation and rhetoric which shone forth so gloriously at the great Church Councils of the fourteenth and fifteenth centuries. A Hessian, Heinrich von Langenstein, when still a member of the University of Paris, sketched the main features of that Church-policy which resulted in the Councils, and of which Johannes Gerson was later on the most distinguished exponent. Heinrich von Langenstein attacked astrological superstition, and at Vienna, which was the scene of his labours from the year 1383, he paved the way for the great astronomers Peuerbach and Regiomontanus. A Frenchman in later times asserts that Heinrich transported the science of mathematics from Paris to Vienna, and thus was the means of spreading it throughout Germany, where it gave birth to the three inventions of gunpowder, printing, and the art of navigation, which led to the great geographical discoveries of the fifteenth century. But we have as yet hardly any real evidence of a connection between the learning of the universities and the progress of invention.

Gutenberg arrived at the discovery of printing without any aid from science, simply through observations made in con- Invention of nection with the goldsmith's art. Johannes Müller of printing, Königsberg in Franconia, surnamed Regiomontanus, circa 1448. was, it is true, a scholar and also a mechanic. He considerably advanced the studies of mathematics and astronomy; Regiomon- he built the first observatory in Nürnberg, established tanus. a printing-press, and published the first German Calendar, and was the director of a workshop for making astronomical instruments, compasses, and globes. Many legends are told of him which prove how much people in these times were still inclined to ascribe to the investigator of nature a supernatural power over nature itself.

In Regiomontanus we have an instance of great scientific achievements going hand in hand with classical learning. Georg
Peuerbach. Peuerbach, his teacher, was the first man to give lectures on classical studies in Germany (1454); he expounded Virgil, Juvenal, and Horace at the University of Vienna, and in the year 1461 Regiomontanus joined him in his labours.

Æneas Sylvius. Æneas Sylvius of Siena, who was secretary in the Imperial Chancery from 1443 to 1455, did his utmost to bring classical studies into favour with the Emperor, the Austrian princes, and his colleagues.

The principles advocated by Æneas with regard to the training of princes were realised to a certain extent in the education of Maximilian I; and this emperor became, not only the last of the knights, but also a Mæcenas after the Italian model, the patron of learned men, authors and artists, and a promoter of classical studies in particular.

The earlier Universities of the fifteenth century, Leipzig (1409), Rostock (1419), Greifswald (1456), were still founded after the old model; but the founders of Freiburg (1457), Basle
Advance of classical studies. (1460), Ingoldstadt (1472), and Tübingen (1477), seem to have been actuated by an interest in classical studies; and at Wittenberg (1502), and Frankfurt on the Oder (1506), foundations in which Kursachsen and Brandenburg emulated each other, the promotion of classical studies seems to have been a matter of course. Soon after Peuerbach had begun his lectures on the classics in Vienna, wandering classical scholars, 'Poetae' as they were called, began to appear at other Universities, where they dared to attack the traditional learning of the Middle Ages. These scholars were all eclipsed by the wandering preacher of Humanism, Konrad Celtis, the
Konrad Celtis, 1459-1508. son of a peasant at Wipfeld in Franconia, who began his career of agitation in favour of classical studies in 1485, at the age of twenty-six. Celtis gave lectures at various Universities, founded literary societies and wrote a description of his travels and love-adventures in elegiacs, after the model of Ovid's 'Amores.' He subsided at length into a Professor of Rhetoric and Poetry, first at Ingolstadt from 1492

to 1497, then at Vienna, where he continued till his death in 1508.

But the New Learning in Germany was not destined to follow in the paths which Celtis wished to prescribe to it, after the example of the Italians. The aim of the great majority of the German Humanists was not a secular-æsthetic culture with a colouring of paganism, but a thorough, systematic education with constant reference to religious matters. Animated by this idea, we find, as early as the close of the fourteenth century, the 'Brotherhood of the Common Life,' led by Gerhard Groote, taking the reform of the German system of education into their own hands, and founding a school at Deventer, which became more influential than many universities. They insisted that the laity should read the Bible in the mother-tongue, and in all learning they only prized that which advanced the sanctification of life. At the same time they did not hold aloof from those new studies which came from Italy, but insisted on the mastery of classical Latin and the study of Greek. From their school Westphalia and the Upper Rhine drew their first teachers of the New Learning. Their school produced the witty philologist Erasmus, a man who could fully value a refined secular life. He sought by numerous writings to promote the general acquirement of an elegant and correct Latin style such as he himself wrote, but still he looked upon the application of the philological method to the writings of the New Testament as his greatest and noblest task.

Gerhard Groote's educational reforms in Holland.

Erasmus.

The philological method required that students should go back to the original sources of tradition and information. By seeking the best authorities and abandoning the bad ones, men were learning to set themselves free from authorities altogether. Peuerbach and Regiomontanus, in penetrating to the original text of Ptolemy and communicating his knowledge to their contemporaries, were preparing the way for the work of Copernicus. The physicians, by returning to Hippocrates, were preparing the way for the anatomical discoveries of Vesalius. The way to Nature lay through the study of the Greek writers. At first men saw only what had been seen before by the

Tendency to independent views.

ancients, but soon they learnt to look for themselves. Juristic science began to pass over the mediæval teachers and to keep to the *Corpus Juris.* Theology began to disregard the scholastic writers and the Fathers and to keep to the Bible. It is true, theological study did not at this time go further than this; it did not exercise its criticism on the Word of God itself, but it refused to be satisfied with the Latin translation, which had been recognised throughout the Middle Ages. In the New Testament men returned to the Greek text, in the Old to the Hebrew, and in pointing out numerous mistakes in that version of the Bible which had been exclusively used and authorized by the Church, the new theologians were putting out a hand against the power of the Church itself. This step was taken by Erasmus in one country, by Reuchlin in another, by neither of them with any destructive intentions, but simply in the honest search after truth. Still, it was from the text as supplied by Erasmus that Luther made his translation of the New Testament.

If on the one hand the religious humanists turned their attention to artistic literature, on the other hand they were also much influenced by the popular comic writings. Erasmus' ironical 'Encomium Moriae' ('Praise of Folly') is written in imitation of Brand's 'Ship of Fools.' Heinrich Bebel, a Professor at Tübingen, the son of a Swabian peasant, made a Latin version of a well-known popular song ('Ich stund an einem Morgen'); he also made a collection of proverbs and comic anecdotes, and in his 'Triumphus Veneris' he has given us a satire on the influence of love on all classes, in the style which was so popular in the Carnival Plays. These satirists always directed their sharpest weapons against priests and monks; anti-clerical satire reached its climax in the so-called 'Epistolae obscurorum virorum,' a work of great historical importance, which proceeded from the University of Erfurt, and produced an effect through all Europe, for it was the hardest blow dealt at the clergy before the Reformation.

At the beginning of the sixteenth century, a band of young scholars had come together in the University of Erfurt; this circle produced many renowned Latin poets, such as the witty

The Humanists influenced by the popular literature.

Crotus Rubianus, chief writer of the 'Epistolae obscurorum vi- rorum,' the worthy Eobanus Hessus, who afterwards The Erfurt translated the Iliad and the Psalms into Latin, the circle of epigrammatist Euricius Cordus, whom Lessing es- writers. teemed highly, and from whom he gained many ideas for his epi- grammatic poems ; Ulrich von Hutten also for a time formed one of this band. These young scholars all honoured as their leader, Konrad Mutianus Rufus, Canon of Gotha, a gifted man, who despised the honours of literary renown and found satisfaction in personally influencing a few. Mutianus implanted his own bitterness against the Roman Church in the minds of the talented youths who surrounded him. Classical studies freed men from prejudices and inclined them to tolerance in an intolerant age. Mutianus preferred certain ancient philosophers to many Chris- tian theologians, and took a pleasure in the splendid sayings of the Koran. Reuchlin's Hebrew studies had enabled him to enter into the Jewish spirit, and he believed that valuable secrets lay concealed in the Rabbinical writings. When, therefore, the baptized Jew Pfefferkorn advocated the burning of all Jewish books with the exception of the Old Testament, Reuchlin undertook their defence (1510), and became involved in a controversy with the Cologne theologians. In this quarrel all the German disciples of the New Learning were on Reuchlin's side, and the Erfurt poets, the 'Order of Mutianus' as they called themselves, turned his enemies to ridicule in the so-called 'Epistles of The obscure men,' an imaginary correspondence between 'Epistolae a number of clergy, whose characters are revealed obscurorum by their letters. A certain dramatic element is again virorum' apparent in this work, and the letters show a power (1515 and of character-drawing superior to anything ever at- 1517). tained by the mediæval drama. The characters do not stand before the public and simply enumerate their faults, as in the Carnival-plays, but are made to reveal their secrets to each other in confidence, and are supposed to be overheard in so doing. The semblance of probability is strictly preserved; the charac- teristic features are piled up for caricature, but every feature is true. The delightfully comic dog-Latin, the ignorance of classical literature, the foolish subjects of controversy, the serious arguing about mere nothings, the reports of quarrels with the poets and of bad treatment sustained at their hands, the naive confessions of convivial pleasures and love-affairs are all based on reality. The unity of the whole is cleverly secured by the device of a chief addressee in Cologne, and by constant reference to the course of the Reuchlin controversy.

The merit of having originated the idea of these letters belongs
Crotus Rubianus originated them.
to Crotus Rubianus, who was also the chief contributor to the first part, which appeared in 1515. In the second volume (1517), Ulrich von Hutten took a leading part, and not altogether to the advantage of the work, for he allows his lofty seriousness, his pathos, and even his better Latin occasionally to break through, and sometimes goes beyond the bounds of probability.

This was the most brilliant period in the career of the University of Erfurt, but it was unfortunately of short duration. In the year 1519 eight classical professorships were established there. Eobanus Hessus was the most favourite teacher, Erasmus the ideal of learning to which they all aspired. But the University soon suffered from the storms of the Reformation.

In the year 1501 Martin Luther began to study theology at
Martin Luther at Erfurt, 1501-1506.
this very University; he was not a member of the Erfurt circle of poets, though acquainted with Crotus Rubianus. He afterwards entered the Augustinian monastery there, but was summoned in 1508 to the University of Wittenberg, which he was destined to make, during his life-time, the intellectual centre of Germany.

CHAPTER IX.

THE REFORMATION AND THE RENAISSANCE.

THE epoch of the mediæval Renaissance had its movement of Church Reform, which proceeded in the tenth century from the Burgundian monastery of Cluny, and in the eleventh century even triumphed over the Papacy. Similarly, the epoch of the modern Renaissance was at the same time the epoch of the Protestant Reformation, the epoch which produced Martin Luther. Germany, which has so often been led by foreign influences, then for the first time took upon herself, for a short period, the intellectual leadership of Europe.

The Reformation and the Renaissance were kindred movements, but their interests were not identical. The deeply exciting questions raised by the Reformation interrupted that promising intellectual movement which had been called forth by the revival of classical learning. The jesting tone of the 'Epistolae obscurorum virorum' soon changed into one of bitter earnestness; the literary war gave place to a real struggle of reckless violence. In German literature as in German history the years from 1517 to 1530 are entirely absorbed by the Reformation; this movement enlisted all powers in its service; the Muses were silenced, and the voice of Theology alone was heard. It was not till the third and fourth decades of the century that æsthetic interests ventured again to assert themselves; after the religious peace of 1555, intellectual life began once more to spring up vigorously in all directions. After that, though Protestant theologians might tear each other to pieces, though the Jesuits might advance boldly, organizing a counter-

The Renaissance interrupted by the Reformation.

The Religious peace of 1555.

reformation, still, side by side with religious questions, other human

Short revival of literature about 1600. interests again began to obtain a hearing. From about the year 1600 German literature began noticeably to increase in merit and influence. The Drama came more and more decidedly to the front, and dramatic art was greatly improved. It is true that we do not meet with any authors of first-class powers among the writers of Latin and German plays of this period, but such as they were they seemed specially destined to prepare the way for some great master, as whose predecessors they would have been named with honour. The drama in Germany at this period had reached the

Interrupted by the Thirty Years' War, 1618. same stage as it had in England before the appearance of Shakspeare, and there seemed no reason why Germany should not also have produced its great dramatist. But all the hopes and promises of German literature were shattered by the Thirty Years' War, which proved most fatal for some time to all intellectual progress in Germany.

MARTIN LUTHER.

It was Martin Luther who created the Reformation in Germany;

Luther determined the Reformation in Germany. his mind and his will determined the character of the whole movement. The numerous remarkable men whom the New Learning had formed, and who afterwards entered the service of the Reformation, had either to attach themselves to Luther or to sink into insignificance beside him. Even Zwingli could only succeed in gaining a local influence ; in his mind the New Learning and the

Zwingli. Reformation were not opposing interests, and he hoped to meet in heaven Socrates, Aristides, the Scipios, and other good heathens. He displayed all the practical common-sense of the Swiss; he was first a purifier of morals, and afterwards a Reformer. His cheerful temperament knew nothing of inward struggles such as those through which Luther gained

Luther. the power of confronting the Pope and the Old Church, and carrying the nation with him. Luther, too, had imbibed elements of humanistic culture, but he was not a true

Humanist. He could esteem a few didactic productions of classical
poetry and science, but the beauty of the classical authors left no
impression on him. In the Scriptures he found both beauty and
wisdom, and that sufficed him. It was for the sake of the Bible
that he became a philologist. Erasmus and Reuchlin led him to
study the Scriptures in their original form, and by his translation he
made them accessible to the German people.

Before Luther, no German had, so far as we know, been ener-
getic enough to grapple with the whole of the Scriptures. No one
had followed the example of the Goth Ulfilas. Under
Charlemagne a translation of the Gospel of St. *Translations*
Matthew was the only work done in this direction. *of the Bible*
The ninth century was content with extracts and *before*
metrical paraphrases; the tenth and eleventh demanded *Luther.*
German texts with commentaries, such as Notker's Psalms and
Williram's Song of Solomon. From the twelfth century we possess
fragments of the Gospels in German; and in the fourteenth and
fifteenth centuries, notwithstanding the papal interdiction of the
Bible, these translations of single portions continued to increase,
and gradually embraced the whole of the Scriptures. The Emperor Wenceslaus ordered a splendid copy of the whole Bible,
decorated with many pictures, to be made from these various
translations. The German Bible was first printed in 1466, and
before the year 1522 it had been printed fifteen times. But
these editions all followed one and the same translation, the
different parts of which were very unequal in merit. They
were of little help to Luther in his work; he not only had to
correct mistakes but to substitute a clear, graphic, thoroughly
German prose for the old text, which was uncouth and often
incomprehensible, and which slavishly followed the original without
ever attaining to its excellence. Luther reproduced *Luther's*
the Greek and Hebrew Scriptures in a German form, *Bible.*
after having passed them through the medium of his own thought.
In the Greek portions he adhered more literally to the original,
in the Hebrew he allowed himself more freedom, as the genius
of the two languages seemed to require; in the former he was
dependent almost entirely on his own knowledge, in the latter

he drew more help from his friends. He had the highest idea of the importance of the task he had undertaken. He knew what art, industry, knowledge, and wisdom were required to make a good translator. 'Interpretation,' he says, 'is not an art for everyone; it needs a very pious, faithful, industrious, diffident, Christian, learned, experienced, and practised soul.'

Luther was an enthusiastic lover and admirer of his mother-tongue, and he spared no trouble to make his translation a monument of German style. He devoted himself to the work with the greatest seriousness and conscientiousness; he tried to absorb the spirit of the original, and his thorough knowledge of the popular tongue, together with his firm resolution not to write for the court or for scholars, but for the people, enabled him to make his Bible a true people's book.

The work issued from the Wartburg, and shed fresh glory on that place of ancient literary renown. Luther began his great

Luther begins his translation, 1521.

work at the age of thirty-eight, when he was at the height of his popularity after the diet of Worms. In the winter of 1521, about Christmas time, he formed the resolution, and, though it sounds almost incredible, by the time he left the Wartburg, on the third of March, 1522, he had already finished the New Testament. In two months the work had been done so far that it only required a final revision; Melanchthon helped in this revision, and in the month of September of the same year the book was published. While the New Testament was being printed, Luther set to work upon the Old. But it

The whole Bible published, 1534.

was not till the year 1534 that the whole Lutheran Bible was published at Wittenberg by Hans Lufft, in six parts. In the year 1541 it was remodelled with the assistance of expert collaborators, and this version afterwards received a few amendments in the editions of 1543 and 1545.

The translation of the Bible is Luther's greatest literary achieve-

Importance of Luther's Bible.

ment, and at the same time the greatest literary event of the sixteenth century, or even of the whole period from 1348 to 1648. It laid the foundation of a common culture for all ranks of society, and opened a whole intellectual world to the people. Luther's Bible was an inexhaustible source of grand and edifying thoughts, a noble and imperishable literary monument, a treasure often worshipped to the point of superstition and abuse.

Luther's Bible permanently fixed the literary language of Germany. Though the Reformation increased the divisions within the German nation, though it rent asunder Protestant Germany and Catholic Germany, yet, on the other hand, it softened the contrast between South Germany and North Germany by definitely imposing on the Low Germans a High-German literary dialect. In this respect, the Reformation laid the foundation for modern German literature and for that unity of intellectual life which we at present rejoice in.

It made High-German the literary language.

Before Luther's time the High-German, though it enjoyed a certain literary pre-eminence, had not been able to put a stop to the literary employment of other dialects. The form of German used in the Imperial Chancery was, when Luther began to write, the one generally recognised as a pattern to which others should conform; but though the Chanceries of the various princes and of the towns as a rule followed this form, they yet continued to mix their own dialect with it.

When Luther first began to write he adopted the form of German employed in the Saxon Chancery, and adhered pretty closely to the Saxon dialect. Gradually, however, he succeeded in freeing himself from it, and attained to a form of language which approaches very nearly to that of our day, though not coinciding with it. His language became the authority for all writers and printers. In Strassburg we find that books written about 1515 had already to be modernised in 1540. The first German grammarians, Fabian Frangk (1531), Albert Ölinger (1573), and Johannes Clajus (1578), based their rules consciously or unconsciously on Luther's form of speech. And the Bible was and continued to be the classic in this language. It made its way from the centre of Germany into the countries round. In Switzerland it supplanted the 'Schwyzer Dütsch,' which had still been written by Zwingli; it supplanted Platt Deutsch in the North and the Cologne

Wide influence of Luther's Bible.

dialect in the North-West. Even the Catholics participated at once
in the advantages afforded by Luther's Bible. 'They steal my
language from me,' said he; but it was a triumph to him to have
taught even his enemies how to speak. Hieronymus Emser corrected Luther's New Testament according to the Latin text recognised by the Catholic Church (1527); Johann Dietenberger of
Mainz did the same for the whole Bible (1534); Johann Eck's
more independent translation, made in 1537, could not assert itself
against Luther's.

But Luther not only gave the German Bible to his Church;
he not only made the Bible the centre of his theology, but on the
basis of the Bible he reorganized the sermon and the Church-hymn.

The sermon had continued to flourish since the time of Berthold

The Sermon von Regensburg and of the Mystics. In the course of
as Luther the fifteenth century it received an extraordinary addi-
found it. tion of material, and its sphere was also much widened.
The best German preacher of this century was Geiler von Kaisers-

Geiler von berg, a Swiss by birth, but brought up in Alsace,
Kaisersberg, who occupied the pulpit of Strassburg Cathedral from
1445-1510. 1478 till his death in 1510. He was an orator of
far-reaching fame, but he often sacrificed the dignity of the pulpit
to the popular desire for a realistic mode of expression, and would
entertain his listeners with unsparing satire on all classes of society.
Though a man of wider culture than Berthold von Regensburg
he was yet inferior to him, and he carried Berthold's mannerisms
to excess. Like Berthold he would start from common things,
and hang religious teaching on to them. In one of his sermons
he makes Brand's 'Ship of Fools' the foundation of his discourse,
and takes each fool singly and treats each bell on his cap as a
separate sin. Any passing interest of the day, and even the most
ordinary occupations of everyday life, were not too mean to serve as
material for his allegorical 'Moralisations.' Other preachers of
this period shared Geiler's faults, and added others to them. We
notice in all of them a false striving after realistic effect, much obscure and barren learning, and a mass of satire and anecdote, of
frivolous and comic ingredients. Such was the condition of the
sermon at the time when Luther appeared.

He replaced all this by simple teaching; he did not condescend to work on people's feelings and imagination, but simply appealed to their reason and conscience. *Luther's Sermons.* His sermons were mostly interpretations of the Bible. His chief desire was to bring home the Scriptures to the understanding of every one of his hearers, and to point out their application to every-day life. This he did with great power and clearness, and in his own peculiarly simple and attractive style. Ordinary rhetoric played but a small part in his sermons, but for this very reason he appealed more to the hearts of his audience. He could not, however, hinder the sermon from sinking again in later times into allegory and dogmatism, into pedantry and polemics.

The sacred song had passed through all the various phases of German literature. Walther von der Vogelweide and many other Minnesingers and Mastersingers wrote religious poems. *The Church-hymn.* But it was not every religious poem that could become a Church-hymn, or even a popular religious song. The Mystics, too, had cultivated this branch of literature, but it was not till the end of the fourteenth and beginning of the fifteenth century that there arose religious poets, such as the Monk of Salzburg and Heinrich von Laufenberg, who made it their special object to increase the existing store of Church-hymns, and thus to break the power of the secular ' Volkslied.' *Heinrich von Laufenberg's hymns, circa 1400.* Heinrich von Laufenberg in particular adhered, as far as possible, to the spirit of the ' Volkslied;' he retained the popular melodies and sought to infuse a spiritual meaning into the conventional phrases, but he really accomplished the very opposite of what he had intended. His elegant and melodious hymns sounded far more secular than religious; they shed an unholy splendour round the sublime subjects which they sang of, and drew divine things down to an earthly level.

Luther, on the contrary, revived the best traditions of the Christian Church-hymn. The Psalms had been the basis of the oldest Church-songs, and Luther in his hymns *Luther's hymns.* returned to the Psalms and the Bible, though without despising those glorious Latin hymns and ' Sequences' of the older Church, which were really developments of the Psalms. He also remodelled a few old German songs, as, for instance, the Easter song, ' Christ is arisen.' Moreover, he embodied his hatred for the Pope in some original verses, in which he teaches his followers to pray thus :—

> 'Erhalt uns Herr bei deinem Wort,
> Und steur des Papst's und Türken Mord.'

> ('Keep us, Lord, in Thy Word,
> And frustrate the murderous designs of Pope and Turk.')

In another hymn, the first which he wrote for congregational use, he adopted the tone of the popular roundelay, and sang the redemption of man in the dramatic style of a ballad; but the dignity of the subject does not suffer in the least from his treatment of it.

Most of Luther's hymns were written in the years 1523–24. A manly tone rings through them all, such as was yet unknown to German lyric poetry; and they are all written in that impersonal spirit which is a characteristic of this whole epoch. As the dramatist vanishes behind his creations, and speaks through the souls of strange characters, so Luther in his hymns makes his own personal feelings retire into the background, and expresses in powerful language the feelings and sentiments shared by the whole congregation of the faithful.

Some of Luther's hymns are in the narrative form, others again are instructive, while some are in the form of a confession of faith. The character of the Christian knight, which we have met with in various metamorphoses throughout the Middle Ages, is the true ideal of the age of the Reformation, and nowhere is this ideal more gloriously represented than in Luther's famous hymn : ' Ein' feste Burg ist unser Gott.' This hymn, for which Luther probably composed the melody as well as the text, is based on the 46th Psalm, and was written in October 1527, at the approach of the plague. It is the reflection of a moment of great distress and difficulty, and at the same time it affords us a true picture of Luther's own strong and noble soul. But of his inner experiences he only reveals to us those which everyone might feel alike, those which in their moral aspect recur in all ages, whenever a brave man, conscious of the goodness and greatness of his cause, arms himself against the attacks of the world.

It is in his hymns that Luther shows most of the artist; but he is an artist also in his pamphlets. And while in his songs he suppresses all subjective emotions, in his pamphlets he allows them free course. His translation of the Bible, his sermons, his hymns, all served as weapons in a peaceful agitation for the Protestant *Means of agitation employed by the Reformers.* cause. But side by side with these, he also availed himself, from the very beginning of the conflict, of all the stronger means of agitation, which, in the then existing state of German culture, lay at his command. Those who could not read might have their feelings roused by woodcuts. Luther therefore invited Lucas Cranach to produce 'The Passional of Christ and Antichrist,' in which the sufferings of Christ were contrasted trait by trait with the pomp and luxury of the Pope. The latest news might be spread through printed songs or prose-writings; thus Luther described the burning of two Evangelical martyrs at Brussels (1523) in an excellent song, and also published many accounts of important contemporary events, with or without criticisms, but never without a decided purpose. Other short writings might also be spread by the aid of printing; thus we find papal letters of indulgence among the earliest productions of the press, and Luther caused his own celebrated theses against indulgence to be printed for circulation. Living and enkindling speech could now be replaced by printed words, and weapons of attack and defence might by this means be put in the hands of thousands; Luther made extensive use of the polemical pamphlet and accom- *Luther's pamphlets.* plished great things by its aid. The historian of German literature must class these controversial writings with the polemical poetry of Walther von der Vogelweide. The object of attack is the same; the effects produced and the rhetorical weapons employed are in both cases closely allied, and only the literary form is slightly different in each. By means of his pamphlets Luther spoke to thousands, and made his voice resound throughout Germany. Most of them show a certain want of coherence in the development of thought, consisting as they do of a series of numbered assertions, proved one after the other, without any attempt to gather them into a logical whole. Their tone varies greatly according to the different audiences whom the author is addressing, but he always takes care that his meaning shall be clear to all. He is less successful in temperate discussion than in passionate attack; in pamphlets of the latter character he adopts a tone of unaffected popularity, using all those arts which he scorned to employ in his sermons, in such a way as often to remind us of Brother Berthold and Geiler von Kaisersberg.

Luther's pamphlets are quite as popular in tone as the writings of Walther von der Vogelweide, and some of the characteristics which we have noticed in Walther appear still more marked in Luther, such as natural imagery, pregnant phrases, proverbial expressions, exaggerated utterances of anger or scorn and a power of imaginative and vivid representation resulting in highly dramatic effects. **Luther and Walther von der Vogelweide.** Luther is very fond of personification; he speaks of Romish avarice, for instance, as the worst thief and robber, to be handed over to the punishment of thieves and robbers—hanging or decapitation. In his polemical pamphlets he always directly addresses his opponent, running him down, pouring out a torrent of abuse against him, and thus involuntarily drawing a grotesque caricature of the man. He never indulges in monologue, but always gives us a portion of a dialogue. Luther's whole personality is represented in his pamphlets: his bursts of passionate violence, his strong emotions, his fiery activity, his bold outspokenness, his deep humility and trust in God, his strong self-reliance, arising from the conviction of being engaged in a good work, and finally his boyish high spirits, leading him to make fun of his opponents, and to spare kings and princes as little as his theological colleagues. He himself disapprovingly compares his style to a restless and turbulent fighter, always struggling with terrific monsters, and he laments the want in himself of that loving and peaceful spirit which he admires so much in others. But he comforts himself with the assurance that the Heavenly Father in His great household must need different kinds of servants, the hard one for hard work, a common hatchet for common logs.

Neither in Germany, nor elsewhere, has there ever arisen a man who was able to appeal with such power to the whole nation as Luther did. No other writer has ever gained such vast and immediate influence through his writings; no other professor has ever afforded such an emphatic contradiction of the charge of pedantic

Influence of Luther on the intellectual life of Germany.

conceit. In spite of his school and university training, in spite of the monastery and the professorial chair, Luther remained at heart a son of the people, and it was this that made him the people's hero. His disciples extolled him for having, as they expressed it, freed the noble German people from the Roman and Babylonian captivity like a true Samson; but Luther did far more than this: his nation was threatening to sink into mere frivolity, he recalled it to earnestness and a serious view of life.

Whether we glorify or condemn Luther's action it is impossible to deny that he had the support of the people, and also that the Reformation was of the greatest benefit to the intellectual life of the German nation. Those districts where the preaching of the Gospel did not prevail, or where it was suppressed, remained for a long time shut off from any great intellectual or literary development. Without the enthusiasm of the reformed religion, without the educational influence which the Lutheran pastors exercised on the people, there was no mental progress. As long as Luther lived he was the centre of Germany; scholars streamed to Wittenberg from all parts, and then spread the spirit of reform throughout the world. With Luther died the unity of German Protestantism. In the Smalkaldic war Wittenberg passed to the other Saxon line; Melanchthon did not exhibit the firmness which the occasion required, and Luther's University lost its supremacy for ever. Luther's memory, however, remained sacred to all Protestants. Exhaustive editions of his works were published, a collection was made of his letters and table-talk, and the pastor, Johann Mathesius, of Joachimsthal, narrated his life in an excellent and truly popular style. Luther's pre-eminent authority was not altogether a blessing for his Church; it became also a weapon of intolerance, and a source of dissension. But the influence of his powerful mind continued to make itself felt after his death far beyond the circle of those who counted themselves as his rightful heirs.

LUTHER'S ASSOCIATES AND SUCCESSORS.

The movement of the Reformation caused an immense increase in literary production. The number of German printing-presses increased ninefold in the years 1516 to 1524. It is useless to attempt to give even an approximately complete description
Literature of the literature suddenly called forth by the great
of the religious movement, or to think of reviewing the theo-
Reformation. logians of this period according to their literary capacities. Men wrote in German and in Latin, in verse and in prose, in the tone of bitter controversy, and in that of quiet discussion.
. Luther found enemies to right and left. The radical Anabap-
Luther's tists cultivated that mysticism in which he too had
opponents. once found comfort, but which had failed to exercise any decisive influence on his thoughts. The Anabaptists disseminated their doctrines among the people by means of small pamphlets, and also wrote hymns from their own point of view. Two
Anabaptist of their sect, Denk and Hätzer, anticipated Luther in
writers. the translation of the Old Testament prophets, and Sebastian Franck of Wörd acquired most literary fame among them as a historian, geographer, and collector of proverbs, while the noble Kasper von Schwenckfeld was the one who lived longest in the memory of his disciples.

If we exclude the opposition of scholars like Eck, Emser, Coch-
Thomas läus, and Erasmus, Thomas Murner (see p. 257) must
Murner. be reckoned as the most prominent among Luther's opponents on the Catholic side. Murner had formed his literary style on that of Sebastian Brand and Geiler von Kaisersberg. He attacked the Reformation in a satire in rhymed couplets, entitled ' Der grosse Lutherische Narr ' (' The great Lutheran fool '). The work is cleverly planned, though somewhat carelessly carried out, and it rises in some parts to a quite dramatic interest.
Luther's On Luther's side were arrayed Humanists like Ulrich
associates. von Hutten and Willibald Pirkheimer, popular writers like Hans Sachs, Eberlin von Günzburg, Niclas Manuel, Utz

Eckstein, and many other writers whose names have not been preserved. The Frankish knight, Ulrich von Hut- Ulrich von ten, had already fought in Reuchlin's cause, and had   Hutten. been an active coadjutor in the 'Epistolae obscurorum virorum.' Longing for new activity he now espoused Luther's cause, and handled the pen as though it were a sword. He wrote Epigrams, Invectives, Speeches, Dispatches, Complaints, and Dialogues—all in the youthful chivalrous tone which is peculiarly his own, and all at first in Latin. But at the end of the year 1520, three years before his death, he began to write in German. He wrote in rhymed couplets complaining of the 'unchristian power of the Pope.' He addressed words of urgent warning to Charles V, and narrated the history of the various struggles between Emperor and Pope. He produced stirring songs   His songs in connection with the great religious struggle in   and Germany; among these we may specially mention dialogues. the brave and earnest song beginning: 'Ich hab's gewagt mit Sinnen,' which appeared in 1521. He also translated some of his Latin dialogues into German. From 1517 to 1521 he wrote in dialogue-form, and made it the fashionable style for the controversial literature of the Reformation. Thus he represents Duke Ulrich of Würtemberg, the murderer of Hutten's cousin, as meeting in the lower world with the most celebrated tyrants of antiquity; or he makes a German, lately come from Italy, enumerate all the sins of Rome in order. In one dialogue Helios and Phaethon are supposed to be looking down on the Diet of Augsburg in 1518, and Helios is made to describe all ranks in the German nation. In another, a Papal Bull is introduced fighting with German Liberty; many allies on both sides mingle in the fray, and finally the Bull bursts, and out of it come Indulgence, Superstition, Ambition, Avarice, Hypocrisy, Deception, Perjury, and Voluptuousness. The dialogue, 'Arminius,' published after Hutten's death in 1529, first introduced the Hermann-worship into German poetry. Tacitus' praise of the old chief of the Cherusci and Velleius' report of the battle with Varus, which had only lately become known, inflamed the patriotic hearts of the German classical scholars. Here they had at length a sure basis for national pride, a reason for glorying over the Italians. Hutten's Arminius, when in the Lower World before the judgment-seat of Minos, makes a claim to be recognised as the first general, and he gains at least the acknowledgment of having been first among the Liberators of their country.

The literary war called forth by the Reformation was continued most vigorously till 1530. In 1520 the Nürnberg classical scholar, Willibald Pirkheimer, wrote his Latin dialogue, entitled 'Eccius dedolatus' ('the planed Eck'), directed against Dr. Eck, Luther's most famous opponent at the disputation in Leipzig. In 1523 the Nürnberg shoemaker, Hans Sachs, composed his 'Wittenbergisch Nachtigall' in praise of Luther, and in 1524 he wrote four excellent prose dialogues, exhorting to reconciliation and moderation. The Franciscan Eberlin von Günzberg published in 1521 his 'Fünfzehn Bundgenossen' ('Fifteen confederates'), a series of essays on the Reform movement. Niclas Manuel, a Bernese painter, statesman, and soldier, wrote dramas advocating the principles of the Reformers, as well as a poetic dialogue in which a girl refuses to go into a nunnery, and an excellent prose dialogue, entitled 'Die Krankheit der Messe' ('The Illness of the Mass'), published in 1528. The pastor Utz Eckstein, of the Canton of Zürich, published similar but less successful conversations and dramas in 1526 and 1527. A great many anonymous dialogues appeared at this time, most of them argumentative or instructive in tendency, but showing great variety in outward form. We will give a few examples of the subjects of these pamphlets. Luther and Murner meet by chance in the house of the peasant Karsthaus; Murner runs away, and Luther wins over the peasant to his doctrines. An Augustinian converts a Dominican to the new doctrine; a peasant converts a monk; peasants take their pastor to task; Luther struggles successfully with his opponents, who appear in the shape of animals, as he himself loved to describe them; Emser as a goat, Murner as a cat, and so on. The Pope allies himself with Hell in order to make a futile onslaught on Heaven. The questions of the day are also discussed in letters: a nun is made to give utterance to evangelical sentiments, or the question of leaving

Other polemical writers of this period.

Anonymous dialogues.

the convent is talked over.   The Pope holds a correspondence with the Devil; Lucifer praises the priesthood, thereby revealing the corrupt state of the Church.   In a report of the Diet of Worms a parallel is drawn between Luther's life and the history of Christ's passion.

Printed reports or criticisms of the latest events were even then sometimes called 'Zeitungen' (Newspapers).   The first of these appeared at Augsburg in 1505, and contained intelligence about Brasil, published by the Fugger family[1].   In the second and third decade of the sixteenth century these newspapers became more frequent.   But regularly numbered journals first began to appear in the year 1566, at the time of the Turkish scare; and serial newspapers in half-yearly or monthly numbers were started in the year 1585 in Cologne, Frankfurt, and Augsburg.   Side by side with these the printed songs and poems in rhymed couplets, which had been the older instruments of journalism, continued to thrive with undiminished popularity till about 1650; the style and treatment in these poems was not by any means more poetical than in the newspapers.

The first newspapers, circa 1500.

The octosyllabic prose-like rhymed couplets, which had once enjoyed such fame as the metre of the chivalrous epics, experienced a kind of revival shortly before their final disappearance.   It was found now, as in the fifteenth century, that every kind of matter could be poured into this form.   Dramas were almost exclusively written in this metre, and it was also a favourite form for tales, and for all religious and didactic themes.   But the lyric stanza was at this time used equally indiscriminately for the most various subjects.   Many of the Mastersingers, the representatives of the oldest traditional forms of lyric poetry, joined the Reformation movement.   In their poems they ascribed reformed opinions to the founders of their art, amongst whom they reckoned Wolfram von Eschenbach and Walther von der Vogelweide.

Verse.

Many parts of the Bible were now turned into verse by Mastersingers and ministers, and even a versified abridgement of the whole Bible was produced.   In this form, often set to a well-known melody, the Scriptures could best be impressed on the memory of

---

[1] A great merchant-family of Augsburg, the 'Rothschilds' of the fifteenth and sixteenth centuries.

the people. No less than seventeen rhymed versions were made
of the Psalms, and Church-hymns were constantly drawn from this
source. In hymn-writing Luther led the way and incited his friends
to help him. In 1528 he published a hymn-book containing
thirty-seven hymns by various authors. Their number was greatly increased during the sixteenth century,
and the Lutheran hymns excited a wholesome rivalry
in other religious circles outside the Lutheran sect. Many of
these hymns were written in imitation of Luther's style, and have
a bold and manly ring about them even when written by a
woman, as in the case of Elizabeth Cruciger. They are not remarkable for elegance of diction, but their simplicity and sublime
earnestness appeal most powerfully to our hearts.

Hymn-writing after Luther.

But this only applies to the best among the older Lutheran
hymns, those which, like Luther's, only embodied the general
feelings of a Christian congregation towards its God. Soon after
Luther's death feeble repetition, verbosity, and triviality began to
assert their power, and a few poets developed an amazing fertility
in hymn-writing. Besides the congregational hymns giving
utterance to the feelings of the worshippers, we now find many in
which the Christian is made to express his individual feelings,
perhaps in some special circumstances; hymns of the dying are
particularly numerous. The best hymns, about the year 1600, are
more tender in sentiment, more ornate in form than the earlier
ones, and sometimes rather trivial in tone.

The language of the Song of Solomon now came again into favour,
and the soul was made to address Christ in words such as these:
'Ei mein Blümlein, Hosianna, himmlisch Manna das wir essen,
Deiner kann ich nicht vergessen.' ('Ah, my floweret, Hosanna,
heavenly manna which we eat, Thee I never can forget.') Since
the year 1570 it had again become the fashion to transform large
numbers of popular songs into sacred hymns, and owing to this
the hymns acquired a more cheerful character. On the other
hand many a well-meaning pastor recognised no fixed
boundary between the sphere of religious teaching and
religious song. In the writings of the excellent Bartholomäus Ringwald, who died about 1600, we find both united,

Bartholomäus Ringwald.

and sacred song was not improved by the union. Ringwald wrote two didactic poems, one of which gives a description of Heaven and Hell in the form of a vision, while the other deals with the conception of the Christian knight. Both are full of satirical elements, and their strongest point is detailed description. But this abundance of detail often makes poetry insipid, and this is perceptibly the case in those hymns where Ringwald has chosen subjects which had been already handled by Luther.

Calvinism, which after Luther's death had become powerful in the South-West of Germany, in the Palatine and in Hesse, now began also to assert its influence in the sphere of Calvinist religious poetry; it constituted an international ele- hymns. ment in German culture, and established a special bond of union with France. The Calvinists would admit nothing but the Psalms as Church-hymns, and the French version of these by Clément Marot and Theodore Beza, with the melodies of Goudimel (1565), spread wherever the followers of Calvin gained a firm footing. In Germany Paul Schede, called Melissus, a celebrated Paul Schede. Latin poet, began a translation of the Psalms at Heidelberg in 1572. The complete version published in 1573 by Ambrosius Lobwasser, professor at Königsberg, became the authorized hymn-book of German Calvinists. It was a servile imitation of the original, and was sung to the foreign melodies. Generally speaking, French influence becomes perceptible in the South-West of Germany about 1550, but without entirely supplanting native taste. Kaspar Scheid of Worms, who had some connection with the Court at Heidelberg, quoted French poems and intro- duced French works to Germany, but he also joined the school of Mastersingers at Worms, and trans- Dedekind's lated into German rhymed couplets the Latin poem 'Grobianus,' 'Grobianus,' written by Friedrich Dedekind in 1549. 1549; Sebastian Brand had invented the character of 'St. translated by Grobianus' (grob=coarse, rude) an embodiment of 1551. the obscenity and indecency which so unpleasantly characterized this age.

Friedrick Dedekind, who became in later years an earnest Churchman and a religious dramatist, was, when he wrote

'Grobianus,' a gay student at Wittenberg. The work contains excellent material for satire, which the author, however, did not succeed in bringing into good shape; Scheid, in his translation, managed to increase the indecencies, without improving the style.

Johann Fischart was a nephew and pupil of Kaspar Scheid, and Johann came from Mainz or Strassburg. He wrote chiefly Fischart. between the years 1570 and 1590, and during that period developed a marvellous literary fertility. In 1574 he was made 'Doctor of Law' at Basle, and later on he held various offices in the legal profession. Long journeys and wide reading contributed much to the development of his mind. For years he lived an independent life at Strassburg, trying his hand at various forms of literature, and always with success. Like Scheid he directed his attention to the popular poetry, and in versifying the coarse History of Eulenspiegel, he was carrying out a project of his teacher's. Like Scheid he wrote many elucidatory verses to His comic accompany pictures, and made translations from Latin writings. and French; and like Scheid he chiefly contributed comic writings to German poetry. Fischart chanced to light on the ironical praises of 'Podagra' (gout) in the literature of the Renaissance, and made these the foundation for his 'Podagrammisch Trost-büchlein' ('Book of comfort in gout') published in 1577. In French literature he owed much to the writings of Rabelais, which furnished him with the materials or the idea for three of his works, namely, his 'Aller Practik Grosmutter' (1572), a satire on the prognostications and prophetical calendars then so much in vogue [1], his 'History of Gargantua' (1575), and his satirical Book-Catalogue, 'Catalogus Catalogorum' (1590). Fischart's 'Gargantua' was not so much a translation as an expansion of the first book of Rabelais' celebrated romance; Fischart exaggerated Rabelais' peculiar style, and thus sacrificed the epic to the satiric interest of the book, but his work is hardly worthy to be called a satire, consisting, as it does, of a formless mass of comic allusions and digressions, puns, anecdotes, jingling rhymes, perverted proverbs, popular expressions, piled-up synonyms, quota-

---

[1] This kind of prophesying was then called 'Practik.'

tions from ' Volkslieder,' and notes on games, food, manners, &c. The rhetorical device of accumulating words, so frequently employed by Luther, is the leading artistic principle of this work of Fischart's. 'Gargantua,' like 'Grobianus,' is a satire on rude manners, while it was also meant to ridicule monasticism, mediæval education, the universities and the Schoolmen, and to glorify the intellectual progress of the age. The book ends with a prophecy of the persecution of the Protestants and the final triumph of truth.

In one respect Fischart stood far above the mild and inoffensive Scheid; he was a champion of Protestantism, a friend of Calvinism, but not an enemy of Lutheranism; he only attacked Lutheran intolerance, as embodied in the ' Formula Concordiae ' of 1577. He was the most powerful Protestant controversialist after Luther, though less popular and less eloquent. His original writings were mostly in verse. He began his career with Protestant polemics, and his first darts were directed against a renegade Pro- His polemical testant and against the mendicant orders. He wrote in writings. Latin and in German against the Jesuits, or ' Jesuwider ' (contrary to Jesus) as he calls them; his ' Jesuiterhütlein,' written in German (1580), was founded on a French poem which represented the Order as the work of the Devil and his grandmother. Fischart followed with active sympathy the fate of the Protestants in France. Through translations of French pamphlets, to which he was fond of adding a few rhymes, he endeavoured to awaken sympathy for the persecuted Huguenots among their German co-religionists. He translated from the Dutch Philip Marnix's ' Bee-hive,' a comprehensive Calvinistic satire on Catholicism, to which he made some additions. He repeatedly argued against compulsion in matters of faith, and he published older writings advocating liberty of conscience. In his own immediate circle he agitated for the union of Strassburg with the Protestant towns of Switzerland; his ' Glückhaft Schiff,' published in 1576, describes a voyage of the men of Zürich with some broth which they are supposed to bring to Strassburg still warm from Zürich. In 1588 he wrote in praise of the alliance between Zürich, Bern, and Strassburg, by which these towns sought to defend themselves against the aggressive policy of Spain. And when, in the same year, the

Spanish Armada was destroyed, and the great European crusade
against Protestantism thereby frustrated, Fischart wrote a trium-
phal poem in honour of Queen Elizabeth, and a mocking greeting
to the Spaniards full of the joy of victory and the love of freedom.

But it is not only as a controversialist that Fischart may be
reckoned among the literary successors of Luther.
He wrote psalms and other sacred hymns, and exhorted his fellow-citizens to bring up their children
in a Christian manner. Like Luther he wrote in
praise of music, and he placed Luther, as the reviver of psalmody,
by the side of King David.

His hymns and didactic works.

In his study of ancient literature he, like Luther, was chiefly
attracted by the common-sense philosophers, such as Plutarch and
Horace: from the former he derived his 'Ehezuchtbüchlein'
(Marriage-book), (1578), while he imitated the latter in singing
the praise of rural life. He shared Luther's humble reliance on
God, as well as his strong patriotism and his delight in domestic
happiness.

Fischart occupies a high place among the German poets of the
sixteenth century. He has great wealth of material, and treats it
in a graphic manner, and he could equally well express the most
serious and the most comic, the most sublime and the most vulgar
ideas. His power of figurative language is far above the ordinary
level, and his verse is clever and lively, and free from mere padding.
He possessed many of the qualities which make a great poet, but
he was deficient in taste, in sense of proportion, and in artistic
power. He represents the peculiar excellences and also the
peculiar defects of the age in which he lived.

SECULAR LITERATURE.

The Reformation, as a religious movement, was as hostile to
secular interests as the mediæval priesthood had ever been. The
reformed religion countenanced no art except music, no science
except theology ; poetry was in its eyes only a means for theological
ends, philology only a key to the Scriptures. But the representatives of the Reformation were not merely religious reformers.

Their intellectual sphere was not entirely confined to religious interests. If they wished to be the leaders of the nation it was necessary for them to assert their power, if not over the whole intellectual life, yet over the whole instruction of the nation.

This task fell to Melanchthon, the great-nephew of Reuchlin and the friend and colleague of Luther; he was called 'Praeceptor Germaniae,' and he well deserved the name. The German school-system, as it existed from the sixteenth down into the eighteenth century, owed its organiza- **Melanchthon founded the German school-system.** tion to the hand of Melanchthon, and this organization also served as a model to the Jesuits. It was, however, not an original creation, but only a realisation of the thoughts which from the beginning had characterized the Renaissance movement in Germany. Latin was learnt in order to use it elegantly in speech and writing; Greek was learnt in order to read the New Testament in the original text: all other aims were subordinate to these. Many schools and universities, such as Marburg (1527), Königsberg (1544), Jena (1558), Helmstädt (1576), Altorf near Nürnberg (1581), were founded afresh under the influence of the Reformation, and it was Melanchthon who wrote the standard text-books for these schools and universities. He wrote manuals of Greek and Latin grammar, of rhetoric and dialectic, of theology, ethics, physics, and psychology. He also promoted the study of law, and he deserves some praise for his sketch of universal history. In everything he insisted on a clear system. His was an organizing but not a creative mind. The great scientific discoveries of the age were made by others around him.

The astronomical discoveries of Copernicus were made known to the world in 1543. About the same time other Ger- **Science. Copernicus, Gesner, and Paracelsus.** man investigators in the field of natural science began to abandon the study of books for the study of the objects themselves; Conrad Gesner of Zürich admirably sum- marised the traditional and the newly acquired know- ledge of plants and animals, and another Swiss, Theophrastus Para- celsus, recalled chemistry from alchemy to the service of medicine. Paracelsus propounded a fantastic natural philosophy, whose prin-

ciples were later on united with the kindred doctrines of mys-
Philosophy. ticism, and thus led to the theological views of
Jacob Jacob Böhme. Beyond mere dreams of this sort,
Böhme. however, German philosophy in this period pro-
duced little original thinking. But the true Protestant spirit showed
itself in the critical and historical researches of the
History. so-called Magdeburg Centuriators, Mathias Flacius
The and his colleagues. Secular historical research in this
Magdeburg period produced nothing to rival the work achieved
Centuria- by these writers in ecclesiastical history, in criticising
tors. authorities and in showing up ancient forgeries. Many his-
torians now turned their attention to their own national history,
and the art of historical narrative found worthy representatives in
Histories of paths as yet untrodden. The Middle Ages had only
Germany. dealt with universal history; in the year 1505 the
Alsatian scholar, Jacob Wimpfeling, an enthusiastic patriot, wrote
in Latin the first history of Germany. In 1555 Johannes Sleidanus
wrote the History of the Reformation and of Charles V, also in
Latin, and in the style of Cæsar ; it was written from the Protestant point of view, but without any exaggerated party-feeling, and
it obtained for its writer a European renown. Sebastian Franck
published a universal history in 1531, and in 1534 a people's history of Germany. Bavaria found its historian in Aventinus,
Switzerland in Tschudi, Pomerania in Kantzow. Biography was
Biography. also zealously cultivated, for men not only took
pleasure in the record of the great events which
they had lived through, but also held in grateful remembrance
those by whose efforts the great advances of the age had been
brought about. By the year 1600 a large number of Latin bio-
graphies of various scholars had appeared, which, however, did not
succeed in giving a really clear idea of the character of the men
whom they commemorated. The German autobiographies of this
date, on the contrary, furnish graphic pictures of contemporary life :
in aristocratic circles we have those of Götz von Berlichingen,
Sebastian Schärtlin, and Hans von Schweinichen, in the learned
world those of Thomas and Felix Platter, in the bourgeois-class
that of Bartholomäus Sastrow.

The Latin poets, who were then so numerous in Germany, were not able to express the inner life in their poetry. **Latin** Their descriptions of travels, their idylls, and their **poetry.** occasional poems seldom go beyond mere incident or rise above conventional phraseology. Love-poems became more frequent about the year 1600, but they continued to adhere to the traditional forms. In poetry as in prose, religious subjects were most in favour, and these were treated sometimes in epic, sometimes in lyric form, sometimes almost dramatically.

· One of the natural aims of the Renaissance was to make the Classics accessible to wider circles. Translations were made from Greek into Latin, and from Greek and Latin into **Transla-** German. But men were far from wishing the Classics **tions.** to enter into any rivalry with the Scriptures, and the character of the age is clearly intimated in its choice of authors for translation. The classical lyric poets were entirely passed over, and Homer and Virgil did not receive much attention. For the Metamorphoses of Ovid the modernised translation of the thirteenth century was for a long time considered sufficient; Greek and Latin romances received somewhat more attention, but the foremost place was accorded to Roman comedy, from which men slowly passed to the Greek Drama. Equal favour was shown for the didactic prose-writers— Cicero, Plutarch, Vitruvius, Vegetius, but especially the historians; Livy's Roman history nourished the patriotism of German burghers. For the masses of the people the literary Renaissance meant little more than delight in a few of the thoughts and deeds of the ancients.

The classical fables also enjoyed great popularity. They furnished moral teaching in a pleasant form, and afforded a wealth of worldly wisdom in graphic language ; and moreover **Classical** this was a class of poetry long known to the Germans, **and** one in which they themselves had tried their skill with **German** success. Luther appreciated both the classical fables **Fables.** and 'Reinecke Fuchs,' and declared the 'Fable-book' to be the most useful book, after the Bible, for knowledge of the world. The 'Fable-book,' which he refers to, was a certain popular collection of German prose-fables, bearing the name of Æsop on the title-page; Luther himself had begun in the year 1530 to write a masterly new version of this book. The best writers of fables in verse at this period were Erasmus Alberus, a pupil of Luther's, Burkard Waldis, and Hans Sachs. They mostly give their materials a German colouring, and transfer the scene to German localities, which they describe somewhat minutely; they speak as if they had themselves been present. at the time, and they even introduce personal experiences, contemporary allusions, and

Rollen-hagen's 'Frosch-mäuseler,' 1595. Protestant sentiments into their moral teaching. Georg Rollenhagen of Magdeburg, who had studied at the University of Wittenberg, expanded the Homeric war between the frogs and mice into a manual of politics and a history of the Reformation, in which Luther figures as the frog 'Elbmarx' (1595). Fischart in his 'Flea-hunt'

Fischart's 'Flöhhatz,' 1573. (1573) developed, with many comic additions, a sub-ject already treated in an older poem, namely, the war of the women and the fleas. Fischart evidently meant to clothe this work in the form of a legal trial, but with his usual want of artistic power he has not consistently adhered to this plan throughout. Animal-poetry is further represented, in

Spangen-berg's 'Gans-könig,' 1607. somewhat different form, by Master Wolfhart Span-genberg's 'Goose-king,' published at Strassburg in 1607. This poem, written with a Protestant bias, is an ironical eulogy of the goose, representing the bird as a noble creature, which annually on St. Martin's day voluntarily suffers death by fire for the good of humanity. In return for this, the goose is admitted to the paper-heaven of calendar saints, which is graphically and humorously described. This work shows more power of imagination than any of Fischart's writings.

In the thirteenth century we noticed that the distinction between **Tales and Proverbs.** fable and tale was hardly perceptible, and that both were furnished with a moral; and this is still the case in the sixteenth century. These two branches of literature are as indistinguishable in Hans Sachs as in Stricker. Formerly the moral was often expressed in a proverb at the end; now the process is reversed, and a proverb is made the text, and then illustrated by fables and short anecdotes. It was in this form that didactic poems like Freidank's 'Bescheidenheit' were continued in the sixteenth century. All kinds of didactic, anecdotic, and narrative material, comic and serious, in verse and in prose, were woven in motley tissue round a thread of proverbs, of proverbial expressions, or sometimes even of maxims invented by the writer himself. Collections of this kind had been begun by Erasmus, Bebel, and other scholars of the German Renaissance. One of Luther's own circle, Agricola of Eisleben, made them the vehicle for Protestant sentiments. The Anabaptist Sebastian Franck patriotically endeavoured to show that the Germans possessed not less but more of these treasures of wisdom than other nations: 'Wherever,' he says, 'the Latins, Greeks, or Hebrews have one proverb, we have ten.'

Meanwhile, the prose literature of amusement had long attained an independent existence. In his book entitled 'Schimpf und Ernst' (Jesting and Seriousness), published in 1522, Johannes Pauli collected a mass of mediæval anecdotes, such as had been used for illustrations in sermons. Pauli was an Alsatian Franciscan and a faithful follower of Geiler von Kaisersberg. The Latin farcical stories, most of them very coarse, of the Re- Farcical naissance scholars, of men like Poggio and Bebel, anecdotes. became the foundation of later German collections, which, however, also borrowed from oral tradition, from Boccaccio and from other sources. Between the years 1555 and 1563, not less than eight of these compilations appeared, with attractive titles: Wickram's 'Rollwagenbüchlein' (Carriage-book), Frey's 'Gartengesellschaft' (Garden-party), Montanus' 'Wegkürzer' (Journey-shortener) and 'Ander Theil der Gartengesellschaft,' Lindener's 'Katzipori' and 'Rastbüchlein,' Schumann's 'Nachtbüchlein,' and Kirchhof's 'Wendunmuth' (Cheer for Low-spirits). In the years immediately following the Religious Peace, men took great delight in funny stories; they loved to spice their conversation with them, and did not even spare the ears of women. Protestant zeal found great satisfaction in reporting in such stories the evil things narrated by the scholars of the Renaissance concerning the Catholic clergy; but still, Protestantism maintained an attitude of decided hostility towards two branches of literature,—the secular 'Volkslied' and the novel.

Luther expressly contrasted his songs and those of his colleagues
with the 'Love-poems and fleshly songs' of the period. He
wished, like Otfried long before him, to supplant secular songs by
religious poetry. But he succeeded in his purpose no better than
the old monk, although he was able to apply to the task powers
far superior to Otfried's. On the contrary, we find that in the
Secular   course of the sixteenth century the secular part-song
songs.   greatly increased in power, and became a favourite
form of recreation among the bourgeois families. Songs were
now no longer circulated by mere hearing, but by music-books.
They passed beyond the masses of the people into more cultured
circles. About the year 1600 songs begin to be international;
we meet in Germany with Italian melodies, with canzonets, motetts,
villanelles, galliardes, neapolitaines, &c. The words of these
foreign songs were translated or imitated, and thus the German
songs about this time began to be adorned with foreign expressions and allusions to ancient mythology. These songs are
generally spoken of as 'Gesellschaftslieder,' social songs; still
they owe their origin to the 'Volkslied,' and are but a development of it. They borrowed from foreign sources, but without despising the native treasures. A song might call itself a galliard,
and yet begin in true German fashion:—

> 'Ach Elslein, liebstes Elslein mein,
> Wie gern wär ich bei dir.'

The Lutheran clergy were also hostile to the prose-novel, al-
Novels.   though the romance of 'Die schöne Magelone'
appeared with a commendatory notice by Luther's
friend Spalatinus. But the prose-novel, like the 'Volkslied,' succeeded in asserting its claim to general popularity in spite of the
clergy. Novel-writers continued borrowing from foreign sources,
as in the fifteenth century, but at the same time the original creative power of the Germans began to exert itself more vigorously
and in a nobler manner than before. The spirit of the Reformation is clearly stamped on a People's Book called 'Kaiser Friedrich,' which appeared in 1519; it narrated the treacherous and
overbearing conduct of the Pope towards the Emperor, and told

how the latter would one day come forth from his mountain-cave to punish the priesthood.

Between the years 1533 and 1539, after the storms of the Reformation had somewhat subsided, five novels were introduced from France, and soon attained great popularity; these were, the tale of the heathen giant 'Fierabras,' and that of the four 'Haimonskinder,' stories of fighting and bloodshed full of wild force and rude poetry, reflections of a bygone barbarous age which appealed to the rude taste of the present period. Besides these two tales there were the romances of 'Kaiser Octavianus' and 'Die schöne Magelone,' telling of separation and re-union, and lastly 'Ritter Galmy,' a tale of injured innocence finally triumphant.

Soon after this the first step in original novel-writing was taken by Jörg Wickram of Colmar. He was a most active writer, a Mastersinger, a dramatist, a collector of tales, a moralist, and for a long time the only original novel-writer in Germany. His four stories were written between the years 1551 and 1556. In 'Gabriotto und Reinhard,' the fortunes of two noble pairs of lovers suffer shipwreck owing to difference of rank. In the 'Goldfaden' the peasant's son Leufried triumphs over the hindrance of his low birth, and wins the Count's fair daughter Angliana. The 'Knabenspiegel' (Mirror for Boys) relates the story of a prodigal son, who afterwards repents and returns home. The 'Gute und böse Nachbarn' is a commonplace family history, introducing no inward conflicts, but merely outward dangers which are happily warded off. Wickram wrote for the youth of Germany, from his own provincial and bourgeois point of view. It is not love and chivalrous life that interest him most, but marriage and the bringing-up of children. Even when he transports his characters to distant regions and makes them go through romantic adventures, their speech and their sentiments still remain those of German burghers. His creations were derived from his reading of the older popular romances, and the incidents and ideas which he combines can in general be easily traced to their original source. His works bear the same relation to the borrowed romances of the fifteenth and sixteenth centuries that the original

Marginal notes:

Five novels borrowed from the French, 1533–1539.

Jörg Wickram's Novels.

narratives of the thirteenth century bore to the classic chivalrous epics.

After Wickram foreign elements again begin to intrude, and
Translated translations of classical, French, and Italian romances
romances. were offered to the German public. The long-winded
romance of 'Amadis of Gaul' in particular, with its exaggerated
form of chivalry, its conventional gallantry, its affected and stilted
style, its long moralisings, in short with its general artificiality,
won the hearts of the German nobility. Between the years 1569
and 1594 it was expanded to twenty-four volumes.

Meanwhile in Germany itself new popular romances had sprung
Collections up in the form of collections of short tales of similar
of stories. purport, which were attributed to one author, often
a historical character. These popular books appeared later than
the collections of funny stories which we mentioned above, and
drew largely from them. The 'Finkenritter' was a collection of
wildly improbable stories, which appeared about the year 1560.
Claus Narr, who was a jester at the Court of the Elector John
Frederick of Saxony, and died in 1532, became the popular
centre of all fools' stories ; his 'Historie' appeared in 1572. Hans
Clauert of Trebbin, first glorified in print in the year 1587, has
many points of similarity to Eulenspiegel. Stories of magic
centred round Doctor Faustus, and appeared first in a collected
form in 1587. The foolish things told of provincials were immortalised in 1597 in the 'Schildbürger' (Citizens of Schilda).

The literary worth of all these works is very small. The
The 'Schildbürger' stands relatively highest among them.
'Schild- It is better put together than any of the others, and
bürger.' it shows the hand of a cultivated author, who was,
however, unable to adhere consistently to his first intentions or to
express his ideas in lively narrative. Of all these stories, those
Stories of which centred round Faust were alone destined to
Faust. have a great future. 'Eulenspiegel,' the 'Finkenritter,' and the 'Schildbürger,' and all these jesters, clowns, and
wags, aimed only at satisfying the fun-loving tendency of the age ;
but the story of Faust contained food for more serious minds.
The comic stories supplied material for the clown of the drama,

and Claus Narr actually became a name sometimes used for this character in German plays; but the story of Faust furnished material
for a tragedy. These comic stories were only an episode, a recreation, so to speak, in the intellectual life of the sixteenth century,
but the spirit of the Reformation had a share in producing the
character of Faust. Faust represents the attitude of the Reformation towards science and the pleasures of the senses, in fact, towards the secular world in general.

There was a historical Faust whose life can be traced in the
records of his contemporaries from the year 1507 till   The legend
after 1530. He was a man of licentious character,   of Faust.
who travelled about as a magician, astrologer, and soothsayer, and
boasted of being able to work all the miracles of Christ. He
had been seen in many places, and men believed that he was
finally carried off by the Devil, who accompanied him during his
life-time in the form of a black dog. Stories were told of
him such as were told in the Middle Ages of Simon Magus,
of Albertus the Great, and others. The man of science was then
popularly supposed to be endowed with a magical power over
nature, a power given not by God, but by the Devil. But the
Faust of the legend is not only a magician, but also a classical
scholar. He audaciously attempts to restore the lost comedies of
Plautus and Terence, and he gives lectures in Erfurt on Homer,
and calls up the old heroes in person before his audience. He conjures up Helen of Troy from the lower world, in order to enjoy
life with her, and the child that she bears him reveals to him many
future events that are to come to pass in all countries. He
takes to himself eagles' wings and wishes to explore all the
depths of Heaven and Earth. He defies God, like the ancient
Titans who stormed heaven. His defiance has its source in the
Popish religion. The corruptions which Faust has witnessed in
Rome had hardened him in his sins; he lacks steadfast faith in
Christ, and holds the grace of God to be an impossible thing.
In fact, the Faust of the legend is the exact contrast to
Luther. Luther believes where Faust doubts; Luther reverences
the Scriptures, but Faust waives them aside; Luther distrusts
reason, Faust is an independent enquirer; Luther struggles with

the Devil and triumphs over him, while Faust succumbs to his power.

One of the best pamphlets of the Reformation-period describes how a devil appeared to Luther in monk's attire, and conveyed to him the proposals of hell: he shall be a cardinal if he will hold his tongue. But Luther struggles against this temptation with prayer, and repels the messenger with strong words. This story is a faithful reflection of Luther's mind, and his own strong belief in devils descended to his followers. In the time of the religious peace it became customary to refer the various vices to separate devils, and to attack them in moral and satirical writings. The Faust-legend stands in close connection with this devil-lore. Its hero—like the priest Theophilus and others—makes a compact with the Devil; Faust is not however, like them, saved through prayer, but falls a victim to eternal damnation. This was the form which the story took in print, and in the same form it was soon represented on the stage.'

THE DRAMA FROM 1517 TO 1620.

The two dates which I have chosen as limits for the period

Hans Sachs' first Carnival-play, 1517. 'English Comedies and Tragedies,' 1620.

which we are about to consider in the history of the German drama are associated with the following events: Hans Sachs's first Carnival-play was written in the year 1517; in the year 1620 appeared the 'English Comedies and Tragedies,' a work which furnishes the most important literary evidence of the influence which the English drama had exercised on the German since about the year 1590. Till that time the German drama had been confined to the same forms which existed before

Three types of German drama prevalent till 1590.

the Reformation, and all the plays which were written in Germany might be divided into three classes. They either had many characters and displayed an epic breadth of treatment, like the Passion-plays of the fifteenth century, or they were short and sketchy, like most of the Carnival-plays, or else they were constructed after the stricter models of ancient comedy. The first two groups of plays were popular; the dramas of the third class were 'school-plays' ('Schul-dramen'), acted at the various schools and universities by the scholars and students[1]. The popular plays were written only in German, the school-plays in German or Latin. The link between the popular drama and the modern German drama is to be found in the Latin plays based on classical models. Terence was read in the schools, was acted in the original by the scholars, and imitated *Influence of the Roman plays.* by the teachers. A multitude of translations of Terence appeared in the sixteenth century, and the numerous Latin imitations of the same poet were either translated into German or copied in the vulgar tongue.

Italy, France, Holland, and England had produced a new kind of Latin drama, based on the ancient drama, and the poetical productions of these countries were introduced into Germany, where, through the medium of the school-plays, they also exercised an indirect influence on the popular drama.

The Reformation, by improving the schools, gave a new stimulus to the school-plays. Every German Gymnasium (public school) dating from that period has its theatrical history, though unfortunately but little is known of it. Luther was no enemy of the drama; on the contrary, he believed that it was represented in the *Influence of the Reformation on the drama.* Old Testament; he thought that the books of Judith and Tobit were originally plays, the former a tragedy, the latter a comedy. He recognised in Terence's plays a fair reflection of the outer world, and favoured the representation of them as a good exercise in language. He considered the religious drama as an instrument for spreading evangelical truth, and only required that it should be serious and moderate in tone, not farcical as it had been under the Papacy. The Church festival-plays, especially the Christmas-plays, were continued under the Protestant *régime*; the genuine Passion-plays alone *The Protestant drama.* were banished from within the sphere of Luther's immediate influence, for he disapproved of the sentimental view of

---

[1] The acting of plays at schools and universities was also the fashion in England at this period. A relic of these 'school-plays' remains in the Westminster play.

Christ's sufferings, and said it was not right to mourn and lament over Him as one would over an innocent man. Those dramas too which were founded on sacred legends ('Lügenden,' lyings, as they were termed by the controversialists) were banished by the Protestants. But on the other hand, the drama acquired a great increase of material through the popularity of the Bible, and all parts of the Scriptures were ransacked to furnish subjects for plays. A great number of polemical dramas, written with a Protestant bias, were also produced, closely resembling in character those satiric dialogues which were called forth in such numbers by the Reformation. Sometimes a polemical colouring was given to an already existing subject, sometimes the polemical element was confined to the moral which was at that time appended to every play.

The various dramatic forms of the fifteenth century, Mysteries, Moralities, Farces, and 'Sotties,' can still be clearly distinguished. But the school-drama only recognised tragedy and comedy, and in doubtful cases tragicomedy. The popular carnival-play formed a class by itself. The 'Sottie' or Clown-play proper became rarer, but to make up for this, in some districts the clown and his jokes made their way even into the Biblical plays, notwithstanding Luther's disapproval. The Farces received important additions from the comic tales and jest-books, the Moralities from the parables of the New Testament, the Mysteries from the History of the Children of Israel, from the life of Christ and the Apostles, and from current tales and novels. German history contributed but little material to the drama of this epoch. Now, as in the fifteenth century, the play-writers seldom tried to be original in their choice of material, and did not hesitate to make use of former plays on the same subject. The earliest dramatic version of a story often became the model for all succeeding ones.

Various classes of drama in the sixteenth century.

Dramas based upon the story of the Prodigal Son always introduced flattering parasites, after the manner of Terence, and described profligate life, or else they attacked an effeminate and indulgent education, sometimes with a special application to student-life at the Universities. The stories of Rebecca and of Tobias furnished an opportunity for dwelling on the

Biblical dramas.

beauty of family life, courtship and marriage; the parable of
Dives and Lazarus brought forward the subject of social ine-
quality; Judith and Holofernes were made to suggest Turks and
Christians.

The stories of Joseph and of the Prodigal Son were successfully
dramatised by two Dutch scholars; the story of the Prodigal Son
was treated by Gnapheus of the Hague in 1529, that of Joseph by
Cornelius Crocus of Amsterdam in 1535. Both these plays are
written in Latin. The story of Susanna was first dramatised in
German and in Latin in the year 1532, by a South German
scholar, Sixtus Birk by name.

It can hardly have been possible in any part of Germany to draw
a fixed line between the regular drama and the popular drama. But
the relation of the one to the other and the prevalent subjects and
forms of composition varied according to time and locality.

In Switzerland we find at first all branches of the Drama represented. A short play on Wilhelm Tell was pro-
duced in the province of Uri. At Bern, Niklas   **Swiss plays.**
Manuel wrote elaborate dramas meant to convey special truths,
and composed in the style of the carnival-plays. In 1522 he
published the 'Todtenfresser' (Dead-eaters)—i. e. the clergy who
live on masses for the dead; also the 'Unterschied zwischen
Papst und Jesus Christus,' in which the hosts of the Pope and the
Saviour march against each other just in the manner depicted by
Luther and Lucas Cranach. In 1525 Manuel wrote the 'Ablass-
krämer,' describing the 'Indulgence-monger' who no longer finds
any favour in the villages, and is forced to acknowledge his
wickednesses. All this is most dramatically conceived and carried
out, in a realistic manner calculated to appeal most strongly to the
popular mind. Heinrich Bullinger of Kappel was the author of
a play, 'Lucretia,' written before 1529. In 1531, at Zwingli's instigation, Aristophanes' comedy of 'Plutus' (Wealth) was performed
at Zürich, in the original Greek. A year before this, Petrus
Dasypodius had produced a Latin play with a miser as its central
character. Sixtus Birk began his career as a dramatist in Basle in
the year 1532, and continued the same at Augsburg, thus handing
on to Swabia and Bavaria the fashion of writing simple school-

dramas on Bible subjects, written either in German or in Latin. These Protestant plays soon had to compete against the gorgeous representations arranged by the Jesuits.

Subsequently, however, we find most in vogue in Switzerland diffuse Scriptural dramas, lasting many days and introducing masses of actors. In these dramas nothing was made known by mere narrative, but everything passed before the eyes of the spectator in strict se-

The drama in Alsace. quence of time. The taste for such dramas also prevailed in Alsace. In Jörg Wickram's 'Tobias' every

Jörg Wickram's 'Tobias.' single incident is represented in full detail, and every sad or joyful family event is accompanied by the inevitable condolences or congratulations of the neighbours. But while in Switzerland these diffuse dramas were still increasing in popularity, in Alsace, on the contrary, their power was declining. The influence of Hans Sachs and other writers was beginning to assert itself. Short tales were dramatised, and in other ways too an effort was made towards greater conciseness of treatment. In the Strassburg Gymnasium and Academy the Renaissance Drama was cultivated after ancient classical models.

In Franconia it was Nürnberg—'the eye and ear of Germany,'

The drama in Nürnberg. as Luther called it—which set the fashion in plays for the other towns. Nürnberg remained what it had been in the fifteenth century, the classic home of the carnival-plays. But the Nürnberg dramatists ranged far beyond

Hans Sachs. the old farces. As for Hans Sachs, the Nürnberg shoemaker, who surpassed all his colleagues in fertility and artistic power, there was no province in which he did not try his hand, no interest of the time which did not find an echo in his writings. Only in his versification he persistently adhered to the worst traditions of the close of the Middle Ages. He had no idea that there could be any fixed relation between matter and form. In no writer of the sixteenth century is the want of æsthetic culture which characterizes the epoch so apparent as in Hans Sachs. At the same time he is not incapable of artistic composition, like Fischart, and we may even say that he is the greatest poetical genius that had appeared in Germany since the Minnesingers. Although a Protestant, he had not the combative temperament of

a Hutten, a Murner, or a Manuel. His poetry was not inspired
by indignation; he retained his poetical composure   Peaceful
in the midst of the troublous times in which he wrote.   character
His power of easy creation resulted from the peace-   of his
fulness of his nature. He looked on the world with   writings.
an untroubled glance, and could enter into its life with a sympathy
free from all egoism. What he himself observed he was also able
to reproduce in words. But he endeavoured to represent many
things which had never fallen under his observation, and he
made the mistake of thinking that every form of poetry was suitable for every theme. He treated many of his subjects in verses
for singing and in epic rhymed couplets as well as in dramatic
form, viz. in a dialogue in rhymed couplets. It is a pity that he
did not likewise treat them in prose, for his Reformation pamphlets
show us that in prose-writing he commanded a clear and flexible
style. He made use of all forms of writing in his efforts to diffuse
information on various subjects. He was a real teacher of the
people, and his teaching was of a comforting and conciliatory
character, springing from his own kind and gentle nature. He
always unites description and reflection ; he is a   His style.
master of description, and makes use of it on every
possible occasion, but his reflections are for the most part trivial.
He pictures graphically to himself all the scenes which are within
his power of imagination. As an instance of this power we may
mention his story of the pedlar who goes to sleep in a wood, and
has his wares plundered, and his clothes damaged by apes. The
heat, the weary pedlar, the quiet of the wood, the shade, the cool
spring inviting to rest, the pedlar's dream which conjures up before
his eyes a vision of a village festival and of large receipts, the de-
vastation caused by the apes, and the exact contents of the basket
ransacked by them—all this is most vividly described. Hans Sachs
does not think of telling us at the outset what the pedlar's pack
contained, we only learn it when the things themselves come to
light; action thus takes the place of mere description. In other
cases, too, we notice that he tries to give his story a poetic form.
Thus, when wishing to describe the latest victories of Charles V,
he pictures himself as coming one day into Nürnberg from the

country to make purchases, and seeing with astonishment many signs of festal rejoicing, and at length asking an explanation from an old man, who then gives him a short narrative of the events. In this way he succeeds in producing suspense in the reader's mind.

In his tales and dramas, Hans Sachs frequently endeavours to connect action with motive and to develop character; but he as frequently neglects this altogether, or attempts it only in the most superficial manner. He does not go so far as summarily to dismiss his characters from the stage, when he no longer requires them there, but the reasons for their exit are often very insufficient. He divides his comedies and tragedies into acts, but the number of acts is quite capricious, and the division is often made at a most unfitting place. He twice dramatised the pretty story of Eve's good and bad children being examined by God in the doctrines of faith, and some of them answering badly in their examination. Each version has its special merits, but in the second the close of the act is made to come in the midst of the examination, where it is utterly out of place. With regard to his character-drawing, it is in treating serious subjects that Hans Sachs furnishes us with truly individual personalities, for then he draws them from his own experience. He represents in a touching manner the banishment of Adam and Eve from Paradise, and effectually enlists our sympathies on the side of our first parents, whom affliction only binds more closely together. Specially charming is his description of Eve's naive fear of God, whose visits alarm her; or of Adam as a father, instructing his boys how to behave before the good God, how to take off their caps, to bow and to give their hand. In Cain, the poet has given us an excellent picture of a naughty boy. The impetuosity and imprudence of the porter of Heaven, St. Peter, are drawn with inimitable humour in all Sachs's farces and dramas. Frequently he paints not individuals but types, like the masks of Italian comedy; in this he was influenced by the German poetry of the day, whose strength lay in satirical caricature. One or more of these typical figures regularly appear in every farce: the Catholic priest and his housekeeper, the cheating landlord, the wicked and quarrelsome old dame, the sharp-witted wandering scholar, the unfaithful wife, the jealous husband, and many

His dramas.

others. In his invention of dramatic situations, striking speeches, and comic scenes, as in his creation of characters, the poet has certain fixed moulds at his disposal, which he further embellishes by traits drawn from his own observation.

Hans Sachs's literary activity extended from 1514 to 1569. According to his own reckoning he had by the year **Sachs's great** 1567 written 4275 Master-songs, 208 dramas, 1558 **fertility in** comic stories, fables, histories, figures (*Figuren*), com- **writing.** parisons, allegories, dreams, visions, lamentations, controversial dialogues (*Kampfgespräche*), newspapers, psalms and religious songs, street and tavern songs, as well as seven prose dialogues —in all, therefore, 6048 larger or smaller works. It is in his farces and fables that he best satisfies the usual requirements of art, less in his carnival-plays, and still less in his other dramas. His first tragedies, 'Lucretia' (1527) and 'Virginia' (1530), dealt with stories of Roman liberty. It was not till 1533 that he turned his attention to the Scriptural Drama, and not till 1545 that he began dramatising tragic subjects drawn from tales, especially from Boccaccio. The period of his greatest dramatic activity falls between 1550 and 1560; in these years he wrote masses of plays, seizing alike on scriptural, classical, or romantic subjects. Sachs represents throughout the sketchy style of drama; he only gives slight outlines, and does not develop, but compresses.

Hans Sachs died in 1576 in the 81st year of his age. Through his influence the Nürnberg school of dramatic art **Hans Sachs** became the example not only for the towns in the **died, 1576.** immediate neighbourhood, but also for Magdeburg, Augsburg, Breslau, and Strassburg. And even in the present day relics of Hans Sachs's dramas may still be found in the plays acted by the German peasants of Upper Bavaria, as far as Hungary and Silesia. In those districts they have lived on, like popular songs.

A short time after Hans Sachs had begun to cultivate the Scriptural drama, and about the time when the Ger- **Dramas** man Bible was finished, several Biblical dramas and **produced** dramas written with a fixed purpose were produced in **in Luther's** Luther's immediate circle. Joachim Greff wrote seven **circle.** or more such plays, none of which show anything worthy of remark.

Johann Agricola of Eisleben, the collector of proverbs, wrote a tragedy of ' John Huss.' Paul Rebhun followed Birk's example, and even tried to outdo him in efforts to improve the technique and versification of the drama, dividing his pieces into five acts, and making each act end with a chorus.   His endeavours in th's

Thomas direction were continued by other play-writers. Lastly, **Naogeorg's** there was Thomas Naogeorg, who ranks highest as **Protestant** a writer of dramas with a Protestant bias.   It is true, **plays.** he only wrote in Latin, but his plays were often translated, and he found an excellent German-writing disciple in Johannes Chryseus.   Naogeorg came from Bavaria, and was for a time pastor at Kahla in Thuringia; later on, a disagreement arose between himself and Luther, and he had to give up his living.   His first work, published in 1538, represents the Pope, under the name of ' Pammachius,' as Antichrist and as an ally of the Devil.   The second, ' Mercator ' (1540), introduces us to a dying merchant, who can find no relief in all the Roman Catholic means of salvation, but to whom St. Paul's doctrine of justification by faith at length brings comfort and peace.   His third work, ' Incendia ' (1541), was written to ridicule Duke Heinrich of Brunswick, against whom Luther was at the same time writing his pamphlet entitled ' Wider Hans Worst.'   Naogeorg also made a detailed study of the character of Haman in a drama directed against bad ministers, hostile to the Gospel (1543); he depicted Jeremiah in his conflict with idolatry (1551), and branded in the person of Judas Iscariot all traitors to the Protestant cause (1552). Naogeorg's nature was essentially manly, and he confined his plays, as far as possible, to male characters.   His art did not improve, but rather deteriorated in his later works.   He worked hastily and superficially; his plays are full of dramatic defects, and he did not keep the requirements of the real stage sufficiently in view.   But his first dramas are full of quite Aristophanic scenes, and exhibit a mixture of the terrible and the grotesque, which cannot fail to exercise a powerful influence on all who come in contact

Chryseus. with it.   His disciple, Chryseus, in his ' Hofteufel' (1544), chose the prophet Daniel as his hero, but filled the play with allusions to contemporary events and interests. Daniel is represented as the ideal of a Protestant pastor, and the idolatry which he scorns is called 'thoroughly Roman;' the 'Court-Devil,' who wishes to ruin him, is a venerable priest in a monk's robe, and his allies at Court are some of them Bishops and Cardinals.

The plays which arose in Luther's immediate circle belong to the class of schoolplays founded on Terentian models. This kind of drama gradually spread itself over the whole of North Germany, and acquired fresh vigour from its competition with the Jesuits. About 1540 we find writers in Berlin making efforts in the direction of original literary production; but Prussia, Pomerania, Mecklenberg, Brunswick, and Westphalia were not roused to activity till after the conclusion of the peace of Augsburg (1555), or even till considerably later.

The chief dramatist of this later epoch was again a South German, Nicodemus Frischlin of Tübingen, who Nicodemus wrote classical comedies, mostly in Latin; they were Frischlin. produced between the years 1576 and 1585, and were first performed before the court of Stuttgart. The plots are feeble and full of glaring improbabilities. The comic characters alone show any attempt at character-drawing, and the dialogue is disjointed and lively to excess. Still, Frischlin has many happy ideas and a decided comic talent. He specially delights in introducing the slaves and swaggering parasites of Roman comedy. In his play of 'Rebecca,' he turns Ishmael into a boisterous youngster, whom he draws to the life. 'Susanna' is a satire directed against lawyers and inn-keepers. Another of his plays introduces us to life and ways of beggars and tramps. In one play, the idea of which is quite original, he describes the tortures which the Roman grammarian Priscian suffers at hearing the corrupt mediæval Latin, and takes occasion to sing the praises of Melanchthon as a philologist. A second original play glorifies Luther and the Würtemberg Reformer, Brenz, while Zwingli, Karlstadt, Schwenckfeld, and the whole Council of Trent are represented as carried off by the Devil. And in a third, and that the best of all, he represents Cæsar and Cicero as coming up to Germany from the lower world, and being filled with amazement at the glory of the German nation, with its gunpowder, its art of printing, its Empire, and its modern Latin poetry,

while they are confounded at the condition of two of their countrymen, a Savoyard pedlar and an Italian chimney-sweep. These
plays give dramatic expression to three great features of the age :
the classical Latin, the Lutheran faith, and the patriotic rivalry with
the Romance races. The passion and bitterness of a Naogeorg
have vanished in Frischlin; his view of life is more serene, and
his poetry rests on the firm basis of an established order of things.
His spirit was not cramped by the daily conflict of a new idea
gradually and with difficulty struggling up into recognition.

Frischlin's plays extend almost to that period when the more
highly developed dramatic poetry of England was destined to
exercise a powerful influence on the German Drama. The
German actors of the sixteenth century, whether scholars or
students, whether Mastersingers or simple bourgeois, were mere
dilettanti. In England an art of acting had been developed
The which was soon to learn to do justice even to the
Stage in creations of a Shakspeare. The predecessors of
England. Shakspeare already possessed some measure of that
art in which Shakspeare surpassed them all. They knew how to
choose powerful subjects for their plays from all quarters. As soon
as the German book of 'Faust' appeared in 1587, Christopher
Marlowe converted it into a masterly tragedy. About that time
English some English players entered the service of a German
players in prince, and shortly after 1590 they became a recog-
Germany. nised institution at two of the German courts. Duke
Heinrich Julius of Brunswick and the Landgrave Maurice of Hesse
each kept a troop of English players, and each wrote plays for their
comedians. The Landgrave's productions have been lost, but the
Duke's are still extant. These players must soon have learnt
German; they used to make long tours and would most probably
recruit their forces from native talent. Their stage was no longer
that of the popular dramas of the fifteenth century, which had hitherto
been retained throughout Germany, but resembled in principle that
of our modern theatres. It consisted of a raised platform as the
scene of action, having an opening in the floor from which the
Devils and Spirits might ascend. This stage was the scene of
murders, executions, martyrdoms and sudden deaths, of duels,

battles, and conflagrations. Gorgeous processions were made to pass across it, guns were discharged and fireworks let off with great noise and smoke. There was much music and singing, trumpeting and drumming, and the jests and pranks of the clowns ran through all. Great realism was aimed at in representation, and no efforts were spared to drive the audience to tears and laughter.

Jacob Ayrer of Nürnberg was a decided follower of the English school, and grafted the English dramatic art on to the style of Hans Sachs. His sixty-nine plays consist of tragedies, comedies, carnival-plays and operatic-plays (*Singspiele*), the latter a new class of drama introduced from abroad. But his productions are far inferior to those of Hans Sachs. He revels in scenic effects, writes in uncouth rhymed couplets, and in his plots seldom rises above a mechanical level. Jacob Ayrer's sixty-nine plays, 1595–1605.

Duke Heinrich Julius showed much more originality, and much more discrimination in borrowing. He adopted from the English dramas their prose-form and the ever-present clown, although the latter was not an utterly unknown character in earlier German plays. The Duke's play of 'Susanna' is borrowed from Frischlin's drama of the same name; his 'Vincentius Ladislaus' Plays by Duke Heinrich Julius of Brunswick, 1593–94. is the Capitano of Italian farce, the loquacious, bragging and lying, but cowardly soldier. His farces are simply comic tales in a dramatised form. It is only in his tragedy of the Prodigal Son that he reminds us of the horrors which formed so favourite an element in the earlier English plays.

Jacob Ayrer's dramas were produced between the years 1595 and 1605, those of Duke Julius between 1593 and 1594. About the same time, important advances were also made in the older forms of drama. After the year 1570, several translations were made of the Scotch poet Buchanan's two biblical dramas; these set the example of treating sacred subjects in the severer style of classical tragedy, especially in the manner of Seneca. About 1600 Buchanan's example began to be followed by poets of central Germany and of the Upper Rhine, who in their Latin plays, Improvements in the drama at the beginning of the 17th century.

if not in their German, observed the unities of time and place.
On the other hand, we find that at the annual theatrical re-
presentations given by the Strassburg Academy-Theatre, which
obtained great renown between the years 1597 and 1617, the
ancient dramas were produced together with entirely modern pieces.
Plays of Æschylus, Sophocles, Euripides, Aristophanes, and
Plautus were acted together with those of Naogeorg and Frischlin.
One dramatist even had the audacity to modernise the 'Ajax' of
Sophocles, and to represent things on the stage, which in the
Greek play are only reported. A number of new dramas were also
put on the stage, the most remarkable being a play on 'Saul' by
an unknown writer, and the works of Kaspar Brülow of Strassburg.
These dramas all show an improvement in style, a greater mastery
of the means of dramatic effect, and a more intricate plot. In
Pomerania, Brülow's native province, and in Mecklenburg the
German and Latin drama flourished about the beginning of the
17th century. Whilst the earlier German drama, even down to
Frischlin's time, had always inclined to comedy, we now, on the
contrary, find tragedy more and more gaining the preponderance.
The comic element was not, however, entirely banished, for farcical
episodes were countenanced in tragedies; for instance, peasants
were introduced, speaking their own uncouth dialect. The comic
interludes were now made into regular underplots; thus, side by
side with the marriage of Isaac and Rebecca the dramatist would
introduce a story of rustic married life, drawn with great fidelity to
Choice of   nature. A change also took place in the choice of
subjects   subjects; secular subjects came more into favour, and
widened.   ancient myths and Roman, mediæval, and modern
stories were dramatised. A number of types of character were now
more fully developed, such as parasites, braggarts, soldiers, peasants,
and witches. The interest then taken in medicine and psychology led
to the representation of various temperaments, for instance, that of the
melancholy man. Love, madness, and overweening pride were repeatedly depicted; and though in the conception of love finer sentiment was still wanting, this was in some degree made up for by
the introduction of touching scenes of child-life. Maxims of somewhat trivial wisdom still continued to adorn the dialogue. In the

construction of the play the excitement was enhanced by retarding
the climax, and more unity was introduced into the plot even where
the strictly classical form was rejected. Though all
this applies more immediately to the Latin dramas, yet
the change in these exercised its influence on German plays also. All the elements for making a great
dramatist existed at that time in Germany; it was only necessary
for these various elements to be united and brought to bear on each
other. And, in fact, this process was actually going on. In Strassburg there existed, beside the Academy-theatre, a play-house of
Mastersingers; Wolfhart Spangenberg, who furnished this German
play-house with pieces of a strongly moralising tendency, at the same
time wrote many of the German text-books which were supplied as
aids to the unlearned among the audience of the Academy-theatre.
The transition would seem easy from this to the writing of German
tragedies in the style of Brülow and of the modernised version of
Sophocles mentioned above. In the neighbourhood of Brunswick
we find a writer of school-plays, Johann Bertesius by name, who
shows great skill in the construction of German rhymed couplets,
writing them in the form employed by Paul Rebhun and quite
coming up to his level. We do not know whether this play-writer
succeeded in attracting more than the passing notice of Duke Heinrich Julius of Brunswick. At Cassel circumstances
were most favourable for the development of the
drama. The Landgrave Maurice built a theatre of his own, the first
Court-theatre in Germany. He chose the actors for his play at first
from among the pupils of the court-school (*Hof- und Ritterschule*),
which he himself had founded; later on he employed English
comedians. The school-boys had acted classical plays, amongst
others the 'Antigone.' With the advent of the English comedians
translations and imitations of English plays were added to the *répertoire*, and thus it came to pass that even the external form which
Shakspeare made use of, namely the alternation of prose and blank
verse, was transplanted to German soil. However German the
English comedians may have become, they did not entirely give up
their connection with England. They brought Marlowe's 'Faustus'
to Germany and several of Shakspeare's plays, amongst others

[margin note: General improvement in composition.]

[margin note: The theatre at Cassel.]

'Romeo and Juliet,' 'Hamlet,' 'Lear,' and 'Julius Cæsar.' They

Collection of English Comedies, published in 1620. also appropriated many features of the native German dramatic art. The collection of English comedies in German published in the year 1620 offers many examples of lively and truly dramatic prose-dialogue, sounding like an anticipation of Goethe's 'Götz von Berlichingen.'

But the English comedians could not found a truly great German school of drama. They merely provided for their *répertoire* whatever they thought would best amuse their audiences on their professional journeys. No creative poet arose, who, while learning from the English players, as Duke Heinrich Julius had done, should at the same time unite and develop in himself all the resources of the German drama, and become a rival of Shakspeare.

The Thirty Years' War stops all development. The development of the drama, which had begun in so many different quarters, was interrupted at its most promising stage. All the hopes cherished with regard to the German drama were wrecked by the Thirty Years' War, and also by the want of a capital town with an appreciative artistic audience. Germany had no capital to attract every great talent to itself and render the stage independent of the favour of single princes.

THE THIRTY YEARS' WAR.

It was not only the drama that made important advances in the

General progress in literature immediately before the war. first decades preceding the Thirty Years' War; there were signs of progress in knowledge and taste at that time in all the provinces of literature. Johann Kepler

Kepler. began to publish his important astronomical works in the year 1596, writing in an extremely clever and lively Latin style. His Swabian countryman, Valentine Andreä, ridiculed the perversities of the age in correct Latin

Valentine Andreä. dialogues and parables, and also wrote some excellent German poems, and some small romances partly in German and partly in Latin prose. In one of these romances he draws a picture of an ideal Christian state, and also gives a scheme for an Academy of Natural Science.

Another furnished the suggestion for the mysterious society of the Rosicrucians, which soon put all Europe in a state of excitement. Johann Arndt of Ballenstädt wrote some excellent popular devotional works, remarkable for their clearness and elegance, and for the noble and tolerant spirit which animates them. They are entitled 'Das wahre Christenthum,' 1605–1610, and 'Das Paradies-Gärtlein voll christlicher Tugenden,' 1612. Jacob Böhme began his theosophical writings in 1610. In scholastic theology we find short moral reflections asserting themselves side by side with interminable dogmatic teaching. Philosophy strove after a standpoint above the strife of religious parties; political science found excellent representatives and philologists, literary historians, historical students, and geographers were beginning to display extraordinary activity.

Johann Arndt and Jacob Böhme.

Theology, philosophy, &c.

A German dictionary was begun, and already the interest of a few scholars was being attracted towards Middle High-German poetry. In the realm of secular poetry, the social song, at once international and popular in character, was flourishing, and Church-hymns were beginning to take a gentler and more individual tone. Prose style was becoming decidedly more flexible, and in many writers was no longer disfigured by foreign words and phrases; still we must acknowledge that now, as in the eleventh century, the mixture of languages was one of the essential characteristics of the literature, reflecting the strong influence exercised on it from foreign sources.

Poetry.

In the years 1600 to 1617 there was an extraordinary increase in the German book-trade, which even the war did not succeed in checking at once. It was not till about 1632 that the trade began decidedly to decline. In these first decades of the seventeenth century, a large amount of foreign poetry was brought into the German market. Translators were very active. Spanish works were imported *viâ* Munich, French productions *viâ* Mömpelgard and Strassburg; the latter consisted mostly of romances like 'Amadis of Gaul,' which found an audience in aristocratic circles, and were many of them translated by noblemen.

Increase in the book-trade, 1600–1607.

Translations.

The pastoral romances were already beginning to appear, and
Pastoral were destined to cause a transformation in the con-
romances. versation of the cultivated classes, and to force even
love-poetry into a pastoral costume. Catholic Germany entered
into sympathy with the culture of the South; the Calvinists continued to adhere to Dutch and French models; the Lutherans
alone remained for the most part faithful to what was distinctively
German. The aristocracy as a whole was now becoming more
cultivated and refined through travelling; the German nobles were
Increased beginning to follow the example of the aristocracy in
interest in other countries, and once more to honour their native
German literature and language by their active sympathy. In
literature. the German Renaissance movement before the Reformation we noticed nobles and scholars working in common,
and this seemed now to be repeated. Then we saw Germans
striving to equal the Italians in classical learning, and to secure
the general recognition of German merits and German titles to
fame. The same patriotic pride meets us also after the Reformation, only its sphere is extended from Latin to national literature.
South-West Germany now as then took the lead in the intellectual
Weckherlin movement. At the court of Stuttgart about 1617, we
at find Rudolf Weckherlin writing elegant drinking-songs
Stuttgart. and love-songs, and describing the glories of the ducal
festivities, just as Nicodemus Frischlin had done some years before
Zincgref in Latin. In Heidelberg we find Julius Wilhelm
and the Zincgref following in the steps of Paul Melissus and
Heidelberg mentioning Fischart's name with reverence. In his
poetic poems Zincgref sometimes copied foreign models,
circle. and sometimes adopted the popular tone; later on
he made an attractive collection of the ' wisely uttered wisdom of
the German nation.' Other young men with the same aims and
ambitions gathered round him. In the summer of 1619 Martin
Opitz joined the circle; he was then only twenty-one, but had
already in a Latin pamphlet written two years before recommended
German poetry to the attention of scholars, and announced himself
as its reviver. Through him East Germany was drawn into the
movement. About the same time too, we find sympathy for the

native language and native poetry beginning to stir in central Germany. On the 24th of August 1617, the 'Fruit-bringing Society,' as it was termed, was founded in Weimar. It was an imitation of the Italian Academies, especially of the Florentine 'Academy della Crusca' ('Crusca'=chaff). The German society borrowed from the Italian one the idea of purifying the mother-tongue from the 'chaff' of foreign words or dialect expressions, and the example of the Della Cruscans was also rigidly followed in all the rules of the society, in the badges worn by its members and the names adopted by them.

'The Fruit-bringing Society' at Weimar.

The 'Fruit-bringing Society' included princes, nobles, and scholars, without reference to their religious beliefs, and the Calvinistic Prince Ludwig of Anhalt, who was their President for many years, deprecated every attempt to confine it to the aristocracy, and expressly declared that scholars were also noble 'by virtue of the liberal arts.' In assuming this attitude the society rightly pointed out the only basis on which a new German literature could prosper. By making it one of the duties of its members to express themselves moderately and courteously, and to abstain from unseemly speech and abusive ridicule, it helped to banish the coarse tendencies of the sixteenth century. It discouraged the use of foreign words among its members, and set up a standard of pure German which future writers endeavoured to come up to. It also aimed at improving versification; it sought to reduce grammar, dictionary, and prosody to rules, and it encouraged good literary work. By all these various efforts the 'Fruit-bringing Society' helped to lay the necessary foundations of modern German literature.

Refinement of literature, through its efforts.

But all this progress which we have noticed was checked by the Thirty Years' War. The Heidelberg circle of poets was scattered as early as 1620 by the Spanish troops; the 'Fruit-bringing Society' had to pursue its aims under great external difficulties. The Thirty Years' War was a fatality not only to the drama, but to all the other branches of literature, and to all intellectual progress generally in Germany. The fact that the literary life of Germany did not

Fatal effect of the Thirty Years' War.

quite succumb under it is a proof of the vigour which it had already acquired. German literature after 1618 is not a new departure, but the meagre continuance of the movement which had begun before the war and was checked by it. The union of popular, classical, and modern elements of culture which seemed to be imminent in the drama and in lyric poetry, never came to pass. The popular style which had enjoyed such complete supremacy in literature since the fourteenth century, now had to give way; Church-hymns alone remained faithful to this style, and though lyric and dramatic poets still occasionally returned to it, yet generally speaking we may say that they now struck out in other directions.

The scholar-poets now set the standard in literature, and they Scholar- despised the national German poetry instead of im- poets. proving it. They founded a class of poetry meant for scholars and men of refined culture. They continued in German the style which they had hitherto pursued in Latin. As they were accustomed to acquire the art of Latin verse from books, so they now wrote manuals to teach the art of German poetry. But in this schism with the national poetry these writers lost their independence, and translation and imitation remained their highest art. They introduced foreign styles of poetry and foreign metres, and allowed themselves to be carried away into foolish and inartistic tricks of writing. For the most part it was only lyric and didactic poetry that they cultivated with any perseverance. The eulogy (*Lobgedicht*), a feeble copy of the classical hymn, became the most favourite form of writing, appearing in various guises, chiefly as complimentary verses on special occasions, such as births, marriages, or deaths. This low order of occasional poetry was further promoted by the system of literary patronage and by the fashion of mutual eulogies among scholars; great scholars now begged for recognition and reward just like the despised gleemen of the Middle Ages. Only in two directions were the hopes raised by the period before the war fulfilled, namely in the purification of metrical construction and in the adoption of what is generally called the Renaissance style in poetry.

The verses of the sixteenth century, which simply counted the

number of syllables, and in which the metrical accent might therefore fall on an unaccented syllable, now disappeared.   Improve-
Though the poets of this period did not at once   ment in
return to the beautiful freedom of metre which char- versification.
acterized the poetry of the twelfth and thirteenth centuries, yet their
versification now followed rules calculated to produce a similar re-
result.   The rhymed couplets, which formerly enjoyed such popularity, were now despised as doggrel, and were abandoned without
any attempt at improving them.   Their place was taken by the far
more monotonous Alexandrine, the favourite metre of French and
Dutch poetry, which by its peculiar construction naturally resulted
in constant enumerations and antitheses.   The reign of the Alexandrine is contemporary with the most unfruitful period of modern
German poetry, i.e. the time before Klopstock and Lessing.

The merit of having carried out the reform of German versification must chiefly be attributed to the versatile and   **Martin**
talented Silesian poet, Martin Opitz. His 'Buch von   **Opitz's**
der deutschen Poeterey,' which appeared in 1624, **'Buch von der deutschen**
became the chief authority on the art of poetry in the   **Poeterey.'**
period immediately following its publication. It not only contained
precepts and hints on versification, but also on composition and
style in general, supported by the author's own practice. Opitz
wished to make German poetry more rich and varied and at the
same time more regular. He tried to separate poetic style from
prose-style and to raise poetry above the level of colloquial speech.
He endeavoured to introduce into German poetry something of that
beauty of form which he observed in the classical writers. He
wished to establish a definite style for each class of poetry. In
comedy and in the idyll, he says, the style may be homely and
simple, but in tragedy and in the epic, in the ode and the didactic
poem stately language is required to suit the subject.

These and many other of Opitz's views are derived, either directly
or indirectly, from Julius Cæsar Scaliger, whose Art of   **Opitz**
Poetry, published three years after his death, in 1561, **borrowed**
was considered by the scholars of the age to embody   **from**
the highest theoretic wisdom on the subject. In this   **Scaliger.**
work garbled maxims of Horace are mixed with rules of classical

rhetoric, criticisms on ancient and modern poets, observations on borrowed poetical ideas, and parallel extracts showing the treatment of the same subjects by various authors. The whole affords us a thorough insight into the art of poetry as first practised by the Renaissance-scholars in Latin, and then transferred to the vulgar tongue by poets of classical education. Writers were now authoritatively referred to the classics, just as Horace had enjoined on his Roman colleagues the duty of reading the Greek masterpieces by day and night. Among the mediæval poets, the scholarly Petrarch alone was recognised as worthy of the name. For a long period the influence of classical antiquity had been confined to the subject-matter of works; now, writers aimed also at imitating the classical perfection of form. Translations had hitherto been unwittingly somewhat of parodies, but now words, syntax, and figures of speech were to be closely copied. This close imitation of the classics produced the Renaissance style of poetry. The movement in favour of the classical writers began in France with Ronsard, and his example was followed in Holland by the celebrated philologist Daniel Heinsius. Ronsard and Heinsius were Opitz's much admired models. Opitz was, however, not the first to introduce the Renaissance style into Germany; he had been anticipated in this by a man of greater talent than himself, the Swabian Weckherlin, who was thirteen years older than the Silesian poet. Weckherlin had lived many years in France and England, and had studied the Renaissance-poetry of those two countries before appearing as an author in his own native land. His fame, however, was eclipsed by that of Opitz. Weckherlin adhered in his versification to the counting of syllables, and did not, like his ambitious rival, strive to gain a reputation by forcing himself into the acquaintance of German and foreign scholars. From about 1620 till his death Weckherlin lived in England. His political poems, written in praise of the Protestant generals of the Thirty Years' War, did not appear in print till after 1640. Hence it happened that it was Opitz's name, rather than his, which 'became associated in Germany with the improvement of

[Marginal notes:]

Strong influence of the classics, in France, Holland, and Germany.

Weckherlin introduced the Renaissance-style into Germany.

versification, the creation of a new literary style, and, as it seemed, the inauguration of a new literary epoch.

No writer has acquired an important place in the history of literature with so little title to it as Opitz. He was **Martin** born in 1597, and when he died in 1639, in the full **Opitz,** vigour of manhood, his zeal for poetry had long **1597–1639.** cooled down, the fame of learning having proved more attractive to him. His talent was best suited for the lighter forms of poetry. He was well fitted to raise the social song to a higher level, and to write easy, flowing verses on spring and love, moonshine and the song of birds. In this style he produced a few really excellent poems, some original and some borrowed. He also succeeded fairly well in sacred hymns, some of his being incorporated in the Church hymn-books. But his spirit aspired to higher things than these; he tried to make himself artificially what he was not in reality, and hence his more pretentious works are worthy of little praise. In the drama and the novel he never got beyond translation. His tiresome 'Hercynia,' a prose idyll with verses occasionally introduced, was really intended as mere flattery. Like Fischart, he imitated Horace in singing the praises of rural life, but he overloaded his work with details. His mournful contemplation of nature is carried to exaggeration, though there seems an undertone of true feeling in it. His descriptions in verse often sink to the level of prose, and only differ from the didactic rhymings of Hans Sachs in the Alexandrine metre, the introduction of a few Renaissance flourishes here and there, and the absence of all pleasing *naïveté*. The same may be said of his hymn on Christ's birth, and of his praise of Mars. His poems of consolation in time of war give us a lurid picture of the horrors which had broken over Germany, and contain some strong words against religious intolerance; but they too are spoilt by endless moralisings, in which the commonplace nature of the poet is fully revealed. Still, however low may be our estimate of Opitz's more ambitious works, they satisfied the taste of his contemporaries, and even in the last century, before the age of Frederick the Great had caused poetry to take a higher flight, men still looked up to him with admiration.

Opitz's fame spread rapidly in the years of the war, and his

Silesian countrymen diffused his views all over Germany. In the
School of University of Wittenberg August Buchner, though re-
Opitz. taining his independence in details, yet helped on the
whole to spread the Opitzian taste. In Leipzig Paul Fleming became
Paul his enthusiastic admirer. Fleming had the advantage
Fleming. over his master in this, that he really possessed a
slight amount of genius, and also had the benefit of one great
experience in his life, i.e. a journey to Persia; but he died in
his thirty-first year in 1640, and it was not till 1646 that his
collected poems were published by a friend. They are not free
from barren passages, highflown mythology, piled up maxims, far-
fetched wit, and all kinds of artificialities; but side by side with all
this we find true feeling, epigrammatic conciseness and melodious
and animated verses. Fleming's poetry gives us the personal
experiences of a happy and upright man. He wrote interesting
occasional poems, told the sighs and rejoicings of love, and above
His hymns. all composed sacred hymns, such as the traveller's
song: 'In allen meinen Thaten Lass ich den Höch-
sten rathen,' and the manly and brave poem: 'Lass dich nur
nichts nicht dauren.' But the world of spiritual experience still
remained a closed mystery to the poets of this period. They only
approached it by the circuitous paths of wit and wisdom.

In Königsberg Simon Dach became the centre of a poetic
Simon Dach society which followed Opitz, and wrote hymns as
in well as social songs. It was for this circle of friends
Königsberg. that Dach wrote the poem beginning :

> 'Der Mensch hat nichts so eigen,
>   So wohl steht ihm nichts an
> Als dass er Treu erzeigen,
>   Und Freundschaft halten kann.'

He was the author of 'Aennchen von Tharau,' a song now sung
all over Germany, and which was originally written in Low German
as a marriage-song. Dach's poems have the same smoothness and
ease as Fleming's, the same fluency, sometimes all too great. In
his religious songs he is fond of contemplating death; he does not
however paint it in glaring colours, but only in slight outlines, and
it is not fear that inspires him, but a quiet melancholy, which loves

to gaze into the beyond. Dach died in 1659 at the age of fifty-four.

German taste was not everywhere subject to Opitz. In the South and North it struck out in other directions, which found their expression in other literary societies. These were formed after the model of the Fruit-bringing-Society, but were either in direct opposition to it, or at least asserted their independence of it.

The 'Upright society of the Pine-tree' had been founded in Strassburg in the year 1633; it played off Weckherlin **'Society** against Opitz, and was to a certain extent a con- **of the** tinuation of that South-West German circle of poets, **Pine-tree'** with which Opitz had at an earlier period come in **in Strass-** contact at Heidelberg. **burg, 1633.**

In 1644 the poets of Nürnberg formed their 'Society of the Pegnitz shepherds, or the crowned Flower-Order on **The 'Pegnitz** the Pegnitz.' Its most distinguished members, Hars- **Shepherds'** dörfer, Klaj, and Birken threw themselves with special **in Nürnberg,** enthusiasm into the pastoral fancy. The florid Re- **1644.** naissance style became with them mere bombast and wordiness, and we find them following Italian models, in opposition to the French and Dutch taste to which Opitz paid homage.

Thus Strassburg and Nürnberg once more proved true to their ancient literary reputation, and produced the last followers of Sebastian Brand, Murner, Fischart, and Spangenberg on the one hand, and of Rosenblüt, Folz, Hans Sachs, and Jacob Ayrer on the other. But new circumstances now contributed **Hamburg** to make Hamburg and its neighbourhood an impor- **becomes a** tant centre of learning and poetry. The North-Sea **literary** towns, Hamburg and Bremen, succeeded in preserv- **centre.** ing a prudent neutrality during the war, and thus developed great prosperity in the midst of the general misery. While German trade was everywhere else falling into decay, and England and Holland were enormously increasing in power and importance, these two towns were engaged in conveying foreign wares into the interior of Germany, and thus profited by the prosperity of the English and Dutch. But while Calvinistic Bremen played but little part in German literature, Lutheran Hamburg on the contrary developed, side by side with great material prosperity, a highly active intellectual life. There Joachim Jungius taught and Balthasar Schuppius preached, and it was also the home of many other distinguished scholars. Opitzians and independent poets here met together, and each party sought to increase its importance by starting a poetical society of its own. The minister Johann Rist was established at Wedel on the Elbe in the neighbourhood of Hamburg, and in Hamburg itself Philip von Zesen went to rest, after a chequered and wandering life. Rist came from Ottensen near Altona; he was born in 1607, and died in 1667. Zesen, who came from Central Germany, lived from 1619 to 1689. Rist first made his appearance as an author in 1634, Zesen in 1638. Rist founded the 'Order of the Elbe Swans' (*Elbschwanenorden*) in 1658; Zesen was from 1643 the president of a 'German-feeling Society' (*Deutschgesinnte Genossenschaft.*)

Rist, like Fleming and Dach, was one of those Opitzians who
Johann Rist, surpassed their master in talent. His secular songs
1607-1667. produced a great effect in their time, and amongst his religious poems we must mention the sublime hymn beginning: 'O Ewigkeit, du Donnerwort.' But Rist spoilt himself by overwriting. His fluency became shallow insipidity, his grandeur degenerated into pompous verbosity, and he never knew the right point at which to stop.

Zesen, who was an author by profession, was not less productive
Philipp von than Rist, and wrote excellent love-poems and novels.
Zesen, He was sentimental and mystical by nature, and
1619-1689. possessed a great variety of superficial knowledge. He developed great activity as a translator, particularly of Dutch works, and stood forth as a champion of liberty of conscience. He wrote works on metre, grammar, and morals, also a guide to politeness, a history and description of Amsterdam, and various devotional works. His treatment of his subject is never wanting in thoroughness, and his language is always polished, his style as finished as he could make it. Zesen sometimes carries his thoroughness to exaggeration, and appears as a scholar where we only expect the

poet. He can put no limit to his description of psychological states, and he tries to surpass all his contemporaries in purity of expression. No other German writer has taken up the patriotic war against foreign words so thoroughly in earnest, and in consequence none has so exposed himself to ridicule. Where Opitz makes ostentatious use of names of ancient mythology, Zesen tries to replace them by German ones. Pallas was to be called *Kluginne* (*klug*, wise), Venus, *Lustinne* (*Lust*, pleasure), Jupiter, *Erzgott* (arch-god), Vulcan, *Glutfang* (glow-catcher). He proposed replacing all foreign derivatives by words of purely German origin. But in his own writings, Zesen did not strictly adhere to these Germanisms, and he never set himself up as an unimpeachable authority in the matter of language.

The activity of most of the above-mentioned poets was continued on into the years succeeding the war, and the writings of some of them seem to anticipate the literature of the following period. Almost all of them devoted themselves chiefly to religious or secular lyric poetry ; but Zesen also cultivated the novel, and Klaj, Rist, and Dach tried their hand at the Drama. The real dramatist of this period was Gryphius, a Silesian like Opitz, **Andreas** and a man whose influence was as great as that of **Gryphius** Opitz. He introduced the Renaissance style into **and the** tragedy, and formed a special school of dramatic **drama.** writing. His poems too are noteworthy, and in everything he forms the link between the French-Dutch Renaissance of the Opitzians on the one hand, and the Spanish-Italian bombast of the later Silesians on the other. He is more imaginative than the former, and not so exaggerated as the latter. In contrast to the sanguine and versatile lyric poet Opitz, Gryphius was a serious and resolute man, with a tragic basis of character. Opitz used his talent against his evangelical co-religionists, but Gryphius remained all his life a loyal Lutheran. Opitz poured flattery on distinguished men, but Gryphius never thus lowered his personal dignity. Opitz devoted his energies exclusively to the Renaissance movement, and formed his ideas on the ancients and on the Dutch; Gryphius, while he followed Opitz's example for the most part, yet at the same time had some connection with the popular drama, and carried on both in tragedy and comedy the style which had been prevalent before the war. We have said that everything seemed prepared in German literature before the war for the appearance of a Shakspeare; owing to that war Germany produced instead of a Shakspeare only a Gryphius.

The Renaissance-drama in Holland attained its highest level in **Gryphius** Joost van den Vondel. Andreas Gryphius, who was **influenced** a scholar of many-sided talent, and had studied and **by Joost van** taught for six years at the University of Leyden, **den Vondel.** translated one of Vondel's tragedies, and learnt much from him, both in general choice of subjects and in single dramatic motives. These two writers closely resemble each other in the technique of their art, in their adherence to the regular five acts, in their endeavours to observe unity of time, and to a certain extent unity of place, in the introduction of a chorus mostly at the end of the acts, in the use of the Alexandrine side by side with lyric metres in the chorus, in the alternation between long speeches and short ones, and finally in their stirring dialogue, adorned by similes and ingenious modes of expression. Both adhere to the modern school of Seneca, which furnished the leading type of tragedy for the whole of the Renaissance literature, and was already represented in the German school-plays about the year 1600.

In the general character of his pieces Gryphius approaches more **Character-** closely to Seneca than Vondel; he piles up ghost-**istics of** scenes and generally revels in the horrible. When **Gryphius'** he does depart from the manner of Seneca, it is to **plays.** follow the English and German tradition; as, for instance, when he puts a prologue into the mouth of a personification of Eternity, or makes the catastrophe take place on the stage itself, instead of adopting the stereotyped form of report by a messenger.

Gryphius lived from 1616 to 1664. He was born in the year of Shakspeare's death, and died a hundred years after Shakspeare's **Melancholy** birth. A succession of sad experiences had early tinged **tone of his** his mind with sadness; the dreadful Thirty Years' **poetry.** War threw its shadow over his youth. A melancholy tone prevails in many of his lyric poems, and brave endurance is

the chief theme of his tragedies, some of which were written in
the last years of the war.   Later on, as Syndic of his native town
of Glogau, he may have taken a more cheerful view of life ; it was
in this period that his comedies appeared.

Love is hardly touched on in Gryphius' poems, and even in his
Sonnets we seldom find any praise of women's beauty.   But he
often sings of his own experiences ; his birthday or the New year
generally disposes him to serious reflections.   Satire Religion his
too is not strange to him, but his chief theme is re- chief theme.
ligion.   He is the author of the two hymns beginning : 'Jesus, meine
Stärke,' and 'Die Herrlichkeit der Erden Muss Rauch und Asche
werden.'   He is absorbed in the thought of his own sinfulness, and
of the sufferings of Christ.   He wrote a Latin epic, taking the scene
on the Mount of Olives as the central point of interest.   This work
shows perfect unity of composition, but is spoilt by the author's delight in descriptions of earthly misery, of all the horrors of sickness
and death.   Gryphius strongly appeals to the imagination of his
readers.   He succeeds in giving life to the dryest subjects, and
renders even occasional poems interesting ; and when he means
to be simple, and lays aside all 'poetic fancies and colours,'
he impresses us by his true feeling, and by a great flow of language.

His earliest tragedy, 'Leo Armenius,' treats of a successful
palace-revolution at Constantinople, and contains many Gryphius'
protests against tyranny and reflections on the tran- tragedies.
sitoriness of all earthly glory.   Three other tragedies of his have
martyrs as their heroes.   The martyr to religion is depicted in
Katherine of Georgia, who resists the suit of a heathen prince ; the
political martyr in Charles I of England, whom Gryphius glorified
in the drama immediately after his death ; and the martyr to duty
in Papinianus, who will neither approve an imperial act of violence,
nor yet save his life by revolutionary means.   'Cardenio and
Celinde' is a piece which breathes strictly Christian sentiments.
It differs from the other plays, in not introducing any of those
princely characters, which were at that time thought essential to
tragedy.   It resembles the later class of bourgeois-tragedy, and
replaces the ordinary declamatory style by language more true to

reality. Like many dramas of the sixteenth century it is founded
on an Italian tale, of which the following is a short outline. Cardenio, being passionately in love with Olympia, wishes to murder
her husband; Celinde, who has been deserted by Cardenio, tries
to win him back again by magic spells; but both are cured of
their passion by the intervention of higher powers in the shape
of terrifying and warning ghosts. The glow of earthly passion
seems extinguished by the view of death, and the whole purport of
the play is expressed in the warning: 'Think every hour of dying.'
The first act is long and confused, and the fifth is taken up in telling us things which we know already; but the three acts between
show us the best that Gryphius ever accomplished in the sphere of
tragic poetry. Here we have truly dramatic effects, genuine tragic
emotion, and a perfect reflection of real life. The characters are
clearly sketched, though perhaps not fully developed; and above
all we have, in place of mere excited speeches, an interesting and
well-developed plot.

We here feel ourselves in an atmosphere akin to that of Shakspeare's plays, and Gryphius' comedy of 'Peter
Squenz' actually deals with one of Shakspeare's own
themes, namely, the acting of the 'mechanicals' in the Midsummer
Night's Dream. The subject had been brought by the English
comedians to Germany, where it was afterwards frequently made
use of. This amusing farce takes with Gryphius the form of a satire
on the dramatic attempts of the Mastersingers, but the best and
leading ideas of the piece are, as we have said, not original.
Another comedy, of Gryphius' own invention, entitled 'Horribili-
cribrifax,' introduces us to two military braggarts and several pairs
of lovers. One of the soldiers mixes French words, the other
Italian words with his conversation, the schoolmaster Sempronius
affects Latin and Greek expressions, and a Jew makes frequent
use of Hebrew words; an old woman misunderstands the foreign
tongues, and gets enraged through her mistakes. But these jokes
of language, which presupposed a great knowledge of languages in
the audience, are driven to death in this piece. There is too much
repetition, the action often stagnates for a long time, and unity is
destroyed by the interweaving of several plots.

'Die Geliebte Dornrose,' a rustic piece in the Silesian dialect, gives us far more real life than any other of Gryphius' plays. The idea of it was, to a certain extent, sug- gested by Vondel, though peasant-scenes of this kind had long been a favourite theme with German dramatists. The comic treatment of dialects was an idea introduced in the sixteenth century. Sometimes the rustic piece formed an interlude to another play, alternating with it act by act, and this practice too was· derived from the older German drama. Gryphius' 'Dornrose' is an interlude of this kind. The plot is clear, con- nected and sufficiently interesting. A pair of lovers are separated by a quarrel between their two families; the quarrel is in the end made up, and the youth and maiden are united. An un- successful suitor of the girl's is also introduced, and a hag-like old woman who would like to have the youth for herself. Finally, the whole party are brought before the judge. The characters are not wanting in individuality; the dialogue is in prose, as in all Gryphius' comedies. The play to which 'Dornrose' forms the in- terlude is a comic operetta (*Singspiel*), entitled 'Das Verliebte Gespenst'('The ghost in love'). It stands in contrast to 'Dornrose' by its conventional verses and conventional motives. Gryphius made some other successful efforts in this new class of poetry; his two operatic festival-plays, 'Majuma' and 'Piastus,' are quite excellent. In addition to all this, he translated a Latin religious drama, and wrote German versions of Italian and French comedies. Gryphius thus represents all branches of the drama of that time, and we can see that his writings were affected by almost all the native and foreign influences which could possibly be brought to bear on a German dramatist of that period. He justly became, therefore, a recognised authority among dramatists, nor was his work quite without result among the professional players. The wandering players managed to keep up their trade, though with difficulty, as may be supposed, through the long years of the war. The civic plays and the school comedies, for want of development and support, and for want of a capital to attract all the best talent, sank to the level of mere local amusements, and thus became useless for the

Marginal notes: 'Die Geliebte Dornrose.'

Operettas.

Wandering players during the war.

general development of the drama; but these wandering troupes of actors carried their art into all parts of the country, and kept their stage open to every available production. In the course of the seventeenth century they adopted Italian, French, Spanish, and Dutch plays and themes; they endeavoured to draw what benefit they could from the dramas based on classical models, and at the same time retained what had formed the original basis of their *répertoire*, namely, English pieces. Among the latter, one attained special popularity, probably because it was drawn from a Ger-

Marlowe's man source; this was Marlowe's tragedy of 'Doctor
'Faustus.' Faustus,' which in the course of time assumed a more concise and effective form on their stage, and was handed down to posterity by means of oral tradition. Thus the tradition of the popular drama was preserved by the wandering players, just as, at an earlier period, the heroic songs had been preserved by the strolling gleemen. We have seen how the old Nibelungen legend attained in Middle High-German poetry to a position of new importance; even so the legend of Doctor Faust became the centre of modern German literature, and engaged the attention of those great German writers to whose efforts German literature owes a new period of glory and splendour.

CHAPTER X.

PEACE came at last, in 1648.   It placed the three Christian sects in Germany legally on the same level, and thus laid   Peace of
the basis of modern toleration.   The war left Germany   Westphalia,
poorer by two-thirds of its population; its prosperity   1648.
was shaken to its very foundations, its position among the nations greatly lowered, but the spirit of its people was still unbroken. The struggle to rise again to new vigour and prosperity called forth all the nation's strength, and its successful efforts in this direction were of benefit to its intellectual life.   The peace of Westphalia in 1648 inaugurates the last great epoch
of German history, the period in which we still stand.   Beginning of
a new period
It marks a new development in economics, politics,   in history
and science, which, in spite of single relapses and in-   and
literature.
terruptions, still continues to progress; it also marks
a new movement in literature and music,—a movement which reached its zenith about the beginning of our century and since then has gradually declined.   In the last epoch the tone had been set by the taste of the lower classes, and a plebeian stamp had thus been impressed on the writing of the period; but about 1600, the nobility had begun once more to bestow their favour on literature, and had soon united with the scholars in endeavouring to improve both literature and language, through the means of academies like the Fruit-bringing Society.   Most of the German provinces took part in these praiseworthy efforts.   In 1650 the influences of that

period of aspiration which preceded the war were still living and active, but later on, literary tendencies died away in most quarters under the stress of exhaustion and misery. The sphere of German literature of any higher order remained confined for some time to Hamburg, Silesia, and Saxony, till Berlin in 1690 and Switzerland in 1720 entered the circle. The Fruit-bringing Society had till 1651 been presided over by its first chief, Prince Ludwig of Anhalt, and from that year till 1662, by Duke Wilhelm of Sachs-Weimar; but after the death of the latter, it led but a phantom sort of existence. The other linguistic societies and literary circles also now came to an end, or else sank into utter insignificance. Single poets still continued to be recruited from the ranks of the aristocracy, but the upper classes, as a whole, now withdrew their

The aristocracy subject to French influence. co-operation from native literary efforts, and paid tribute to the political, industrial, commercial, and literary superiority of their Western neighbours, by striving after French culture; this attitude they retained, until confronted by native productions which quite rivalled the French in merit. If the nobility thus held aloof, it

German literature now appeals to the middle classes. became all the more necessary for German writers to win and strengthen the allegiance of the middle-class reading-public, and for this purpose to cultivate the more popular branches of literature. The learned *élite*, who would only write for a learned and cultured audience, now began to disappear. In counting the books annually brought into the German market, we find that till 1639 Latin poetry had a steady preponderance over German, but

Latin gives place to German. after two decades of fluctuation, we find that from 1659 onward there is just as decided a preponderance of German poetry over Latin; and it is the same with prose writing. We find German asserting its power in scientific works, and even penetrating to the lecture-rooms of the Universities. Professors now became journalists and poets, and diffused generally useful knowledge. They did not, like their predecessors in the sixteenth century, condescend to the popular level, but sought to raise the taste of their readers to a higher standard. They were the leaders of public opinion, and the educators of those generations whose national ambition produced the great literary achievements of the eighteenth century. They first formed from amongst the men and women of the nobility and of the middle classes that middle stratum of the 'cultivated,' which since that time has made up the 'public' of Germany.

Now, as in the beginning of this period, writers generally spring from the ranks of the learned classes, that is to say, they have generally had a university education. The first representatives of this new period either imitated Opitz, or were directly opposed to him. The pastor Paul Gerhardt improved the tone of sacred poetry; Professor Johann Laurenberg wrote splendid satires; the lawyer Andreas Gryphius published his dramas; the theologian Bucholtz produced long-winded novels. It might appear from *Literary efforts at the beginning of this period.* this that the new literature was destined to infuse new life simultaneously into all the branches of poetry, but such was not the case; only the lyric, epic, and didactic forms of writing were to rise to any permanent excellence. The German drama has not to our own day succeeded in establishing any fixed tradition; Andreas Gryphius belongs rather to the expiring than to the opening epoch, and even during his lifetime, a party arose which condemned the theatre as sinful and worldly.

Religious tendencies had a great deal to do with the rise of the new literature, and now, as in the eleventh and twelfth centuries, we meet with an attitude of decided antagonism to the world, and with serious attacks even on innocent *Religious influences.* pleasures. Once more men's souls melted in the fervour of religious devotion, and again we find religious poetry striving after earthly glories in its own sphere. The emotion awakened by religion soon sought earthly objects, and the love of God promoted the love of man. Emotion in itself was now considered sacred, and the exalted state of sentiment and thought gave full life and varied form to all classes of poetry. At the zenith of this period religious poetry had to yield the first place to secular, and the church lost its hold over men's minds, till in the nineteenth century, as formerly in the thirteenth, its power revived anew.

The new literature was to a great extent determined by princely favour or disfavour. Those scientific men, who took any share in literature, were for the most part professors, schoolmasters, Princely or librarians in the service of princes; and more patronage. than once the founding of a University, or the period of its greatest renown, marks a decided advance in the intellectual and literary life of Germany.

Now, as in the Middle Ages, the Guelphs were reckoned among Brunswick. the patrons of the national literature. Duke Julius of Brunswick (son of that Duke Heinrich whom Luther attacked in his pamphlet 'Wider Hans Worst') introduced the reformed faith into his dominions, and founded the University of Helmstedt. He was followed by his son Heinrich Julius, the dramatist, a tolerant and cultivated ruler. Duke August the Younger, who was reigning in Wolfenbüttel (Brunswick), at the time of the peace of Westphalia, founded the library at Wolfenbüttel and patronised the liberal theologians of Helmstedt; this Duke was himself a learned theologian, and had compiled a Life of Christ from his own translation of the Gospels. His son Ulrich was vain, gallant, and fond of splendour, and took Louis XIV. as his model. He wrote a number of German Church-hymns, which were corrected by his teacher Schottelius, also diffuse novels like those of Bucholtz, and patronised the classical drama of French origin. One of his successors gave appointments in Brunswick to various German poets, and made Lessing librarian at Wolfenbüttel. The Hanoverian-Guelph line (which ascended the English throne) succeeded in attaching Leibniz to its service; it was a prince of this house too, who in the year 1733 founded the University of Göttingen, where exact research soon flourished, and where an exchange of ideas took place between England and Germany.

In Saxony the old university of Leipzig long formed a literary Saxony and centre of varying importance, and threw the once so Prussia. celebrated Wittenberg more and more into the shade. It was a most important event for the intellectual life of Germany, when the Electoral House of Saxony, which had hitherto favoured Lutheran orthodoxy, turned Catholic for the sake of the Polish crown, and Prussia thus became the champion of progress in Pro-

testantism, and gave entrance to more liberal views in Church
matters. The Prussian Calvinistic sovereigns who reigned over
Lutheran subjects did great things for the cause of toleration; they
received the fugitive French Protestants, and founded Universities
like Halle, Berlin, and Bonn, which became each in its own way
centres of a free intellectual life. All the Prussian rulers since the
great Kurfürst Frederick William (1640-1688), took an active interest in German culture, and advanced it either   Frederick
directly or indirectly. Frederick the Great did most   the Great
in this direction, through his Liberalism in Church   begins to
matters, his patriotic wars, his active sympathy with   reign, 1740.
literary culture and his glorious example in patronising distinguished men of letters, an example which was imi-   Period of
tated among the other German princes by men like   prepara-
Karl August of Weimar, the patron of Goethe. The   tion, 1648
period of the first aspirations of modern German   to 1740.
poetry and science, the time of preparatory development before
the accession of Frederick the Great, that is to say, the ninety-
two years from 1648 to 1740, form the subject of the present
chapter.

RELIGION AND SCIENCE.

When Johann Kepler published his 'Harmony of the World,' in
the fatal year 1618, he accompanied it with these   Kepler's
words of proud confidence: 'Here I throw the dice,   'Harmony
and write a book to be read by contemporaries or   of the
posterity, no matter which; it may wait thousands of   World,'
years for its reader, since God Himself has waited six   1618.
thousand years for one who should contemplate His work aright.'
Kepler lived on with unimpaired faculties till 1630, to the benefit
of science and to the glory of his nation. He was for a long time
the only German who, in the glorious century which produced
Galileo, Descartes, Bacon, Hobbes, Boyle, Harvey, Huyghens, and
Spinoza, could dare to plant his name by the side of these great
foreigners. The development of philosophy, mathematics, and

natural science fell at first to the share of the Western nations, the French, Dutch, and English. Germany did not produce any

No other great German scientist till Leibniz. other great man of science besides Kepler, till Leibniz established his fame, by the side of Locke and Newton. It was not till Leibniz's time that centres of research began to be founded in Germany, such as England possessed in the Royal Society, and France in the Paris Academy.

The Thirty Years' War broke in like a devastating flood over

Deplorable effect of the Thirty Years' War. religious and secular knowledge. The burning passion for scientific progress, which had animated Kepler, was stifled. Theology alone retained its power; but it showed its strength only in doctrinal controversies, and did nothing for the improvement of morals. It abandoned the people to the increasing spirit of coarseness, and to that code of military morality which, under the name of *Reputation*, spread even to the lower classes,—a morality which replaced conscience and true honour by a conventional respect for the claims of those of the same social rank, and a brutal disregard of the rights of those lower down in the social scale.

But it is only the dominant majority that presents such a melancholy picture; in secret, those forces were working which preserved the ideals of earlier times for the benefit of posterity. Johann Valentine Andreä was still living. The writings of Johann Arnd had not yet fallen into oblivion, and their readers drew

Joachim Jungius and Balthasar Schuppius. from them a purer form of religion. The philosopher and naturalist Joachim Jungius, a moderate Baconian, was director of the academic Gymnasium in Hamburg, and made it widely renowned as a seminary of learning. Marburg enjoyed the teaching and preaching of Balthasar Schuppius, who was also later on called to Hamburg. He was a popular orator and writer who, like the satirists of the sixteenth century, devoted his attention to real life, and inculcated practical Christianity. Putting aside controversies of doctrine, he attacked vice in all its forms, and by his realistic power of description he brought things home to men's minds, and was able at once to instruct and to amuse. At the University

of Helmstedt we find as teachers Georg Calixtus and Hermann
Conring, the former an enlightened theologian, who
sought out the points of agreement between the   Georg
                                                    Calixtus
two Protestant confessions (Lutherans and Calvinists),   and
and insisted that these only were essential, the   Hermann
latter a scholar of marvellously wide learning, a theo- Conring.
retical and practical physician, a theologian, politician, and unprin-
cipled journalist, and at the same time the founder of the history
of German law.   In the neighbouring town of Wolfenbüttel, and
in the service of the same Guelph line as the two   Justus
scholars just mentioned, lived Justus Georg Schotte-   Georg
lius, the most distinguished grammarian of the time. Schottelius.
He not only published a most valuable manual of correct speech,
but also made a survey of the history of the German language,
and intended to produce a dictionary on a very sensible plan, by
the collaboration of various scholars.

All these men arose within the Lutheran pale, and all of them
lived to see the religious peace of 1648; Andreä died in 1654,
Calixtus in 1656, Jungius in 1657, Schuppius in 1661, Schottelius
in 1676, Conring in 1681.   Among the Catholics also polemical
writing did not absorb all energy.   In Bavaria the   Catholic
Alsatian, Jacob Balde, wrote his highly imaginative   writers.
and elaborate Latin poems; on the Rhine and the Moselle Friedrich Spee was composing his tender, graceful German hymns.
Outside the ruling Churches, the doctrines of Schwenckfeld and
Jacob Böhme retained their vitality, and the mediæval mystics
acquired new hold over men's minds.

But it was not till after the peace of 1648 that all these good
tendencies were brought to maturity.   A tolerant   Spirit of
spirit, a reconciliation of differences, mark the coming toleration
period.   Party ties were weakened and individuals   after 1648.
found a way of accommodating themselves to each other; religious
feeling and practical Christianity took the place of religious controversy.   We can trace this tolerant tendency in all the various sects
at this period; a peaceable disposition might now again exist in
company with the strictest faith.   Just before the middle of the seventeenth century the songs of Friedrich Spee became known among

z

the Catholics and those of Paul Gerhardt among the Protestants, and however these two poets may differ from each other, yet we can trace in both kindred features, characteristic of the new period.

Friedrich Spee, a Jesuit of noble descent, who came from **Friedrich** Kaiserswerth on the lower Rhine, was a gentle soul, **Spee.** and one of the first opponents of the outrageous judicial murders committed in the trial of witches. Spee died at Treves in 1635, at the age of forty-four, and it was not till 1649 that his posthumous German works were published, namely his 'Güldnes Tugendbuch' and his 'Trutznachtigall.' The former is a devotional work in prose, with poems inserted in it, and the latter a collection of sacred hymns. In both the ideas and spirit of mysticism and of the Song of Solomon are predominant. The soul worships Christ as her bridegroom, and embraces Him with fervent devotion.

Spee's poems are connected with the Latin hymns of the **Character** Middle Ages, and continue the sentimental style of **of his** the Mystics; but the Renaissance has imbued them **religious** with its splendour and its audacity, and here and there **poetry.** we catch in them the tone of the social song. They are full of disdain of the world and delight in nature, longings for death and lamentations over sin; the poet delights in personifications of abstract conceptions, in childish playing with words and feelings, and sentimental enthusiasm. Pure, heavenly love is called Cupido, is blind, and wounds the soul with its arrows. In one poem Christ is praised as the good Shepherd Daphnis; in another the moon leads the stars out to pasture and sings them a sacred pastoral-hymn. The prevailing tone is idyllic, and a spirit of reconciliation and mercy runs through all the poems. We feel that a true poet of tender feeling is here pouring out in solitude before his Creator complaints of love and songs of praise.

In Johann Scheffler of Breslau (1624–1677), the genius of Fried-**Johann** rich Spee appears deepened, widened, and mingled **Scheffler.** with other elements. Scheffler published his most important poetic works under the name of Johannes Angelus Silesius. He began as a Protestant doctor, and ended as a monk.

The Silesian adherents of Jacob Böhme put him on the track of the mediæval mystics, and he was soon entirely captivated by the religion of the Middle Ages. In 1653 he became a Catholic, was consecrated to the priesthood, and allowed himself to engage in the most bitter controversy with his former brothers in the faith. The character of Scheffler's poetry also changed in later life; his style became more harsh, and he passed from ideal creations to pompous descriptions of externals. In his 'Cheru- His 'Cheru-
binischer Wandersmann' (1657) he teaches the mys- binischer
tical way to God; this work is full of profound Wanders-
sayings and gives pregnant expression to thoughts mann.'
tinged with pantheism. His 'Heilige Seelenlust' contains sacred pastoral songs of Psyche to her beloved Jesus, which His
remind us strongly of Spee's idyllic mannerism. 'Heilige
But Scheffler can also strike other tones than these. Seelenlust.'
He sings a more vigorous strain in the hymns: 'Auf, auf, O Seel', auf, auf, zum Streit,' and 'Mir nach spricht
Christus unser Held, Mir nach ihr Christen alle.' His hymns.
And in the third of his greater works, his 'Sinnliche Betrachtung der vier letzten Dinge,' he paints the pleasures of heaven and the horrors of hell in unsparing detail.

The Life of Jesus was written with much feeling by the Capuchin Father Martin of Cochem, who thus furnished one of
the best Catholic works of devotion. He, too, was Life of
indebted to the mystical literature of the Middle Jesus, by
Ages, and whatever holy men or women pretended to Father
have learnt in visions about the life of the Redeemer, Martin
or the feelings of His mother, was received by him as of Cochem,
important historical evidence. Moreover he allowed his own ima- 1691.
gination full scope in expansion and romantic description.   He divides the story of Christ's life into short sections, each of which is followed by a prayer.   The narrative itself is far removed from the simplicity of the Gospels, but is by no means without merit. If Martin's purpose was so to present the subject, that even the dullest heart should be roused to feelings of compassion and piety, then he has probably obtained his end in the best way imaginable. Every-thing is very graphically and exactly described, in a manner best

calculated to suit the popular mind. The author even knows the dimensions of the cave in which Christ was born, and the number of hammer-strokes which nailed him to the cross. A strong appeal is always made to the feelings, and every situation and sentiment is fully exhausted. Father Martin outdoes the most thrilling and horrible elements of the religious popular plays, and carries to a climax that sentimental view of Christ's life, which Luther had so strongly deprecated. The scourging and the crucifixion are horrible to read; but Martin is equally successful in idyllic scenes, and shows great tenderness of feeling in his account of the birth of Christ and his picture of the life of the Holy Family. Father Martin thinks that he is helping on the salvation of his reader by exciting his emotion. He does not terrify the sinner with hell, but shows him a God of mercy, and addresses him in these words : 'Take courage and despair not, however low thou mayest have fallen ; read often with devotion in this book ; endeavour to move thy heart to compassion, and be assured that there is still help for thee.'

Sentimental character of the work.

The Augustine monk, Father Abraham a Sancta Clara, a contemporary of the Capuchin Cochem, was the most celebrated Catholic preacher of that time ; he was a fruitful writer, and his style, like Cochem's, was popular and graphic. But where Cochem seeks to edify, Abraham endeavours rather to interest and amuse. The former, in his depth of feeling, resembles his countryman Spee, and reminds one of older Rhenish writings, full of mystic fervour; but the Swabian Abraham, who found his chief sphere of activity as a Court-preacher to the emperor in Vienna, leans rather to the plain-spokenness of mediæval Bavarian writers and to the satire of Upper-Rhenish authors of later date. In his writings he is always an orator, and we may say without exaggeration that he is one of the greatest oratorical geniuses that Germany ever produced. He is able, better than any other writer of the seventeenth century, to rivet the attention and work up the interest of his readers by suspense and surprise. His oratorical devices are not always refined, and are often most unsuited to the dignity of the pulpit; but the scurrilous style of preaching

Father Abraham a Sancta Clara, 1644-1709.

His oratorical genius.

had the authority of a long tradition to back it, dating as it did
from the Middle Ages. Among Protestant preachers, Schuppius
may be compared with Abraham, but the Catholic preacher far
surpassed the Protestant in system, and in fascinating power of
language. Abraham is filled with an honourable hatred of vice,
and tries bravely to reform morals by his preaching; the Court-
preacher does not spare the Court, nor the priest the clergy.
Where he means to be profound, he is to our mind almost absurd,
but he always shows great force in satire. He draws typical
characters, describes emotions and passions, and is inexhaustible
in appropriate anecdotes, similes, and jokes. He makes skilful use
of his heterogeneous information; his writings are full of minute,
dramatic genre-pictures drawn from his observation of the life around
him, pictures in which he brings graphically before our   His
eyes the Vienna of that period, with all its love of plea-   pictures of
sure, its curiosity, frivolity, and affected gentility. His   real life.
intellectual stand-point is that of the sixteenth century, and the
objects of his satire are all to be found already in Thomas Murner.
His way of looking at the world cannot be compared with the
contemplative gaze of Hans Sachs, but with regard to literary art,
the school of the Renaissance has raised him far above such predecessors. There is hardly a trace of deep religious thought in
his writings, and in this respect Father Martin von Cochem is
decidedly superior to him. The temple into which he leads us
resembles a cabinet of curiosities, and beyond it we gaze not into
the great realm of nature, but into a theatre for burlesque. The
power of the Church over the minds of men was as little increased by exhibiting holy things in the light of sparkling wit,
as by teaching the soul to find the mystic way back to its divine
source through pious sentiment, without the aid of any priestly
mediator.

Abraham a Sancta Clara died in 1709 at Vienna. He reached
the age of sixty-five, and had been engaged in literary activity
since 1679. He formed a special school of writing, and his
memory long continued to live both in the scene of his labours
and also in wider circles.

Meanwhile the Protestant world had produced its Spener and

its Leibniz, and had risen to a far higher level both in spirit and

Protestant writers. in knowledge. At the head of the new movement stood Paul Gerhardt, who is generally held to be the greatest Protestant hymn-writer after Luther.

Gerhardt's earliest church-hymns were published in 1648, and in

Paul Gerhardt, 1606-1676. 1667 appeared the first collected edition of 120 hymns. He came from Gräfenhainichen, in the neighbourhood of Bitterfeld, and studied in Wittenberg; from 1657 to 1666 he was Deacon at the Nicolai-Kirche in Berlin, and he died in 1676 at the age of seventy as Archdeacon in Lübben. He was a faithful Lutheran, and was firmly convinced that in the poor ' Formula Concordiae' of 1580 he possessed the truth which alone could bring salvation. He refused to sign a rescript of the great Kurfürst, which forbade the Lutherans to revile the Calvinists, and was on account of this deposed from his Berlin incumbency. His conduct in this matter was prompted by conscientious scruples, not by a natural impulse of character; his was a peaceable nature, and a peaceful spirit breathes also in his hymns, which were inspired by

His hymns. pious feeling, and appealed to pious feeling. Many of them have really become sacred popular songs, in which millions of faithful souls still continue to find edification. These hymns combined all that could appeal to wide circles of readers— narratives of sacred events in ballad-form, instructive and pregnant thoughts, devout fervour, a sublime view of divine things, and poetic glorification of domestic bliss. Gerhardt often draws from the Psalms and from other parts of the Bible, but he also made use of Latin poems by St. Bernard of Clairvaux, and of prayers by Johann Arnd. Where he does follow his own inspiration, he is not particularly original, but it was just by giving a poetic form to wellknown subjects that he was able to appeal to all hearts. Gerhardt is more serious and more simple than Spee, and does not diffuse so much earthly lustre over his poetry. He is less serious than Luther, whom he surpasses, however, in elegance of form, while on the other hand he is inferior to Spee in melody. He seldom attains to Luther's pregnant force, and where he treats the same ideas, he is always weaker. Sometimes Gerhardt becomes quite prosaic, and sometimes he passes the limits of good taste, but his best hymns are written in a beautifully tender and harmonious tone; peaceful acquiescence in God's will seems to have dissolved all thoughts into soft music (*cf.* the hymn beginning 'Nun ruhen alle Wälder ').

His religious earnestness does not exclude cheerfulness, and cheerfulness forms, indeed, the leading moral cha- *Their* racteristic of his poetry. Whereas with Luther the *serious,* world is full of storm and tempest, with Gerhardt, *yet cheerful* on the contrary, it lies in perpetual sunshine; every- *tone.* thing, he thinks, is so beautifully calculated for the good of man; death and hell have long lost their power, and the soul rejoices in the certainty of salvation; we must throw our cares on God, for God cares for us, and if we succumb, He will extend His mercy to us. Luther resists evil like a man, but Gerhardt over-looks it like a youth. Even sin he thinks is of some use: ' Had I no guilt of sin on me, I had no part in Thy mercy.' While Luther's hymns are congregational, Gerhardt's express *Their* the feelings of the individual soul, and as such they *individual* are the beginning of modern German lyric poetry. *character.* What Gerhardt began in the religious sphere was completed by Goethe in the secular, and it is by no mere chance that we find these words of Gerhardt echoed again by Goethe : ' How long shall I be sorrowful, and eat my bread with tears?'

Gerhardt did not purposely seek out those situations in which a religious hymn would be suitable. One might think that many of his poems were the expression of his own inner experience, but their personal character never hinders their general application. Every devout mind can follow him when he calls forth memories of the Saviour in connection with the church-festivals; everyone can find in his hymns consecration of joy, and comfort for dark hours. The whole of life, seen from the Christian *Gerhardt's* point of view, is spread out in his poems. He praises *pictures* the morning and the evening, and accompanies *of life.* us in summer through the flowery land. He describes earthly bliss and earthly sorrow. He praises marriage, and gives us a picture of the Christian wife in her household. Gerhardt tries to rob death of its sting and to make parting easy to the dying : he tells us that we are only guests on earth and points us to our home above. He speaks in the name of a father who has lost his little son, and who imagines he can hear him helping the angels singing, and breaks into tears of joy at the thought. Or Gerhardt makes the dead child speak to its parents, and tell them not to weep for him. These poems were produced in connection with real events, and were written by Gerhardt in fulfilment of his spiritual calling. He was a thoroughly human poet, and knew how to pour balm on wounded souls.

Besides Gerhardt's, many other sacred poems were written about this time; the second half of the seventeenth century and the beginning of the eighteenth were in this respect more fruitful than the century after the Reformation. Noble ladies and women of the middle classes mingled their voices in the holy choir, and gave their enthusiastic sympathy to that development of religious feeling which followed on Gerhardt, and is mostly connected with the names of Spener and Zinzendorf. Gerhardt, Spener, and Zinzendorf belong together; they all three departed from the bigoted, dogmatic type of Lutherism; they all three transferred the centre of religious life to the feelings of the individual, and endeavoured to extract the gold of pious sentiment from the depths of inward experience. But whereas Gerhardt never wavered in his allegiance to the established Church, Spener felt strongly drawn toward the small churches within the Church, while Zinzendorf actually gathered some of these into a new sect.

Development of religious feeling.

Spener was an Alsatian by birth, and passed his life in Frankfurt on the Main, in Dresden, and in Berlin. In Frankfurt he published the ' Pia Desideria ' (1675), which afterwards became the programme of Pietism. He declared that with regard to Christian morals and life the Reformation was not anything like completed, and he strongly condemned the prevalent bitter strife between those of different faith. He wished to banish pedantry and artificial rhetoric from the pulpit. He proposed private assemblies for the promotion of domestic piety, as well as public services. He wished the idea of a universal priesthood to be taken more seriously, and the propagation of

Spener's ' Pia Desideria.'

Bible knowledge to be more energetically carried out. He penetrated from outward faith, outward virtues, and outward prayer, to
the inner man, the 'heart,' as he says, and declared everything
hypocrisy which did not flow from that source. He refers to the
writings of Johann Arnd, whose fundamental doctrine was that one
must not only believe in Christ but also live in Christ, and like Arnd
he praised the works of the mediæval mystics as a school of piety.
Spener shows very little originality, but he entered into the deepest
wants of thuŋeʏ ə, and gave them adequate expression. He became
a spiritual leader in the widest circles of the Lutheran Church. In
Saxony, it is true, he and his followers had to yield to the hereditary orthodoxy, but in Prussia they attained great power. Spener
acquired a decisive influence over most Church appointments, and
at the new University of Halle his disciples found a sure sphere
for their activity. Starting thence, Pietism spread   Spener
over the whole of Lutheran Germany. In all parts   founded
small communities of the pious were formed, who   Pietism.
strictly separated themselves from the children of the world, seeking
to sanctify their life, and who made self-examination a sacred duty,
shedding tears over their sins.

At the same time, and even earlier, similar tendencies may be
traced in the Calvinistic or Reformed Church. Differences of
doctrine and creed retired visibly into the background. Attempts
were made to effect a union between the two Protestant creeds,
and Count Zinzendorf gave to both equal rights in his Moravian
community.

Spener was not a first-class writer, nor a great poet. His prose
is heavy and his few poems are only rhymed reflections. But contemporary with him, and independent of his influence, though
somewhat resembling him in character, we find Chris-   Christian
tian Scriver of Rendsburg, a powerful preacher and an   Scriver.
excellent writer of devotional works. He was somewhat older than
Spener, and Magdeburg was the chief scene of his   'Gotthold's
labours. In 'Gotthold's Occasional Meditations,' Scriver   Zufällige
follows the example of an English writer, and connects   Andachten,'
religious reflections with the events and scenes of   1663.
everyday life. His much-esteemed 'Soul's Treasure' (1675–1691),

describes the original high dignity of the soul, its fall and repent-
The 'Seelen-schatz.' ance, its holy life, sorrows, and temptations, its longing for the Eternal and its preparation for death. The best parts of this work are full of beautifully developed similes, and the style often moves in grand periods; it contains many references to the real world, much miscellaneous information and anecdote, all penetrated with high thoughts, which feed and exalt pious imagination.

Within the Reformed Church the pietistic movement produced
Joachim Neander's hymns, 1679. Joachim Neander, who died young in 1680, in his native town of Bremen. A year before his death he published his sacred hymns, by which the German Calvinists also gained a share in the treasure of German hymnology, after having so long contented themselves with a dull translation of Marot's Psalms. Neander's poems are mostly the expression of his inward intercourse with God; surrounding humanity disappears for him when he soars in pious aspiration to his Creator. The Church feasts are not celebrated in his poems, but the Sacrament of the Lord's Supper holds an important place; otherwise the hymns all deal with sanctification of private life. Evil is much more strongly dwelt on than in Gerhardt; the fearful soul, and Christ its Comforter, are often introduced in a dialogue, and the latter says that He feels His heart breaking in Him from pity for the sinner. The poet imagines quite a human relation between Christ and himself when he says: 'The world, the devil, and sin have torn me away from Thee; I am sorry for this, and return to Thee again; there is my hand, be mine, and I am Thine.' Most striking is the way in which he abruptly breaks off when he is losing himself in the thoughts of eternity; 'Reason, be still, the sea is far too broad and far too deep.' Those of Neander's poems which are most correct in form are by no means his best. Much fault might be found in detail with the celebrated hymn:—'Lobet den Herrn, den mächtigen König der Ehren.' But there is a ring in it like the sound of trumpets, and it presents to the imagination sublime ideas in striking similes.

The pietistic hymnology, such as was produced at Halle in

particular, dealt mostly with the inner life of pious men, which was
described with the minutest details. We can trace
in all these hymns a tendency towards mysticism, and
towards the language and ideas of the Song of Solomon. In the religious life of this period we meet
again with all the exaggerated features of mediæval mysticism,
such as visions, ecstasies, and significant dreams, which now
appear under the name of penitential struggles, awakening and
regeneration; and the pietist hymn-writers, too, are inclined,
like the older mystics, to enlarge on the union with God, and
to paint with earthly colours the relation of the soul to her
heavenly bridegroom. Johann Scheffler's writings still exercised
an influence on Protestant poetry, and many of his poems
were incorporated in the pietistic hymn-books. The lighter and
more effeminate style of writing, which appeared among the
Protestants about 1600, and was continued in the Catholic
Spee, is predominant in all these first efforts of modern lyric
poetry.

Character of the hymns pietistic.

One of the best and most original of Scheffler's pietistic successors was Gottfried Arnold, of Anneberg in Saxony.
He was a disciple of Spener's in his Dresden period,
but afterwards entered on somewhat eccentric paths.
In his 'Impartial history of Church and Heresy,' an
important work of vast scope, he took the part of the
heretics against the Church, or rather he deprecated all
religious persecutions, and in his poems he carefully
avoided everything ecclesiastical, so as to give new and varied
expression to mystic contemplation and rapture.
His hymns consist largely of religious love-songs,
and his lofty and bold flights of fancy sometimes remind us of Schiller. Like Scheffler he bids farewell to earthly
things, and says good-night to mountains, vales, and meadows. In
his poems, as in the old Minnesang, sympathy with nature is associated with the rapture of love. Far from the tumult of the city,
Arnold praises God in the greenwood; there he seems to have
found Paradise, there everything smiles on him in loveliness, there
truth and simplicity reign. Love, he says, bears the soul aloft

Gottfried Arnold's 'Unpar- teiische Kirchen- und Ketzer- historie.'

His religious poetry.

into calm air, beyond the wild waves of all earthly things. Love creates the deepest peace of God, and leads to eternal life. He implores God's aid against the thraldom of the senses, entreating him to crush, break, and tear in pieces the evil power.

Arnold has a wonderful power of directly communicating to us
Arnold's an attitude of the soul, and at once drawing us into his
manner. own feelings, but it is seldom that he succeeds in retaining our sympathy. He is so far in advance of the average powers of his age, that we feel all the more keenly in his writings any of the usual offences against good taste, any imperfections of form and expression.

Among the later pietistic poets Gerhard Tersteegen is specially remarkable. He was a common man, a ribbon-maker by trade, but at Mühlheim on the Ruhr he exercised a great religious influence by his edifying discourses, and lived quite in the spirit of mysticism. He belonged to the Reformed (Calvinistic) Church,
Gerhar and died in 1769 at the age of seventy-two. There is a
Tersteegen's peculiar calm and tenderness in his poems. He says he
religious would like to become a child, for then God and Para-
poetry. dise would come into his soul. He wishes to be calm and patient, and to live in sweet simplicity without much enquiry or much thought. He would live like a true pilgrim, a stranger to the world and its cares, for he knows that his life is but a wandering to the great Eternity.

Unwillingly we turn our eyes from the modest mystic Tersteegen
Count to the world-renowned Count Zinzendorf, who put
Zinzendorf. visible symbols in the place of the mystical flight of the soul from the creatures of earth, furnished grossly sensuous food for the religious imagination, and drew Protestant hymnology deep into the slough of bad taste. Zinzendorf was born in Dresden, but acquired a spiritual bias for life among the Pietists at Halle. His soul lived in cheerful certainty of salvation and in
Founded most intimate communion with the Saviour. He or-
the ganized the Moravian brotherhood of Herrnhut on a
Moravian system derived partly from monasticism, and partly
sect. from the early Christian communities. He succeeded in spreading its members as one order over the old and new world,

and from the year 1734 he established for them a theology which
dealt only with the person of Christ, His sufferings, His blood, and
His wounds ; the latter became the object of an extravagant worship, for which Catholicism, and even some of Gerhardt's hymns
borrowed from mediæval sources, had prepared the way. As a poet,
Zinzendorf belongs to the school of Scheffler.   He could improvise
with the greatest ease, and has written more than 2000 poems ;
but he and the poets of his community who succeeded him, con-
temned perfection of form, and were drawn away into   Moravian
thoroughly childish twaddle.   In verses full of empty   hymn-
wordiness, they sang the praises of the Lamb, and   writers.
expressed their passion for the Saviour, and their ecstasy over His
wounds.   Their profane familiarity with sacred things is such, that
they designate the Trinity as Papa God, Mama God (i. e. the Holy
Spirit), and Brother Lamb.

But the essential characteristics of the Moravian brotherhood
did not consist of such blasphemous follies ; later on   Character-
too, as these began to give general offence, they were   istics
more and more modified.   The distinguishing mark   of the
of the Herrnhut brothers, that which in the second   Moravians.
half of the eighteenth century attracted adherents from all quarters,
was the spirit of brotherly love which united them, the earnest striving
after sanctification in which they all shared, and the bond of sympathy which bound together all the members throughout Germany,
England, and America.   They represented a quiet confederation
of pious people, which maintained itself in the midst of a hostile
and increasingly free-thinking age, which furnished an external
rallying-point for Christians of the same opinions, and everywhere
roused respect by that holy simplicity of heart, which its members
esteemed as the deepest wisdom, the greatest power, and the
fairest ornament.

Besides pietism in all its various forms, orthodoxy also found
utterance in the hymns of this time (about 1700).   The Silesian
pastor, Benjamin Schmolck, was a most fertile writer   Benjamin
of poetry ; sometimes he offers beautiful thoughts   Schmolck,
well expressed in flowing verse, but he frequently   circa 1700.
proves the truth of his own saying : 'If the trees are too often

shaken they let fall unripe fruit.' He offers points of resemblance to Gerhardt on the one hand, and, like the Pietists, to the Song of Solomon on the other. He strove after simplicity and clearness, but often degenerated into the commonplace. The same may be said of several other poets contemporary with him; dry common sense, which had not been wanting even in the earlier religious poetry, now attained great importance, owing chiefly to the fact that it offered a pleasing contrast to mystic extravagance, and also harmonised more with the increasing enlightenment of the age.

Hymn-writing now became didactic and reflective, and endeavoured to suit itself to all the various possible situations in which poetry might be acceptable to a man. Careful attention was paid

Hymns for various classes. to the difference of persons according to rank and profession; in 1716 a Mecklenburg clergyman made a collection of poems for 147 various vocations; in 1737, a Saxon clergyman published a Universal Hymn-book, in which he supplied hymns for christenings, for complicated law-suits, for lameness, blindness, and deafness, for anxiety due to a large family, also songs for nobles, ministers, officials, lawyers, surgeons, barbers, fishermen, drovers, shopmen, and many other positions in life. In an advertisement of this work the author remarked that there were still wanting songs for jugglers, rope-dancers, conjurors, thieves, gipsies, and rogues, and begged to have this want supplied.

Thus in the subject-matter of hymns, the tendency to individualism asserted itself to the point of caricature.

Increase of individualism in hymn-writing. The music which accompanied them fell under the same dominating influence. The Protestant Church-hymn of the sixteenth century had been popular, congregational song, but in the seventeenth century it lost this character; the popular element had to retire before a more artificial manner, the fetters of the stanza were abandoned, and greater freedom of form was introduced, together with a highly emotional and declamatory style.

Even the choir was no longer supposed to express the general feeling of the congregation, but to give a characteristic rendering of

every feature of the text. The chorus was supplemented by the
aria, which was not sung by the congregation, but by   Similar
the trained choir, and soon became secular and trivial   change in
in character. The accompaniment of instrumental   the Music.
music, which had formerly been totally absent, was now thought
necessary to adorn the singing. This whole movement is due to
Italian influence, and especially to the opera, a musical form which
arose in Italy and had for its chief object the individualisation of
song. Poetry tried to adapt itself in various forms to the needs
of the musical composers, and at the same time sought to derive
some advantage for itself from these forms.

Erdmann Neumeister, one of the chief opponents of Pietism,
produced, after the year 1705, innumerable Cantatas, Neumeister's
which were set to music by Johann Sebastian Bach.   Cantatas
At the beginning and end of these there is a text   with Bach's
from the Sunday Gospel, or an old church hymn   music.
arranged as a chorus and chorale, and thus corresponding to the
old congregational song; but in the middle, the subjective modern
piety finds expression in recitatives, arias, duetts, &c.

Barthold Heinrich Brockes, a Town Councillor of Hamburg,
adopted the easy rhyming recitatives of the texts used in the
Hamburg opera, and adding to them arias and ariosos, Brockes'
produced those poems which form the basis of his work 'Irdisches
entitled, 'Earthly Pleasure in God.' In this poem he Vergnügen
absorbs himself, like Spee and others of his stamp, in in Gott.'
all the detailed life of nature ; he tries to describe it faithfully and
exactly, and recognises in all a witness to the wisdom and
goodness of the Creator. The recitatives expound the subject
to us, the arias and ariosos are devoted to natural description
and pious sentiment. The poet describes the presence of music in
nature; the twittering descant of many birds, the rippling tenor
of the crystal drops flowing over smooth pebbles, the high alto
in the whispering rustle of the trees and bushes, the deep bass in
the pleasant humming of many thousand bees flying after honey.
In the midst of so much harmony, he calls on his heart also
to let its songs be heard, and then the aria falls in with these
words:—

'Sing, my soul, the Lord His praise,
Who in His great wisdom's ways
Decks the world so gloriously.'

Brockes achieved his first literary success in 1712, with the
text of a Passion-Oratorio.   The Passion music had
passed into the Protestant Church from the Catholic;
the text of one of the Gospels was divided among
various individuals, and sung like a Psalm, and at
the beginning and end of the oratorio the congregation would sing a suitable hymn.   In the latter half of the
seventeenth century this psalmody was replaced by recitative, and
four-part church-hymns were introduced at intervals.   At the
beginning of the eighteenth century, under the hands of the
Hamburg opera-poets and opera-composers, the German Passion-
music assumed quite the form of the Italian Oratorios; neither the
Scripture words nor the congregational hymns were retained, and
when the clergy remonstrated against this, a compromise was
effected, and either the Bible-words or the church-hymns were
again admitted.   Thus, Brockes has put rhymes of his own
invention in the place of the Gospel words, but he has also
woven in verses of Church-hymns.   As in the earlier Hamburg
Passion-texts, so here sentiment finds expression in the arias and
ariosos; either the acting characters themselves indulge in monologues, or the 'Daughter of Sion,' or the 'Faithful Soul,' is introduced, and gives vent to feelings and reflections.   This poem of
Brockes is a work of great imaginative power and full of dramatic
effects, so that all who heard it must have been quite carried away
by it.   The poet used the same strong means which Father
Cochem had employed to render the life and sufferings of Christ
as touching and edifying as possible.   It is no wonder that the
book enjoyed great popularity, was translated into foreign languages,
and set to music by several composers, amongst others, by Handel.

*Bach's
Passion-
Oratorios.*

Sebastian Bach borrowed from it the words for the
arias in his St. John's Passion; he, however, did away
with all operatic features, and in his St. Matthew's
Passion (1729), brought this class of music to the highest point of
perfection.   The text for the latter was furnished by an insig-

nificant Leipzig writer, Henrici by name. He supplied the elements which Bach required: on the one hand the fixed church tradition, the congregational chorales, and the simple narrative of the Evangelists, which was rendered dramatic by assigning the cries of the populace to the chorus, and the separate speeches to solo singers; on the other hand, the emotional reflections on the Passion of Christ, or expressing the feelings of the human soul conscious of its sin, longing for redemption, and filled with gratitude to the Saviour. There is hardly a trace in Henrici's work of mystical and pietistic tendencies, or of expressions borrowed from the Song of Solomon; all frivolous and trivial elements are banished, and the whole stands on about the same level as Gerhardt's hymn: 'Ein Lämmlein geht und trägt die Schuld.' Gerhardt's words too are chiefly used in the chorales.

The depth of feeling revealed in Bach's Passion-music shows us that he too was under the influence of that emotional revival which had set in since Gerhardt's time and which had been due in the first place to Pietism.

Handel stands on quite different ground from Bach; he dived deep into secular music, to which Bach all his life   Handel. remained a stranger. He passed from the Opera to the Oratorio. Till 1716 Handel composed the music for pietistic texts, and for Passion-oratorios in the Hamburg operatic style; then, however, he turned to the more vigorous words of the Psalms, and finally discarded the sentimental conception of the Saviour for the Messiah of the old Hebrew prophets. His immortal Oratorio of that name stands in spirit and aim far higher than all the other Passion-oratorios, and is a grand hymn on Christianity. In his conception of Christianity and of classical antiquity, as revealed in his 'Messiah,' and in his musical dramas of biblical and classical origin, Handel is a true representative of the age of enlightenment and of classical studies. Bach represents purely German art, but Handel owed much to the Italians. The genius of the former is national, that of the latter, cosmopolitan.

The same difference of national and international genius is apparent between Spener and Leibniz; but in this age all differences were merged in the common effort, conscious or unconscious, to free

A a

man from traditional authority, and make him self-dependent. The

Increasing independ- ence in religion and science. power of feeling strengthened individuality in sacred poetry and music, while in science individuality was strengthened by the power of thought. Feeling and thought combined together to break the power of the Church, of law, and of every authority generally which laid claim to the intellectual guidance of the individual; every man now sought for himself the way to salvation.

Contemporary with Spener we observe a remarkable activity in the

Pufendorf. field of secular learning. Spener was born in 1635; Pufendorf, Stieler, and Schilter in 1632, Morhof in 1639, Leibniz in 1646. Samuel Pufendorf was a strong patriot, and an elegant Latin author. In a spirited satire he ridiculed the monstrosity of the German imperial constitution of that day, and endeavoured to liberate German statesmanship from the influence of theology; he demanded liberty of conscience for the individual, and the subordination of the Church to state-supervision, while he also defended the idea of a Protestant union. He composed in uncouth German a History of European States, from the political point of view, and wrote in dignified Latin the history of the Great Kurfürst of Brandenburg. Kaspar

Stieler, Schilter, and Morhof. von Stieler published a carefully compiled German dictionary, the first complete one since the attempts of the 16th century. Johann Schilter undertook a great compilation of early German, and especially of Old High-German literary monuments. Daniel Morhof sketched the history of German and foreign poetry. In all branches of learning, energetic efforts were made to retrieve what had been lost through the war, and no one achieved more in this respect than Leibniz, the founder of German rationalism. Leibniz commanded all the knowledge of his own and of previous ages, and sought to systematize this knowledge and turn it to the good of mankind.

Leibniz is the first great European name that Germany can show

Leibniz. in the history of philosophy since the Middle Ages, since the Dominican Albert the Great (p. 229). And as Albert was the mediator between Greek Philosophy and the Church, so Leibniz sought to effect a compromise between religion and the Anglo-French rationalism of the seventeenth century. He

assumed, in a characteristically German manner, a hostile attitude
towards the contemporary science of other countries, an attitude
which is in some measure explained by the views prevalent at that
time in Germany, views in which he himself participated. The
Anglo-French philosophy was mathematical and mechanical, and to
some extent materialistic; in contrast to this, Leibniz, himself also
a great mathematician and mathematical physicist, but at the same
time a friend of Spener, the founder of German Pietism, established
the claims of the inner life and of the unseen world. He placed
force in antithesis to matter. The Frenchman
Gassendi had successfully revived the ancient doctrine   **His**
of atoms; Leibniz transformed the atoms into souls,   **philosophy.**
and thus arrived at the idea of his ' Monads.' The number of these
is infinite, and each has its own individuality, in which it mirrors
the whole world; all of them are in process of unceasing change,
and all are harmoniously determined by their common cause, the
Divine Will. Leibniz found an explanation of the universe in the
assumption of innumerable individuals, each of the nature of a soul.
Soul is thus to him the essence of things. The conception of the
individual soul, round which the whole theology   **Its connec-**
and religious poetry of the time turns, asserted its   **tion with**
supremacy also in Leibniz's imagination, and became   **Mysticism**
the centre of his philosophy. And more than this: for   **and**
                                           Pietism.
the human soul, according to his view, is not only a
mirror of the world, but also an image of God, and intended to hold
communion with its Creator. Thus Leibniz expressly adopted
the mystical doctrines of submission to God, and of the presence of
God in the heart. Love of God was to him religion; from love
sprang morality and right. Here Leibniz's connection with
Mysticism and Pietism is clearly visible, and he also reduced to a
system that Optimism which so attracted us in the writings of Paul
Gerhardt. The peaceable, tolerant disposition which   **His**
animated the best men of the age, was shared by   **Optimism,**
Leibniz. He worked hard to effect a union of the   **tolerance,**
various Protestant sects, and for years exerted himself   **and**
                                           patriotism.
in the cause of a reunion of Protestants and Catholics.
He was an untiring and subtle negotiator, a man full of schemes,

weak and somewhat naive as a politician, but a good patriot according to his lights. He was unwearied in advocating the foundation of learned societies, as a means of raising German science; the Berlin Academy, founded in 1700, is a living His efforts monument to this day of his endeavours in this to raise direction. And even though he wrote mostly in Latin German and French, so as to attract the attention of cultivated science. people and of foreigners, yet he had the cause of the German language at heart. He condemned the excessive use of foreign words, and took up Schottelius' judicious schemes for a German Dictionary. His own German prose has about it something fresh, clever and animated, praise that cannot be given to many of his colleagues.

Leibniz, as we know, had found patrons in the Guelphs, and Leibniz lived for forty years as librarian at Hanover. All the patronised three branches of the Guelph line made him their by the historiographer; in Berlin a Guelph princess, Queen Guelphs. Sophie Charlotte, helped him to carry out his schemes. Yet he died alone in 1716, and but little zeal was shown in furthering the publication of his literary remains. His chief philosophical work did not appear till 1765, and his History of the mediæval Empire not till our century.

Through aristocratic patronage Leibniz was raised above the intrigues of the Universities, but in consequence of this he failed to exercise a direct influence on the younger generation. This influence which he missed, fell to the lot of his successors, Christian Thomasius and Christian Wolff. The former was born in 1655, the latter in 1679. The former was a follower of Pufendorf, the latter of Leibniz. Both helped to popularise their great predecessors, and to introduce their thoughts into the curriculum of academic instruction.

Thomasius was a true apostle of 'Enlightenment' (*Aufklärung*) Christian in the ordinary sense. He hated the Middle Ages, Thomasius and ranked Hans Sachs before Homer. He always a champion of 'Enlight- preferred an appeal to a man's common-sense to a enment.' strictly scientific proof, and laid great stress on the general utility of science. He was no mediator between the old ideas and the new like Leibniz, but an innovator, a champion of so-called enlightened views, an intellectual liberator. The monsters whom he wished to vanquish were either prejudices, or pedantry, and hypocrisy. He wished to follow the French example, to give to the learned classes a practical secular training, and to break down the barriers of intellectual aristocracy. He was the first University teacher who gave a course of lectures in German; this was in the winter term of 1687–88. He was the first to publish a literary periodical in German, i.e. the 'Monatsge-spräche,' which appeared in the years 1688–89. As Spener may be said to have carried on Luther's religious movement, so Thomasius carried on his pamphleteering and extended it to a wider sphere. His natural style was plain-spoken and satirical; he did indeed pass through a piet-istic period, in which he became a mystic and strove to acquire a more serious style, but later on he returned to his old manner.

Starts the first literary periodical in German.

In contrast to Thomasius, Christian Wolff had nothing of the impetuous innovator and nothing of the mystic about him. His intellectual development took the steady direction of a consistent rationalism. His system claimed to comprehend the whole world by means of reason, and yet could not make any advance in knowledge without secretly taking counsel of experience. By the aid of the Leibnizian ideas, somewhat diluted, Wolff founded a new scholasticism, a system which could be easily expounded, and which impelled even average intellects to thoroughness of thought and argument, and to methodical and clear demonstration; moreover, his system could also live in peace with orthodoxy, and hence it gradually esta-blished itself in all the German Universities. Wolff wrote and lectured in German, and by a carefully formed terminology he achieved what Leibniz had longed for, and rendered it possible for Germans to philosophise in their own language. He took up and carried on the work of the mediæval mystics, and rendered the Ger-man language capable of moving easily in the realm of ideas. In his philosophy Wolff paid his tribute to the prevalent tendency of glorifying the individual. According to him, God has regulated everything in the world for the

Christian Wolff, a rationalist.

He modified and popularised Leibniz's philosophy.

His tendency to indi-vidualism.

advantage of man, and to discern in all things the beneficent intention of the Creator is man's task, and forms the basis of religion.
Wolff's views are clearly related to those of Gerhardt and Brockes.
Even the state is to him only a police institution for the advantage
of the individual. . But this individual himself, for whose happiness
everything is calculated, has, according to Wolff's ideal, no heart,
but only intellect; rational reflection is his sole motive of action.
Thus Wolff's rationalism stands in its conception of the moral
world in direct antagonism to Spener's pietism; and the two
systems were actually to come into collision, as we shall see.

Pufendorf, Leibniz, and Thomasius were Saxons. All of these,

Saxony and Prussia. and besides them August Hermann Francke, Spener's
most distinguished disciple, and later on Christian
Wolff himself, found their first footing in Leipzig.
But they were all in some way or other rejected by Leipzig, and
being driven away from there they all seemed to find in Prussia
the best field for their activity and influence. Pufendorf had been
since 1688 in Berlin; in 1690 Thomasius had already begun

Intellectual supremacy of Prussia under Frederick I., crowned King, 1701. lecturing at the Ritter-Academie in Halle; in 1691
Spener exchanged Dresden for Berlin; in 1692
Francke came to Halle, and two years later the new
University was opened there, at which he and Thomasius were teachers. In the year 1700 Leibniz
was made President of the Berlin Academy, and in
1706 Wolff received a professorship at Halle. Under the liberal
government of its first king, Prussia decidedly took the lead in
the intellectual movement.

But under the parsimonious soldier-king, Frederick William I.,

Change under Frederick William I., 1713-1740. all this was changed. The young academy declined;
science, as such, found no patronage; pietism alone
flourished, and its outward power did not contribute
to its inner improvement. Wolff's pietistic colleagues
sought to overthrow him, and through mean intrigues
succeeded in obtaining a cabinet decree from the king, deposing
the philosopher and banishing him from Prussia on pain of
hanging (1723).

Contemporary with this intellectual retrogression in Prussia

Saxony rose again to importance. From the year 1724 the East-Prussian Gottsched represented the Wolffian Literary philosophy in Leipzig, and applied its principles to importance questions of taste in German poetry. Through him of Leipzig. and his pupils the University of Leipzig acquired great literary fame for a few decades.

THE REFINEMENT OF POPULAR TASTE.

The history of religious poetry is inseparably connected with the development of religion, but many writers of this period contributed to the store of sacred poetry who were not clergymen by profession, nor exclusively religious poets. Religious poetry is the strong point of this period; in the secular poetry of the time we find nothing to be compared with the rise of the evangelical church-hymn, with the wide popularity of Paul Gerhardt's hymns, with the tender grace of Spee, and the thoughtfulness of Scheffler. Of the manifold productions of a poet like George Neumark, who enjoyed great reputation in his day, hardly anything has survived but the beautiful hymn: ' Wer nur den lieben Gott lässt walten.'

But just as in religious lyric poetry the unbroken tradition of the sixteenth century revived to new vigour as soon as the war was over, so in secular poetry satire once more made its appearance, and introduced a popular element into the pedantic scholar-poetry of the time. And as individual feeling was the most marked characteristic of the religious poetry, so individual criticism was the strongest feature of the secular poetry of this new period. In the preachers Schuppius and Abraham a Sancta Predomin-Clara, and in the law-students, Pufendorf and Tho- ance of the masius, we already noticed a strong tendency to Satire. satire, and this tendency becomes still more apparent in the secular poets. Satires were written in strophes, in Alexandrines, in prose, and even in the old despised rhymed couplets of the sixteenth century. The church-hymn and the satire now exercised the greatest power over the nation. They were both a legacy of the Middle Ages, and had struck the deepest roots in all classes of the people ; they both have their origin in moral pathos, which in the hymn breathes devout aspiration, and in the satire criticises reality from an ideal standpoint, in a bitter or a laughing mood; and they are both essentially German in tone, and carry on the popular style of the sixteenth century. These two forms of writing held sway in the coming period till the death of Gellert and Rabener, who are the last representatives of this popular tendency.

Parallel between costumes and literary styles of this period. German poetry in the seventeenth century seems at first sight like a wrestling-ground of foreign fashions, just as was the case in the costumes of that time; and indeed a parallel might fitly be drawn between the costumes and the literary styles of this period.

About 1600 the Spanish costume, close-fitting, stiff, and elegant to excess, reigned supreme. In the Thirty Years' War this affectation was followed by naturalism; stiffness gave way to comfort and usefulness, and the courtier's costume was replaced by a martial garb. Under Louis XIV. naturalism was dismissed, and fashion once more made everything courtly and magnificent, stately and precise. It was not till the eighteenth century that opposition began to be roused in Germany; King Frederick William I. of Prussia invented the *queue* (*Zopf*), and in it created a German symbol of that stern and sober respectability, which prefers the practical to the beautiful; he also took a step towards naturalism in making people wear their own instead of false hair.

All these fashions are paralleled in the literary system of the time; there too we see mannerism succeeded by naturalism, and this in turn followed by the French classicism of the age of Louis XIV. which finally gave place to a popular tendency. But the popular tendency in literature did not only come to light with Frederick

Rise of a popular tendency. William I.; it had already been extant for a long time in literature and in life, but had not excited much attention and found but slight and passing favour with the nobility or the courts. Still this popular tendency steadily gained ground, and all the foreign influences which were apparently adverse to it, all the bad taste and foolish imitation which flourished for a time, in the end only contributed to the refinement of this popular taste.

If we consider the changes in general taste more closely, we shall observe, first of all, corresponding to the Spanish costume, a literary style which bore different names in the various literatures of Europe, but which was everywhere of the same character. In Spain it was called *estilo culto*, 'the cultivated style,' or *Gongorism*, after the poet, Gongora; in Italy *Marinism*, after the poet, Marini; in England *Euphuism*, after John Lyly's novel, 'Euphues;' in France the same style appears in connection with the *beaux-esprits* and the literary ladies, the *Précieuses* who were made 'Précieuses Ridicules' by Molière, when the fashion had reached its decline. In Germany this fashion is spoken of as the 'Italian style' or else simply as 'bombast' (*Schwulst*).

The affected style in various literatures.

Bombast is the Spanish fashion in literature. This style originally developed itself in the province of conversation and of letters. It was the incense offered to gentlemen of rank, or to ladies; it was a language of flattery and servility, wishing to keep as far away as possible from the talk of the people, and aiming at being uncommon, choice, and witty. The wildest epithets were coined, and conversation and writing were loaded with metaphors, plays on words, exaggerated expressions, remote allusions, far-fetched ideas, and subtle antitheses; hence this style frequently resulted in artificiality, eccentricity, obscurity, and bad taste. Instead of the *sun*, poets said, 'the torch of heaven;' instead of the *sea*, 'the salt foam of the waves;' instead of *blood*, 'purple ink,' or 'milk of life.' Love is called the 'golden light and eye of this world, the sapphire, the vault of Heaven.' A lover, who cannot forget his lady, remarks that the soap of scorn is not capable of washing out her image from his heart. In a tragedy written about this time we find the following: 'If mothers sometimes hurt us, it is but a spoonful of pain, which cannot exhaust the sea of their goodness to us.'

The bombastic style in Germany.

The sublime here passes into the ridiculous. Nevertheless, this fashion marks the beginning of the moral and literary influence of women in modern society, and the introduction of more refined manners among the men who bowed to their judgment. Bombast was the cradle of modern gallantry, and of modern politeness. It holds the same place in literature as the *baroque*

style does in art. Like the latter it was international, and like
the latter it went hand in hand with ecclesiastical and political
absolutism. Its source may be traced very far back.

Luther roused the masses of the people to activity. The Reformation and the German Renaissance, as well as
the German art of the fifteenth and sixteenth centuries,
as represented in Dürer, Holbein, and Hans Sachs,
rested on a popular basis; they were determined by
the towns, the middle-classes, the people, and are all
marked by stern and manly characteristics. But as
early as the beginning of the sixteenth century certain feminine
aspects of human nature begin to appear again. First
in Spain and then in Italy there arose a strong desire
for personal distinctions and outward adornment.
Titles came up, and cumbrous designations took the
place of a simple mode of address in letters and in conversation.
Men separated themselves from those whom they thought lower
in rank; those who considered themselves equals sought to add
to their importance by forming themselves into societies and
academies, and aspired, above all things, to sun themselves in the
light of royalty. Art became aristocratic, academic, and courtly.
Even God, it was thought, must receive the faithful in His house
with princely splendour. The Jesuits were the leaders of the
ecclesiastical reaction of the sixteenth century, as the Mendicant
Orders had been in the thirteenth; and wherever the Jesuits penetrated they brought with them the splendour of their churches,
the pomp of their ceremonies, and the magnificence of their
theatrical spectacles. A love of luxury and ornament seized on
all spheres of life. Even the scholars of the latter half of the
sixteenth century began in their Latin style to aim at the uncommon; they no longer took the Latin of classical writers, but
that of pre-classical and post-classical epochs as their model;
Cicero retired into the background, and Tacitus and the orators
and Fathers of the Hadrianic and following times were set up as
patterns; instead of system and perspicuity, writers now preferred obscurity, affected brevity, and the bombast of the African
Latinists.

Marginal notes:
Popular character of the Refor-mation and Renaissance in Germany.

Aristocratic movement in the 16th century.

Society now sought for some diversions to fill its unbroken leisure. The ruder pleasures were not agreeable to the ladies; games, masquerades, and all kinds of refined amusements were more to their taste, and what they were naturally most interested in was the affairs of love. But the usual ceremonies and usual phrases of conversation were soon exhausted, and something more exciting was demanded; accordingly, sentimental affectation of pastoral life on the one hand, and the representation of horrors on the other, now came into vogue. The literature of this period shows us mannerism in the idyll and naturalism in tragedy. And in poetry and art Pietism endeavoured to assert its supremacy over all æsthetic tendencies; it dominated a poet like Tasso, and painters like Guido Reni and Caravaggio. This religiosity could furnish, on the one hand, the raptures of ecstatic souls, on the other, the horrors of martyrdom; the beginning of the Saviour's life supplied an idyll, while the end afforded the most affecting tragedy. Friedrich Spee owed his literary fame to this mixture of æstheticism with sentimental piety, and a number of Protestant poets followed his example; if in his own writings sentimentality preponderates, in those of Count Zinzendorf, on the contrary, naturalism is carried to extremes. Pietism, since it could embrace such extremes, might be truly called Catholic.

Mannerism and naturalism in literature.

These two currents of sentimental æstheticism and crude naturalism, represented respectively in Spee and Zinzendorf, were by no means confined to the religious writing of this period; they are also strongly marked in secular literature, where the one was represented in affected idyllic poetry, the other in realistic tragedy, both being combined with a certain amount of bombast.

The classical idyll had already been revived in the Carlovingian period. It is represented in Middle High-German poetry by Neidhart's songs and by the village-stories. It came up again with Petrarch, and remained in power during the whole of the Renaissance, reaching its zenith in the *baroque* period. The pastoral affectation swamped lyric poetry, made itself at home in the novel, and even gained a place in the drama. Tasso and Guarini furnished the chief models for the pastoral

Idyllic poetry.

drama, the former in his 'Aminta,' the latter in his 'Pastor Fido.' For the pastoral romance, which always combined prose narrative with inserted poems, the recognised authorities were the Spanish romance 'Diana,' by Montemayor (1542), Sir Philip Sydney's 'Arcadia' (1590), and the Frenchman d'Urfé's 'Astræa' (1610). The pastoral costume soon became obligatory for love-poems; every lyric poet played the pipe, pretended to be leading lambs to pasture, and protested that he had written his love's name or even whole poems in the bark of the trees. Opitz calls himself a shepherd of the Rhine, and thus describes the pains of love which he feels : 'The flock it has grown thin, and I am no longer I.' Under the mask of Corydon, he tells his 'dearest Field-goddess,' that he is but a peasant-boy. Fleming, too, sometimes adopts the guise of a shepherd. The poets of Nürnberg and Königsberg, and the members of the Order of Elbe-Swans in Hamburg assumed shepherd-names ; in Nürnberg the pastoral fashion gained a specially strong hold. The customary wedding poems were now frequently clothed in bucolic form, and the number of German pastoral poems was legion. They are not the most unpleasing portion of the poetry of the seventeenth century ; some of them are very pretty and graceful, though one must always be prepared for occasional barbarisms. They aim at ease and simplicity, and are, on the whole, tolerably free from bombast. Weckherlin, it is true, had brought a few new flowers of speech from England, and adorned his love-poems with them ; and the same ornaments blossomed afresh in Opitz, who really introduced the fantastic style into Germany. But, generally speaking, the verse of this period is freer from bombast and affectation than the pastoral prose, that is to say, the idyllic narratives. These had their origin in the pastoral romance, and their essence lay in painting minute particulars in full detail, and in eking out a meagre theme with all sorts of flourishes and embellishments. Nature and love were the chief subjects of these romances, and the high-flown prose was supposed to deepen the sympathy of the reader. If we open Opitz's Hercynia, we come at once on such phrases as : 'Night, the mother of the stars;' or, 'The eye of the world, the sun;' or,

Idyllic prose-narratives.

'The guide of the body, the mind;' or the reader is warned that if he wishes to flee love, he must sail with blindfolded eyes and stopped ears, to the harbour of Sorrow, to Patience, who with her mother, Time, can alone give him the wished-for deliverance. The close observation of external Nature led to the imitation of natural sounds and noises, in which the Nürnberg poets specially distinguished themselves, and though this may seem puerile to us, yet it reveals a new flexibility in the language.   Philip von Zesen led the pastoral romance back to a field which had already been cultivated by the popular art of the sixteenth century.   Zesen's His 'Adriatische Rosemund' (1645) reminds us of Jörg 'Adriatische Wickram's 'Good and bad neighbours' (see p. 297), Rosemund.' for it moves in the sphere of every-day life, and the chief event which it narrates is the separation of two lovers, Rosemund and Markhold.   And these lovers are not transferred into a remote and ideal world; Rosemund comes from Venice and lives in Amsterdam, and Markhold is about to journey to Paris.   During his absence, the love-sick Rosamund transports herself into an artificial pastoral life, and *bleu mourant*, the colour of loyalty, 'death blue' ('*sterbe-blau*'), as Zesen translates it, is the livery of her sorrow; her clothes, her rooms, her furniture, are all of this colour.   Nor does Markhold's return bring happiness, for he is Protestant while she is Roman Catholic, and her father requires that she should retain her religion, and that any daughters of hers should be brought up in the same.   Markhold will not yield to this demand, and Rosemund succumbs to her sorrow.

We see clearly that what interested the poet in this work was the problem of mixed marriages.   He expands his simple and even meagre theme with descriptions of places, houses, furniture, pictures, and dresses; he weaves in amusing and instructive conversations, and thus seeks to raise the private life of the middle classes into a higher sphere of feeling and culture.   But in   Pastoral this he found no successor.   In fact the whole school   writing supof pastoral writing had in the latter half of the tenth   plemented century to give way to tragedy and to a more ex-   by a more citing class of literature, to many-volumed novels and   exciting sensuous poems.   Bombast now entered on its naturalistic stage.   style.

The English comedians had already transplanted naturalism to Germany, the coarse naturalism of blood and horrors ; but the same naturalism might be clothed equally well in the rhymed couplets of the sixteenth century as in simple prose. In the writings of Gryphius, where naturalism does not appear in its most repulsive form, we perceive for the first time an effort to preserve an exalted and embellished style throughout.

Hoffmanns-waldau (1618-1679) and Lohenstein (1635-1683). The Silesians, Hoffmannswaldau and Lohenstein, the literary magnates of the years 1660–1680, carried bombastic poetry to its climax. Hoffmannswaldau lived from 1618–1679, Lohenstein from 1635–1683. The former distinguished himself in poems, the latter in tragedies and novels. In Hoffmannswaldau sentimentalism passes into frivolity; in Lohenstein the tragic tendency degenerates into mere love of the horrible. Hoffmannswaldau, who belongs to the school of Ovid, aims at being graceful, and revels in the light play of wit; Lohenstein, as a disciple of Seneca, affects the sublime and delights in mere bombast. Hoffmannswaldau did succeed in attaining a certain soft and attractive sweetness, but Lohenstein never rose above rude splendour and pedantic obscurity. Both were excessively admired in their own time, and found many disciples; both seem merely repulsive and tedious to the readers of to-day. Nevertheless, the form as well as the matter of their

Efforts after originality. poetry shows a strong play of imagination. Poets now no longer cared to borrow the adornments of their poetry from the ancients, as Opitz had told them to do, but sought to give their compositions a beauty of their own; their bad taste thus really sprang from their effort after originality, which was in itself the first step towards a nobler freedom. Poetry had to diffuse itself over a wide range of subjects before it could give profound utterance to any one. Imagination had to run riot in the wide domain of the improbable, before it could gain new creative power.

The bombastic style, though of foreign origin, was quite compatible with warm patriotic feeling, for all this imitation was only emulation, only an endeavour to produce works of equal merit with those of other countries. The joy of the German Humanists at

the re-discovery of ancient German times in the works of Tacitus
and in other Roman writers had not diminished, but
rather increased. Tacitus became the favourite author
of the German classical scholars of the seventeenth
century. In the year 1616, Philip Cluverius of Dantzic
published a detailed scientific description of the ancient Germans, a book which long retained great
authority. In 1643 the history of Arminius, written in German,
was published at Nürnberg in a miniature volume,
and had a very wide sale. The novel-writers of this
period loved to lay the scene of their stories in old
Germanic times, and Lohenstein chose Arminius as the hero of one
of his novels. The patriotic purist, Philip von Zesen, gave German
names to the characters in his novels, such as Rosemund, Adelmund,
and Markhold. German scholars never tired of praising in the
strongest terms the old German tongue, the language of the ancient
German heroes; some even tried to derive Greek and Latin from it,
and most of them were united in their hatred of foreign speech, dress,
and cooking. Hans Michael Moscherosch (see p. 386), in one of his
prose satires, gathers together the heroes of the past, Ariovistus,
Arminius, Wittekind, and others, at the castle of Geroldseck in the
Vosges mountains, and brings before them a fashionable young German, Philander von Sittewald, who is sternly reproved by them for
his affectation of foreign manners and his effeminacy. Moscherosch
is an indiscriminating hater of the French, and does not recognise
the value of that refinement of manners which came to Germany
from France. But such exaggeration is an evidence of the strong
patriotic feeling at this time, and we can understand that this
patriotism would be of use to poetic style, in making some poets
turn away from the grandiose foreign style of writing, and return to
the popular art of the sixteenth century.

The popular style of the Reformation writers, of Murner, Luther,
and Hans Sachs, is chiefly represented at this period
in church-hymns and in comic writings; but it is now
raised to an altogether higher grade of art, being
made more perfect in syntax, versification, melody, and form.
Even the clown of the popular drama was not quite unaffected by

Margin notes:

Patriotic
sentiment;
Cluverius's
'Germania
Antiqua,'
1616.

History of
Arminius,
1643.

Refinement
of popular
style.

this refining influence, and it was only the lowest buffoonery, the jokes of the wandering jugglers and singers and of the mechanical writers of occasional verses that resisted all refinement. We have seen how in the church-hymn Paul Gerhardt combined religious themes with a popular style and artistic form; the comic poetry and prose of this period embodied in an artistic form the typical characters of satire, the realistic style of representation, the popular plain-spokenness, the anecdotes, proverbs, and loaded epithets of the popular literature of the sixteenth century.

In the satirists of the middle of the seventeenth century patriotic hostility towards everything foreign went hand in hand with a coarse realism in style. This is especially the case with worthy Johann Lauremberg of Rostock, whose 'Four comic poems,' published in 1652, fascinate us even in the present day. Whilst all the literary world was striving after stricter versification Lauremberg wrote in Platt-Deutsch, and allowed himself the greatest licence in his poetry. He boldly declared: 'My rhymes are as bad or as good as the rough cap which my grandmother wears.' ('*Meine Reime sind so schlecht und recht, wie die rauhe Mütze, die meine Grossmutter trägt.*') He says he does not wish to thunder and affect high-flown language after the new fashion; he sticks to the old fashion and means to keep his simple manner. He introduces popular coarseness and obscene wit wherever it suits him; he has a wealth of appropriate humorous similes at his command, and like the writers of the sixteenth century he only occasionally has recourse to the ancients for subject-matter, and does not wish to imitate their form. His pictures of life are always interesting, though sometimes his characters do not keep true to their part. It cannot justly be said of Lauremberg that he appealed by low means to a low audience; he shows the greatest skill in his use of the doctrine of the transmigration of souls in a satire on all classes of society, and he has carefully secured an artistic connection between his four satires. Throughout his writings we can trace thoughtful composition, a remarkable talent for artistic arrangement, and a great command of language. Lauremberg was a many-sided scholar and poet; from 1618 to 1623 he was

[Marginal note:] Satire. Johann Lauremberg's 'Vier Scherzgedichte,' 1652.

Professor of Poetry at Rostock, and from 1623 till his death in 1658 he was Professor of Mathematics at the University of Soroe in Seeland. His 'comic poems' were also published in Danish, and found as great favour in Denmark as in Germany.

Joachim Rachel of Ditmarschen received his education in Rostock, and was at first an adherent of Lauremberg's school; a Low-German poem of his, in which a peasant woman sings the praises of an excellent youth to her daughter, has become a true popular song and lives on as such to our day. Later on Rachel devoted himself to High-German poetry; his satirical poems of 1664 are written after the model of Persius and Juvenal, but they still betray the influence of Lauremberg.

Joachim
Rachel's
satirical
poems.

The revival of the Satire led to the revival of the Epigram, which according to the theory of the age was only an abridged form of satire. The Silesian, Friedrich von Logau, did as much for the epigram in the poetry of the Renaissance as Opitz had done for lyric poetry and Gryphius for the drama. In 1654, a year before his death, he published a classified collection of epigrams ('Sinngedichte'), comprising over three thousand poems; they are mostly very short, and deal with many well-known themes of older or contemporary satire, such as court-life, the degeneration of the Fatherland, the decay of morals, various failings of character, all handled with bright wit and with a serious purpose, but in a somewhat general manner; his description of the state of public affairs in particular shows a great want of individual traits. Logau carries his hatred of foreign fashion in dress so far as to say that he would rather allow the Germans their immoderate drinking than the worship of fashion. His personal convictions appear to the best advantage when he is preaching Christian charity, branding hypocrisy, and demanding liberty of conscience. 'Lutheran, Papist, and Calvinist,' says Logau, 'all these three faiths exist, yet there is reason to doubt where Christianity is to be found.'

Friedrich
von Logau's
'Sinnge-
dichte,'
1654.

After the Thirty Years' War the anonymous popular songs and social songs gradually disappear, but the style of these songs was continued by poets of artistic culture. The authors of the new

pastoral poems tried to strike a light and popular tone. A poet
Poems in like Jacob Schwieger of Altona, the true Minnesinger
popular of the seventeenth century, was always better in the
style. popular and comic than in the cultivated and serious
style, better in the love-ballad than in the artistic song ; the Leipzig
poets Finckelthaus and Brehme, both friends of Fleming's, and
later on Schoch and other poets wrote rollicking students' songs,
festal songs, drinking songs, and satirical songs in which the
ancients are mocked at, lovers are rejected, and peasants are
favourably contrasted with the devotees of fashion. Some of
these songs soon penetrated into the guard-houses and taverns.
Most lyric poets took care that their songs should be spread
abroad accompanied by appropriate melodies, and a few particularly favourite tunes, such as the beautiful melody to Rist's
pastoral song—'Daphnis ging vor wenig Tagen über die be-
grünte Heid,' were frequently made use of. About the year 1660
we find in song-books which were meant for wide circulation poems
by Opitz, Rist, Finckelthaus, and Greflinger, printed side by side
with the later 'Hildebrandslied,' with historical songs of the fifteenth
and sixteenth centuries, and love-songs of old renown, such as
'Wär ich ein wilder Falke.'

Christian Weise of Zittau (1642–1708) joined the ranks of the
Christian Leipzig poets. From 1660 to 1668 he studied and
Weise, gave lectures in Leipzig, and he made his first appear-
1642-1708. ance as a poet about 1670. His youthful poems are
marked by that easy flowing style combined with meagreness of
subject-matter, that jesting and frivolous tone, that mixture of
reflection and sentiment, which remained for long the fashion in
Leipzig, and which even appears in Goethe's earliest lyric poems
written in that town. Weise bids farewell to mythology and to the
Character fantastic school of writing; he makes fun of the
of his Purists, renounces the pastoral style, and prefers to
poetry. adopt the mask of a porter or a sexton. He wrote
love-dialogues and other poems in dramatic form, for instance,
a love law-suit; he describes dancing in a dance-song, gives us
a picture of the young gallant of that day, and draws a parallel between love and a chase. Weise is always inclined to interweave witty

observations and descriptions in his lyric poetry, which betray the hand of the satirist just as much as the novels and dramas which he wrote (see pp. 389, 396). Weise exalted his peculiar manner into a canon of art, and even defended it on theoretic grounds. He is continually exhorting authors to write in a natural and unconstrained manner. He himself expressly aimed at a popular style, and avoided everything artificial, wishing, as he said, 'not to earn the name of a lofty and inspired, but of a simple and clear writer.' He was thus the very opposite of Lohenstein. But the more his influence increased, the more empty and superficial did his poetry become. As Professor in Weissenfels (1670), and later on as Rector in Zittau (1678), he attracted the young nobility around him, and found an opportunity of claiming for German poetry a place as a recognised branch of an aristocratic education; but his verses of this period approach more and more the style of the mechanical occasional poetry which we have already noticed, and in place of Lohenstein's bombastic obscurity he can only offer us a dull, insipid, vulgar, would-be-witty kind of poetry, well suited to mediocre taste and mediocre capacities. This style now asserted its sway in all branches of literature, and *His wide* thus prepared the way for the enlightenment of a *influence.* trivial rationalism, and at the same time for the influx of French taste.

In France too the bombastic style prevailed for a time, and there too it met with opposition, and was overthrown earlier than in Germany. In the time of Louis XIV. Molière, *French literature.* Boileau, Lafontaine, and Racine led the revolt against *Molière,* fustian in literature. In 1659 Molière wrote his *Boileau,* 'Précieuses Ridicules;' in 1674 Boileau produced *Lafontaine,* his 'Art Poétique,' in which he inveighed against *and Racine.* brilliant nonsense, and exhorted writers to reason and healthy common-sense. But while in Germany the opposition, of which Christian Weise was the leader, only gave rise to a weak and insipid poetry, mere rhymed prose full of didactic commonplaces, in France, on the contrary, there arose a great literature, whose influence soon spread to England, and which later on derived from England many new ideas and suggestions. The chief representative of

this literature and the leader of Western European culture in
the eighteenth century was the philosopher, historian,
and poet, Voltaire.

Voltaire.

Already in the seventeenth century the new French poetry began
to exercise an influence in Germany. Educated men
of the world, such as the Prussian Christian Wer-
nicke, began to adopt its standard of taste, and to
mock at the German verse-makers. About 1700 we
find a number of poets who had begun as Lohensteinians and had
then been converted to French Classicism. These writers betray a
certain connection with Christian Weise, but they endeavour to
rise above his common-place level; they have also some features
in common with Hoffmannswaldau, but they aim more at intellect
and refinement than at exuberant descriptions. The best among
them, poets like Canitz and Neukirch, are satirists, and thus far
followers of Lauremberg and Rachel, but they take Boileau and his
model Horace as their examples. At the same time poetry became
once more aristocratic, and for a time it seemed as if Berlin were
to be the centre of the French influence. The first
King of Prussia, Frederick I., surrounded himself with
literary men. He patronised or attracted to himself
Pufendorf, Spener, Leibniz, and many French Protestant preachers.
He gave appointments in Halle to Thomasius, Francke, and Wolff,
and in architecture and the plastic arts he left behind him visible
monuments of the rising greatness of his country. Baron von
Canitz was a member of his Privy Council; the poet Johann von
Besser was the director of the royal festivities; Benjamin Neukirch
held an appointment in Berlin. But the poetry of those times was
far from coming up to the level of what Andreas Schlüter accomplished in architecture and sculpture, and in the year
1713 the accession of Frederick William I. put an end,
for the time, to all hopes of literary or artistic development. Schlüter went to St. Petersburg, Besser to
Dresden, Neukirch to Ansbach; Canitz had already
died in 1699. A certain Pietsch, an artist by calling,
was indeed made Professor of Poetry at Königsberg in return for
having written a pompous eulogy on the victory of Prince Eugene

French influence in Germany, circa 1700.

Berlin under Frederick I.

All progress stopped by accession of Frederick William I., 1713.

at Temesvar ; but his disciple Gottsched, who pronounced Pietsch the greatest poet of the eighteenth century, was obliged to keep away from Berlin, for fear lest his strong build and lofty stature should attract the attention of Frederick's zealous recruiting officers. He went to Leipzig, where all the earlier literary movements had found a rallying-place, and which he now made in addition the centre of French classicism in Germany.

We have already noticed in Leipzig Fleming and his friends as well as Christian Weise. There was no North German town where the fantastic style gained so little ground as Leipzig as in Leipzig. Neither secular nor pietistic bombast a literary found any favour there, and though we find Thomasius centre. enthusiastically praising Lohenstein and Hoffmannswaldau, yet he also sets up the French as models. As early as 1682 the 'Acta Eruditorum' had been started, a Latin learned newspaper, after the model of the Paris 'Journal des Sçavans.' Neumeister and Henrici, who had the honour of writing the text for some of Bach's cantatas and oratorios, belonged to Christian Weise's school. Professor Burkard Menke, who in 1707 succeeded his father as editor of the 'Acta Eruditorum,' also wrote satires and satirical occasional poems in Weise's style; his poems show little merit, but he recognised and encouraged youthful talent in Günther and Gottsched, and he founded and directed the 'German Society,' a students' literary association, which later on developed into a kind of academy, and was used by Gottsched as the pedestal of his fame.

Johann Christian Günther was a kind-hearted but wild and dissolute character, who came to a miserable end in 1723, Johann when only in his twenty-eighth year. He was a Christian Silesian by birth, and was at first a follower of Lohen- Günther, stein, but later on he chose his countryman Neukirch 1695-1723. as a model, though without giving up that higher flight of fancy which he had already developed in the bombastic school of writing. In addition to this, Günther was influenced by the student-poetry which he became acquainted with as a student at Wittenberg and Leipzig, and it was his peculiarity to confide to his verses his own joys and sorrows, his friendships and enmities, his love, his ill-health, his faults and his repentance, and to demand the sympathy of posterity for the same. The picture which he gives us of himself is not pleasing, but the various influences which acted on him, together with his own powers, raised him above the level of his contemporaries. He could describe with great imaginative power, and was most successful in sketching small scenes. He wrote satirical occasional poems like Menke, also affecting religious hymns and serious, passionate, and audacious love-songs, seldom in the pastoral style, sometimes in ballad-form, and generally drawn from his own personal experience. Frankness and truthfulness are characteristic of all his poems, but this frankness sometimes degenerates into coarseness.

Compared with Günther, Gottsched (see Chap. XI. § 1) makes a very poor figure as a creative poet. His best gifts lay in another direction, but he could not discern the limits of his powers ; he was so arrogant in exercising the authority which he had gained in literary matters, so obstinate in his narrow-minded devotion to French Classicism, that opposition to Gottsched was the first task to be performed by the rising literature of the last century. All the young poets, on whose powers the future prosperity of German poetry depended, first came into notice as opponents of Gottsched, and in the work of rendering German poetry more truly national, the Prussian soldier-king, Frederick William I., the inventor of the *queue*, also did his part.

Gottsched.

The patriotic German satires of the seventeenth century, which we have noticed above, were the expression of a wide-spread feeling, a feeling which was not confined to the middle classes but animated even some of the German princely families. The Duchess Elizabeth Charlotte of Orleans adopted a homely and popular style in her splendid Letters to Germany; she was a Princess Palatine and maintained her upright and honourable German ways in the midst of the Court of Louis XIV. The patriotic, simple, upright type of German character was most strongly represented in Frederick William I. of Prussia. He was by no means content with mere opposition to what he stamped as foreign affectation and refinement ; his activity also took the direction of a grandmotherly solicitude for the welfare of his people, an enlightened despotism, and an

Frederick William I.

His opposition to foreign influence.

attempt to imprint upon his subjects his own qualities of simplicity, frugality, punctuality, and military discipline. He made a crusade against fashion and kept French influence at a distance. The chief factors in German education since the Reformation and Renaissance, namely Biblical Christianity and classical literature, were thus able to exercise more direct and exclusive power on the young Prussians than on other Germans; the fashionable French culture stood less in their way, and the great models of antiquity were not obscured for them by an affected and sometimes petty taste calling itself classical. Thus it was by no mere chance that the Prussian University of Halle gave birth to that poetic movement which the Prussian Klopstock later on carried to its highest point, that Winckelmann was a Prussian by birth, and that Lessing owed to Berlin the stimulus which determined his later development.

English influence (which we have already noticed at an earlier period in this history) was likewise destined to play a part in the literature of the coming epoch. **English influence.** Gottsched himself was for a time affected by it, though he afterwards discarded and even opposed it.

In the first and second decades of the eighteenth century, under the reign of Queen Anne, English literature assumed a distinctively middle-class character. The connection with France was not broken off, but France now became in some respects a debtor to England. Pope was a follower of Boileau, whom he imitated in the **English literature under Queen Anne.** satire, the didactic poem, and the burlesque epic; but Pope developed the philosophical didactic poem in a manner peculiar to himself. Jonathan Swift seems in his satirical narratives to revive the style of Rabelais, but also shows great originality. We shall meet again with Daniel Defoe, the author of 'Robinson Crusoe,' in connection with German novel-writers. (See next section.) In the 'Tatler,' the 'Spectator,' and the 'Guardian,' Steele and Addison founded an important branch of older journalism, the moralising weekly papers; **The 'Tatler,' 'Spectator,' and 'Guardian.'** their chief excellence lay in their satirical and humorous sketches of current manners and social conditions and in their popular and attractive manner of treating literary and religious questions. These papers exercised the greatest influence on the culture of the middle classes, and were imitated at once almost throughout Europe. In Germany, between the years 1714 and 1800, we can count over a hundred periodicals, more or less of this description. The earliest appeared in Ham-

German newspapers on the same model.

burg; Zürich, Hamburg, and Leipzig were the first to attain to excellence in this branch of literature. The Zürich 'Discourse der Maler' (1721) were published by John Jacob Bodmer and his friends, the Hamburg 'Patriot' (1724) by Brockes and his friends, and Gottsched was the editor of the two Leipzig papers, entitled the 'Vernünftige Tadlerinnen' (1725), and the 'Biedermann'

Gottsched and Addison.

(1727). Gottsched also had translations made of the 'Spectator' and the 'Guardian,' and he owed to Addison the only one of his tragedies which is in the least suited for acting, i.e. his 'Cato' (1732). He simply adopted Addison's tragedy as the basis for his own, only adding to it a few ideas borrowed from a French tragedy. The taste which Addison represented was in the main shared by Gottsched. But Addison stood far higher as a critic than as a poet. His own poetical works were mediocre, but as a critic he showed a thorough appreciation of Milton, Shakspeare, Homer, Biblical poetry and popular ballads. In this respect Gottsched could not come up to him, but the Zürich scholars, Bodmer and Breitinger (see p. 423), certainly did.

Feud between Gottsched and the Swiss school.

In consequence, there arose a difference between their theoretical views and those of Gottsched, and this difference became the germ of a bitter feud. In addition to this, Switzerland as well as Hamburg could point to poets of original genius, whom neither Gottsched nor his disciples could equal, namely Haller and Hagedorn.

Both these poets had acquired part of their literary culture in

Haller and Hagedorn compared.

England, and both have some connection with Pope. They both wrote didactic poems and satires; but Hagedorn is less noted for these than for his many slight poems, fables and stories in verse, after the model of Lafontaine and other poets. He is bright and sprightly where Haller is heavy and serious. Haller recognises Virgil's uniform sublimity as his highest model, but Hagedorn strives to attain the elegant conversational tone of Horace. Haller seeks to reproduce in poetry the grandeur of Alpine scenery, but Hagedorn is content with the modest charms of town and level country. The former is sunk in religious melancholy, whereas the latter is a thorough child of the world. Haller, notwithstanding his efforts, never quite freed himself from his Swiss-German, but Hagedorn attained to perfect finish and smoothness of expression. Haller's writings are full of profound thoughts, and bear the stamp of a high intellect; Hagedorn, on the contrary, loved a light and easy treatment of his subject. Haller generally used the Alexandrine, Hagedorn less frequently. Hagedorn has far more of the modern spirit than Haller, and yet it was the latter who exercised the greatest influence on posterity. The Swiss poet Haller is more German; the Hamburg poet Hagedorn more international.

Albrecht von Haller of Berne holds in German literature a place close to Günther. His celebrated 'Ode to Doris'—for **Albrecht** whose ardour he thought it right in his old age to offer **von Haller,** an apology—is a moderately passionate Güntherian **1708-1777.** love-song. Haller too had in his youth embraced the Lohensteinian exalted style, and had retained enough of it to prevent him from ever sinking into common-place twaddle. He held a very peculiar position, being equally noted as a scholar, a critic, and a poet. He lived from 1708 to 1777, and thus saw Gottsched's highest glory and also the dawn of Goethe's fame. His best poems were written between the years 1725 and 1736, and the first collected edition of them appeared in 1732; they are few in number, and he treated them as quite secondary work, but still was never tired of repolishing them. In his old age he tried his hand at writing political novels; his 'Usong' (1771) deals with Oriental despotism; his 'Alfred, König der Angelsachsen' (1773) treats of limited monarchy; his 'Fabius and Cato' (1774) describes that form of government under which he had himself grown up, and in whose service he ended his life—i.e. an oligarchy. His wide **His** scientific knowledge, his power of work, and his **scientific** capacity for collecting and classifying masses of facts, **knowledge.** were quite marvellous. His contemporaries placed him on a level with Leibniz, and like Leibniz he had no equal among his contemporaries. His chief interest was medicine, and especially anatomy and physiology; he studied in Tübingen and Leyden, in London, Paris, and Basle, and from 1736 to 1753 he taught in Göttingen, acquiring an ever-increasing reputation. But notwithstanding his success, he could not bear his exile from his native land, and in 1753 he gave up all the honours and influence which the University could bestow on him, and even the possibility of strict scientific research and discovery in his own favourite department, in order to accept an unimportant office in the State of Berne. This office did indeed later on open to him a sphere of great general usefulness, but did not offer him any scope for political activity. His devotion to his fatherland is attested by many passages in his poetry. As a student in Leyden he gave vent to his home-sicknesss in verse. A

His poetry. 'Die Alpen.' botanical excursion in the Bernese Oberland called forth his poem 'The Alps,' which contains descriptions of nature and men, full of truth and showing great power of language. Haller omits the ideal shepherd of contemporary lyric poetry, and yet manages to shed over his poem the rosy light of a golden age, for he imagines himself to have discovered primal innocence and virtue among the shepherds of his native mountains. He sarcastically censures the corrupt morals of the period as he saw them in his own native town, and displays, in so doing, the same patriotic zeal against everything foreign, which we noticed in the older satirists. Yet he could also appreciate the greatness of the age in which he lived, and praises its enlightenment, while he expresses his hatred of the Middle Ages, of Catholicism and the priests. He is a Protestant of strong convictions like Leibniz, whose philosophy he adopted, but his treatment of the problem of the origin of evil, in his longest didactic poem, is not very successful.

Poem on Eternity and others. Some fragments of a poem on Eternity, on the contrary, are really magnificent, especially his picture of Newton, whom he conjures up in order to ask him unanswerable questions, and thus to show, in a truly Faustian

Haller's style. mood, the nothingness of human knowledge. Haller was tolerably well master of the collective wisdom of his time; his thoughtful monologues are based on exact knowledge, but he always tries to embody abstract ideas in an imaginative form and to give poetic expression to stern moral problems, and at every turn he refutes the false opinion that the didactic poem is a low order of poetry. He likes to begin his poems with a description of external nature, sometimes reminding us of Brockes, whom Haller zealously studied and imitated in his youth; but whereas Brockes, like all the poets of the seventeenth century, never knows where to end, and often becomes trivial, Haller, on the contrary, keeps the true artistic mean.

Friedrich von Hagedorn belonged to Brockes' circle of friends. He was of the same age as Haller, but died in 1754. He won his literary spurs in writing for the Hamburg 'Patriot.' But while Brockes stuck fast all his life in the Lohensteinian bombast of the Hamburg opera-poets, Hagedorn entirely freed himself from it. His first collection of poems, published in 1729, showed that he had not quite thrown off the older taste; he praises Besser, Gottsched, Brockes, and Pietsch as true poets, and describes in Brockes' manner; he also writes a political ode in the style of Günther, and sings the praises of wine in the uncouth verses of the students' song. It is in his poetic fables and tales, published in 1738, and in the odes, songs, didactic poems, satires, and epigrams, which appeared in a collected form in 1753, that his whole talent is revealed. Hagedorn made great advances in poetic form and was the first to re-introduce into German literature the taste and correctness of the Minnesingers. He knew how to make his style not only elegant but also generally intelligible, and though several of his poems would appeal only to more cultivated readers, others are addressed to a very large public. Hagedorn's life and circumstances strongly influenced his poetry. He was of noble birth and grew up in the best society; he imbibed French culture in his home and English culture in London. His three years of student-life in Jena probably made him acquainted with German popular poetry in the students' songs. He afterwards settled in Hamburg, a town where the 'Volkslieder' still enjoyed the favour of the middle classes. There he lived in comfortable

Friedrich von Hagedorn, 1708–1754.

His early poems, 1729.

His later poems, 1738–1753.

His life.

circumstances, and his office of secretary to a commercial company
left him ample leisure for social enjoyments and also for the intellectual pleasures of reading and poetry.   He expected the same
appreciation of science and art from the Hamburg merchants as
he had met with in the English ones.   Hagedorn was a refined
Epicurean, and a man of a bright and cheerful disposition.   Like
his beloved Horace, he praised contentment as the only happiness.
Liberty and friendship seemed to him the most desirable things,
His fables while he depreciated power, riches, and luxury.   He
and tales. wrote fables and tales in verse after French and
English models, but he was not unacquainted with his German
predecessors of the sixteenth century in this branch of literature.
In the seventeenth century this class of poetry had been entirely
ousted by the pompous didactic poetry and the grandiloquent
novels then in vogue, and it had never gained an entrance into
the realm of popular song; now, the increasing sense of form and
the consequent demand of finer charms even in narrative-writing,
the pleasure in what was profitable and amusing at the same time,
the love of satire, wit, and pregnant sayings brought the fable and
tale into new favour.   Lafontaine and Lamotte enjoyed the greatest
popularity in Germany; it was some translations of Lamotte's
fables, published by Brockes, which first suggested that style of
writing which was afterwards so successfully developed by Gellert,
and this whole class of writing prepared the way for the rhymed
epic.   Hagedorn was not one of the best story-tellers, but he was
the first to gain great success; he prepared the way for Gellert,
and a few of his characters, such as 'John, the cheerful soap-boiler,'
are yet unforgotten.   In his tales he revived a vanished type of
German bourgeois-poetry and gave it a French colouring, and in
his lyric poetry he joined the ranks of those older writers, who,
His 'Oden like Christian Weise, carried on the popular style.
und His 'Odes and Songs' contained free translations of
Lieder,' Horace and imitations of Anacreon, and for the rest
1747. poems on well-known subjects, only more finely conceived and more wittily carried out than usual, and often ending
in an unexpected way, after the French manner.   In this collection there are social choruses, drinking songs, and pastoral songs;

love and wine are sung of in lyrics, dialogues, ballads, and reflective poems, while we also meet with beautiful pictures of nature, serious and ironical eulogies, and songs put into the mouth of certain characters. Various types of character are often treated satirically from one special point of view, and there are altogether many satirical elements in these poems, but there is a marked absence of serious and affecting love-poems. There is a special charm in a few short songs consisting only of one stanza, which Hagedorn says he derived from French models.

Haller and Hagedorn both liked to draw types of character, and their delineation of human nature is mostly confined to this; but Haller also drew ideal figures, and Hagedorn constructed a framework of narrative for the characters of his satire. In their satire both these poets meet on the same ground; both were influenced by that current of satire, which we have traced since Lauremberg, which was continued after him in the Leipzig poets, in Canitz and Neukirch, and was strengthened by the moralising weekly papers. Prose satire, in the shape of literary criticism, must also be mentioned under this head. Hagedorn's friend, Christian Ludwig Liscow, who was, like Lauremberg, a native of Mecklenburg, ridiculed, with first-rate humour and in a clear and readable style, insignificant characters, such as bad preachers, bad writers, tasteless scholars, servile flatterers, or theologising lawyers. He fought in the cause of enlightenment for the rights of reason, liberty, and manly dignity. In the year 1739 he made a collection of his satirical writings; after that he wrote no more, and he died in 1760 at the age of sixty. *Christian Ludwig Liscow. Literary critic.*

There is an undeniable connection between the movement in favour of enlightenment and rationalism, and the class of poetry represented by Hagedorn, in which taste, intellect, and wit predominate over imagination and feeling; and this connection becomes specially apparent if we compare Hagedorn's poems and Liscow's satires, for both of these were the work of men of an equable temperament, both were the fruit of an independent attitude of mind, and both show dignity and correctness in form. *The enlightenment movement and Hagedorn's poetry.*

German literature had made a long step from Gerhardt's

church-hymns and Lauremberg's satires through the Italian bom-
Gradual
improve-
ment of
popular
taste from
the 16th
century. bastic style to French classicism and the English
influence; yet on the whole it was a direct path, at
least for the favourite forms of literature in that time.
The religious, patriotic, and moral pathos of the
church-hymn and the satire kept true to the simple,
popular style of the sixteenth century, and when that
style threatened to sink into mere platitude French and English
influences came to its aid. The literature of orthodoxy as well as
of rationalism adhered to the popular style; romances, secular lyric
poetry, and the drama, on the contrary, fell entirely under the
dominion of bombast, and even the pietistic writers were sometimes
carried away by the tendency : but pietistic literature possessed independent sources of strength in the Song of Solomon and in
the old German Mystics, and never quite lost its sympathy with the
people. Still, the best religious poetry never exercised an elevating
influence on the secular, but, on the contrary, endeavoured to
approximate to secular poetry. It was not till Klopstock that the
highly imaginative pietistic poetry bore fruit in deepening and
sanctifying earthly emotions. But this whole development was
really the slow rise of popular poetry from the degradation it had
sunk to in the sixteenth century.

Imagination and clearness were first combined in Wieland (see
Chap. XI). Haller's style was not popular, and his form not always
correct. Through Hagedorn correctness of form penetrated about
the year 1740 into popular poetry; till then both the drama and
the novel were without it. But in both these branches of literature the popular style achieved the greatest successes ; in novel-
writing Grimmelshausen gained the chief honours, in the drama
Christian Weise.

THE NOVEL.

After the versified romances of the Middle Ages had given way
Romance
of
'Amadis.' to prose, it was in the story of 'Amadis of Gaul' (see
p. 298) that the spirit of the chivalrous poetry was best
preserved, and this romance, with its kindred successors,
became the school of fine manners and good taste. It retained this

position even when the new romantic style, which was flourishing in
Spain and other countries about the beginning of the seventeenth century, was introduced into Germany by means of numerous translations. 'Don Quixote' was translated into German, but did not excite
much notice. Certain changes, however, set in in German romance-
writing, which look as if Cervantes' ridicule had been   The
taken to heart., About the middle of the seventeenth   Spanish
century the chivalrous novels began to be attacked;   influence.
some people condemned the romance of 'Amadis' as   17th
immoral; they feared that it contained snares of the   century.
devil, and were offended by its fabulous and magical elements.
About the same time German novel-writers began to try their hand
at original invention, and endeavoured to cultivate in Germany the
various classes of novels which were in vogue elsewhere, and to
dress them up in the newly acquired grandiloquent style.

Little was accomplished at this time in the province of the
pastoral romance. This class of writing belonged essentially to
the period of the Thirty Years' War; Philip von Zesen, as we
know, had developed it in a special direction, bringing it down to
the level of real life (see p. 365), but his example had no immediate
effect.

After the pastoral romances, the hero-ròmances and love-
romances had enjoyed the greatest favour in France   Hero-
and Italy. These romances often spread over many   romances
volumes. They introduced important historical events,   and love-
or else they were transferred to remote regions and   romances.
dark ages, and were spun out by numerous episodes, sometimes
derived from contemporary history, so that the characters of the
narrative might be simply real people, disguised under a slight
mask. We have already had examples of this fashion in the
epics of the Emperor Maximilian, in Rollenhagen's 'Froschmäu-
seler,' and in some of the pastoral romances. Where these romances
were connected with well-known historical or biblical characters,
they differed but slightly from the historical novels of the present
day.

The historical romance was introduced into Germany about the
year 1660 by a Lutheran clergyman, Bucholtz by name. Bucholtz

was professor of theology and afterwards 'Superintendent[1]' in

Pseudo-historical romances. Bucholtz. Brunswick. He hated 'Amadis' and he hated the Jews; he planted his heroes in a fabulous Christian Germany of the third century; he drew his episodes from the Thirty Years' War, and he set forth the whole Lutheran system of dogma in his conversations. In invention Bucholtz seldom got beyond the old ideas of the Greek and the chivalrous romances; the best figure which he created, that of a German Amazon, reminds us of Tasso's Clorinde, or of Virgil's Camilla. Bucholtz meant his pious novels to compete with the secular poetry for the favour of the general public, just as the religious poets of the twelfth century wished their works to supplant the old German heroic poetry.

Duke Anton Ulrich of Brunswick. Duke Anton Ulrich of Brunswick, whom we shall have occasion to notice as a patron of the drama, wrote two chaotic and long-winded romances, one of which gives the history of an ancient German chief whom the venerable Melchisedech had married to a queen of Nineveh, while the other has for its hero the son of Arminius. Lohenstein made

Lohenstein's 'Arminius und Thurnelda,' 1683. Arminius and his Thusnelda the centre of a diffuse history, which appeared in 1689 in two quarto volumes of 3076 pages. This work is a mass of historical, antiquarian, geographical, and ethnographical knowledge. It contains a disguised history of the Habsburg emperors and of the modern religious wars, a fictitious history of early German times, written with a patriotic bias, a number of imaginary incidents and adventures, and sketches of various philosophies, all jumbled together in an unpleasing medley. Herr Heinrich Anshelm, of Ziegler, and Klipphausen in Lusatia, understood far better than Lohenstein the art of effective

Anshelm von Ziegler's 'Asiatische Banise.' and lively narration. His 'Asiatische Banise' appeared the year before Lohenstein's 'Arminius,' and is in comparison with it a book of moderate dimensions. It is full of battles, horrors, and narrow escapes, of love and jealousy, complications and surprises, passionate utterances, and calculating and measured speeches.

---

[1] The highest office in the Lutheran church.

The subject-matter was derived from Oriental history in the sixteenth century, but it has been skilfully treated by the author so as to form a complete romance.   There is a marked absence of pedantry in the work, and the author gives us the usual characters of romance : a noble and persecuted princess, a brave lover, a humorous servant, and a horrible tyrant.   Furnished with these attractions the book quickly found a large audience, and was for a long time the delight of the German reading public.

Meanwhile, in France, the novel had been reformed by the Countess Lafayette, who gave it the stamp of the age of Louis XIV.; she discarded all the improbable incidents, and gave up the principle that the scene of a romance must necessarily be laid in a remote and ideal region.   Instead of the ordinary romance of adventures she wrote a touching modern love-story, full of simple and truthful pictures of human passion and virtue, wishes and sacrifices, joys and sorrows.   But her example was not followed by the German novelists, though Zesen had already made an effort to introduce the same principles into German romance-writing.   The Germans did not need to have recourse to the French for the coarser pictures of real life, and all that French influence did for them was to further encourage the tendency to write mere frivolities and platitudes.   To impart instruction in novels, and to unite the profitable and the pleasurable, continued for a long time to be the aim of many German romance-writers, who really only deserved the name of bookmakers.   And whoever had theological scruples against light literature pure and simple, produced in opposition an allegorical story with a spiritual meaning.   Thus, for instance, Johann Ludwig Prasch, a Protestant living in Regensburg, transformed the ancient myth of Cupid and Psyche into an allegory of the soul, which, after having overcome the temptations of the world, is exalted to heavenly regions.   Other countries had set the example in these spiritual allegories, and in the early drama of the seventeenth century attempts had already been made to give a Christian interpretation to the old heathen myths.

The Countess Lafayotte's novel-writing.

Her example not followed in Germany.

Spiritual allegories. Prasch's 'Psyche cretica.'

c c

In this branch of writing too, Father Martin von Cochem (see

Father Martin's 'Auserlesenes History-buch.' p. 339) deserves honourable mention. His 'Select History Book' is a collection of sacred legends and biblical and secular stories, all told with great skill. At least three of his stories were afterwards reprinted separately, and in this form became thorough people's books; these were 'Griseldis,' a story pretty widely known before his time in various versions, 'Genovefa' and 'Hirlanda,' both of which he derived from a book by a French Jesuit—another proof of the strength of French influence in the sphere of popular romance. About this time the Nibelungen legend was revived

Popular story of Siegfried. once more in the popular story of the invulnerable Siegfried; but even this story purports to be a translation from the French, and in truth, one of the episodes, in which two cowards fight together, must be of French origin.

Thus the ancient German legend had to sail under a foreign flag if it wished once more to gain access to the ears of the people; and we shall soon see that the best productions of German literature in the period after the war were written under foreign influence. We owe to Spanish influence the truest pictures of the war-period, the most life-like descriptions of real life, which have come down to us from this period of the dawn of modern literature, namely, the writings of Hans Michael Moscherosch and Hans Jacob Christoffel of Grimmelshausen.

Moscherosch (1601-1669). His 'Gesichte Philander's von Sitte-walt.' Moscherosch (1601-1669) came from the Upper Rhine and died in Hessia; Grimmelshausen (1625-1676) was a native of Hessia, and ended his days on the Upper Rhine. Both showed their talent in drawing satirical pictures of the life around them; Moscherosch was a real satirist, Grimmelshausen used satire in his novels.

Their literary models belonged to that school of art which is most brilliantly represented in painting by the genre-pictures of Murillo. Moscherosch translated Quevedo's satirical 'Dreams,' and wrote himself some descriptions of the same character; the most noteworthy of these are a picture of the military life of the Thirty Years' War, and the scene at Geroldseck, which we

have already noticed (p. 367), between the fashionable young German and the old Germanic heroes. Grimmelshausen adopted
the style of the Spanish humorous and roguish romances. His
'Simplicissimus,' which appeared in 1668, narrates in autobio-
graphical form the adventures and fortunes of a vagabond,
the various incidents being very similar to those of the Spanish
romances. But while the Spanish vagabonds commit one roguery
after another, and are at the end of the book seldom better than
they were at the beginning, the character of Simplicius
Simplicissimus is conceived in a far more serious and
moral spirit. In the Spanish romances we are reminded of the tricks of the scamp Morold, but in
reading 'Simplicissimus' the comparison to Wolfram's

Grimmels-
hausen
(1625-1676).
His 'Simpli-
cissimus.'

'Parzival' naturally suggests itself. Simplicius, like Parzival, grows
up in solitude, a stranger to the world; he loses his parents
when still young, he discovers his near relations in the course of
his life, and does not learn till late that he is of noble descent.
Dressed in fool's motley he becomes an object of general ridicule.
When he sees riders for the first time he takes man and horse to
be one creature; when asked for his name, he answers 'Boy,' for
so he was called by his supposed parents. His inner development
leads from simplicity to sin, and from sin to repentance and
amendment. Simplicius too has long forgotten God, and as Parzival was directed by a pilgrim knight, so Simplicius has the right
way pointed out to him by a soldier who is just starting on a pilgrimage. For a long time he contents himself with the most
general religious ideas, till at last he chooses a special creed, the
Catholic, and partakes of its sacraments. The place which the
knight Trevrizent holds in 'Parzival' is taken by Simplicius's first
teacher, who, from the very beginning of the story, takes pity on
the poor child, neglected by the peasants who have the charge
of him, and who afterwards turns out to be the child's father.
Like Parzival, Simplicius has soon to leave his wife, and though he
is not faithful to her but succumbs easily to temptation, yet he still
has a faithful friend at his side, who is the means by which his
nobler nature raises itself once more. As Wolfram's poem was
not without fabulous and marvellous elements by the side of pic-

tures of real life, so too Grimmelshausen made artistic use of all
the superstitions of his time, such as witchcraft, exorcisms, treasure-
digging, legends, interweaving them with the extravagantly realistic
descriptions in which he delighted. Simplicius is surrounded by the military life of the Thirty Years' War,
as Parzival is by the life of chivalry.   But there is a
vast difference in the state of morals represented in
the two works; where Wolfram shows us refinement, Grimmelshausen gives us nothing but coarseness, and draws a picture of a
fearful state of moral corruption, in which there is no security for
person or property, and unfaithfulness of every kind is the order of
the day.   Stealing, profligacy, murder, and incendiarism flourish,
and a deadly war is raging between soldiers and peasants; the
towns alone afford behind their strong walls a refuge where quiet
social intercourse, reading, art, but above all low pleasures can
be carried on.   The general level of culture is rather that of ' Rudlieb' than of ' Parzival.'   At times we find ourselves transported
back to the coarseness and the filthy jesting of the sixteenth century.
Women have but slight influence, and that not of a refining
nature.

Scene laid in the Thirty Years' War.

Grimmelshausen's male characters are drawn with great skill and
variety.   His moral judgment is consistent throughout, and the artistic unity of the work is fairly kept in
view.   The narrative is developed according to a
well-considered plan, and the descriptions give us the
impression of being drawn from personal experience and observation.   But occasionally Moscherosch gives way to the prevalent
love of out-of-the-way learning, and sometimes the speeches seem
unsuitable to the characters in whose mouth they are placed.   We
might also wish for more simple and definite outlines in the story
and for a better conclusion.   Just when we think the hero is saved
he has the strangest relapses, till finally, filled with disgust for the
world, he withdraws from it and becomes a hermit like his father.
We cannot help thinking that Grimmelshausen need not have
made his hero bid farewell to the world in the language of a
Spanish Mendicant friar, and might have found some better pro-
vision for him than a hut in the forest.   And it soon appears that

*Excellen-
ces and
defects of
the work.*

even as a hermit he is not to find rest, but is to be forced into action again.

Grimmelshausen wrote many novels and other works before and after 'Simplicissimus.' He created the character of 'Courasche,' a woman who is the wife of a cavalry-captain, a captain of infantry, a lieutenant, a sutler, a musketeer, and finally a gypsy. He introduced to the public the 'curious young scapegrace' (*seltsamer Springinsfeld*) who from a bold soldier has sunk down to a crafty beggar and vagabond. He told the story of the first sluggard (*Bärenhäuter*), who by an agreement with the devil might not for seven years cut his hair and beard, wash his face and hands or blow his nose, and had to use for cloak and bed the skin of a bear slain by himself. He described the degraded conditions of family-life among the peasants and townspeople after the war. He uttered warnings against foreign military service, especially the French. He attacked exaggerated purism, and also the unnecessary use of foreign words in the German language. In reading his works we are often reminded of Hans Sachs and other satirists of the sixteenth century, only that Grimmelshausen possesses the artistic sense which we missed so much in those older writers; in place of doggerel verses we have here a clear, vigorous, and fluent prose.

The influence of Moscherosch and Grimmelshausen is clearly discernible in the novels of Christian Weise, which appeared from 1671 to 1676, but the tradition of the sixteenth century is still more prominent in them. The writer is continually seeking an opportunity for introducing a succession of fools and knaves, after the manner of Sebastian Brand and Murner. He introduces us to one or several travellers who are journeying to discover the three greatest fools in the world, or at another time to find the three wisest men in the world, or yet again to study the effects of that impudence which leads men to grasp at what is not their due. There is no lack of comic characters, and of amusing scenes in these writings of Weise's, and his didactic purpose does not prevent him from being very entertaining.

In adopting the form of a journey for his story, Weise was following a fashion at that time much in vogue in European literature. In the humorous romances frequent change of scene was much favoured. The real journey-romance, a descendant of the Odyssey, could lead its readers to distant countries, could bring before them strange men and strange customs, and could spread geographical knowledge; or, on the other hand, it could be made a *voyage imaginaire*, to the moon, the stars, the centre of the earth, or any allegorical land of fancy. In both these forms it offered a convenient thread for tales and satires, and the experiences and adventures related by the various men whom the traveller met with furnished an opportunity for dragging in all things in heaven and earth. German writers cultivated the journey-romance in all its forms, good and bad. Even when wishing to describe their own country, they bring a foreigner on the scene, who demands information about the state of the country, its manners, and its people. Thus, in his 'Nobleman' (1697), Paul Winkler actually brings a Dutchman to Breslau in order to gain an opportunity of painting the Silesian nobility from the life, and of interlarding his description with endless and wearisome discourses on all sorts of out-of-the-way topics.

The journey-romances.

Paul Winkler's 'Edelmann' (1697).

The journey-romance in its most outrageous form is capitally turned to ridicule in 'Schelmuffsky,' one of the most remarkable books in older German literature, written by a Leipzig student, Christian Reuter, in 1696. It is a handful of lies throughout, but may be considered a classic among fictitious histories, excelling even the 'Finkenritter' and 'Münchhausen.' Schelmuffsky, who relates his own experiences like Simplicius, is a provincial good-for-nothing, who has seen nothing of the world and knows nothing of geography; he makes loaded waggons drive from London to Hamburg, he places Venice on a high rocky eminence, where there is great dearth of water, and furnishes Rome with a large herring-fishery; yet he represents himself to have seen all these places, and to have been on many perilous journeys by land and sea, during which, according to his own account, he made a great impression on

Christian Reuter's 'Schelmuffsky' (1696).

all who saw him, overcame all his adversaries, and was loved by all
the ladies.   Of course he has visited the East, has been to India and
seen the great Mogul, which is the proper thing for the hero
of a journey-romance, and he has also duly suffered shipwreck
and fallen into the hands of pirates. He was able to speak as
soon as he was born, and he has performed feats of which the
giant Gargantua himself need not have been ashamed. Many of
his exaggerations remind us of the swaggering talk of the soldier-
braggarts in contemporary comedy, only they are transferred to a
lower region, and the bombast is replaced by a tone of *naïveté*;
the hero's inventions contain nothing that might not have come
into such a fellow's head when he was once set off. The tone of
his narrative, the constant recurrence of the adjuration, 'The devil
take me' ('*Der Tebel hohl mer*'), and the frequent assurance that
he is an honest man, the similarity of the various experiences which
he relates, the repetition of certain fixed formulas of description,
and the marked vulgarity of language—all this is in perfect harmony
with the supposed character of the narrator.   The author also
shows real inventive genius in the creation of the second swaggerer,
whom Schelmuffsky swears friendship with, and on whose lesser
achievements he looks down with good-natured superiority, and also
in the introduction of the little cousin, who won't believe a word
Schelmuffsky says, and is consequently so annoying to him.
These are particular merits in a work, which as a whole shows
great power of imagination and skilful artistic development.

But the journey-novel could not be stamped out even by the
most biting ridicule. On the contrary, it took a new direction in
the eighteenth century, and assumed a form which the inventive
mind of Grimmelshausen had already introduced in the sequel to
his great novel 'Simplicissimus.' In this second Second part
part Simplicius starts once more on his travels. He of 'Simpli-
does not reach his goal, Jerusalem, but is taken cissimus.'
captive by Arabian robbers in Egypt, and is exhibited for a time
as a savage. After he has succeeded in effecting his escape, he
means to sail round the South of Africa to St. Jago di Compo-
stella, but he is shipwrecked close to a beautiful island; there he
lives at first with his companions, then alone, and cannot be per-

suaded to return even by a European vessel that touches the island.

Grimmelshausen has here introduced an idea which had already played a certain part in Shakspeare's 'Tempest,' and which Defoe made, fifty years later, the centre of his remarkable work, 'Robinson Crusoe.' But the idea started by Grimmelshausen remained dormant until it came before the public in a new form

Defoe's 'Robinson Crusoe,' 1719. from England. Daniel Defoe's 'Robinson Crusoe' appeared in 1719; it was at once translated into various languages, and it continued for a long time to call forth numerous imitations in Germany. Foreign nations as well as native districts were made to furnish names for

German imitations of Defoe's work. all these Robinsons or Adventurers; there was an Italian, French, Dutch, Norwegian, Saxon, Silesian, Thuringian, Swabian, Brandenburg, and Palatinate Robinson, a Swiss, Danish, Dresden, and Leipzig Adventurer. The most celebrated achievement of this literature of Robinsonades, which was continued down into the age of Frederick the Great,. was a four-volume story, which appeared

'Die Insel Felsen- burg,' 1731-1743. between 1731 and 1743, and was called 'The Island of Felsenburg,' after the scene of the narrative. It was written by Johann Gottfried Schnabel, court-agent and newswriter to Count Stolberg. His literary apparatus is on the whole the same as that employed in 'Simplicissimus,' but he gives still greater scope to ghostly and magical elements, he does not mind repeating himself, and he makes no attempt to introduce any higher thoughts into his fascinating narrative of changeful incidents. The island of Felsenburg is supposed to lie somewhere in mid-ocean beyond St. Helena. It is an earthly Paradise, like Simplicius' last habitation. The idea of the shipwrecked people who land there and of their doings was evidently suggested by Grimmelshausen's work. At length there remain but one Adam and one Eve in this Paradise; Adam is a German and becomes the founder of a great race, for his family and subjects are increased by other shipwrecked people, and afterwards by voluntary immigrants. He rules over a realm of peace, and many who have been through troubles and vicissitudes in

Europe find happiness and rest at last in the island of Felsenburg.
Several of these are Germans, and all of them are made to relate
their experiences. We are thus introduced to clergymen, soldiers,
artisans, whose history reflects the general conditions of the age
and acquaints us with many characteristics of German life in the
beginning of the eighteenth century. The citizens of this happy
island seem to have left all their evil passions behind them in their
old Fatherland, but they have not got rid of the stilted forms of
intercourse and the conventional phraseology fashionable in Germany at that time. An elaborate love-letter seems to them more
poetical than a simple heart-felt word. But differences of rank and
religion never form barriers of separation between the islanders, and
in this respect they represent an ideal which was yet far from its
realisation in Germany itself.

THE DRAMA.

In spite of the fancies and superstitions which the authors of
'Simplicissimus' and of the 'Island of Felsenburg' introduced
into their works, we may say, on the whole, that the enchantments
and fabulous marvels, which played so great a part in old romances
like 'Amadis,' were banished from the modern novel in deference
to the demands of a more enlightened age. But marvel and magic
found a refuge in the Drama of this period. The opera and the
burlesque afforded full scope for a lively imagination, and allowed
the author to disregard all laws of probability. The opera and the
burlesque dominated the stage at this time. The opera, like the
fantastic style of writing, derived its strength from Italy; the
burlesque was founded on a popular basis, but was also open
to Italian influence.

The Opera was a true product of the Renaissance. It first saw
the light in Florence, where it sprang from the wish   Develop-
to revive the Greek drama in its original form. The   ment of the
chorus had long existed in the drama; the Recitative   Opera.
was now added to it, and this intermediate between melody and
speech was thought to be the dramatic declamation used by the
Greeks and Romans. The aria was next added as an artistic
necessity, to relieve the monotony of the recitative; then the

chorus began to take part in the action, and the instruments were made to contribute characteristic colouring to it; dancing, rich decorations, spectacular effects, and frequent changes of scene were added to attract the eye, and the drama, thus improved and embellished, was used to impart new glory to grand court-festivals. The first opera, 'Daphne,' with text by Rinuccini and music by

First Opera, 'Daphne,' performed in Florence, 1595.

Peri, was produced in 1594 or 1595 in a private house in Florence; the second, 'Euridice,' also by Rinuccini and Peri, was performed at the ducal Court of Florence in 1600, on the occasion of the marriage of Henry IV. of France with Mary de Medicis. Opitz made a German version of the text of 'Daphne,' and Heinrich Schütz, the greatest German composer of the seventeenth century, wrote new

German version of 'Daphne' produced at Torgau, 1627.

music for it. This first German opera was produced at Torgau on the 13th of April, 1627, at the court of the Elector John George I., to celebrate the marriage of the Landgrave of Hesse with a Saxon princess. Ovid, the teacher of love, sings the prologue, and shepherds form the chorus. Apollo kills the dragon

Python and mocks at Cupid, who resolves to revenge himself and show his power over the god; Daphne enflames the passion of Apollo, flies from him, and is transformed before the eyes of the audience into a laurel tree. Shepherds and nymphs then sing the praise of the laurel tree and of the Saxon rue-plant, and the opera terminates with an anticipation of the much-desired peace.

The protracted war was unfavourable to the development of the opera. It was not till the middle of the seventeenth century

The Opera in Germany.

that operas began to appear more frequently at the court-festivals, and from that time their popularity steadily increased. Love remained their chief theme; to set love-songs to soft music was the highest aim of the early opera-composers, and there were some German poets who declared the opera to be the noblest branch of poetry. Andreas Gryphius and

Prevalence of Italian Opera.

many others wrote German texts for operas. But for the most part Italian operas were performed at Ger-man courts, in the Italian language and by Italian troupes; and if there chanced to be any German singers or com-

posers among them, they were sure to have had an Italian training.
Vienna, Munich, and Dresden were the most important colonies
of the Italian opera; the towns emulated the princely courts in
cultivating it, and it was only in Hamburg that the original German opera attained any true and lasting success.   German
Between 1678 and 1738 more than two hundred and   Opera in
fifty operas were performed there. In the seventeenth   Hamburg,
century some of the operas were still religious in   1678-1738.
character, a continuation of the older Mysteries; otherwise they
were mostly drawn from mythology or history, or else they were
pastoral plays.   There was little modern or patriotic about these
operas, and at last they became almost exclusively mere spectacular
pieces or farces. Among the musical composers, the light but varied
and fertile talent of Reinhard Keiser was the most remarkable. The
writers of texts were, for the most part, quite unequal to their task;
their models were Italian libretti, which they deteriorated rather than
improved.   At last they contented themselves with simply adopting
Italian arias, and in 1740 an Italian troupe established itself in
Hamburg.

The influence of the opera, the delight in splendid accessories,
decoration and machinery, made itself felt in the   Influence
spoken drama also.   The artistic drama and the   of the
popular drama stood at first in opposition to each   Opera on
other, but gradually a *rapprochement* took place   the Drama.
between them; the popular drama influenced the artistic drama,
and both were affected by the opera. The artistic dramas were
written by scholars, and acted by students and school-boys.
The popular drama was fostered by wandering actors, who drew
materials for their plays from all sources, altering them as they
pleased.

The Silesian Andreas Gryphius was the originator of the German
artistic drama.   His countrymen Lohenstein and The artistic
Hallmann tried to outdo him in tragedy, and carried   drama,
his manner to extremes.   They revel in executions, Gryphius,
prison-scenes, ghosts, and the cruelties of torture;   and
the horrors of Shakspeare's 'Titus Andronicus' and Hallmann.
of similar English plays are continued in their works. Strong

realistic effects are combined with bombastic dialogue, moving in stiff Alexandrines.

Christian Weise occupies a far higher place as a dramatic writer
Christian Weise's dramas. than Lohenstein or Hallmann. He cultivated all branches of the drama. He too was influenced by Gryphius ánd by the Opera, but like Gryphius himself he also learnt much from a direct study of the popular stage. Like Gryphius he mingles comic and tragic elements in his plays, and was indebted to Shakspeare for a few of his subjects. He employed prose almost exclusively, and aimed at making his dialogue rapid and dramatic; it is only in moments of great emotion that his style rises above the ordinary level, and on such occasions it generally degenerates into bombast. Weise seeks to produce rapid changes of mood in his audience by means of perplexing entanglements and surprising solutions of difficulties. He wished to give faithful pictures of real life, and hence in his plays the High-German speech is reserved for the princely characters, and all the others speak in dialect. The wealth and facility of his invention are marvellous, but he did not take the trouble to polish and mould his works thoroughly. He wrote more than fifty dramas, and had them nearly all performed by his pupils, when he was Rector in Zittau, from 1679 to 1688 and 1702 to 1705. He also wrote Biblical dramas full of realistic elements drawn from contemporary life, but he avoided New Testament subjects, and he never introduced the Devil on the stage; the kind of play in which that character flourished was evidently dying out at this time. His historical plays, in which he seems to have a predilection for revolutions or the fall of favourites, remind us very much of the tragedies of the Silesian school, without coming up to them in horrors. The exceeding stiffness of the serious parts is somewhat compensated for by excellent popular scenes, delicious humour and a few situations of strong human interest, into which the author seems to have thrown his whole sympathy. In his original dramas Weise began with loosely connected satirical pictures, and ended with concise delineation of life among the lower middle classes. He passed from farce to comedy, but in the latter he is often stiff, loquacious, and dull.

Christian Weise found followers both in schools and elsewhere.
The school-drama in general was still in vogue, though   Dramatic
not so much as it had been.   The Jesuits and other   spectacles
religious orders got up splendid dramatic represen-   in schools.
tations in their schools and colleges, and tried to satisfy the love of
gorgeous spectacles, while at the same time promoting piety.   But
their efforts contributed nothing to the development of the drama
as a branch of literature.

From the beginning of the eighteenth century till about 1730,
the spoken drama disappeared almost completely from printed literature, being entirely supplanted by the text-books of the favourite
opera.   The popular dramas too continued to enjoy   The
the same, or even greater, favour than before, but like   popular
the school-dramas they were not printed, except per-   drama.
haps an outline of the plot on theatre-programmes. Like the poetry
of the mediæval gleemen, they existed solely in manuscript or in
the memory of the wandering actors.   The manuscripts too were
sometimes incomplete, giving mere stage-directions, and leaving free
space for improvisation side by side with fixed parts.   And these
manuscripts, being only intended to help in the production of plays,
like the decorations and costumes, were like them worn out and lost,
so that the popular drama of the seventeenth and eighteenth centuries,
like the popular poetry of the Middle Ages, is wrapt in obscurity,
and only insignificant and chance fragments of it have come down
to us.   The comedians, as we have noticed, wrote their own plays,
and had no scruple in seizing on other people's property; foreign
and native literature, the artistic drama and the school-plays, operas
and romances were all made to supply them with materials.   But
they arranged this material according to their own requirements,
and with reference to their favourite effects, and to the likings of
their audience.   They handled their materials in the same way as
the Strassburg playwrights about the year 1600 handled the Ajax
of Sophocles; they liked to represent everything in   Its style.
detail on the stage, more especially anything horrible,
and to leave nothing to mere narrative.   They loved to introduce
a bloodthirsty tyrant into their plays, a Nero or a Domitian, who
might be made to rage and rant to any extent, and who would

furnish an opportunity for all kinds of horrors. Such tyrants generally have evil counsellors and flatterers by their side; they meet with conscientious opposition, and their tyranny calls forth martyrs and revolutionary spirits; they were the favourite heroes both of the popular dramatists and of their more learned colleagues. Tragedies treating of tyrants, or of kings, princes and other public characters, always formed the main bulk of the *répertoire* of the wandering comedians; they were the chief event in every theatrical representation at this time, and were relieved by comic interludes or by a farce at the end. Later on they became notorious under the name of 'chief and state actions' ('*Haupt- und Staatsactionen*').

It seemed for a short time as if the German stage was to be ennobled by French influence in the seventeenth century, as if the splendid productions of Molière were to point the German dramatic

Translations of Molière, 1670 and 1694.
authors to higher aims. As early as 1670, three years before Molière's death, five of his comedies were published in German, and in 1694 there appeared a German translation of his collective prose works.

From 1685 to 1692 a troupe of Court players was kept in Dresden, of whom Magister Velthen was the leading spirit; these comedians had various plays of Molière's in their *répertoire*. There was also a plentiful supply of translations of French tragedies; several of these appeared in Brunswick between 1691 and 1699, and were represented at the Court Theatre, under the patronage of Duke Anton Ulrich. But with this exception the regular drama found but little support at the German courts, and it

French influence yields to Italian.
was on their favour that it chiefly depended at this time. The French fashion had soon to yield to the Italian, for the latter supplied that most favourite element of the German popular stage: the clown.

Already in the German popular drama of the sixteenth century

The clown of the drama.
the fool had sometimes been introduced as standing jester, and even then the jokes which he had to make were often left to his own invention. The English comedians transplanted their clown to the German stage, and the character was at once adopted by Jacob Ayrer and Duke Heinrich

Julius of Brunswick in their plays. From that time forward, the clown
became more and more the most necessary member of the wandering troupes of actors; he attracted the largest audiences, for he was
the representative of low comedy. He was the heir of all the
popular comic characters in German life and literature; there was
a bit of Morold about him, and a bit of Eulenspiegel; he was a
fool, a Grobianus, a poor devil, and the last metamorphosis of the
wandering gleeman. He was servant, messenger, spy, intrigant,
and conjuror, was dressed in motley and provided with a cracking
whip, like the old gleeman. He was obscene and vulgar, a great
eater and drinker, a braggart and a coward. He was the hero of
farce and the jester of tragedy, and he even forced his way into the
Hamburg Opera. He gained the heart of Christian Weise, and was
only discarded in the comedies written at the close of his career.
He went under different names at different periods, '*Pickelhering*,'
'*Harlequin*,' and '*Hanswurst*' being the most frequent. *Pickelhering* was the comic character of the English comedians, and
flourished throughout the seventeenth century, appearing even in
Christian Weise's works. *Harlequin* was derived from the Italian
Arlechino, a character of ancient renown in the improvised
Italian popular comedy. As early as the fifteenth century,
Italian comedy exercised a great influence on other
nations, and in the seventeenth century it attained an
international popularity. In Paris there existed an
Italian theatre which rivalled Molière's, and from
which he derived some suggestions for his plays.
The first Italian troupe came to Germany about 1670,

*Italian
comedy
in France
and
Germany,
17th century.*

and o course brought their Harlequin with them. The Paris
troupe later on began to act in French; the pieces which they
acted, or outlines of them, were collected in print after 1694, and
the German actors made frequent use of them. The Italian farce
found a favourable reception everywhere, but there was no place
where it struck such deep roots as in Vienna, the
town where farce and every kind of coarse jesting had
flourished vigorously since the Middle Ages. As
early as 1708 a German theatre was established in the

*The stage
in Vienna.
'Hans-
wurst.'*

Imperial capital, and its founder Joseph Stranitzky, a Silesian, made extensive use of the characters and plots of Italian farce : he himself acted Harlequin, to whom he gave the old German name of *Hans-Wurst*, a title borne occasionally by the clown of the earlier drama. He made him appeal more directly to the Viennese. His *Hanswurst* came from Salzburg, just as the Italian *Arlechino* came from Bergamo, and both were made to speak in their native dialect. As *Arlechino* had his own special costume, made of triangular patches of cloth, so *Hanswurst* always appeared as a peasant with the characteristic green pointed hat.

Hanswurst and his kindred are a characteristic production of the period about 1600, and unfortunately this character of the clown committed the popular drama for ever to the level of that period. Literary influence could not succeed in effecting any change in this leading character, and nothing was able to gain any footing in the popular plays that did not harmonise with *Hanswurst* or bring him into stronger relief. The spectacular element was readily increased; the arts of scenic decoration, enchantments, flying machines and transformations found favour on the popular stage as well as in the opera. The bombast too of the artistic tragedy, after the Lohenstein and Hallmann style, established itself in the popular plays; the Alexandrine and the short dialogue alternating in single lines were introduced side by side with prose, and in verse as in prose a stream of highsounding words and well-worn images was poured out to a delighted audience, mingled with the filthy jokes of *Hanswurst*.

Such was the state of the German stage when Gottsched appeared on the scene, and endeavoured to set up the French classical drama as the only authorized model. The opera and *Hanswurst* seemed to him the worst enemies which good taste had to fight against. Hence he greeted with applause Pradon's very mediocre play of ' Regulus,' which was translated from French and German at Brunswick at the command of Duke Anton Ulrich, and was performed by the Hoffmann troupe in Leipzig in 1725. The Brunswick translations formed the basis of a new *répertoire* for the regular drama, and the Neuber company, which sprang from the Hoffmann troupe in 1727, made it its chief business to promote the cause of the artistic drama founded on French models. These actors enthusiastically took up Gottsched's ideas, gave up the 'chief actions' and 'State actions,' confined Harlequin to the realm of farce, and finally banished him from the stage altogether.

Gottsched made the German stage once more dependent on German literature; that was his great merit in connection with the German drama. Unfortunately, he did not get beyond preaching imitation of the French, and practising it himself; he did not think of rescuing and improving the available materials and workmanship of the popular plays, and thus preserving the national character of the German drama. He broke entirely with the past, and in so doing impoverished the German drama for the present and the future. He disdained reform, and undertook his revolution in the cause of a false ideal.

END OF VOL. I.